DEADLINE
EVERY
MINUTE:

THE STORY OF THE UNITED PRESS

BY Joe Alex Morris

GREENWOOD PRESS, PUBLISHERS
NEW YORK   1968

First Greenwood reprinting, 1968

LIBRARY OF CONGRESS catalogue card number: 69-10137

Printed in the United States of America

For MAXINE

ACKNOWLEDGMENTS

The author is deeply indebted to a great many persons for assistance in preparing this history of the United Press Associations, particularly the large number who contributed material or anecdotes that were of importance in shaping the background even though they do not appear in the final version. Hundreds of contributions were received while this work was in progress, and the original manuscript ran to some 350,000 words. The necessity of eliminating many stories and of reducing the wordage by more than half proved to be not only difficult but often painful to the author. Many anecdotes and adventures were regretfully stowed away in the files to await a future historian.

A large part of this volume is based on personal interviews with four of the eight presidents of the company over a period of fifty years. Much important material came from the recollections of numerous former employees, some of whom played prominent roles in the development of the United Press—Ralph H. Turner, Herbert W. Walker, Joshua B. Powers, Don E. Chamberlain, Edward Derr, Earl B. Steele, Tom Reynolds, Martin Kane, E. W. Lewis, John R. Beal, Donald Coe, Roscoe Johnson, Arnold Dibble, Harman Nichols, and others. Mrs. John Vandercook also contributed important material.

Some of the early history of the agency recounted here was drawn from the autobiographical notes of J. H. Furay and from a manuscript prepared by Robert K. MacCormac. A few of the quoted messages in early sections of the book are reconstructed from the memory of persons who sent or received them or from letters written in later years.

The author is also grateful for the information supplied by the following Unipressers: Wendel Burch, director of foreign services; Don Dillon, New York foreign staff; Harry W. Sharpe, Washington Saturday night editor; Robert Musel, London reporter; Bruce Munn, United Nations staff; Al Wiese, San Diego manager; M. E. Stevens, Atlanta telegrapher; Fred A. Parker, Tennessee business representative; Al Stees, Eastern division news editor; Thomas J. Allen, European communications chief; Henry Rennwald, Chicago telegrapher; Leo Soroka, Memphis manager; Robert W. Keyserlingk, British United Press manager; Eliav Simon, Tel Aviv manager; Al Kuettner, Atlanta bureau manager; Roscoe Snipes, Washington foreign department; Francis T. Leary, Central Division news editor; Chiles Coleman, Southern Division news editor; Jack V. Fox, features editor; Joe W. Morgan, night news manager; John J. Madigan, radio news manager; Henry Rieger, San Francisco manager; Alexander P. Bock, assistant treasurer; Jack Gaver, drama critic; William J. Fox, day cable editor; Fred J. Green, superintendent of bureaus; Carl B. Molander, assistant sales manager; A. K. Das, Calcutta manager; William H. McCall, South American news director; Daniel F. Gilmore, United Kingdom manager.

Source of material used in preparation of this history included the following books: *Freely to Pass* (Crowell) by Edward W. Beattie, Jr.; *This Is the Enemy* (Little, Brown & Co.) by Frederick C. Oechsner; *Balcony Empire* (Oxford University Press) by Reynolds and Eleanor Packard; *Barriers Down* (Farrar & Rinehart) by Kent Cooper; *AP, the Story of News* (Farrar & Rinehart) by Oliver Gramling; *Of the Meek and the Mighty* (Nicholson & Watson) by Edward J. Bing; *The Right to Know* (Farrar, Strauss & Cudahy) by Kent Cooper; *A Life in Reuters* (Doubleday) by Sir Roderick Jones; *Forty Years in Newspaperdom* (Brentano's) by Milton A. McRae; *Six Bells off Java* (Scribner's) by William H. McDougall, Jr.; *I Found No Peace* (Simon & Schuster) by Webb Miller; *Springboard to Berlin* (Crowell) by John A. Parris, Jr., and Ned Russell; *The Lindbergh Crime* (Blue Ribbon Books) by Sidney B. Whipple; *Mediterranean Assignment* (Doubleday) by Richard McMillan; *Damned Old Crank* (Harper Brothers) edited by Charles R. McCabe.

DEADLINE EVERY MINUTE

Take Ten....

NEW YORK, June 21, 1907 (By United Press) This is
about the way telegraph copy looked when it was laid on
the telegraph editor's desk during the earliest days of
the United Press Associations. A telegrapher sitting
with his ear close to a small wooden sounding box heard
the dots and dashes coming over the wire in Morse code
and copied them in words on a typewriter at around thirty-five words a minute. If anybody close to him whistled it distracted him and he was likely to miss several
words, so whistling was taboo in newspaper offices.

A couple of times a day the signals would say:
"Take ten...." and that meant the operator could rest
for ten minutes while the wire was silent. Usually he
read the sports pages or rushed out for a cup of coffee.

At the bottom of each page of copy the receiving
operator typed his initials, the exact time of day and
indicated whether the story was complete--

more ejm923a

The operator was and is a vital cog in any press association. In the final accounting, it was what came over the wires, what the operator copied down that meant success or failure. If a reporter had a news story in Miami or Portland or Kansas City and couldn't get it on the wire, the newspaper editor in Pittsburgh or Boston or Denver was out of luck--and so was the press association that sold him a news service.

The press association was and is almost without physical assets. It is a staff of men scattered around the surface of the globe, a comparatively insignificant amount of office furniture, a vast communications network that is leased but not owned -- and confidence. It is the confidence of the staff that it can find and report accurately what is going on all over the world and the confidence of a certain number of newspaper editors in the ability of those men to do their jobs well. If one of them fails, then the value of the property that is called a press association decreases by the importance of his failure. If one succeeds brilliantly, then the value of the property increases by the importance of his success. If this confidence vanished

tomorrow the assets of a press association would be only
a jumbled pile of pencils and paper, of typewriters and
battered furniture.

It is the nature of a press association that men
and women scattered from St. Louis to Bombay spend their
days and nights hunting not only headlines but the small
scraps of news that will interest readers in Centerville,
Iowa, or Albany, New York, or Santa Barbara, California.
There is endless routine and endless drudgery and there
are times when a correspondent feels that the press association does possess certain physical assets after all --
it possesses _him_. At other times, when his story skims
over the wires for thousands on thousands of miles, carrying his excitement and perhaps his name into hundreds
of newspapers around the world, he may feel that he is
the press association. But day after day, the wires are
always open, always waiting for him to produce. Day and
night, on holidays and on days of disaster, the wire is
always waiting.

"Yes, young man," a famous statesman said to a reporter who sought to interview him some years ago, "I'll
be glad to prepare a statement for you. Just tell me

more ejm935a

when is your -- what do you newspapermen call it? --
your deadline."

The reporter sighed. "I'm from the United Press,"
he replied. "Our deadline is now. Someplace around the
world at this instant a newspaper is going to press.
We've got a deadline every minute."

end ejm937a

CHAPTER ONE

In the spring of 1897, Edward Wyllis Scripps was a wealthy, red-bearded, forty-two-year-old newspaper publisher with ambitions and, as he put it later, a cocky feeling that he was going to be "a sort of man of destiny." He was also in a hell of a jam.

Scripps' trouble was easy to understand. His Midwestern newspapers could not exist without a news service to bring them daily reports on what was happening throughout the world. On April 7, 1897, the Scripps papers ceased to have such a news service, and his rivals in the publishing field couldn't easily see where he was going to get another one.

This predicament was largely of Scripps' own making and more or less typical of his methods. He was a purposeful eccentric. He spent much of his time on an isolated ranch in the desert in Southern California, about as far as he could get from the heart of his business affairs. He claimed—falsely, it may be assumed—that for years he drank a gallon of whisky and smoked thirty cigars a day. He had a puckish way of looking at people he didn't like, and even people he liked sometimes thought he had the stare of a dead fish, possibly due to a cast in one eye. He loved to philosophize and, like most philosophers, frequently contradicted himself. He was frank, honest, grasping, sympathetic, devious, boastful, cold-bloodedly logical, penny-pinching, morally courageous, cynically open-minded, bitterly independent, and one of the newspaper titans of his day. He may have been, as not a few colleagues asserted, a genius. In any event he was a complex and extraordinary man.

Scripps had grown up on an Illinois farm, where he preferred to sit on a fence and think rather than work. With a nest egg of eighty dollars sewn into his vest, he went to Detroit in 1872 and, shortly thereafter, became a newspaperman of sorts in the employ of his half brothers, James E. and George H. Scripps, who owned the Detroit *News*. In 1878, he persuaded his brothers to help finance the inauguration of his *Penny Press* in Cleveland, where his bid for readers among the working class and his refusal to align his paper with any political party were startling but successful innovations. Later, he bought a Cincinnati paper, changed its name to the *Post,* and put its business affairs under direction of Milton A. McRae, who became a partner in 1889 and was a tower of strength for Scripps in later years. The Scripps newspaper empire was founded, and other newspapers were added steadily in the following years.

The gathering of news of the world had been a haphazard business in the first half of the nineteenth century until Samuel Morse brought about a revolution in communications by invention of the modern telegraph. During the war with Mexico in 1848, six New York newspapers formed a syndicate to share the expense of covering the news of the day, so far as possible, by telegraph, and later these news reports were shared with papers in Philadelphia and Baltimore. As the telegraph lines spread, American news coverage improved and, with completion of a transatlantic cable in 1858, was extended to Europe. Various news agencies or combinations of newspapers were formed to gather the news and, after the Civil War, there was opened an era of tremendous newspaper progress. The newspaper, in a modern sense, grew up in the last half of the nineteenth century and so did the news agencies.

One of the most powerful news-gathering services in the early 1890s was the United Press, of which Scripps was a client but in which he had no other interest. This agency at one time almost established a monopoly in the United States. But, in 1892, a rebellious group of publishers, led by Victor Lawson of the Chicago *Daily News* and including James E. Scripps, formed the Associated Press of Illinois and raised $550,000 to oppose the United Press. The Associated Press became a co-operative organization and granted contracts or franchises to member newspapers guaranteeing them exclusive use of Associated Press news in their circulation areas.

E. W. Scripps did not desert the United Press, which gave him many special favors that enabled him to get telegraph news to his newspapers at a very low cost. He expected that he would profit for a long time by the battle between the United Press and the Associated Press. But the United Press was badly managed and began to crumble rapidly in 1897. On April 7 it suddenly closed down its wire services and went out of business. Scripps was jolted to find himself "a very insignificant factor" in the news-gathering field as a result—a publisher with a few correspondents in key cities but without a wire service worthy of the name. He was in a hell of a jam.

2.

The Associated Press did not slam the door in Scripps' face in the spring of 1897. The agency's general manager, Melville E. Stone, and other officers expressed willingness to admit some but not all of Scripps' newspapers, and E.W. was urged by Brother James and partner McRae to accept this offer. Scripps had other plans. His newspapers were published in the afternoon and he was convinced that the Associated Press was dominated by large morning newspapers which exerted their influence to give "the morning newspapers . . . a monopoly of all the important news." But perhaps more important was the fact that he intended to start another score or so of newspapers and he was bitterly opposed to the Associated Press policy of granting exclusive franchises to member newspapers. If he were a member of the agency, this policy would prevent him—except under special circumstances—from becoming a competitor of an established Associated Press newspaper, which was what he intended to do in a number of cities.

In order to maintain his freedom of action, Scripps instructed his editor in chief, Robert F. Paine, to start enlarging the special telegraph report which the Scripps-McRae newspapers received from their own correspondents in Washington, New York, and other cities in the East and Middle West. This became known as the Scripps-McRae Press Association and it operated in alliance with a similar telegraph service (later called the Scripps News Association) on the Pacific coast, where E.W. had already established a number of newspapers. Even by combining and improving these services, Scripps still had only a poor excuse for a news agency as compared to the Associated Press, which collected news from its member papers all over the country and had available the foreign dispatches of Britain's Reuters agency.

Scripps believed he could build up the Scripps-McRae Press Association (SMPA) by selling the service to many other newspapers that did not belong to the Associated Press. Unknown to him, however, a group of Eastern publishers headed by J. B. Shale had organized the Publishers' Press Association and grabbed off most of the Atlantic seaboard papers that Scripps had hoped would subscribe to his agency. As a result, he had to make an alliance for exchange of news dispatches between SMPA and Publishers' Press. This alliance was never very satisfactory, but it was not until nine years later that Scripps—prodded by one of his editors, John Vandercook—purchased Publishers' Press for about $150,000 and instructed Vandercook to combine all of these telegraphic services into a single news agency for afternoon newspapers.

The new agency was incorporated in June of 1907. Very little cash was paid out by anybody. It was specified in the certificate of incorporation that the company would begin business with at least $500 capital, and only that amount was paid in. Scripps, however, emerged with $200,000 in preferred stock, which he used to pay various personal debts. The new press association began its existence with liabilities of $300,000 and, according to a later remark by Scripps, "what might be termed a bag of wind."

COUNTY OF NEW YORK
June 19, 1907
We, the undersigned, Hamilton B. Clark, Roy W. Howard and Jacob C. Harper, all being persons of full age and at least two-thirds being citizens

of the United States and at least one of us a resident of the State of New York, desiring to form a stock corporation pursuant to the provisions of the Business Corporations Law of the State of New York, do hereby make, sign, acknowledge and file this certificate for that purpose as follows:

To collect, formulate, transmit and dispose of news by telegraph, cable, telephone and other agencies, in and from the United States and her dependencies and foreign countries; to buy and sell news; to own, lease, manage, buy and sell news agencies; to acquire press franchises and to become a member of and hold stock in associations and corporations for such purposes.

The name of the proposed corporation is
UNITED PRESS ASSOCIATIONS.

3.

In later years, E. W. Scripps liked to talk and write about the United Press and, for that matter, about almost anything else in the world from the high cost of ignorance to the folly of trying to grow old gracefully. He was, as he once acknowledged, a damned old crank and he thoroughly enjoyed the role.

Most newspapers in the first decade of the twentieth century were somewhat partisan in their reporting, particularly of political events, and the Scripps-McRae publications were no exception. The idea of strictly objective reporting, however, had been emphasized in an important manner by Melville E. Stone and Frank B. Noyes in framing the policy of the Associated Press because they knew a co-operative agency could not take sides or show bias if it expected to serve member newspapers of many different political and social complexions.

Scripps fully appreciated the importance of this principle when the United Press came into being. His ideas were summed up later in fragments from his letters and his autobiographical notes:

"I believe in one-man control—in other words the 51 per cent rule—just as firmly as I believe in the distribution or the sharing of profits amongst all of the important and capable administrators of a business. Providing one man is fairly intelligent and is possessed both of reputation and character that makes him dependable, it is better that he should have final authority, not by agreement but by his own individual power and title. . . . The early days [of the United Press] would have been critical had it not been for the fact that I owned so many of the newspapers that were its clients that its financing was a simple matter. All I had to do was, first, to calculate the monthly expense necessary for conducting the United Press; second, to add up the amount of money received each month from clients other than my own newspapers; and, finally, to cause my own newspapers to pay assessments so that their aggregate would be sufficient, taken together with the receipts from other clients, to pay the whole monthly expense.

"After the first year or two, the receipts exceeded its disbursements.

"I imagine that in founding the new United Press, the Scripps papers actually paid out several hundred thousand dollars more than they would have paid out had they been members of the Associated Press. However, notwithstanding these comparatively large payments, I felt that the investment, bad as it was financially in one way, was a good one because it secured, not only to the Scripps papers but to all of the other papers in the country, freedom from the temptation of one huge monopoly. Our corporation was not a mutual one but a stock company for the purpose of profit. We could not legally, even if we desired, refuse a report to any newspaper that wanted it, even in cases where the new newspaper would come in direct competition with one of our own properties. In fact, there have been many cases where some of our newspapers have suffered seriously by that competition. . . .

"I do not believe in monopolies. I believe that monopolists suffer more than their victims in the long run. I did not believe it would be good for journalism in this country that there should be one big news trust such as the founders of the Associated Press fully expected to build up. . . . The men who hold controlling interest in the present Associated Press and Mr. Hearst [William Randolph Hearst had founded a news service about the time UP was formed] would inevitably combine into a trust were it not for us. . . .

"I believe, too, that I have done more good indirectly with the United Press than I have done with it directly, since I have made it impossible for the men who control the Associated Press to suppress the truth or successfully disseminate falsehood. The mere fact that the United Press can be depended upon to disseminate news that is of value to the public and that is against the interests of the plutocrat band makes it not only not worth while, but positively dangerous, for the Associated Press to withhold any information from the public.

"Many times I have contended . . . that the most substantial thing, the thing which is very, very long enduring, is the thing which has no substance at all, has no tangible, seeable, smellable, tastable quality. . . . This thing is the stream of thought, habit, custom, convention, tradition, faith—all of these things, or one of them, which is the same thing. This thing flows through what we call the minds of men; through the existence of one man's life into and through the existence of other men, living or to be born. It is something that spreads through a small group of minds, or through larger and still larger groups. . . .

"As I said, I regard my life's greatest service to the people of this country to be the creation of the United Press. . . . It is quite possible that I am the only man in this country who could have performed this service. I doubt if there was a single newspaperman in the United States, other than those in my employ, who at the time I made the decision to do this believed I would be successful. . . .

"Because I was what I was this condition—called the United Press—came into existence."

CHAPTER TWO

The United Press Associations was born in the summer of 1907 as a company selling daily news reports for profit to 369 newspapers. The incorporation papers were filed on June 21. On June 22, Hamilton B. Clark, an associate of Scripps, was elected chairman of the board, and John Vandercook was elected president. But the mere existence of a corporate organization did not mean that the United Press name suddenly blossomed out in client newspapers. It was not, in fact, until July 15 that Scripps' Cleveland *Press* announced on its front page that the new agency had been formed and that its dispatches would thereafter appear in the *Press*. The same edition carried the first "By United Press" credit line.

In any event, by midsummer the wires of the United Press were humming with as many as 10,000 or 12,000 words a day, and the new press service was preparing to plunge into a long period of intense rivalry not only with the Associated Press but with the newly-formed Hearst News Service. The battle would be directed by a dapper, energetic news manager named Roy Wilson Howard. He was twenty-four years old and the proud owner of one share of United Press common stock worth ten dollars.

Almost everybody in the news-gathering department of the United Press was young, and, in retrospect, it appears likely that only ignorance of the business and youthful self-confidence could have persuaded them that the company had even a fighting chance for survival. It would be years, however, before Roy Howard realized that he and a handful of colleagues had set out to do what almost any experienced newspaperman knew was impossible—buck the Associated Press on a shoestring.

Slight, dark-haired, and bright-eyed, Howard had had an inordinate amount of drive since his boyhood in Indianapolis, where he set some kind of record by earning thirty-five dollars, at space rates, in one busy week as high-school correspondent for the Indianapolis *News*. Upon his graduation, the newspaper rewarded him with a regular job at eight dollars a week. He later worked on the Indianapolis *Star* and then migrated to Pulitzer's St.

Louis *Post-Dispatch,* which he quit because the editor turned him down for the post of telegraph editor in favor of a man about thirty years old.

"They've just appointed an old crock to the job I should have had," Howard wrote his friend, Ray Long, who was managing editor of the Cincinnati *Post.* "Do you have a job for me?"

Long did. In Cincinnati, Howard met John Vandercook, then the editor of the *Post,* and shortly persuaded Vandercook to send him to New York as a special correspondent. When Publishers' Press was purchased by Scripps in 1906, Howard became its news manager in New York at a salary of thirty-three dollars a week. After Publishers' Press was merged into the United Press, he continued in the same job with the new agency.

Howard soon began to see the great possibilities that might be opened up by a lively, aggressive press service. He began making many changes in personnel. He displayed a kind of driving leadership. Under his energetic prodding, reporters might curse him freely but they usually put on a little extra steam, too, and some were infected with his conviction that nothing was impossible if you brought a little imagination and a great deal of effort to the job. Gradually, Howard demonstrated that a large number of able young men—usually underpaid and grossly overworked—could be persuaded to devote themselves to the role of the underdog in overcoming the great advantages held by the Associated Press. It wasn't easy to pick the right men, but he found some. Ed L. Keen, who had helped organize SMPA, had remained in charge of the Washington bureau after the official debut of the United Press, and Keen was Howard's kind of newsman. He could achieve a great deal with a small staff and he had a remarkable knowledge of communications problems.

Howard also hired a young newspaperman from the Louisville *Courier-Journal.* His name was William W. Hawkins and he arrived in New York with a trusting stare in his eyes and a valise in his hand. Wandering across Lower Manhattan from the ferry terminal, he lost his way and finally stopped to ask a policeman how to get to the Park Row building, then the tallest structure in New York City.

The cop pushed back his hard helmet and roared with laughter. "If you don't move," he yelled, "the damn thing is likely to fall on you!"

Red-faced, Hawkins walked in the door and up to the third floor where he joined Howard—for forty years. Bill Hawkins was a steady, sedate man in contrast to the small, sharp-tongued, and aggressive Howard. But almost from the beginning they seemed to complement each other in an extraordinary fashion. Hawkins' voice was calm. Howard's was likely to rise in pitch when he was angry. Howard drove men as he drove himself and often he drove them to the point where they decided they had had enough and would quit. Then, if the man was worth keeping in the organization, Hawkins would come along with a soothing, sympathetic voice to smooth down ruffled feathers, to bestow a pat on the back, and perhaps to lend the victim five bucks.

"Never mind what he said," Hawkins would murmur. "We'll fix that little bastard one of these days."

"I'll choke him!" the victim of Howard's tongue might cry.

"I'll help you," Hawkins would chip in. "But right now would you give me a lift with this story? I've got to have it in ten minutes and you're the only man in the office I can depend on to get it done."

More often than not the victim was back on the tracks, and the next time Howard came into the news room he would be all smiles and compliments. Of course, there were plenty of times when it didn't work and another reporter would go looking for another job, swearing that Howard ran a sweatshop. He doubtless did, but to not a few young newspapermen it was also a day-by-day adventure serial in which they were permitted to stand close to the great events of the day and in which, tomorrow, they might see their names as front-page by-lines.

Things moved rapidly under Howard's direction. Not too long after the United Press was launched, he had gathered together the core of a staff that was prepared to make journalistic history.

2.

By the beginning of 1908 the shimmering wires of the United Press stretched out in a long skein from the Atlantic coast, wound through the Middle West to Chicago and St. Louis—and stopped dead. Between the Mississippi River and San Francisco there weren't enough client newspapers to justify leasing a wire from Western Union, and news dispatches were filed as regular telegrams for transmission from Chicago to the associations' leased-wire network along the Pacific coast.

Howard knew what was going on in the East and, after a fashion, in the Midwest, but he knew little about the Pacific-coast operations. Max Balthasar was in charge of the United Press on the West Coast. He had never been in New York. In January of 1908, Clark directed the two men to exchange jobs for a few months in order to get a better picture of the organization as a whole. Howard headed West and, after various stops along the way, arrived in San Diego in February. His first port of call was to be Miramar, the ranch where E. W. Scripps was in residence.

The New York news manager of the United Press had never seen the Old Man, but he had heard a great deal about him. He knew that Scripps, a big, broad-shouldered man, lived very informally on his ranch, that he wore khaki shirts open at the neck, and that he tucked his pants legs into high boots. He knew, too, that it was more or less customary for officials of the Scripps organization to stop in San Diego at a certain dry-goods store and buy khaki shirt and pants to wear when they visited Miramar because they thought it would please the boss.

But when the leather-topped Scripps automobile chugged around to pick up the youthful manager of the United Press, Howard looked as if he had just stepped out for a Sunday afternoon stroll down Fifth Avenue. His derby hat was at a jaunty angle. His shirt was a neat stripe. His necktie was tightly knotted in place. He wore spats and swung his light stick in careless fashion. Nobody was likely to mistake Howard for a rancher as the automobile bounced him out across the high, arid plateau toward Miramar. New York was written all over his smooth, boyish face.

Well sprinkled with dust, Howard approached the ranch house down a long driveway that led into a circular road around the main building. On all sides were trees that Scripps had planted and, after a great deal of experimentation, persuaded to grow and thus turn the desert mesa—now supplied with water from seven reservoirs—into a pleasant landscape.

John P. Scripps, the publisher's second son, was twenty years old and it was he, rather than his father, who greeted Howard at the door. But it is more than likely that the elder Scripps was looking forward to the meeting, perhaps with a touch of nostalgia and a touch of sardonic amusement. Along with everything else, E. W. Scripps had his share of snobbishness. Almost a quarter century earlier, he had lived for a while in a country house outside of Cincinnati on the old Hamilton turnpike. About a hundred yards from this house was a cottage in which lived the tollgate keeper for the turnpike—a prosperous farmer—and his family. Scripps kept a saddle horse and often rode down the turnpike to visit a young woman whom he later married, but it always irritated him to have to stop at the tollgate. So, on occasions, he jumped his horse over the gate and didn't pay the toll.

It was some years later that he learned from a relative that the grandson of the tollgate keeper, whom he had never seen, was employed on one of his newspapers, the Cincinnati *Post,* as a reporter and that his name was Roy Howard. "Something about the association of young Howard and a very important incident in my life [marriage] caused me to be especially interested in him," Scripps wrote later. "What could be expected of a tollgate keeper's grandson? . . . of course, he was only an employee. I do not suppose he, or anyone else, ever thought he would be anything else."

That last remark made it clearer than anything else that Scripps didn't know Howard. And when his son, John, led the new arrival through the big ranch house to his father's office, Scripps was busy. He had just finished with several other visitors, all of whom by an odd coincidence happened to be small men, and he was sitting on a davenport, wearing an old sweater and skullcap and smoking a cigar as he concentrated on a sheaf of papers. John and Howard stopped near the door.

"Father," John said at last, "this is Roy W. Howard."

Scripps looked up, pushed his steel-rimmed glasses up on his forehead, and flicked his cigar ashes on the carpet.

"My God!" he exclaimed. "Another *little* one?"

"Well, Mr. Scripps," Howard responded, "perhaps another little one, but this time a good one."

Scripps frowned and then put out his hand. It was like a limp, cold mackerel when Howard grasped it. But the Old Man did not seem displeased. "One thing," he grumbled, "you'll never lick anybody's boots." Then he talked for a while about the United Press.

"I tried to run a press association," he said in reference to SMPA, "but I wasn't much of a success. I was probably too closely associated with my newspapers to know how to do it.

"Now there are only a couple of things that I ask of you . . . Always see that the news report is handled objectively as far as it is humanly possible. You must not be biased or take sides in controversies. You won't always succeed in being completely objective but you must always try to tell both sides of any dispute.

"Second, never make a contract to deliver news exclusively to one newspaper in any territory."

Howard tilted his head inquiringly. "Not even in cities where you have newspapers?"

"Never," Scripps replied. "I'm not interested in just making money out of the United Press. I believe there must not be a news monopoly in this country. At one time I could have gone into the Associated Press but it would have limited my own operations and it would have put into the hands of the board of directors of the Associated Press the fate of any young man in America who wanted to start a new newspaper. I believe that any bona fide newspaper in the country should be able to buy the services of the United Press."

When Howard departed, he wasn't sure whether Scripps liked him. Eventually he would come to the conclusion that the Old Man didn't have any real feeling of affection toward him. In two decades, for example, he received only two letters from Scripps, one of them asking him to find out why in hell Brentano's bookshop had failed to send him some volumes that he had ordered. But in time Howard was well convinced of one thing—E. W. Scripps did more for him over the years than for any other man in the Scripps organization.

"He [Howard] was a striking individual, very small of stature, with a large head and speaking countenance, and eyes that appeared to be windows for a rather unusual intellect," Scripps wrote later in his autobiographical notes. "His manner was forceful, and the reverse from modest. Gall was written all over his face. It was in every tone and every word he voiced. There were ambition, self-respect, and forcefulness oozing out of every pore in his body.

"Since those days, Howard has learned to affect some degree of deference in his speech and manner in my presence; but in my first interview with him, he did not reveal, and I do not believe he experienced, the least feeling of awe. However, so completely and exuberantly frank was he that it was impossible for me to feel any resentment on account of his cheek. . . . Of course, he is an upstart, and a very innocent upstart . . . [but his] self-respect and self-confidence, right from the start, were so great as to make it impossible for them to increase."

3.

From Miramar, Howard went to San Francisco. The United Press bureau, in the offices of the *News,* a Scripps newspaper, was between the newspaper's editorial room and the business office. It was long and narrow and there was barely enough room for the eight or ten staff members and telegraphers. Most of the space was occupied by a telegraph desk with positions for four operators on one side and a wire editor on the other. Desks and typewriter tables for reporters were fitted into the corners of the room, and there was a rickety telephone booth that had to be protected on one side by plates of heavy zinc because it was close to the small stove that heated the room. News dispatches were delivered to the *News* through a slot in the wall. Above the slot were two sliding windows, and when the editor of the *News* had a complaint he slid back one of the windows with a bang and yelled. The bureau was not an ideal place to work, especially since the floor was usually littered with discarded copy paper and newspapers, but it served its purpose and was no surprise to Howard when he arrived in the winter of 1908.

One development that pleased Howard while he was on the West Coast demonstrated the future possibilities of transmitting news by wireless. President Theodore Roosevelt had ordered the United States Atlantic Fleet on a voyage to the Far East for the purpose of advertising the nation's naval strength, acquiring prestige, and, possibly, building good will. The fleet was commanded by Rear Admiral "Fighting Bob" Evans, a hero of the day. The United Press arranged for Norman Rose, who was with the fleet, to act as its correspondent, and he made a little newspaper history by transmitting dispatches by wireless from the flagship. His first dispatch was not exactly exciting but it was exclusive and explicit:

BY NORMAN ROSE
United Press Correspondent
WITH ADMIRAL EVANS FLEET, (By Wireless via Pensacola, Fla.) March 8 (UP) *At eight o'clock* P.M. *today the fleet's position was latitude 14 degrees, 37 minutes north and longitude 102 degrees, 1 minute west. We shall arrive at Magdalena Bay on March 12, two days ahead of schedule time. The weather is fine. Our speed is now ten and one-half knots.*

This succinct bit of reporting was front-page news and good for a full-page United Press advertisement in the trade magazine *Editor & Publisher.* The advertisement boasted of United Press enterprise and pointed out that this was the first direct word from the fleet since it left Peru. Due to the distance of transmission, it was "regarded by Navy officials as one of the most remarkable feats in wireless telegraphy yet accomplished. The President and other officials were highly gratified."

A few days later, however, Rose did score what the Seattle *Star* described as a "memorable beat." This time he had some news. Admiral "Fighting Bob" Evans' health had broken at Magdalena Bay, he was relieved of command and returned to Washington. Rose's dispatch was good for headlines all over the country.

During his stay on the West Coast, Howard discovered that the problems faced by the San Francisco manager were greater than he had foreseen. All news from east of the Rocky Mountains arrived in skeletonized telegrams from the Chicago bureau. Normally, this skeletonized service totaled 2000 words a day, transmitted in several batches. In addition to news from the East, the Pacific coast wires carried dispatches originating in California, Oregon, and Washington and adjacent states, which were mostly of regional interest. By the time these and the expanded versions of the telegrams from Chicago had been put on the wire, the network was carrying around 4000 words on an average day. This wasn't enough to keep the wires busy by a wide margin, and Howard couldn't bear the idea of wasting good wire space that was already paid for and, more importantly, might be used to give United Press newspapers better service.

He rolled up his sleeves and pulled his chair up to a typewriter. The early telegraph report from Chicago had arrived and Howard started rewriting it. He was familiar with the background of most of the stories and, by the time he had finished, the first 500 skeletonized words had been expanded to 2000 with the addition of explanatory facts that were at his command. Then the Pacific coast stories began coming in on the wires. Most of them, he noticed immediately, had been picked up with almost no change from the morning newspapers in the various cities. They were obviously yesterday's news. He started the San Francisco rewrite men searching through the dispatches for information about what was going to happen today.

"Put a 'today' angle on it," he said again and again. And orders to get a "today angle" went out to all the Pacific coast bureaus. "Write about what is going to happen today, not what happened yesterday."

By late afternoon, the Pacific coast wires had carried a record number of words, the telegraph operators had missed any chance to study the sports pages, and one rewrite man approached Howard with his hands held out for inspection. "Damn it," he complained, "you've made me grow corns on my fingers since sunrise."

But Howard was just getting warmed up. He ordered an increase in the flow of mail material about coming events to be sent from Chicago, New York, and Washington to San Francisco, where it could be used by rewrite men to build up the regular telegraphed dispatches. This was especially useful in connection with scheduled events such as the inauguration of a president or the launching of an ocean liner, because many colorful details could be written in advance for release when the event occurred. He also had each Pacific coast bureau manager study a well-known "predate" sheet, which was put out by a publishing house and which gave details of coming events all over the country. This material could be used to expand telegraph dispatches if no regular mail background was available. Then he ordered each bureau to use the slack period each afternoon to prepare at least one feature or "human interest" story for the next day's leased wire. Within a few weeks the Pacific coast wires were carrying around 12,000 words a day, and the telegraph instruments were clicking steadily from 7 A.M. to 3 P.M.

Then, one day late in March, Howard got a message from Clark in New York: Vandercook was seriously ill in Chicago and Howard should return East at once.

4.

The United Press had a dozen bureaus scattered across the country in 1908, but except in a few key cities most of them were limited to one newsman with a young assistant and such telegraph operators as were necessary. Sometimes a "bureau" was just one man with a desk in the news room of a client newspaper. In various other cities there were part-time correspondents— called string correspondents or stringers—who were paid according to the work they did. The stringers often were reporters or telegraph editors on local newspapers or perhaps an experienced telegraph operator who could be counted on to relay important news gathered by a client paper.

The bureau at Chicago, an important relay point, had been in charge of Ray Long for a year or so after the United Press was founded, but he resigned in April of 1908 and was replaced by a newcomer to the news agency business, J. H. Furay. Pleasant and persistent, Barney Furay had worked on newspapers in Omaha, St. Paul, Chicago, Indianapolis, and Cleveland— where he had been managing editor of the *Press*—before being hired by the United Press for forty dollars a week. The Chicago headquarters was two small rooms in the Security Building across the street from the old Chicago *Daily News* building. In one room were the telegraph tables at which the operators worked their "bugs." The second room had a few old desks and chairs for the staff.

Furay had hardly had time to warm his chair in the office when Vandercook arrived in Chicago and came immediately to the bureau. He was sitting beside Furay's desk, talking enthusiastically, when he suddenly leaned forward, writhing in agony and clasping his arms across his stomach. Furay tried to help him.

"It's nothing," Vandercook insisted. "Just a bellyache."

But the pains continued and Furay insisted on taking him to a hospital, where a surgeon discovered that his appendix was ruptured. An emergency operation was performed. But Vandercook died about noon on April 11.

By that time, Howard had arrived in New York where the news management of the United Press was now entirely in his hands.

CHAPTER THREE

The character of the United Press Associations in its early years was brashly and naïvely Midwestern, and this may have been an important factor in its ability to survive competition with the Associated Press. By 1908, the Associated Press, reckoning from its modernization in 1892, was sixteen years old. It had achieved stability as no other news agency ever had in the United States, and with stability it developed a certain rigidity. It was operated by men who had long been closely associated with big and generally conservative Eastern newspapers. They had prestige, dignity, and a tendency to conform to set habits and traditions.

The men who ran the United Press hadn't been long associated with anything. They were young and self-confident and hungry. They wanted to get ahead. They had moved from newspaper to newspaper and when they got into the United Press they moved from job to job within the organization, and then a lot of them said to hell with this and went back to newspapering or to selling shoes. But a certain percentage stuck and they were—like Howard—largely Midwesterners who saw a chance to get ahead and who could ignore the condescension of the big city newspapermen toward a reporter who worked for the raggle-taggle United Press. There was another Midwestern quality that helped these young men along, too. They weren't afraid to tamper with tradition or to take a chance with a new idea. What some famous newspaperman had done or not done ten or twenty years before was no precedent for them because they had never heard of it. They went at their jobs with whatever equipment they had, and if that wasn't enough they invented something new.

An example of Howard's enterprising approach to news coverage developed in connection with a vacation trip by J. Pierpont Morgan up the Nile River. While the famous banker was on this trip, rumors began circulating in New York that he had fallen seriously ill. The rumors upset the market but all efforts to get information of any kind from the offices of J. P. Morgan & Company were unsuccessful. The company's spokesman simply clammed up, and newspapers in New York were balked in their attempts to get the facts. But Howard declined to be awed by the wall of silence erected around the Morgan company's affairs. He addressed a personal cable to Morgan in Egypt asking him to clear up—by "collect cable" to the United Press—the rumors about his health. Howard hesitantly risked twenty-five dollars to send the cable but it was a good investment. The next day he received a long prepaid reply from Morgan saying that he had been uncomfortably ill but was better and the doctors did not regard his condition as serious.

When the story hit the afternoon newspaper headlines the market leaped upward. So did the temperature of several Morgan partners. The firm's spokesman indicated to other newsmen that the United Press story was not authentic and then called Howard on the telephone, denouncing him and demanding that he "come down here and bring that fake cablegram."

"If you want to see it you can come up here," Howard replied.

Twenty minutes later he puffed angrily into the bureau. Howard handed him the cable. He read it and puffed angrily out again without a word. Actually, company officers had known all along that Morgan had been seriously ill—he died soon afterward—but had remained silent about it.

The Western Union Telegraph Company was already old and sedate, accustomed to doing business in its own manner even after it encountered competition in the form of Postal Telegraph. Since many newspapers could not afford a regular leased wire to deliver news, a simple system of sending dispatches in the form of Western Union or Postal telegrams had grown up. It was not unusual, however, for the telegraph companies to handle these telegrams haphazardly and slowly. There were many complaints from editors that their news report arrived too late to get into the afternoon edition. Some of them would threaten to cancel the service and frequently did, but they soon discovered that the dispatches were often late whether they came from the United Press or the Associated Press.

The United Press manager in Indianapolis, Kent Cooper, was particularly irked by delays in such service to his client newspapers, and decided to do something about it. He began using the telephone regularly to serve some small newspapers. The long-distance telephone rates were too high to make this practicable generally, but Cooper proposed an arrangement with the telephone company to give him a low rate on a regular daily news budget transmitted by telephone to several client papers simultaneously.

It was a revolutionary idea for the time, but the American Telephone and Telegraph Company was eager to develop new business and quickly fell in with his scheme. With a little practice, it was found that the newspapers could receive more words by telephone than they could get by telegraph for the same amount of money. Furthermore, the bureau manager knew when he hung up the telephone that the report had been delivered on time. This system was called "Public News Transmission" or PNT and eventually the "pony report." It proved a boon to small newspapers and was rapidly adopted by other United Press bureaus with the encouragement of the A.T.&T. With a bureau man who could read clearly and rapidly and with experienced men on the receiving end in each newspaper, a report of 1000 or 1200 words and often more could be transmitted to as many as ten newspapers in fifteen minutes. As the system developed, each newspaper would receive two five-minute periods of news reports and perhaps a third five-minute period for last-minute bulletins at rates as low as ten and twenty dollars a week in some areas.

Other early United Press innovations included the transmission of feature stories—largely human-interest pieces about personalities—on the leased wire, the use of by-lines (the signature of reporters) on important stories and creation of the Red Letter mail service. The Red Letter was a news sheet filled with stories that were not urgent but of general interest, theatrical articles, personality pieces, and copious background on some event—such as a ceremony at the Vatican—that was scheduled to take place on a certain date. Many of the articles were written to supplement telegraphic news that would be on the wires on specific dates, giving the telegraph editors of newspapers a column or so of background material that could be added to the telegraphic news if desired. The Red Letter was especially valuable to small newspapers which could clip out feature stories to supplement their scanty wire reports.

2.

Howard was a busy executive but never too busy to be a reporter. In the summer of 1908 he had appeared in Chicago with his crack political reporter, John Edwin Nevin, to cover the Socialist national convention that nominated Eugene V. Debs for President. He also covered the Democratic and Republican conventions and often dictated the play-by-play account of the baseball World Series. On July 4, 1910, he was in Reno, Nevada, for the heavyweight championship fight between Jack Johnson and Jim Jeffries.

The telegraph service from Reno was not all that could be desired, but Howard had made arrangements for two wires, one leading west to San Francisco and the other leading east to Chicago and New York. Howard's experience with boxing crowds had made him aware of the tremendous noise and confusion at ringside, and weeks before the fight he began to worry about how it would be possible to dictate the blow-by-blow account of the fight to two operators at the same time. Then one day he noticed in the window of a store an old-fashioned gramophone device with long rubber tubes leading to earpieces. He went in and bought one with eight feet of rubber tubing. He also bought an ear trumpet such as was then often used by deaf persons and attached it to the tubing.

When he got to Reno, Howard went out to the arena to inspect the four seats that had been assigned to the United Press in the ringside press box. He had his west-wire operator installed in the first seat, the second and third seats he reserved for himself and Max Balthasar, and the fourth seat was marked for the east-wire operator. Then he produced the strange equipment he had purchased and began arranging an ear trumpet, earpieces, and eight feet of rubber tubing along the narrow table already crowded with typewriters and telegraph instruments.

By the time the famous boxers appeared in the ring the reasons for his preparations had become apparent. The great crowd of men thronging the arena was in a wild, unrestrained mood at the prospect of a championship battle. They roamed crazily through the aisles, they jammed the ringside area, they shouted and roared and, not infrequently, fought each other. The tumult was indescribable and you had to shout to be understood by the man at your elbow. Just before the fight started, Howard seated Balthasar beside the west-wire operator and handed him the ear trumpet that had been spliced to one end of the tubing. He handed the earpieces on the other end of the tubing to the east-wire operator and told him to put them on. Balthasar held the trumpet close to his lips and leaned his head close to the ear of the west-wire operator, who could thus hear his words without artificial aid. And, at the same time, the east-wire operator could hear him through the speaking tube.

The gong rang. "They came out swinging. . . ." Balthasar dictated to both operators, who simultaneously transmitted his blow-by-blow description on the east and west circuits. Howard looked over at the Associated Press sports staff. They were writing out the blow-by-blow account in short "takes" and handing them to their telegraph operators. Howard also was sure they were writing the description in considerable detail so that it would be complete enough to satisfy morning newspapers. As a result, they were rapidly falling behind the concise, graphic account that Balthasar was dictating as it happened.

As the fight progressed, newspapers all over the country had announcers stationed in front of their offices to give the crowds a round-by-round description of the fight. In cities where there were both United Press and Associated Press newspapers, the largest crowds gathered in front of the AP paper's offices. But by the time the fight was four rounds old the word had spread that the United Press description was a round or two ahead. The crowds began to shift to the offices of the United Press clients. When Johnson knocked out Jeffries in the fifteenth round, the United Press blow-by-blow story was complete. Balthasar merely had to describe the last blows—"Jeffries went down. FLASH: Johnson wins by knockout." The Associated Press flash on the knockout was sent in the middle of their description of the ninth round and United Press afternoon newspapers had gone to press with a complete story of the fight long before the AP finished its round-by-round account.

3.

Howard never permitted the United Press or any United Press bureau to settle down into routine. He kept everybody moving. For all of these fast-moving employees he had some stern advice. "Don't try to imitate the Associated Press," he warned whenever he caught up with them, which was frequently. "Other people have tried that with no luck. We've got to do things that have never been done before. Remember what you wanted but didn't get from a wire service when you were a telegraph editor. Ask every telegraph editor you see what he wants but doesn't get. Don't worry too much about the publisher or the editor—keep in touch with the man who handles the wire report in the newspaper office. Study the way Pulitzer and Hearst humanize the news in their papers. Get interviews with people in the news. People are usually more interesting than the things they are doing. Dramatize them."

This approach had begun to pay off in 1909 when Howard had drummed up enough clients to enable the United Press to make a profit for the first time—about $1200 for the year. This may have been the first time in history that any news agency had made a profit derived wholly from the selling of news, because most earlier news agencies also performed other functions for a profit or were, like the Associated Press, operated on a non-profit co-operative basis.[1] By 1909 Howard also had moved his headquarters from the Park Row building to the third floor of the New York *World* building, also on Park Row. The offices in the *World* building were considerably larger, and Howard picked the best spot for his desk—in front of the windows at one end of the room. Unhappily, when he picked the spot he did not realize that a big exhaust fan from the kitchen of a nearby restaurant was just outside the windows. When warm weather came along and he opened the windows he was all but suffocated by the pungent, greasy smell of cooking onions, hamburgers, and beans.

Unaffected by cooking odors but apparently impressed by the growing client list, the United Press board of directors held a special meeting at Miramar in January of 1910 and considered an unusual resolution. Present were Clark, Howard, H. N. Rickey of the Cleveland *Press*, B. H. Canfield, J. C. Harper and W. B. Colver.

"Mr. Rickey," the minutes of the meeting recorded, "moved that the directors instruct the United Press executive officers to make a profit of $12,-000 for the year 1910."

The motion was seconded by Harper and put to a vote. Everybody voted "yes," including Howard, who now faced the problem of making the United

---

[1] Negley D. Cochran, in his book *E. W. Scripps*, states that the United Press was "the first news agency in the history of the world's journalism ever to make a profit that was derived solely from the merchandising of news."

Press return a profit ten times as great as had been possible in the previous twelve months. It meant more scrimping on costs. It meant some United Press men weren't going to get the raises they were expecting. It meant that a lot of ingenuity would have to be exercised.

4.

Out in Chicago, Furay had been exercising plenty of ingenuity as well as a lot of common sense. Just take the Republican national convention that met in Chicago to nominate William Howard Taft for the presidency. Furay had never covered so much as a county convention and was happy to leave the reporting job to the United Press political experts who came on from Washington, but he had to see that their dispatches moved rapidly from Chicago to newspapers all over the country. And he didn't even have a leased wire between Chicago and San Francisco—a fact that the United Press usually tried to keep hidden from the world.

Hawkins was in charge of the Pacific coast bureaus at that time and his only communication with Furay in Chicago was by Western Union telegrams, which meant that the United Press newspapers in the West would get scanty service as compared to the report that could be laid down over the Associated Press leased wire. Both Furay and Hawkins, however, were competitive. Nothing hurt them so much as to imagine that the Associated Press could do a better job for a lot of money than they could do for a little. Prior to the opening of the convention they assembled all possible material on what was going to happen, hour by hour and day by day. They wrote colorful sketches about the men who would play important roles in the proceedings and had the veterans of the Washington staff write descriptive material concerning various formalities which are the same at every national convention.

When the United Press staff at Chicago started writing the story of the convention, Furay sat at his desk with a copy of all the prepared material at his elbow. He passed the stories from the convention hall on to telegraph operators, who began sending them to newspapers on the United Press leased wires in the Middle West and East. Then he scribbled a telegram to Hawkins at San Francisco: "Convention opened release advance one." This he handed to a boy who rushed it to the Western Union operator and saw that it was dispatched to San Francisco.

Meantime, the Associated Press leased wire began carrying at forty words a minute a dispatch about the opening of the convention. It took the reporter on the scene a few minutes to get his copy written. Then it was relayed to the Chicago bureau and then relayed again on the leased wires strung over hundreds of miles to the West Coast. But there is a limit to the distance over which a leased wire can be efficiently operated. In those days there was not an unbroken circuit from Chicago to San Francisco and, in fact, it was necessary for the Associated Press copy to pass through such "relay points" as Kansas City, Denver, and Salt Lake City as it traveled across the country—that is, it had to be copied by a Morse operator and then re-sent by another Morse operator several times. At least a few minutes were lost at each relay and this necessarily slowed down transmission of cross-country dispatches.

Furay's telegram to Hawkins, on the other hand, was brief, and with luck it could be delivered in San Francisco within perhaps twenty minutes. Hawkins then picked up story number one in the copy already prepared for the routine opening of the convention and started it moving on the United Press leased wires in California, Oregon, and Washington. By the time a few paragraphs had moved, another brief telegram arrived from Furay saying something such as:

STUMPF PREDICTS TAFT FIRST BALLOT

Hawkins promptly stopped the story moving on his wires at the end of a paragraph and wrote a new paragraph or two saying that Senator Josiah Stumpf had started the convention off harmoniously by predicting that William Howard Taft, the choice of President Roosevelt, would be nominated on the first ballot, and going on to tell who Stumpf was and why his words were important. He inserted this news in the story and then kept on moving the material that had been prepared in advance until he got another telegram from Furay.

Thus, by the time the Associated Press had delivered to newspapers 500 words of the convention story, the United Press wires on the Pacific coast had delivered perhaps 300 or 400 words, including Senator Stumpf's last-minute statement—all at the cost of a few telegrams. This did not, of course, make the United Press coverage equal to that of the Associated Press. There were times when Hawkins ran out of anything to put on the wire for long periods, and editors would call up to ask: "Say, what's happening at Chicago now?"

Hawkins would dig out his advance program and find, perhaps, that at 2:30 P.M. the governor of New Jersey was scheduled to make a speech.

"Why, they're listening to a speech by the governor of New Jersey right now," he would reply. "We'll have it on the wire just as soon as he says anything worth reporting."

Then he would wait for the next telegram from Furay and dash off a snappy "add running story" to keep the clients up to date. Sometimes he had to wait quite a while because the cost of the telegrams sent to San Francisco was charged against the budget of Furay's Chicago bureau, and Furay was constantly worried about overspending his budget. His telegrams were masterpieces of brevity and he sent them only when necessary. But after a fashion he and Hawkins managed to get by with their system throughout the convention. Sometimes, indeed, they got important news developments on the west-coast wire ahead of the Associated Press. By the time the Democratic convention met later in the year at Denver, however, Howard decided that such makeshifts had to be abandoned. A leased wire was set up from Denver to San Francisco for the duration of the political sessions.

5.

When the leased wire was permanently extended to Denver in 1910 Furay went with it to open the new bureau and remain as Rocky Mountain manager. He was succeeded in Chicago by Edward T. Conkle, a stern-looking man with an acid tongue but also with patience and the ability to train young reporters. Conkle never learned to use a typewriter and wrote all of his copy in longhand. He did not smoke, but he almost always had a stogie in his mouth and he chewed it furiously while at work. His language was profane even for a newspaper office when things went wrong, but he took the responsibility for running his own bureau and many times also took the blame for mistakes committed by his staff. For more than twenty years he conducted the most successful training school in the United Press organization.

Among his "students" were Raymond Clapper, Webb Miller, Miles W. Vaughn, L. B. Mickel, Wilbur Forrest, and many others. He also had a well-known student whom he acquired in an unusual manner. About the time Conkle arrived from Cleveland, where he had been bureau manager, he hired a new office boy in the Chicago bureau. An office boy had many duties. Sometimes he read the "pony" report over the telephone to nearby client newspapers. He ran errands. He made "books"—a dirty job that involved sliding heavy carbon papers between thin sheets of flimsy paper on which reporters and telegraph operators typed six or eight copies of a story. An office boy had to make scores of such "books" every day and was likely to end up with carbon covering his hands and face.

When the new boy reported for work, Conkle was puzzled by something about his appearance. He called him to his desk.

"Son," he said, "there's something different about you today. What is it?"

The boy gave him a challenging glance. "What's wrong?" he demanded. "Don't I look okay?"

Conkle nodded. "Yes, you look fine. But something bothers me today and I think it's you."

The boy shrugged. "All right, my brother was the one you hired but he got a better job. I want to be a reporter, so I took his place."

Conkle chewed his cigar and nodded again. "Okay. What's your name?"

"Pegler, like my brother's," the kid answered. "Westbrook Pegler. But just call me Bud."

CHAPTER FOUR

There was a great deal more than ingenuity involved in the progress the United Press made in the difficult and critical period prior to World War I. There were young men coming into the organization who would rank among the best reporters in the country, and their contributions were of top importance in the slow process of building up the press association's prestige.

One of them was a slim, personable fellow named William G. Shepherd, who not only had the ability to make a story "come alive" but had an uncanny knack for being on the right spot at the right time. Shepherd had been a reporter in Minneapolis and St. Paul, getting most of his experience on the St. Paul *Daily News,* before he wangled a job with the United Press in New York. He hadn't been there long when he stumbled into one of the biggest stories in years. He was walking back to his hotel on Saturday, March 25, 1911, when he saw smoke pouring from windows of the Triangle Waist Company factory, a flimsy loft building that lacked adequate fire escapes.

Shepherd ran about a block down the street to the factory, where flames already were shooting up the stairways and elevator shafts, cutting off scores of women employees on the upper floors. He found a telephone in the window of a building across the street from the factory and called the United Press bureau. Roy Howard was on the desk in the New York office and answered the telephone.

"Roy, I'm across the street from the Triangle Waist factory and there is a helluva fire in the building," Shepherd said. "I can see some girls and boys at the windows above the ninth floor. I think some of them are about to jump—— There goes one! Can you hear . . . oh, my God, there goes another. . . ."

Howard broke in. "Bill, are you drunk?"

"Roy, another one just jumped. There are a lot more trapped. . . ."

"Just wait a second, Bill," Howard said. He turned to the adjacent telegraph desk where four operators were at work. "Everybody break!" he yelled. "Now listen. I'm going to dictate a bulletin. New York, March 25 (By United Press) Fire broke out this afternoon in the Triangle Waist factory and it is feared a number of persons have been trapped in the upper stories. Some have jumped from the windows of the ninth floor. . . ."

"Is that right, Bill?" he asked Shepherd, who could hear over the telephone what Howard was dictating directly to the Morse operators in the office.

"Yes, okay, I can count nine bodies on the sidewalk. There's a boy and a girl on the tenth floor. They've got their arms around each other and are on the window sill. They're kissing. There they go . . . they jumped. My God, Roy, there are more getting ready. . . ."

Howard kept on dictating to the telegraph operators, repeating what Shepherd said to him over the telephone. It was an incredible tragedy that Shepherd reported and all the horror of the scene seeped into paragraph after paragraph as the story went on the wires across the nation. He had reported several score dead before any other reporters could reach the scene of the fire. By the time, more than an hour later, he turned the telephone over to reporters sent to relieve him it was about over and firemen were counting 145 dead in the ruins of the firetrap. Incidentally, the eloquent horror of Shepherd's story did much to bring about later legislation designed to prevent such gross negligence in the safeguarding of the nation's factories against fire.

When Howard had finished dictating the story for the afternoon wires, he suddenly remembered that a story had to be prepared for the Saturday night wire. But he had not written down a word. He slammed his pencil down in disgust.

"What's the matter?" asked Arthur Struwe, who was working the other side of the desk.

"Why, I've dictated a thousand words direct to the wire and we've now got nothing on paper for the night wire," Howard exclaimed.

"Oh yes, we have," Struwe replied. "It's all right here. I took it down on the typewriter as you were dictating."

When Shepherd got to the office late that afternoon he was near collapse. Howard asked him if he could write a personal story of the tragedy he had witnessed. He nodded. But then he sat down at the typewriter and buried his head in his arms for several minutes, trying to control his emotions. When he straightened up he began writing.

BY WILLIAM G. SHEPHERD

NEW YORK, March 25 (United Press) *Thud—dead! Thud—dead! Thud—dead!*

Sixty-two "thud—deads." I call them that because the sound and the thought of death came to me, each time, at the same instant. There was plenty of chance to watch them as they came down; the height was eighty feet.

I was walking through Washington Square when a puff of smoke issuing from the factory building caught my eye. I reached the building before the alarm was turned in. . . . I learned a new sound—a more horrible sound than description can picture. It was the thud of a speeding, living body on a stone sidewalk. . . .

Howard pulled the first couple of paragraphs of copy from Shepherd's typewriter and carried them over to the waiting telegraphers. For an hour Shepherd wrote without pause except to put fresh paper into his machine. He told the story in short sentences that were all the more vivid for their simplicity. Men—hard-boiled newspapermen—standing beside telegraph desks all over the country read the story as operators transcribed it and felt that they were looking over Bill Shepherd's shoulder as the old factory shuddered with flames and girls crowded the windows with hopelessness written on their faces. In some offices the story was tacked on the wall and remained there for months as an example of how to do a job of reporting.

Shepherd's story of the Triangle Waist factory fire was the beginning of a long reportorial career in which he never lost his touch for the simple, factual telling of a story. Whenever anybody asked him how he did it, he had a famous answer:

"Why, there's nothing to it," he liked to say. "I just write for the milkman in Omaha. I figure if he can understand what I'm writing, then everybody can understand it."

Writing for "the Omaha milkman" became a standard phrase in the offices of the United Press, repeated over and over to young reporters who were trying to learn how to tell a story quickly and simply. There was nothing fancy about Shepherd's writing, but he left a mark on the United Press that served as a guide for many years.

2.

The greatest problem faced by United Press bureau managers in the early days probably was the coverage of big news stories that broke in remote areas. This was due to the peculiarities of the communications setup under which the agency operated: specifically, the lack of leased wires and sometimes the lack of even a string correspondent in large sections of the country. A bureau manager in St. Louis, for example, might be responsible for covering anything that happened as far away as New Orleans or Brownsville, Texas. This frequently called for ingenuity of a high order, especially on a shoestring budget, and occasionally prompted the Associated Press to complain, possibly with some justification, that the United Press was not above "lifting" news that had been gathered by its member newspapers. The

United Press occasionally made the same complaint about the Associated Press.

When the Mexican revolution against Porfirio Díaz began late in 1910, most of the southwestern part of the United States and the Mexican border area were just one great open space as far as the United Press was concerned. The agency had a telegraph "pony" client newspaper at El Paso and its correspondents were helpful, as were the editors of the Fort Worth *Star-Telegram*. But there was no leased wire that reached the southwestern region, and such news as the company's stringers could collect had to be filed by telegraph to St. Louis or Denver, where rewrite men wove it into a daily story.

Sometimes this system worked out well. During the early revolutionary period, an attack was made on the town of Torreón by insurgents under direction of Francisco I. Madero, Venustiano Carranza, and Pancho Villa. The United Press correspondent on the El Paso *Herald* studied the daily dispatches received from that newspaper's correspondents in the field and then sent a condensed report by telegram to the United Press in Denver, where Furay was manager. These reports were more colorful than any other dispatches printed in the United States, but it was not until years later that Furay learned most of them were based on dispatches written by John Reed, who was then the *Herald's* reporter at Torreón and who later attracted wide attention for his writing on the Bolshevik revolution in Russia and was buried in the Kremlin wall at Moscow.

There were plenty of other times when the system ran less smoothly. As the fighting spread later to Juárez, across the Rio Grande from El Paso, Furay arranged for a reporter named Cook, who worked for an Associated Press newspaper, to act as correspondent and to file up to 200 words a day to the Denver bureau. Cook did a good job covering the first day of the battle of Juárez and that evening Furay was congratulating himself for having found a capable man when he received still another telegram:

PLEASE ACCEPT MY RESIGNATION. MY PAPER BELONGS ASSOCIATED PRESS MANAGEMENT OF WHICH INSISTS THAT NO STAFF MEMBER BE PERMITTED WORK FOR UNITED PRESS. HAVE ARRANGED FOR COMPETENT REPORTER BROWN TO COVER FOR YOU.

COOK

Furay fretted at the loss of a good man, but on the second day of the battle Brown's telegrams proved to be just as expert as Cook's had been. In fact, Furay observed that, oddly enough, Brown was using many of the same phrases and expressions that Cook had used. His spirits soaring again as the result of a second day's excellent coverage of the battle, Furay sat down to write a telegram of appreciation. He never sent it, because at that moment he received a telegram:

REGRET MUST ASK YOU ACCEPT MY RESIGNATION. BUT HAVE ARRANGED
FOR GOOD MAN GORDON TO PROTECT YOU.

BROWN

More than a little perplexed Furay went home to a restless night's sleep. The next day, however, Gordon proved to be just as competent as Brown and Cook had been and, since the battle was reaching its climax on the third day, his telegrams provided a magnificent description that drew congratulations from many client newspapers. The fact that he tended to use words and phrases in the manner of Brown and Cook was no great surprise to Furay by that time. He was happy to be getting the reports and had no intention of disturbing such a satisfactory arrangement. He wasn't even much surprised when he received a telegram of resignation about 5 P.M.

This time the telegram wasn't signed by Gordon but by the original Cook, who candidly explained that now his resignation was absolute, positive, and final, and there was no substitute in line. He went on to say that he had been able to get away with changing his name for a couple of days and that his editor merely winked at him. But now the Associated Press management had informed his newspaper that its service would be suspended if any member of the staff continued to cover for the United Press. "So this is for keeps," Cook added. Luckily for Furay, the New York office some days earlier had ordered Bill Shepherd to the Mexican border, and he arrived at El Paso that night to take up the burden.

3.

Ed L. Keen was the first United Press manager in Washington. At the turn of the century, he had covered the Spanish-American War in Cuba as correspondent for Scripps-McRae Press Association and had later been sent to the Far East, where he scored a notable beat on the start of the 1899 insurrection, led by General Emilio Aguinaldo, against the United States forces in the Philippines. One reason for Keen's beat on the story was that he filed 600 words at the "urgent" rate of $5.40 for each word instead of using the much slower press rate, and his report reached the United States even before official advices had arrived at the War Department in Washington. "It cost $3240—a tremendous sum for any press association in those days, and especially for ours," Keen wrote much later. "I never forgot the success of that plunge, and it influenced my decisions on many later occasions. But, I have no doubt, I would have been fired if the story had not turned out to be a world beat."

As Washington manager of SMPA and then of United Press, Keen did much to establish the prestige of his bureau, to win equal rights with other correspondents in facilities for coverage of the capital, and to speed up communications. Dot-and-dash telegraphers working the leased wires used the Phillips code—a system of abbreviating words—to speed up transmission of copy. They would send in dot and dash only the letter "t" for the word "the" or "tt" for "that" or "f" for "of the" or "scotus" for "Supreme Court of the United States." There were many such contractions in the Phillips code, and they meant much faster transmission. Reporters soon became familiar with the code and adopted it as a kind of shorthand for taking notes. Keen went a step further in the days when there were few typewriters in the Washington bureau and most copy was written in longhand. He required all members of his staff to learn the Phillips code. Then if a reporter telephoned a story to the office the man on the desk could take it down rapidly in longhand by using the code and pass his copy directly to the telegrapher for instant transmission on the wire if desired. This meant a saving of perhaps five minutes on brief stories and much more on longer dispatches. On many occasions, it meant that Keen's understaffed bureau could get a late start in reporting a story but still deliver it to client newspapers ahead of the opposition.

One of the young reporters on Keen's staff was Perry Arnold, who later put down his recollections of the early days of the United Press: "A United Press man in those days was a man apart. The dynamic influence which had been evident in the [New York] office was beginning to permeate the whole organization. United Press staff men knew our organization would not countenance any combinations or any pool of news resources with others. That viewpoint struck at the foundations of a Washington institution as old as the press gallery itself for 'combinations' were the regular and accepted form of news coverage with everybody helping everybody else."

The Republicans had a firm grip on the national capital in 1909 when Richard A. Ballinger of Washington State, who was President Taft's Secretary of Interior, came under fire. A few months after his appointment, an Interior Department investigator named Louis R. Glavis wrote an article for *Collier's Weekly* charging Ballinger with mismanagement in administration of public lands and hinting at still graver shortcomings bearing on the integrity of the Secretary. Gifford Pinchot, who later became governor of Pennsylvania, was then the chief forester of the United States and a leader in the Progressive branch of the Republican party. Pinchot supported Glavis' charges and in the ensuing political tumult forced the party's congressional leaders to order an investigation by a joint committee of both houses.

While the hearings were dragging along, Arnold ran into an old personal friend, Fred Kerby, who was then private secretary to Ballinger. Kerby told him confidentially that his conscience was troubled because he had transcribed a defense of Ballinger which Ballinger himself had dictated but which was to be made public as coming from the President to the joint committee. In other words, the public official who was on trial had written the letter exonerating himself.

Arnold, later joined by Robert Wilson, the Scripps-McRae newspapers' correspondent covering the hearings, urged Kerby to make a public revelation of the whole affair. He hesitated, knowing that he would be vilified and fired immediately. Arnold also informed Louis D. Brandeis, who was counsel for Glavis, of the situation, but the lawyer, although knowing that Kerby's story could be a decisive factor, said that professional ethics prevented him from approaching Kerby. Finally, however, Kerby went to see Brandeis and told the whole story, backed up by his stenographic notes of Ballinger's dictation. He also agreed that Arnold and Wilson could break the story, which they did the next day.

The joint committee's anger was great and its action rapid. Kerby, Arnold, and Wilson were subpoenaed and Kerby was sworn as a witness while frowning, red-faced senators and representatives looked on. The committee counsel then made a traditional prosecuting attorney's attack on Kerby by questions that clearly suggested he was an ingrate, a liar, a sneak, and probably beat his wife. But Kerby proved to be a good witness. He knew all the details and he stuck to them, usually backing them up with documentary evidence. The committee counsel also described Arnold as a "snake," among other things, but did not call him as a witness.

It was perhaps in the nature of political affairs at the time that the joint committee then closed its proceedings by exonerating Ballinger as it had planned all along. Later, however, Ballinger resigned from the Cabinet.

4.

Two important stories brought special attention to the United Press early in the second decade of the twentieth century. One was the textile workers' strike at Lawrence, Massachusetts, in the bitterly cold winter of 1912, and the other was the so-called Ludlow massacre in southern Colorado during a long and bloody conflict of strikers against the Rockefeller-owned Colorado Fuel and Iron Company.

The Massachusetts strike was being routinely reported when Howard decided that it offered the kind of opportunity he had been seeking to draw attention to the United Press by more vivid, human-interest writing. Marlen E. Pew, who had been in charge of the Newspaper Enterprise Association when Howard first arrived in New York, had later become the United Press New England manager with headquarters in Boston. Howard directed him to go to Lawrence to get the "heart" of the strike story—the story of the people involved, how they lived, what they said and did. Pew arrived at a good time.

Lawrence was a city of 90,000, with many big textile mills employing some 30,000 men and women. They had been working sixty hours a week but only recently had succeeded in getting through the legislature a law that limited the week to fifty-four hours. The manufacturers changed the shifts to conform with the law but they also cut twenty-two cents a day off the pay check of each worker. The strike followed, and there were threats that it would spread to some 200,000 workers in other New England cities.

The International Workers of the World and other extreme left-wing labor organizations were active and most of them were regularly denounced in the newspapers for resorting to violence and advocating socialism. As a result the strike had generally been pictured as the attempt of a small band of radicals to stir up a revolt against the police and the capitalistic system. There were various clashes, which were usually described by the press as attacks by a mob on police.

"I want you to understand," the mayor of Lawrence said to one reporter, "that a crowd of bandits is not going to run this city. I will keep order here if I have to call on the whole federal army, and believe me when I tell you that if the rioting is repeated there will be awful slaughter."

That kind of story from the strike zone was typical, but Pew went further and studied the viewpoint of the strikers, too. He talked with scores of them, learned how they lived and why they were striking. When the mayor later announced that the strike was about over and the strikers were going back to work, Pew knew enough about their attitude to be prepared for a new demonstration the next day by 7000 men and women who attacked streetcars, beat up anyone who tried to return to work, and successfully resisted a bayonet charge by Company G of the 8th Regiment.

He reported, too, the story of a former New York school girl, Elizabeth Gurley Flynn, who had become a socialist and an ardent worker in behalf of the strikers. Pew told it all as he saw it—the fact that it was more often the hired guards of the company than the police who attacked strikers, the harassment of the strikers by the militiamen who broke up their parades, the viciousness of strikers who dug bricks and chunks of ice from the streets to hurl at trolley cars or at factory guards or at factory windows.

Perhaps there was an element of crusading in Pew's stories, although he did no more than would be done by all press associations and most newspapers in later years—try to tell both sides of a controversial story. It was a period in which labor was struggling to win a position in the American community, and the "crusade"—if any—that Howard and Pew waged was merely for the right to present all sides of a question to the public. The stories were a sensational success, led to a congressional investigation, and did a great deal to further the prestige of the United Press.

Coverage of the strike against the Colorado Fuel and Iron Company in 1913 was a difficult job for the United Press because its biggest client in the state, the Denver *Express,* was vigorously biased in favor of the strikers. Furay, in charge of the Denver bureau, had his office in the *Express* building, and was entitled to use the newspaper's dispatches but he could not depend on them for objective reporting. He was then running the bureau without any assistant, not even an office boy, and a fourteen-hour day in a seven-day week was more or less routine for him. It gave him little time to get out and cover a story himself, but he had long since become an expert on the telephone. For the most part he used the *Express* correspondents' stories as "tips" on developments in the strike, which extended over a large part of the state, and then called up the sheriff or some other official at the scene of action so he could report both sides of the story.

This system worked well since the *Express* had plenty of men scattered around the strike areas and Furay could be assured of getting quick tips on whatever happened, as well as a lot of rumors about what might happen. There was one *Express* correspondent, Donald MacGregor, whose stories were biased but brilliant, and Furay often found it difficult to resist using his copy on the wires despite his knowledge that most of them were distortions. MacGregor wrote in a distinct British newspaper style, but in such a fiery manner that his articles were the most interesting to come out of the strike zone.

The strike dragged on, and by September of 1913 Furay had lined up string correspondents in key towns and was able to relax slightly. Then Governor Ammons ordered out the state's single regiment of militia to keep order in the southern area. There were many militants among the strikers during the following winter, and in April there was acute tension at Ludlow, near Walsenburg, where the strikers and their families were living in a tent colony. On April 21 the tension broke into violence. It was not then or later easy to establish exactly what happened. The soldiers charged that the strikers fired on them. The strikers charged that state troops, aided by armed mine guards, deliberately set out to destroy the tent colony and opened fire on the strikers without provocation. The miners, who were armed, returned the fire. The tents were soon blazing and a pitched battle was in progress. Before it ended, twenty-five strikers or members of strikers' families were dead, including two women and eleven children, who died of suffocation in a cave where they had hidden to escape the machine-gun fire.

In the Denver office of the United Press, Furay was making the most of a lucky break. The *Express'* fiery MacGregor was the only staff correspondent of a Denver newspaper at the scene of the battle. Indeed, there was a strong suspicion on the part of Furay that MacGregor was probably leading the fighting. But in any event, his reports to the *Express* gave the United Press an early tip that violence had broken out, and Furay was able to telephone his string correspondents as well as the sheriff's office to get the management's side of the story. By that time the strikers' side of the story had been laid in his lap by the brilliant young Scotsman, who turned in a graphic blow-by-blow account of the fighting, of the burning tents, and of the wounded and dying children. With the viewpoints of both sides in his hands, Furay was able to write a rapid and objective story of the battle that brought attention to the United Press report in spectacular fashion.

The Ludlow fighting shocked the nation and opened the public's eyes to the futility and the dangers involved in such crude handling of relations between management, labor, and the state. The brutality of the attack and the killing of women and children swayed public opinion toward the cause of labor. Strike sympathizers from all parts of the state rushed to Walsenburg, Trinidad, and Ludlow to lend aid, and for a time there was a threat of "civil war" in Colorado. At that stage, President Wilson ordered two squadrons of United States cavalry to the scene, and the troops disarmed both sides. The militiamen were ordered back to their homes and order was restored.

CHAPTER FIVE

The news coverage which the United Press provided for its client newspapers in the first few years of its existence was sometimes very good, and generally a little better than might have been expected of such a new and comparatively small organization. But it was nothing that caused any tremors of fear at meetings of the board of directors of the Associated Press, which had over-all expenses in 1910 of $2,742,492. The older organization sometimes clamped down on its members—numbering close to 800 newspapers—to prevent them from assisting or subscribing to the United Press, but its official view of the upstart press association was strictly down the nose.

Roy Howard had no fault to find with this attitude. It gave him plenty of opportunity to push his own ideas of how a press association should cover the news, and it tended to retard the Associated Press in keeping up with the innovations introduced by the United Press.

Howard had started operations on a shoestring, with 369 afternoon clients, most of them small newspapers. By 1909 the United Press had lost some clients but had gained new ones. The result was that the number was not much larger—392—and the shoestring was not much longer. In that year, for example, Howard's annual budget for correspondents, special services, and foreign coverage totaled only $72,628. The Boston bureau in 1909 was operating on an average of about $300 a month, including the salaries of the staff. The Washington bureau was spending only about $1100 a month and the Chicago bureau less than $1000. There were, technically, twenty-one bureaus in the United States and others in London, Paris, Rome, Berlin, Tokyo, and Havana, but some of them had only one man or perhaps one man and an office-boy assistant. By the end of 1912 there were still only a score of bureaus, but the cost of operating them was $100,800 a year in the United States alone. Over-all news expenses were $165,000 that year. By then the list of client newspapers had grown to 491, and Howard was elected chairman of the board of directors.

The mere fact that the United Press was making money didn't prompt

Howard to expand his shoestring more than necessary. Cutting corners to save on expenses, avoiding waste, keeping the overhead down were all well-established Scripps policies, and with the United Press, Howard kept up the tradition in small as well as large matters. Walking through the news room, he would stop to pick up a new piece of carbon paper that someone had carelessly dropped underfoot and restore it to the pile from which the office boy made "books" for the staff's typewriters. A reporter was expected to get top mileage out of pencils and typewriter ribbons. Expense accounts were closely scrutinized. Perry Arnold of the Washington bureau was once ordered aboard a naval vessel heading for the West Indies on such short notice that he did not have time to pack a bag. His winter suit soon became unbearable and he purchased some white ducks for eight dollars, and listed that amount on his expense account. It was promptly returned to him with a notation that the company didn't buy clothes for its employees, and he had to send in another accounting—in which the eight dollars was carefully concealed as routine expenses—before he could collect.

Until Howard became chairman of the board, the United Press had been so busy developing news-gathering facilities that it had somewhat neglected the establishment of an efficient business and sales organization. In his travels around the country, Howard had been a promoter, a persuader, and a business representative, as well as the spark plug of the news report. But in 1913 he began planning better ways and means of selling the service to additional newspapers.

This thought was uppermost in his mind one day when he stopped in the St. Louis bureau to talk with L. B. Mickel, a new manager there. Mickel had been graduated from Kansas State College a couple of years earlier and gone to work for eighteen dollars a week on Victor Bender's *Evening News* at Springfield, Illinois. There he ate luncheon almost every day with the United Press correspondent in Springfield and noticed that his companion regularly spent twenty-five cents for a piece of beefsteak. Mickel was quickly convinced that he wanted to work for the United Press if its employees could afford to eat so well. He persuaded Manager Ed Conkle at Chicago to give him a job as "pony" editor and, after several months of training, was sent to St. Louis. When Howard visited him, the St. Louis bureau was serving Scripps newspapers in Memphis, Oklahoma City, Dallas, and Houston with telegraphic "pony" reports and Mickel's biggest problem was how to persuade them to put up enough money to pay for a leased wire service to the Southwest. He assumed Howard wanted to discuss that problem, but he was wrong.

"I've been thinking about how to build up a bigger client list," Howard said. "I've got a theory that we can go out and sell the news service more aggressively—the way you might sell shoes or anything else. I'm going to try it out. Would you like to be a salesman?"

Mickel didn't have to think hard about it. He wasn't interested in becoming a salesman and he said so.

"Well," Howard told him, "I think it will work and I think I've got a man who can do it. His name is Karl Bickel."

2.

Tall, lanky, and distinctly Western in his dress, Karl August Bickel arrived in New York in March of 1913. Bickel had been born in Illinois and, inspired by the war dispatches of Richard Harding Davis, had gotten a job on the two-page Geneseo *Daily Arena* while still in high school. Later he had gone to California, attended Stanford University, worked for the San Francisco *News,* and joined the United Press as its first manager at Portland, Oregon, in 1907. He had a desk in the news room of the Portland *Journal* and about all he learned about the news agency business was that there was a querulous little guy in New York named Roy Howard who was always demanding that he spend less money and produce more news six days a week. Howard later remarked that the Portland bureau was the worst in the organization and he was on the verge of firing Bickel when the latter quit to become editor of the Grand Junction *News* in Colorado. In Grand Junction, Bickel worked seven days a week in an effort to make the newspaper pay, became an ardent Bull Moose politician, and almost ruined his health. Late in 1912 he took a leave of absence and went to Florida for a rest, after which he headed for New York with thoughts of getting a new job.

Bickel had known C. D. Lee, who succeeded Vandercook as president of the United Press, when Lee was a telegrapher on the Pacific coast, and he dropped around to see him. Lee took him out to the news room and introduced him to Bill Hawkins, who greeted him warmly as a publisher from Grand Junction. "You must meet Roy," Hawkins insisted, leading him toward an office at the front of the building. Bickel went reluctantly, remembering the little guy in New York whose messages had given him such a headache in Portland. Howard sat at a big desk, wearing a purple and white striped shirt and a black and brown striped suit that was sharp but not gaudy. He leaned back with his feet stuck out. He wore black silk socks —the first silk socks Bickel had ever seen. Bickel thought that he had the most brilliant and intelligent eyes of any man alive.

Howard didn't say much. He, too, may have remembered the days when Bickel was Portland manager. But he was toughly pleasant and carried on a running conversation about nothing in particular for fifteen minutes, after which Bickel departed without any mention of a job. He was waiting for the elevators outside the news room when somebody twitched his elbow. It was Howard.

"Are you in a hurry?" he asked. "I want to talk to you."

Bickel was in no hurry.

"What kind of a newspaperman are you?" Howard demanded. "Are you an executive or are you a reporter?"

"Well, I'm a reporter."

"Hell—what else are you?"

Bickel told him of his experiences in running the Grand Junction newspaper. He suggested that he might be an executive as well as a reporter.

"We've got a bad situation in Connecticut," Howard said. "Hearst has been giving us hell there, trying to grab some of our papers for his International News Service. What would you think about working on it for me?" Before Bickel could reply, he asked: "Where's your furniture?"

"In Grand Junction, Colorado," Bickel replied. Then, seeing Howard frown, he added: "There's not much of it."

Howard nodded. "Fine, I'll pay expenses to New York for you and your wife and half a carload of furniture."

"How much salary do I get?"

"As little as possible—thirty-five dollars a week."

"And what's my job?"

"You'll work for me."

Bickel collected his wife and furniture and went to work for Howard on April 6, 1913. He might be called the first business representative of the United Press—hired to prevent the loss of contracts with some newspapers in Connecticut. But he was a man of great energy and drive and, under Howard's often rough prodding, he soon became intimately acquainted with all of the operations of the organization, as enthusiastic and as full of ideas as the man who had hired him. In Bickel, Howard had found another lieutenant to stand next to Bill Hawkins.

3.

There were various ways to measure the progress of the United Press before World War I. But perhaps the most important gain was in prestige, as illustrated by a highly unexpected development in 1912. Baron Reuter, head of the British press service known as Reuters and the dominating figure in a world-news-service cartel, sounded out Howard on a proposal to exchange news dispatches with the United Press.

This suggestion was impressive to a degree not readily understandable to a layman, despite the fact that Reuter was partly influenced by the personal animus of one of his lieutenants toward the management of the Associated Press. Since 1893 the Associated Press had had an exclusive contract in the United States for exchange of dispatches with Reuters, from which it received most of its foreign news. Reuters was close to the British Foreign Office, and the British Government gave it many special favors in transmission of dispatches over British-owned cables. In addition, Reuter and the heads of half a dozen other news agencies—Havas Agency in France, Wolff's Bureau in Germany, Stefani Agency in Italy, Fabra Agency in Spain, and others—

had agreed among themselves to divide the world into territories in which each would operate exclusively, exchanging news dispatches with one another. The result of this vast interlocking system of agencies was virtually a world monopoly, broken only by special correspondents of large newspapers and smaller news agencies such as the United Press.

Most of the agencies involved in the cartel were regarded as official or quasi-official organizations supported or favored by their various governments, and their dispatches frequently were colored if not distorted by policies of their governments. Such official connections were sharply contrary to American ideas of independent newspapers and objective reporting, but the cartel had such a tight monopolistic grip on government sources of news that it was often difficult if not impossible for outside correspondents to compete successfully against the so-called official agencies. Although the Associated Press received news via the cartel, the dangers of the system had prompted that agency's general manager, Melville E. Stone, to visit Europe several times in an effort to arrange a more equal status for American correspondents dealing with government bureaus. The cartel, however, continued its monopolistic methods and was a very powerful news-gathering organization.

When Reuter considered dropping the Associated Press in favor of an alliance with the United Press, Howard was interested. Such a deal would give him access to the most comprehensive world-news report available—and coverage of foreign news had always been an expensive headache for the United Press. A meeting of the company's board of directors approved a resolution authorizing Howard "to negotiate and conclude a ten-year agreement with the Reuter, Havas, and Wolff agencies for the purchase of news gathered by these concerns." In the spring of 1912 Howard went to London and discussed the proposal with Reuter, who wanted to know many details of operation of the United Press and especially whether it could provide him with comprehensive stock-market reports. Howard apparently convinced him that whatever was needed could be provided, but he was by no means convinced of the wisdom of making an alliance with the cartel. Instead of trying to close an agreement, he explained that he intended to visit United Press bureaus in Europe and would return to the United States to put the Reuters proposal before his board of directors.

Howard had only a few full-time correspondents in Europe, among them Ed Keen in London, William Philip Simms in Paris, and Henry Wood in Rome. But after he had made the rounds he was satisfied. He felt he could depend on his men for alert, objective reporting.

Back in the United States, Howard called a meeting of a group of leading United Press officials and client newspaper editors. When they had assembled in the La Salle Hotel in Chicago he explained to them the proposals of Baron Reuter.

"My purpose here is to get a kind of cross section of opinion as to what we should do," he continued. "If we accept this proposal we will have the services of official agencies that are able to get a great deal of important news ahead of anyone else. On the other hand there are certain grave disadvantages. There is the propaganda danger. Also we would not be able to expand the United Press abroad because the cartel has the world divided up into territories for its various members, and nobody infringes on the other fellow's territory. We would not be able to sell the United Press services abroad."

After the details had been thoroughly discussed, somebody asked Howard for his own opinion.

"I am against accepting the proposal," he said. "I want to see the United Press develop as a world-wide news agency."

Others at the meeting expressed much the same opinion, although there was no formal vote. Howard returned to New York and broke off negotiations on the Reuters proposal.

In some ways, it may have been the most important decision he made for the United Press, and it was one which Scripps approved. The Associated Press, continuing secure in its alliance with the official European agencies, did little in the next two years to build up its own direct coverage abroad, but Howard and Keen had to redouble their efforts to provide a competitive foreign news service. Above all, they strove to get American reporters into the most important bureaus, reporters who knew what would be of interest at home and who were free to report whatever happened as objectively and as honestly as possible. Their success in this endeavor was soon to be a turning point for the United Press. World War I, which would throw the European news-agency cartel into confusion and division, was approaching.

4.

Some of the radical changes that the United Press was bringing about in the news-agency business were emphasized in August of 1912 when editors from all over the country gathered at a National Newspaper Conference sponsored by the University of Wisconsin at Madison. One day of the sessions was given over to press associations. General Manager Melville Stone of the Associated Press, one of the most respected journalists in America, was the first speaker. Gray-haired, dignified, and deliberate, Stone emphasized to the editors the great efforts his organization had made to handle the news without bias. He said that staff writers were sternly instructed not to "color" dispatches but to confine themselves to setting forth the facts as plainly as possible. In the future, he promised, the Associated Press would endeavor to continue to handle the news in unbiased fashion.

The next speaker was the general manager of the United Press. Howard, according to a local newspaper account, had arrived in Madison like a small whirlwind, "wearing a white and black checkered suit and a straw hat tilted sharply to the left. . . . He soon had the conference standing on its ear."

Actually, Howard was not displeased by the tenor of Stone's speech. The Associated Press was noted for its dry, factual dispatches, for its long, over-crowded and complicated "lead" sentences, and for its staid, routine handling of stories. This was, in part, a result of the older agency's policy of avoiding bias although, in fact, a dull, colorless news story could be either biased or unbiased, depending on whether it told all the facts and the way it told them. One of Howard's most effective weapons in competition with the Associated Press was his insistence that dullness and routine were not synonymous with objectivity; that news agency dispatches could be unbiased and also readable—or even lively.

Speaking earnestly and vigorously, the general manager of the United Press told the editors that his reporters were under orders to put plenty of legitimate color into their dispatches in order to give a complete and ac-curate impression. "We now recognize," he said, "that it is possible to color a story in legitimate fashion. . . . We now recognize that the really vicious coloring in a news story comes from eliminating facts which should be told —not in writing them in . . . When I speak of color I do not mean dyeing a story [to distort the facts]. . . . I do not mean eliminating facts so as to rob a story of its true color—the color which truly represents the spirit and atmosphere of the situation. . . . By color in the news, I mean the color which is natural to the complexion of the story. . . . We recognize that it is not possible to edit out the point of view if we are going to have a news story instead of a police blotter or a court record. But our constant en-deavor must be along the line of keeping the point of view in the news report honest, human, and disinterested."

Howard referred to the Massachusetts textile strike coverage. At one point during the strike, arrangements had been made to move the children of strikers at Lawrence to other cities where they would be cared for tempo-rarily. But police and company guards prevented the children from boarding their train, creating confusion and protests from excited parents and, finally, a riot. Howard pointed out that there were many reporters present but that each one saw it through different eyes. Some thought the police action was an outrageous plot to keep suffering children on the scene so that their par-ents would be quicker to abandon the strike. Others believed the incident was a trick by strikers who used the children in an effort to win public sympathy. Some reporters merely wrote in a colorless, factual style that a mob had attacked police.

But, Howard added, the United Press dispatches tried to get as deeply as possible into the facts, to tell the whole story, to give equal space to both sides, and to report the color and the action and the smell of the scene so that readers would be given an accurate impression of what was happening. The manner in which the United Press handled the textile strike story led to several interesting developments. The Lawrence Chamber of Commerce wrote letters to many United Press client newspapers urging them to boycott the news agency. None did. On the contrary, the coverage brought the agency many new editorial friends. The United Press dispatches also were widely credited with bringing about a congressional investigation into working conditions, unsavory company practices, and left-wing agitation in the New England textile area.

Howard's speech pointed up many of the differences between the United Press and the Associated Press and was widely discussed in the journalistic world. Will Irwin, writing in *Harper's Weekly,* described the Wisconsin conference as a clash of old and new ideas. "So the old and the new in journalism met on the same platform and held debate—the old generation clinging to the fallacy that news can be written from a godlike height of abstract truth, biased and knowing it not; the younger generation, perceiving that humanity sees truth only from a point of view, honestly biased and knowing it well," Irwin's article said. "You may dress up your [newspaper] pages with . . . high-class writers and expensive cartoonists . . . but you cannot keep circulation unless you are in some measure talking the language of the people. The members of the Associated Press, mainly old newspapers whose publishers have grown rich and Tory, speak in other tongues. Hence, that area of journalism which it occupies exclusively is shrinking. All of which should be very gratifying to the United Press."

The American Magazine also commented at length on the speech, saying that in coverage of the Lawrence strike "the United Press was true to its responsibility and as a result of its accurate representation of that labor conflict the whole nation was aroused." The magazine added the following: "As the United Press was the only news agency to give the newspapers of the country the whole truth about Lawrence, and it is known that it was reading of these accounts that moved Senator Miles Poindexter personally to investigate Lawrence, it is fair to state that it was this exposure that resulted in congressional interference and inquiry, and the federal probe by the Commissioner Charles P. Neill of the Department of Labor.

"This illustration of the positive democratic necessity of free and independent reporting . . . has many counterparts in the history of the United Press Associations. A recent conspicuous example was the report the United Press correspondents cabled of the coronation of King George and Queen Mary [in England]. The American newsmen of the conventional school wired highly colored word pictures of the splendid spectacle, the beauty of the women, the gaiety of the crowds, the worshipful homage of the King's subjects. . . . The correspondents of the United Press, all American-trained, on that occasion reported all that was true of the brilliancy and dignity of the occasion; but they also saw in the event news facts that had escaped rival correspondents and were of especial importance to Americans. The United Press papers that evening told among other things of the enormous expenditures made for the extravagant coronation display, truthfully estimated the enthusiasm of the crowds from observation rather than from preconceived ideas, and these sharp-eyed American reporters did not miss the fact that lunch baskets thrown away by prosperous Englishmen seated in the expensive street stands were eagerly seized and rifled for crumbs by half-starved men and women of the miserable London army of unemployed people."

5.

The United Press made friends in many ways—by its enterprising way of handling some stories, by its tireless quest for "scoops," by its willingness to cater to the needs of individual newspapers, and by its emphasis on speedy service to afternoon newspapers, which were rapidly increasing in number in this period. The Associated Press day wire service had always tapered off sharply around four o'clock in the afternoon, which meant that afternoon newspapers—especially those in the Midwest and Far West—received very little fresh news for their final editions. Howard, however, put heavy emphasis on the fact that the United Press was operated for afternoon newspapers, and he extended the New York wire closing in order to cover final sports results and other late news breaks. It meant more work for everybody, but it paid off in the long run.

The United Press policy of promising to provide almost any news that a telegraph editor desired also added to the burden of the staff. There was, for example, a telegraph editor in Pittsburgh who loved nothing better than a story about a good big fire for his first or street-sales edition. The New York office heard from him frequently over the leased wire.

BADLY NEED FIRST EDITION HEADLINE. GET ME A GOOD FIRE.

Perhaps there was a worth-while fire in New York that could be written quickly but, if not, the word went out on the wires to Boston, Albany, Cleveland, and elsewhere to look around for a fire story. Usually, somebody found one that would serve the purpose of a first-edition headline in Pittsburgh.

Beating the Associated Press on important news developments, however, was a better way to win the favor of editors, and this was done occasionally in an impressive manner. In mid-April of 1914, there was a serious outbreak of fighting against General Huerta, the ruthless and rather reckless dictator of Mexico. An oil plant at Tampico was damaged and United States gunboats were endangered. Several United States marines who went ashore at Tampico were arrested by Mexican officials. This resulted in an international crisis, and Secretary of State William Jennings Bryan later announced that the U. S. Atlantic Fleet was being sent to Vera Cruz to take such action as necessary to enforce recognition of the rights and dignity of the United States.

Bill Shepherd was the United Press correspondent in Mexico City, but he soon discovered that he could send out very little news because of a stiff censorship. Fortunately, he had arranged a system of code words with the New York bureau and he was on friendly terms with the manager of the Western Union office in Mexico City. On the day Bryan announced in Washington that the fleet was en route, Shepherd got through a story that two trainloads of Americans had left Mexico City for Vera Cruz. Then there was silence from both Washington and Mexico City. The world anxiously waited for word on the arrival of the warships. Would there be war? Would Huerta fight or give in?

In Mexico City, Shepherd waited, too—in the office of his friend who was manager of the Western Union. The manager was a former telegraph operator and he had a key in his office so that he could exchange messages with his chief operator in Vera Cruz. They talked back and forth on the wire from time to time and, finally, the Vera Cruz operator said he could see the warships approaching. He began describing the scene. The Mexican forces fired on the ships, which put out small boats and sent marines ashore against the resistance of snipers. There was scattered fighting in the streets and at last the Vera Cruz operator signed off, saying that "they're now shooting through this building. Good-by."

Shepherd wrote out a brief urgent message about the landing and asked the manager to send it to New York.

"I can't possibly do it," he replied. "There is a censorship in effect and they might shoot me."

"Well, I've got another message I want to send," Shepherd said a little later. "I mailed some photographic film yesterday to a friend and I guess I'd better let her know that it's on the way. I'll get the censor to okay it."

He strolled around to the censor's office and wrote a telegram addressed to Margaret Howard in New York. It said:

FILMS FORWARDED VERACRUZ STOP JOHNSON RETURNING VIARAILROAD MEXICITY

The censor noted the words Vera Cruz and at first refused to approve the telegram, but Shepherd talked him around and it was dispatched to New York. As soon as it was received, Mrs. Howard telephoned her husband at the office and read the message. A few minutes later a bulletin went out on the United Press wires:

MEXICO CITY, April 21 (United Press) *American troops are in Vera Cruz and will report their occupation of the city to Washington from there over the cable lines to which they now have access. Mexican forces are retiring by rail toward Mexico City.*

As it turned out, no report was made to Washington that afternoon and no other word seeped through the censorship from Mexico City. In Washington, the Navy Department and the Department of State denied any knowledge of the Marines landing at Vera Cruz and the Associated Press carried a dispatch suggesting that reports of the landing were faked. It was about seven hours after the United Press story had been published that Washington officially announced the landing, giving the landing time as less than an hour earlier than the time Shepherd filed his code message.

Meantime, Shepherd had caught a train for Vera Cruz but he was worrying all the way that the New York office might send him a message of congratulations. "I had had a fierce time getting the 'films forwarded' cipher dispatch past the censor," he said later. "He was frankly suspicious. Later I realized that if I did put over a beat and anyone in the New York office was so thoughtless as to send congratulations, it would turn the censor's suspicions into conviction and convert me from a correspondent into a prisoner in one of Mr. Huerta's privately conducted jails. Nobody sent a message, however, and I am much obliged to New York—for being alive."

6.

Shepherd might be a kind of one-man news agency in Mexico, but covering major news in Europe was quite another matter in 1914. There was, for example, the high cost of cable tolls and the low level of the United Press budget. When Keen arrived in London the quota of words that he was authorized to send by cable from that great capital every day was less than 100. Of course, he could average his quota out over a few weeks or a couple of months by sending nothing on some days and sending more words on days when there was important news but, as he mildly remarked later, "operating out of London on [that] quota was rather difficult." Other bureaus such as Rome and Paris were expected to get by with even smaller quotas unless they had a big story on their hands. Cable rates were twelve and a half cents per word for press material, which was slow. There was also a "full-rate" classification at twenty-five cents a word and "urgent rate" messages at seventy-five cents a word.

The necessity of economizing on cable tolls from Europe was, of course, a handicap to the United Press, but there were also certain advantages to be gained by a man like Keen, who was a master of the art of getting the greatest possible return for every penny spent. For example, then and for many years afterward, Keen developed a remarkable system of sending mail copy from all over Europe to New York. All scheduled events, big or small, in London or in a remote corner of the Balkans, were written up by United Press correspondents well in advance as background copy to be released at the proper time by a very brief cable. Hundreds of such mailers were always on file in London and New York, describing some annual festival in Roumania or the celebration of the King's birthday in Spain or the entries in the Derby in England.

Since these were written when correspondents had plenty of time, Keen insisted that a great deal of work go into them. Take the advance mailer on the English Derby at Epsom Downs. It might run to 1000 words and include a careful description of the course, a dozen paragraphs about the crowd, the candy butchers, the bookmakers, and the royal box as well as some odd historical facts about past races that had been dug up in the library. Then there would be a separate chart that contained the names of all the horses entered, a description of each one, the name of the jockey, and the name of the owner. This chart was ingeniously arranged so that on the day of the race the London office would have to cable only a few words to New York. The New York cable editor merely had to fill in a dozen blank spaces on his mail copy and he had a complete, colorful, and carefully written story ready to go on the wire with no delay. The result was that the United Press story frequently was faster and more satisfactory for fast-moving afternoon newspapers than stories sent by cable from the race track. Not to mention the fact that the cable tolls amounted to practically nothing.

The Keen system of advance mailers was highly important in United Press foreign coverage until the 1930s when radio transmission at cheap rates opened the way for sending voluminous stories over great distances at a cost lower than the price of air-mail stamps required to send the same copy to the various bureaus involved.

Another factor that enabled the United Press to economize on its foreign service until 1914 was the tendency of a considerable majority of American newspapers to ignore the "heavy" political and economic news from abroad, in which Reuters excelled. There was a demand in most newspapers only for the more sensational news such as the Paris trial in 1914 of Madame Caillaux, wife of a former Premier, for the fatal shooting of a French editor who published her love letters of an earlier day. The Caillaux trial was the big news of the day when a young Bosnian student assassinated Archduke Franz Ferdinand, heir to the Austro-Hungarian throne, at Sarajevo, on June 28, 1914. The threat of tragic developments burst briefly into the headlines. European diplomats were fearful of war and William Philip Simms scurried around Paris gathering information and cabling ominous dispatches to New York. But after a few days most American editors were not much interested. Americans apparently couldn't believe there was a possibility of a European war, and the story of a crisis in the Balkans faded out of the headlines in most cities. In July, Simms was still cabling ominous reports—but not for long. Cable Editor Fred S. Ferguson sent him a sharp message:

> PRESS UNIPRESS PARIS
> SIMMS DOWNHOLD WARSCARE UPPLAY CAILLAUX
> FERGUSON

A few days later—on July 28—the armies of Emperor Franz Josef marched against Serbia. War took over the newspaper headlines, and it would keep them for many, many grim months.

CHAPTER SIX

His rimless glasses perched firmly on his nose, Ed L. Keen sat at a desk in the United Press office in Temple Chambers, London, one August evening of 1914 and—like Sir Edward Grey at the Foreign Office a few blocks away—watched the lights go out all over Europe. Except that, in Keen's imagination, it wasn't lights going out as war claimed the Continent; it was telegraph lines going down. The cables to Germany would soon be cut and, in one country after another, the dark hand of censorship was seizing the wires over which reporters might tell the world what was happening.

Keen was forty-four years old, a sedate, persuasive, and indefatigable man with a wide mouth, a firm chin and graying hair parted on the right side and falling in a gentle wave across his forehead. Looking more like a diplomat than a newspaperman in those days, he dressed immaculately, and the wide necktie on which he wore the gold emblem of the Washington Gridiron Club was neatly knotted under his high stiff collar. In an unassuming, patient way, he got through more work in the average day than most men did in a week, but in his already noteworthy career as a correspondent he had never faced such a challenge as was thrust upon him by the beginning of World War I.

His problem was the one that a press association correspondent can seldom forget—communications. It did no good to dig up a headline story if you couldn't get it to the cables, get it to New York, get it to the telegraph desks of United Press newspapers all over America. This problem was never far from Keen's thoughts and he knew as much—frequently more—about the telegraph lines of Europe and the transatlantic cables as did the experts of the communications companies. He knew which routes were crowded with traffic and which ones, at certain hours, might be least busy. He knew that sometimes you could send a message by a roundabout way—say from Paris to London to Buenos Aires to New York—faster than you could send it directly. Now he was ready to put his knowledge to the test.

In the first twelve days of August declarations of war were made by Great

Britain, France, and Germany. Correspondents were expecting the declarations and knew approximately when they would be issued. In each capital the news was available to all reporters at the same time. In each instance the United Press flash on the declaration of war passed through Keen's hands —Paris and Berlin cables were often relayed via London—and arrived in New York from a few minutes to four hours ahead of any other dispatches. These were major news beats.

Keen's success was largely due to the fact that, when the flashes came across his desk, he filed a duplicate on every available route from London to New York. The direct cables were so jammed with official business that even urgent messages were greatly delayed, but Keen's messages over alternate and longer routes found freer channels and were sped to their destination instead of lying for hours under a pile of government dispatches. A little knowledge and a little thought had started the United Press off handsomely in coverage of the war.

Keen had no intention of relinquishing that advantage. The long-standing and effective alliance among the Reuters agency and the official agencies of European nations, by which the Associated Press had always profited in foreign coverage, was damaged from the beginning of the war. First, its effectiveness suffered when each belligerent government began using whatever means was available for propaganda purposes—to get its own often distorted version of events before the rest of the world, especially the United States. Second, the start of actual hostilities closed the frontiers against direct exchange of news between the Central Powers of Germany and Austro-Hungary and the Allied Powers of Britain, France, and Russia.

Holland remained neutral, and Keen quickly set up a pivotal relay bureau in The Hague. Censored German news could be received in Holland and could then be relayed to London. Through the same relay Keen could communicate with his correspondents in Berlin and Vienna, sometimes almost as rapidly as if there had been direct lines. He also quickly discovered that British censorship of news from Europe could be circumvented by sending mail dispatches via Dutch boats from Amsterdam to New York, and much valuable copy was sent that way early in the war.

Roy Howard had made a tour of Europe before the war began and had worked out certain emergency precautions. As a result, Keen was able to strengthen his bureaus almost overnight. Percy J. Sarl was hired to bolster Karl H. von Wiegand's staff at Berlin. William Slater joined the London bureau, and F. C. Bryk was in charge of coverage at Vienna. In addition, New York offered to send reinforcements. A message from New York to Keen said:

CAN YOU USE SHEPHERD STOP DO YOU NEED FUNDS
HOWARD

Keen promptly replied:

URGENTLY REQUEST SHEPHERD UNWORRIED ABOUT FUNDS
KEEN

Unhappily, in the first days of the war, the British censors were highly suspicious of all messages and closely examined them for possible code words. They had been warned, for example, that proper names were often used as codes. So, before passing Keen's message on to the cable operator, the censor deleted three words and the message arrived in New York reading:

URGENTLY   REQUEST   FUNDS
KEEN

Howard went into action and on the next steamer to England was a box containing $15,000 in gold for the United Press in London. This came as a shock to Keen, but his shock might have been much greater if both Howard and Bill Shepherd had not also been on the same boat. Howard had decided to send Shepherd even if Keen didn't request him, and to come along himself for a few weeks.

2.

The first phase of the war found the United Press prepared to cope with many handicaps that had not been anticipated by the Associated Press because of its connections with the European cartel. Urged on by the knowledge that the official agencies would be favored on news releases, the United Press correspondents worked twice as hard to get the news, and frequently got it ahead of Reuters or Havas or Wolff—all of which were under wraps and particularly cautious because of official connections.

As a result of these efforts by correspondents, of Keen's knowledge of communications, and of the fact that the United Press processed the news for an American audience, the associations' prestige mounted sharply. Editors were impressed, and the list of United Press clients increased to 595 by September. This caused no joy in the headquarters of the Associated Press, where a certain number of complaints from newspapers were received. In the August 15 issue of *Editor & Publisher,* General Manager Stone was moved to make a statement in defense of the Associated Press coverage. He pointed out that censorship and crowded cables were delaying dispatches from Europe as much as seventeen hours.

The Associated Press management lost little time in taking steps designed to bolster its war coverage. But it had been hard hit in the first round, and in the next few months the United Press produced some of the most sensational enterprise reporting of the war. Furthermore, its correspondents were writing their stories in a simple, direct way that caught the eye of American editors.

As early as August 3, a United Press dispatch from London had illustrated this tendency:

LONDON, August 3 (UP) *The first "battle of the air" has been fought. The craft in the combat were a giant German zeppelin and a French aeroplane. The Frenchman sacrificed himself and his machine to ram the zeppelin. Both were wrecked and dashed to earth and 8 Germans and the lone French aviator were killed.*

This story was no "scoop" because it was generally available to correspondents, but most of them reported it as "nine dead in air crash." The United Press, seeking an "angle" on its coverage, emphasized that it was the first air battle ever fought.

Bill Shepherd didn't waste time after arriving in London. He went around to see a former war correspondent named Winston Churchill, who was then First Lord of the Admiralty. Churchill knew that Britain needed a favorable press in the United States, and when Shepherd asked for an interview he was agreeable. They talked for a while and Churchill asked him to come back. The next day he dictated what he wanted to say in the interview and Shepherd returned in the evening with 700 words of copy. Meantime, Churchill had visited the King and the Prime Minister, Herbert Asquith, and that evening he added new material to the draft that Shepherd had prepared. Among other things, he referred to German "atrocities" at Louvain, in Belgium. Then he called in the chief censor of the Admiralty to approve the copy and told him to issue instructions to the cable censors to pass it.

When the formalities had been completed, Shepherd ran to a telephone and called Keen with details of the Louvain incident, which had not been released previously. Keen put the story on the cables to New York ten minutes before it was released by the official press bureau. Then he and Shepherd went to the cable office where the interview was filed and transmitted to New York in the remarkably short time of fifty minutes. In the first interview he had ever granted as a cabinet minister, Churchill made a strong plea for American sympathy and support in the war but, aside from its special pleading, it was a major news break and was headlined across the United States.

Twenty-four hours later it was released for use in British newspapers, which published it with credit to the United Press. "This has been a great day for the United Press in England," Keen wrote to New York on August 30. "Every London Sunday paper prominently features Shepherd's unprecedented interview with Winston Churchill. I don't suppose the average newspaper reader at home appreciates what a tremendous achievement this was. It was more than a personal expression of views. He was speaking for the government itself."

The Churchill interview was not Shepherd's only triumph in Great Britain. The eager-eyed reporter was in the middle of everything and wrote a vivid story of the first German zeppelin raid on London, which the censor promptly killed. No dispatches describing the raid were permitted to leave the British Isles. Shepherd fumed. So did all the other correspondents. Keen didn't fume easily, but it happened that at the American correspondents' club luncheon the next day he sat next to Arthur Balfour, then a member of the British Cabinet. Keen told Balfour of the "magnificent story" that Shepherd had written and expressed the belief that it was the kind of news the British Government should want to see published in America because it would arouse sympathy for the people of London.

"Send it to me this afternoon," Balfour replied. "I'll see what I can do."

Keen got a copy of the story to Balfour's desk almost before Balfour himself got there, and two hours later received a telephone call from the cabinet minister's office saying that the dispatch was on its way to New York. Not long afterward, a message from New York said that nobody else had any description of the zeppelin raid, and that the United Press dispatch had been a clean sweep of headlines. Shepherd was in high spirits. Keen was pleased, too, but he was not entirely happy and his face betrayed it.

"What's the matter, Uncle Ed?" Shepherd asked with a broad smile. "You think I should have also interviewed the zep commander by megaphone?"

Keen smiled but his eyes were serious. "I was just wondering," he said, "whether I was quite ethical in doing what I did. I took advantage of the fact that I had been seated next to Balfour at the club luncheon and spoke to him about getting the zep story released. Do you think I was completely correct in taking this advantage over my confreres?"

It seems likely that Keen was the only correspondent in four years of war who paused to wonder whether it was completely fair to make use of a lucky break to scoop his confreres.

3.

In Germany foreign correspondents had a difficult time. Those who were natives of enemy countries were interned, and news service to Reuters and other members of the European cartel ceased, except indirectly by way of neutral countries. Karl H. von Wiegand left Berlin soon after the declaration of war, trying to get to the front. The slight, bespectacled American correspondent made slow progress but he did manage to pick up a great deal of information about Germany's reaction to the war, and then made his way across the frontier to The Hague where he was able to file several dispatches. Later he got to Aix-la-Chapelle for a vivid story of the German attack with their new eleven-inch field guns on Liége and sent his dispatches by courier to The Hague for transmission to New York. He also interviewed a Sergeant Wernes of the German aviation corps, who gave him details of what was probably the first battle between heavier-than-air craft—a subject that was front-page news everywhere.

But Von Wiegand was just getting warmed up. The Russian Army had been advancing ponderously against the Central Powers on the eastern front and a great battle had been fought at Lemberg, the capital of Austrian Galicia, before the Germans and Austrians began striking back. The United Press correspondent doubled on his tracks and, accompanied by three officers of the German general staff as "guides," made his way by train and automobile to Russian Poland early in October. There the German armies were about to turn the tide of fighting in the East and he got a close look at the fighting:

BY KARL H. VON WIEGAND
United Press Staff Correspondent

WIRBALLEN, Russian Poland (On the Firing Line, via The Hague and London) October 8 (UP) *At sundown tonight after four days of constant fighting, the German Army holds its strategic and strongly entrenched position east of Wirballen. As I write this in the glare of a screened automobile headlight several hundred yards behind the German trenches, I can catch the occasional high notes of a soldier chorus. For days, these soldiers have lain cramped in these muddy ditches, unable to move or to stretch except under cover of darkness. And still they sing. They believe they are on the eve of a great victory.*

Today I saw a wave of Russian flesh and blood dash against a wall of German steel. . . .

From the outset of the advance the German artillery began shelling the onrushing mass with wonderfully timed shrapnel.

On came the Slav swarm—into the range of the German trenches, with wild yells and never a waver. Russian battle flags, the first I had seen, appeared in the front of the charging ranks.

Then came a new sound. First I saw a sudden, almost grotesque melting of the advancing line. It was different from anything that had taken place before. The men literally went down like dominoes in a row. Those who had kept their feet were hurled back as though by a terrible gust of wind. Almost in the second that I pondered, puzzled, the staccato rattle of machine guns reached us. My ear answered the query of my eye.

For the first time, the advancing lines here hesitated, apparently bewildered. Mounted officers dashed along the line urging the men forward. Horses fell with the men. I saw a dozen riderless horses dashing madly through the lines, adding a new terror. . . . Then with the withering fire raking them even as they faltered, the lines broke. Panic ensued.

This was raw stuff from the battlefield, and the American newspapers subscribing to the United Press made the most of it. Almost overnight, Von Wiegand had made a world-wide reputation as a war correspondent. The

Germans, too, liked his portrayal of their armed might and a few days later had rushed him again to the Western Front to report from St. Mihiel, France —via Metz, Berlin, The Hague, and London—on the fighting along the road toward Paris. It was a front dominated by the army of the Crown Prince of Germany—and it was here, late in November, that Von Wiegand scored the most spectacular reportorial feat of the war to date:

BY KARL H. VON WIEGAND
United Press Staff Correspondent

HEADQUARTERS OF THE ARMY OF CROWN PRINCE, In France (By courier via Namur, Aix-la-Chapelle and The Hague to London, by cable to New York) November 20 (UP) *"Undoubtedly this is the most stupid, senseless and unnecessary war of modern times. It is a war not wanted by Germany, I can assure you, but it was forced on us and the fact that we were so effectually prepared to defend ourselves is now being used as an argument to convince the world that we desired conflict."*

In these words, Frederick William, the German Crown Prince and heir to the throne of the Kaiser, opened the first interview he has ever given to a foreign newspaperman and the first direct statement made to the press by any member of the German royal family since the outbreak of the war.

This time Von Wiegand probably didn't miss the eight-column banner headline in any United Press newspaper in America. It was a sensational interview, pleading the German case, of course, as Churchill had previously pleaded the British case before the American people, but it represented the first broad declaration of the German Government and as such it was important news. In November the United Press gained twenty-two new clients in thirty days, making a gain of 103 for the year. And as the year drew to a close, Von Wiegand came up with one more headliner—an interview with German Grand Admiral von Tirpitz warning that intensive U-boat warfare would be launched against British shipping. It was an outstanding news beat, the kind that United Press men called a "world shaker" or a "bell ringer."

4.

Even as a neophyte, William Philip Simms looked like a foreign correspondent, and it is quite possible that he was born looking like one. Tall, thin, and handsome as a matinee idol, he was as nonchalant as any veteran of the Quai d'Orsay. Even his colleagues were impressed then and later by the imperturbable Simms.

"Simms of the United Press . . . so sincere, so friendly," wrote Gellett Burgess from Paris in *Collier's Weekly.* "So up he comes, with his pearl-grey shoes, and his pearl-grey hat and his pearl-grey scarf, and his pearl-grey eyes. . . . Simms asserts, in his pearl-grey way—right in the middle of a chill rainstorm, mind you—that never was Paris so beautiful. I shiver. Simms' clear-cut, sensitive face has a poetic calm; he really means it."

The agency's office was on the third floor of an old building that had once been a monastery at 121 Rue Montmartre. A worn stone circular staircase ran up to the office but the stairwell was always dark because there was no electricity in the building. Kerosene lamps were used in the office, which was a small room and a still smaller storeroom that had once been a kitchen. The only advantage of the location was that it was near the cable office in the Bourse.

When Simms took charge the company had a variety of cable addresses for its various offices and services. Some of these were complicated combinations of words and difficult for Simms to remember. After struggling with them for some weeks, he advised everybody that he was registering a new cable address to cover all services: UNIPRESS. In time the word UNIPRESS became the company's cable address in practically all parts of the world, and correspondents became UNIPRESSERS.

Simms also claimed another distinction as Paris manager. After the war started and the Germans had advanced close to the French capital he was sitting at the Café Viennoise, on Boulevard Montmartre, when a little German monoplane flew over the city at an altitude of less than 1000 feet. Stepping to the curb, Simms could plainly see the pilot of the plane as he leaned over the side and hurled something toward the ground. It was a small bomb and it struck in a courtyard directly across the street, exploding with a big bang, breaking windows and tearing a hole in the ground. Simms wrote an eyewitness story of the first airplane bombardment of a large city in history.

In the next few days Simms started for the front, leaving the official communiqués of the generals and statesmen to his subordinates in Paris. By automobile he made his way to Soissons and picked up one of the first detailed stories of fighting as the Germans drove toward Paris. But the tide of conflict was against France in the following weeks and military authorities under General Joffre clamped down on the movements of correspondents. Everywhere Simms attempted to go, there were French soldiers on the road to turn him back to Paris.

Finally, with Wythe Williams of the New York *Times* he secured a military pass in Paris from General Gallieni and chartered an automobile to drive to the battlefields of the Marne. They had luncheon at Soissons, where they heard artillery fire concentrated nearby. A cavalry detachment had concealed its horses in a woods near one end of the town but the Germans bombarded them. The detachment moved its horses to another woods, but again the Germans found the range. It was obvious to the cavalry officers that somebody in the town was signaling to the German artillery, which was on a ridge to the north. Who would do it except a foreigner? And who were the foreigners in town? Two characters having luncheon at the inn, of course.

With several other suspects, Simms and Williams were taken into custody and imprisoned at a farmhouse where their only freedom was a courtyard in which there was a dunghill as high as the Alps. The mayor of the village was away, and for several days they were held in detention. Meanwhile French soldiers occasionally arrived, led away some of the detained persons, and shot them against a nearby wall. In the absence of the mayor, the town was under the direction of a woman whom both Simms and Williams had previously met. Eventually they were taken before her and she asked the army officials of the area to send them back to Paris. En route back to the capital with several other reporters, including Richard Harding Davis, they decided to detour to a French army camp. There they were met by a French officer who tore up their credentials and declared that he, not General Gallieni, was in command of that area. They were sent to the Cherche Midi prison in Paris, where they eventually managed to telephone at four o'clock in the morning to the United States Ambassador, Myron Herrick, who arranged for their release. The French obviously didn't want reporters at the front.

"They said: 'Get out! We don't want you!' " Simms wrote later. "The old-time war correspondent with freedom of movement passed out in the first month of the war."

Simms, however, was a persistent fellow and, with a war on hand, he kept on trying to report it and complaining bitterly of his troubles in his dispatches as well as in his conversations with French officials. When the Germans and Austrians permitted correspondents such as Von Wiegand and Bill Shepherd to go to their fronts, Simms emphasized to the French that they were losing a chance to build up their own case in the newspapers of neutral nations. It was not until late October that the French yielded, but then they selected Simms as the only American correspondent to be attached to General Joffre's headquarters.

"Now France, after refusing for nearly four months to accredit any foreign correspondent with her army, selects a United Press man as the one best fitted to tell the story of her arms and her men to the English-speaking world," boasted the agency's house organ, *The Hellbox*. Back in Paris later, Simms wrote that the war reporter had finally come into his own. "Every country at war has learned that 'it pays to advertise,' " he added. "Every country wants public opinion on its side and the legitimate properly accredited war reporter has been given a recognized position."

5.

The period of World War I, and particularly the first year of that conflict, was of great importance in the development of the United Press. The agency's record was outstanding and its American-trained reporters abroad played a not inconsequential role in bringing about revolutionary changes in foreign news coverage. This did not mean, however, that the United Press fought the war all by itself or suddenly achieved status comparable to the Associated Press at home. It didn't.

The Associated Press had and continued for years to have incomparably superior facilities for gathering and transmitting news in the United States. In number of clients, in personnel, and in financial resources it kept far ahead and its many able correspondents regularly turned in news beats that sent tremors of anger and frustration buzzing along the United Press leased wires from New York to San Francisco. It was the most formidable news agency in the country. It served the biggest and richest newspapers. If it was tradition-bound and slow to adjust to changing times, it nonetheless enjoyed high prestige and, when the war began, it was generally regarded as almost invulnerable to serious competition.

This situation was less unfavorable to the United Press than it seemed on the surface. By its very nature it forced the younger agency to adopt an attitude of bitter, sometimes crude rivalry in which it took advantage of every opportunity to claw its way ahead. A later generation might not always comprehend the intensity of this rivalry or might feel that there were times when the tactics employed were not exactly gentlemanly. But, in fact, the era was one of rude and raucous competition in the journalistic world generally and—as Jack Alexander later wrote in *The Saturday Evening Post*— the United Press developed "the belligerent attitude of an intoxicated field mouse squaring off against an elephant." The feeling behind this attitude was a strong and a very real thing—and highly important in the history of American journalism because it enabled the United Press to survive as a competitor.

The very fact that the Associated Press was the paramount news agency and could adopt a nonchalant attitude toward its rival kindled a kind of do-or-die spirit in many "underdog" United Press reporters. It often persuaded them to work long hours at modest pay for the occasional satisfaction of getting a story on the wires two minutes or ten minutes ahead of the opposition. It encouraged them to use their ingenuity, to try something new. Sometimes they fell on their faces with a thud. But many times the agency's innovations were successful and its product attractive to editors. And on those occasions the "underdog" United Press usually felt it was entitled to boast, which it did boisterously in a manner that was in keeping with the times, although later it might seem crudely unrestrained.

But the net result was a great deal more than a band of brash and sometimes rowdy newsmen resorting to almost any device to get the news first. The vitally important result was, as E. W. Scripps had foreseen, the establishment of competition that was so essential to the future of journalism. It meant, over the years, a constant speeding up and improvement in gathering and transmitting news to newspapers and radio and television. It meant that the citizen in Sioux City, Iowa, could know more quickly and in greater detail what happened this day in Bombay or Buenos Aires or Boston. It meant the end of any possibility—however remote—that any clique could ever gain control of or influence over news distribution in the United States.

The Associated Press made repairs to its damaged prestige after the first months of World War I and kept right on being the most comprehensive and the largest if not the liveliest press association in the country. But someway things were never the same again. The possibility of a news agency so powerful that there could be no serious competition had vanished. The idea of a news monopoly—always rejected by the Associated Press leaders—was outdated. The myth of invulnerability had been shattered in a way that could leave no doubt of a flourishing competition. And the United Press, not unduly afflicted with modesty, never let anybody forget it.

One of the ways in which the United Press bolstered staff morale and put across its story to editors was through publication of a lively, combative, and often boastful little company periodical which Howard called *The Hellbox* —the name for the box into which compositors dumped type that had been set but not used. *The Hellbox* carried personal stories about correspondents, told of changes in personnel, bragged about "scoops"—a word that became badly overworked and eventually was almost dropped as a newspaper term— and printed many compliments as well as a few complaints from United Press clients. It often exaggerated the agency's triumphs but it was also capable of kidding itself at times as it did in admitting that the handling of an important heavyweight fight in Paris had been something less than perfect. "If the dear old Associated Press will lean over, we'll pin a rose on it," the article on coverage of the fight said. "They sure did put it over on us on the Johnson-Moran fight. It was absolutely on the level. We just got a beautiful little trimming and we want to give the other fellow full credit. Several years of observation of the use of 'alibis' by the opposition has convinced us that they don't get anywhere with up-to-the-minute editors. As a matter of fact, it had been so long since we experienced the sensation of being trimmed that we didn't really appreciate how badly the opposition must feel so much of the time."

Usually, however, *The Hellbox* was on the offensive, as illustrated by its lead article during surrogate court proceedings in New York to fix the value of the estate of Joseph Pulitzer shortly after the noted publisher's death. The judge had asked Don C. Seitz, business manager of the New York *World,* if the Associated Press was a corporation.

Seitz answered: "The Associated Press is a fish and game club. That is, it is organized (as a non-profit co-operative) under the New York law providing for the organization of fish and game clubs."

This was a good springboard for *The Hellbox* and an article signed by "Hawkshaw, the detective" said:

"We long suspected it. . . . Not knowing quite what it was, if it wasn't a press association, we were content in the past to let it go at that. After all, it might have been a press association—once.

"But, now it appears this one has never been a press association, even once. Don Seitz has revealed on the witness stand its secret character. It is a fish and game club. . . . A fish and game club! Ye gods, how the name fits! A fish and game club is an organization of amateurs who have leisurely occupations, long imaginations and incurable credulity." In later years such blatant attacks on opposition news services would seem crude, but in 1914 newspapers generally were more given to taking a whack at their competition, and frequently some editor chipped in a contribution to *The Hellbox*. "Ever since the first pop of the first gun over in Europe," wrote News Editor J. E. Richards, of the Alpena, Michigan, *Evening News,* "the local Associated Press paper started yowling its head off about the never-ending virtues of the Associated Press. We stood it and said nothing except to point out where the United Press was first whenever we got a chance. Our real opportunity came when the Detroit *News* took on the United Press last week and spread UP all over its first page. Then our opposition put out an extra last Sunday morning, copying verbatim, except for the date lines, stories from Brussels telling of the Belgians refusing to grant an armistice to the Germans at Liége, and from Copenhagen telling of the invasion of Russia by Germany, which appeared in Saturday's *News.* We rather called their attention to it in an editorial . . . To think that they would drag low the wonderful AP by printing United Press dispatches clipped from our paper 24 hours after they were printed."

6.

The war had reached Rome only indirectly in the autumn of 1914, since Italy had refused to join the Central Powers and remained neutral, but United Press manager Henry Wood made his contribution to European coverage on Wednesday August 19. On that day, Pope Pius X lay gravely ill in the Vatican. He had been stricken earlier, had seemed to be recovering, and then suffered a relapse. Wood was intimately acquainted with the ways of the Vatican and with officials close to the Pontiff. He knew, for example, that it was customary for the Italian government to order all cables held up for some hours immediately after the death of a Pope, in order to permit the Vatican to make official announcement as it saw fit. This fact had been in his mind earlier when he communicated to London and New York his plans for coverage in event the illness proved fatal.

Shortly after noon, waiting at the Vatican, Wood realized from the activities of officials that the Pope was sinking rapidly. He checked with his sources and was told that His Holiness had become unconscious at noon. A little later he privately received the word that had been expected. Wood hurried to the cable office and wrote two different messages about a business deal and addressed them to the private residences of two officials of the United Press in New York. He dispatched them at the urgent rate. There was nothing to connect him or them with the United Press. But when they arrived in New York a story went on the wires.

FLASH—
ROME POPE PIUS DEAD

BULLETIN
ROME, August 19 (UP) *Pope Pius X died today. His Holiness, who had been sick for some days, suffered a relapse this morning and became unconscious at noon. The physicians could do nothing. The Pontiff's death was attributed to grief over the war.*

The news was carried on the wire from New York in midafternoon, and for the rest of the day no other press association had a word about the Pope's death. In fact, they had no word at all from Rome, because soon after Wood's two "business" cables had been dispatched the Italian government stopped all cable news out of the capital. Not until nine hours later did the Associated Press carry a dispatch saying the Pope had died.

The next day the Associated Press charged, according to *Editor & Publisher,* that the United Press story had been a fake. "It was four hours and five minutes *before* the Pope actually passed that the United Press distributed formal announcement that the Pope was dead," the Associated Press said. "The announcement was false."

The United Press didn't even pause before it struck back: "The absurd statement that the United Press announcement was false is obviously based merely on the contention that the official proclamation had not been issued at that hour (3 P.M. Wednesday, New York time). When Pope Leo XII died there was a long interval between his actual death and the announcement. The Vatican also held back announcement of the death of Pius IX for twenty hours. . . . The fact that immediately after Wood's telegrams the Italian government refused to allow any other telegrams of any kind to leave Rome is conclusive proof that the Pope was dead when Wood filed them."

The argument went on. The Associated Press got a letter from an attending doctor saying the Pope died at 1:15 A.M. Thursday and a statement from Italian officials saying that it was not possible to send code messages from Rome because of the war in Europe. These documents were not particularly effective since the United Press acknowledged that the "official" time was correct and since Wood's code was in plain English and not recognizable by the censor as a code. The United Press went right on calling the attention of editors to Wood's scoop on the big story of the year from Rome.

It might as well be mentioned here that in 1922 there was similar confusion and dispute over the death of Pope Benedict XV but with the situation reversed. Wood again had arranged a special code for the death of the Pope:

SEND TRUNKS IMMEDIATELY

One Saturday morning before the wires had opened, New York Bureau

Manager Hugh Baillie arrived at the office and found his desk literally covered with urgent cables sent via half a dozen different routes from Rome. All were signed by Wood. Half of them were the code words for the death of the Pope, but the other half said:

UNSEND TRUNKS IMMEDIATELY

Due to the fact they had been sent by various routes, it was impossible for Baillie to know which had been filed last by Wood but he came to the logical conclusion that the "unsend trunks" message was the latest and was intended to correct the earlier cables saying the Pope was dead. He ordered the cable desk to hold everything. An hour later, messages flooded the office from many clients who screamed that other news services were reporting the death of the Pope. Baillie began to sweat but he was stuck with his decision. His messages to Rome were not answered and he took a terrific mental beating until late that afternoon when Wood cabled a bulletin issued by the Pope's doctor saying he was weak but still alive. Other agencies had to correct their stories. The Pope did not die until the next day.

Controversy raged for days over the story, and some editors compared it with the 1914 episode when the United Press reported the death of Pope Pius X hours before the official announcement. This didn't sit well with Roy Howard.

"The difference is," he usually replied, "that our Pope stayed dead."

CHAPTER SEVEN

Business was booming everywhere in America during 1915, and the United States, which had been an agricultural debtor nation, began growing up into a great industrial power to which Great Britain and France looked for food, arms, and credit.

The United Press grew, too. Newfangled telegraphic printer machines to replace the old dot-and-dash system were tested by the company that year, the first keyboard machine being tried out on a circuit from New York to New Jersey. The printers frequently broke down, and the old-time Morse telegraphers seldom lost an opportunity to give the keyboard operators—known as punchers—a big loud horse laugh. Teletype maintenance experts had to be in almost constant attendance and sometimes they had to spend all night taking the machine apart and putting it back together again in time for the opening of the wire. But gradually the printers were improved and gradually they replaced the Morse operators.

By 1915 the United Press leased wires stretched from New York to New England and Montreal, southward through Washington to New Orleans and Dallas, and westward through a complex network to Denver and the Pacific coast. The 625 client newspapers—"the largest number of afternoon newspapers ever served by any press association," said *The Hellbox*—were in every state except New Mexico and Utah. Twenty-four bureaus on the network fed many of the smaller newspapers daily "pony" reports, usually by telephone. But the agency's many beats in war coverage, its feature stories, and its breezy style had also prompted a large number of additional newspapers in big cities to buy the service as a supplement to the Associated Press's staid daily report.

The United Press also had profited during the war by the fact that the biggest news of the day from Europe usually was received in New York from about ten o'clock in the morning to two o'clock in the afternoon, because of a five-hour difference in time. This was in plenty of time for publication in afternoon newspapers, which got most of the headline "breaks" on war developments. The morning newspapers frequently had nothing except further details on news stories that had already been published in the afternoon editions. Such a situation was highly satisfactory to Howard, who had geared the United Press for afternoon newspapers and kept hammering at editors with his agency's slogan: "TODAY'S NEWS TODAY!"

As the United Press grew under the stress of wartime there were many shifts and changes in personnel. Karl Bickel had taken over as business representative at Chicago and was roaming from Minnesota to Texas on a nonstop selling spree. J. Westbrook Pegler graduated from office boy to "pony" editor and finally to war correspondent, abandoning the initial "J." in the process.

Superintendent of Bureaus Ed Conkle made a trip to Milwaukee in October of 1915 that paid important dividends in the next few years. The Milwaukee manager, Hal O'Flaherty, wanted to move on to bigger cities and he strongly recommended to Conkle a young man named Jerry L. O'Sullivan as his replacement. Conkle said he would like to meet O'Sullivan and, after they had shaken hands, offered him a black, crooked Pittsburgh stogie. O'Sullivan accepted it and went to work on it so expertly that Conkle didn't waste any more time.

"Okay," he said, "I guess from the way you handle that stogie that you will do for the job."

O'Sullivan later handled many important jobs for the agency in the Middle West and trained or directed the activities of dozens of able newspapermen, including Earl J. Johnson, Herbert Little, Marquis Childs, Edward Derr, and Carl Victor Little, during their long or short careers with the United Press.

Once, when O'Sullivan was directing news operations in the central division, he sent Carl Victor Little to southern Illinois to cover the story of a deacon who was suspected of committing a murder. The next morning Little sent in a long story by telegraph, including the confession of the deacon. There was no explanation of how he got the confession and O'Sullivan called him on the telephone.

"Whom did this fellow confess to?" he asked.

"To me, stupid," Little answered, and slammed down the receiver. O'Sullivan then called the sheriff and was informed that Little had been admitted to the suspect's cell and had persuaded him to make a full confession, a copy of which was turned over to the sheriff.

O'Sullivan also helped develop the talents of two crack police reporters in Chicago, Robert T. Loughran and Harry Heydenberg. They had so many friends in so many key spots in Illinois that they were seldom beaten on news from the courts or police stations. When grand jury indictments were returned against members of the 1919 Chicago White Sox baseball team on charges of conspiring to throw the World Series games, a member of the jury went from the grand jury room directly to a telephone booth to call

Heydenberg with news of the indictments two hours before they were announced.

On another occasion the police of several states were vigorously searching for a bank messenger who took off with almost a million dollars in government bonds. O'Sullivan was just ready to leave the office for luncheon one day when Loughran called him and said that a friend on the police force had received word that the messenger was in custody at Heyworth, Illinois, having been captured in a pool hall there. O'Sullivan got the Heyworth telephone operator on the telephone and discovered that the only telephone in striking distance of the pool hall was in a restaurant a few doors away. He talked to the restaurant proprietor, persuaded him on promise of twenty-five dollars to go to the pool hall and get the details of the capture, which included the fact that the sheriff had created a local sensation by dumping the million dollars' worth of bonds on a pool table to count the loot. "We had a tremendous scoop," O'Sullivan remarked later, "but Ed Conkle, who was then superintendent of bureaus in New York, complained for weeks about having to pay the twenty-five dollars."

When O'Sullivan finally left the United Press to become dean of the School of Journalism at Marquette University, he telegraphed his resignation to Karl Bickel in New York. Bickel sent back a message over the trunk wire to Kansas City urging him to stay on the job and asking him why he had resigned. O'Sullivan summed up the sentiments of a considerable number of able newspapermen who had quit the United Press when he replied:

> KAB NX
> HOURS TOO LONG WAGES TOO LOW LIFE TOO SHORT
> JLOS KP

The reporters at the war fronts in Europe dominated most newspaper headlines throughout the war, but there were days when other developments made the big news. One such day came early in May of 1915 when the British liner *Lusitania* flashed a wireless message that she had been torpedoed by a German U-boat off the Irish coast. There were many Americans on board and the great question of the day was the fate of the 1924 passengers.

In London, Ed Keen got off the first flashes on the sinking and then immediately instructed a new recruit, Wilbur Forrest, to get to Queenstown, Ireland, closest port to the sinking, with the greatest possible haste. Young Forrest grabbed his hat and ran. He just made the 8:30 A.M. train from Paddington Station and was the only American correspondent to greet survivors of the *Lusitania* brought to port by rescue boats. He identified the bodies of a number of Americans brought ashore and had cabled 1500 words by the time other reporters began arriving. That afternoon in America it was not believed at first that there had been a heavy loss of life in the *Lusitania* sinking because the ship was not far from the shore. One Washington newspaper, for example, carried an eight-column headline: "None Perish on *Lusitania* When Ship Is Torpedoed." But United Press newspapers coming on the street at the same hour had Forrest's story. The Washington *Times,* for instance, carried an eight-column banner: "Many Lose Lives." In all, 1198 persons, including 114 Americans, perished.

The *Lusitania* torpedoing brought the United States closer to participation in the war and it brought Secretary of State William Jennings Bryan into almost immediate disagreement with President Wilson on neutrality policy, although this split was hidden for some time under official statements that all was harmonious in the Cabinet. In the first week of June, the United Press bureau in Washington pried the lid off. John Edwin Nevin, a big, lumbering man who sweated and suffered under the steaming Washington sun, smelled out the details of the disagreement and wrote a complete and exclusive story about Bryan's attitude and his intention to resign. Shortly afterward, however, when Bryan actually resigned, the United Press apparently had caught cold in its "nose for news" and the Associated Press's David Lawrence, aided by a cabinet official's tip, broke the story so far ahead of everybody else that *The Hellbox* could only moan that "we got one beautiful wallop on the official announcement."

German submarines prowling the Atlantic coast of America continued to make news during the remaining months of United States neutrality. In October of 1916 several submarines appeared off the New England coast and one of them put into Newport Harbor briefly before the pack began attacking British ships beyond the territorial limits of the United States. United Press client newspapers weren't thinking much about war on the afternoon that the story began breaking. They were thinking about baseball. The Brooklyn Dodgers and the Boston Braves were meeting in the World Series at Boston, and the Braves had a strong-armed young left-handed pitcher named George Herman Ruth but usually called Babe because of his boyish face.

The United Press leased wire to Boston was hooked directly into the baseball park's press box so that the account of the game could be relayed play by play to newspapers, and, once the game started, nothing else was carried on the wires unless there was a news break of the greatest importance. All operators were under instructions not to break in on the wires to interrupt the baseball service—even if they missed a few words—until each inning was completed. Fred Ferguson was in charge of the baseball park staff, which included the Boston manager, Frank W. (Bob) Getty, Sports Editor H. C. Hamilton, George Barton, and Chief Operator William F. Lynch, working the key. About the third inning, Lynch seemed to be having trouble with the wire. He nudged Ferguson.

"Somebody's trying to break me," he said, meaning that a telegrapher somewhere along the lines was attempting to take over the wire.

"Nobody's allowed to break," Ferguson snapped.

"Yeah," said Lynch, "but he's still trying."

"Well, let him in. We'll give him hell later."

Lynch let him in, and it was the New York operator with an urgent message from Bill Hawkins:

> FSF BH
>
> ROCKS SAYS UBOAT OFF NEW ENGLAND COAST NEED SAP
>
> WWH NX

Translated into English this was a service message addressed to Ferguson (FSF) at Boston (BH) saying that the Associated Press (Rocks) was carrying a story that German submarines had been seen off New England and a United Press story was needed as soon as possible (SAP). It was signed by Hawkins (WWH) at New York (NX). The code word "Rocks" was a play on the name of the AP general manager, Melville Stone.

Ferguson—a little man with snapping eyes and black hair combed in a pompadour—fairly leaped from his seat, the ball game all but forgotten. A big story was breaking next door and the Associated Press already had scored a beat on it. Leaving Sports Editor Hamilton to clean up the game, he and the rest of the staff rushed to the Boston office for details. It soon developed that the German submarines were out for the kill, and in the next thirty-six hours they sank half a dozen Allied ships in the Atlantic sea lanes, including the liner *Stephano*. Ferguson sent Getty to Newport, Rhode Island, where rescue vessels had put out to pick up survivors and scattered other available men to key points to cover the news.

Getty's problem was to cover the stories of survivors being brought to Newport by the U.S. torpedo boat *Ericsson*. It wasn't an easy job because orders had been given not to permit anyone to board the torpedo boat until the passengers had been examined by the health officer and the boat had docked. But on the Newport dock Getty struck up an acquaintance with the health officer and the crew of the tug on which the officer was to go out to meet the *Ericsson*. And just before the tug left the dock, it signed on a new "assistant health officer"—Getty. He went aboard the *Ericsson* with the health officer about dawn, talked to many of the rescued women and children, and departed with the officer aboard the tug. The *Ericsson* then steamed on toward the dock where a crowd of reporters was waiting to interview the survivors. Getty called Ferguson at the Boston office before the wire opened at 7 A.M.

"Good story, Bob?" Ferguson asked eagerly.

"I've just got notes but pretty good. I haven't slept for so long I'm not sure."

"Get a cup of coffee," Ferguson ordered, "and look over your notes. Call me back at five minutes of seven."

Getty called back at the appointed time. "Okay," Ferguson said. "The wire is just opening. Start dictating."

Ferguson, meanwhile, had put together another story from facts collected by the staff. In all some 220 survivors appeared to have had ships shot out from under them by at least three U-boats in the area. Except for occasional breaks to permit other important stories to move on the wire, the Getty and Ferguson stories ran for several hours. It was late morning when they had cleaned up their work and a weary, red-eyed Getty hung up the telephone. Ferguson sent a message to New York:

> WWH NX
> THAT CLEANS US UP. WE HEADING BALL PARK
> FSF BH

The staff then grabbed a hot dog and a cup of coffee and got back to work at the ball park, where Babe Ruth had to go fourteen innings to win a bitter two-to-one game. The United Press men were a little ragged around the edges due to lack of sleep, but there wasn't anybody else to keep the client newspapers up to date on the World Series. The coverage of the World Series, incidentally, was right good. "We beat the opposition each day," commented the Oklahoma City *News* in a report to *The Hellbox*. "It was the best service ever."[1]

2.

One spring day in 1915, Bickel stopped in Kansas City in a sour mood. He told Bureau Manager L. B. Mickel that there was trouble in Illinois, where the International News Service was regularly beating everybody else on news from the capital at Springfield.

"I'm not surprised," Mickel said. "The INS correspondent there is Bob Bender, whose father owns the *Evening News*. He knows everybody in the government and they probably give him a break."

Bickel thought this over for two minutes, got on a train, and went to Springfield, where he hired Bender for thirty dollars a week, or five dollars more than he was getting. Bender was promptly ordered to New York, where he walked in unannounced and introduced himself to Bureau Manager Fred Ferguson. Ferguson didn't seem to be much impressed by the young recruit

---

[1] To keep the record straight, especially in regard to *The Hellbox*, it should be noted that in the 1916 World Series the Associated Press set up for the first time in press association history a system of direct play-by-play transmission from the Boston press box to many large newspapers across the country. This meant that the customary relay points were eliminated and a 26,000-mile single circuit was established to make transmission of the play-by-play report instantaneous—as long as there was no wire trouble. This system, devised by the AP's Kent Cooper, "worked flawlessly" and was "a sensation in the newspaper world," according to the Associated Press' official history, which showed that it could sometimes toss flossy adjectives around just as adroitly as *The Hellbox*.

and looked at him with a cold eye that evening. "How soon can you get out of town?" he asked. "I want you to join the Washington bureau."

The war had led to many changes in the Washington staff, and for some months the United Press had been lagging behind its rivals on news developments, especially from the White House and State Department. President Wilson was then at his summer home in New Jersey, and Bender was assigned to keep watch over him, a task he performed so expertly that he was made regular White House correspondent. He quickly made friends in the right places and was able to develop a number of exclusive stories, possibly due in part to the fact that he was one of the few Washington reporters who owned an automobile and frequently taxied Joseph Tumulty, the President's secretary, to his home at the end of the workday.

Bender rarely got a day off, but one afternoon he risked going to the golf links—and was beaten on a White House story. He received some harsh messages from New York as a result and told Tumulty that he might be fired. Tumulty said he would try to help out. A few evenings later the telephone rang at Bender's home and his wife answered. The caller was friend Tumulty, who said: "Just tell Bob that it's Newton D. Baker."

Mrs. Bender relayed the message and the next morning the United Press had an exclusive story on the appointment of Baker as Secretary of War. Bender's ability to develop personal contacts with officials led to many exclusive stories, including President Wilson's determination not to accept the German policy of unrestricted submarine warfare, his definite request for recall of German Ambassador von Bernstorff, and his decision personally to attend the Paris Peace Conference.

Later, when Bender was in charge of the Washington bureau, he frequently lectured his staff on the importance of the direct approach to news coverage. At one time a rumor circulated that Mrs. Alice Roosevelt Longworth, daughter of the former President, was pregnant. This was not the kind of story an agency usually worried about in those days, but "Princess Alice" was a famous figure in her own right, as well as wife of the speaker of the House. Every reporter in town was soon busily but vainly trying to check the rumor. Mrs. Longworth's friends would say nothing. Her doctor was not available. When Bender learned of these futile reportorial efforts he grunted in disgust, picked up the telephone, and called the Longworth residence. The mistress of the house answered.

"This is the United Press," Bender said. "Are you pregnant, Mrs. Longworth?"

"Hell, yes," the lady answered happily. "Isn't it wonderful?"

3.

The biggest political news triumph of the United Press in 1916 did not originate in the Washington bureau but in the little town of Eureka on the California coast north of San Francisco. It was there that, unknown to most of the world, the climax of the 1916 presidential campaign was played out at the end of one of the country's most remarkable political dramas.

President Wilson had campaigned on the slogan "He kept us out of war." Charles Evans Hughes, stepping down from the Supreme Court, had waged a vigorous fight as the Republican nominee, and the outcome was doubtful in the minds of most political experts when the voting started on November 7. That evening, however, returns from New York showed that the state had been carried by Hughes, and in the next few hours he piled up a commanding lead in the eastern states. Newspapers such as the influential New York *World* and the New York *Times,* both of which had supported Wilson, conceded the election to Hughes on the basis of these returns, and the former Chief Justice was convinced that he had won the presidency. Neither the United Press nor the Associated Press declared Hughes elected, although it seemed almost certain until Wednesday morning when final returns from Ohio unexpectedly gave Wilson that state's electoral votes. Minnesota, which also had been slow in a final count, went to Hughes by only a few hundred votes, giving him 254 electoral votes. But soon afterward Wilson forged ahead and had 264 electoral votes—just two short of the necessary margin. The counting in California, however, had not been completed, and by Wednesday evening everybody knew that the outcome would depend on who won that state's thirteen electoral votes.

Hughes originally had been favored to carry California, but he had made the mistake of alienating the Progressive wing of the Republican party led by Hiram Johnson. As a result, incomplete returns Wednesday evening showed Wilson running neck-and-neck with the GOP nominee. There were a number of counties in the state that were more or less isolated, and returns from them were extremely slow. Returns from many other counties were so close that the votes had to be checked and rechecked for errors. Correspondents went over the returns time after time. On Thursday the result was still in doubt, but it had been narrowed down at last to a single county, Humboldt, which appeared likely to be decisive.

In Humboldt County, the United Press string correspondent had been Morris DeHaven Tracy, a newspaperman in Eureka, the county seat. He had proved such an able reporter that Barney Furay, the manager at San Francisco, brought him into the bureau not long before the election as a staff member. Tracy knew everybody in Eureka, where he had grown up, and was intimately acquainted with political affairs in the county. All Thursday afternoon he kept the telephone line open to his boyhood friend, who was clerk of Humboldt County, suggesting checks on this or that precinct in an effort to get a final decision. But at 6 P.M., with the telegraph wire to New York still open, the result was so close that the county clerk said it appeared to be a tie between Wilson and Hughes. Some 925,000 votes had been cast in California and at that hour Wilson's tabulated unofficial vote in the state gave him a lead of less than 400—by no means enough to make the outcome certain.

At 6:30 P.M. (Pacific coast time) Thursday, two days after the polls had closed, the New York bureau signaled for the telegraphers all along the line to take a thirty-minute supper period but to remain as close as possible to their posts. Nothing happened during the supper period and the telegraphers returned to work at 7 P.M. They were hardly seated, however, when the telephone rang in the San Francisco office and Tracy's friend, the Humboldt County clerk, was on the wire.

"I got it," he yelled. "I just found an error in counting. About 1800 votes were erroneously put in the Hughes column. Really, they are Wilson votes and he carries the county by about 3600 votes!"

Bureau Manager Furay studied the figures a moment and walked a few steps to the telegraph desk, checking and rechecking in his mind. Returns from all over the state had been verified again and again. Now, with the correction from Humboldt County, Wilson had a lead of approximately 4000 votes. Under the circumstances it was enough. Furay instructed the operator to break in on the news story being received from the East, and the word went on the wires:

FLASH WILSON CARRIES CALIFORNIA

Before anything else could be put on the wire, another flash came back from election headquarters of the United Press in New York:

FLASH WILSON ELECTED

Morris DeHaven Tracy's intimate acquaintance with Humboldt County had produced the news that the nation was waiting to hear. But it was close. The Associated Press flashed the election of Wilson at 7:20 P.M.—just ten minutes later.

CHAPTER EIGHT

Coverage of the European war demanded more and more reporters, and a dozen new men, including Carl W. Ackerman, Westbrook Pegler, Lowell Mellett, Frank J. Taylor, and Webb Miller, were added to the staff in belligerent countries. The boss was on the move too. In September of 1916, Roy Howard showed up again in London, as dapper and bright-eyed as ever and sporting a mustache that apparently was intended to give him a look of maturity. He was, as he had remarked to an interviewer, damn tired of having strangers come into the New York bureau and mistake him for an office boy.

The war had developed for the time being into a kind of grim stalemate. The Germans had been halted by the Allied armies, but they held large areas that had been seized in their early offensives and nobody was very certain what Britain and France could do about it. There were various rumors that the Pope might take the initiative in trying to arrange for a negotiated peace or that President Wilson might advance some plan for ending the war. The Germans may have encouraged such rumors in the belief that any negotiated peace would be to their advantage. After Howard arrived in England, he soon discovered that the British people had mustered their strength and had no intention of settling for less than victory. He also received word from Colonel House, advisor to President Wilson, saying that Democrats of German ancestry were bringing pressure on the White House to suggest some kind of peace move. House apparently was opposed to any effort by Mr. Wilson toward intervention.

This situation presented an opportunity for an enterprising reporter. Howard thought over the possibilities and then went to call on his friend, Lord Northcliffe, who published *The Times* of London. Northcliffe agreed with Howard that the time was right for a story on the peace rumors and that the best way to approach it would be through an interview with a high British official.

"Do you want to interview Asquith?" he asked in reference to the Prime Minister.

"Frankly, I think a better choice would be David Lloyd George," Howard replied. Lloyd George was then Secretary of State for War. "He reminds Americans of Teddy Roosevelt and we like the things he says."

"Very well," Northcliffe said. "If I were you I would go right now to his office, send in my card, and ask for an interview."

Howard protested that such a thing was ridiculous, that nobody would pay any attention to him at the Secretary's office. But Northcliffe pressed his idea and Howard went to Lloyd George's office and—after a long and heated argument with a scornful policeman at the door—managed to get his card sent inside to the Welsh statesman. "It's useless," the policeman repeated. "He won't see you if you have no appointment and don't even know him." But, two minutes later, the astonished policeman received orders to send Howard immediately to Lloyd George's private office. Presumably Northcliffe had paved the way by telephone but he would never admit it to Howard.

It had been Howard's intention merely to explain his idea and ask for an interview at a later date, but Lloyd George began giving his views on the subject of a negotiated peace and giving them in sporting terms. "If I am to speak plainly so that all the people will understand," he remarked, "perhaps sporting terms will have to be used." Three quarters of an hour later he paused and said: "In view of all the circumstances, I will have to ask you to let me see a copy of your article before it is published."

Howard, who had hoped only to arrange a date for a formal interview, had not taken any notes and was startled by this announcement, but he rushed to his hotel room and quickly wrote down everything he could remember of the conversation. He returned to Lloyd George's office the next day with his story. "Hurried fellow, isn't he?" the Secretary remarked to an aide as he read the interview. He deleted four words in the copy and added a phrase at the end. Prime Minister Asquith also approved the story, and it was agreed that the British Information Service would make it available to the world press twenty-four hours after it had been released by the United Press in North and South America.

The interview went on the United Press wires at a time when the world was wondering whether Europe was in for a long military stalemate, for new offensives, or for peace negotiations. The world got the answer in an unprecedented fashion. For the first time in the history of any great war, the British Empire's top military official dropped the stilted language of diplomacy and spoke out in the language of the people—in sporting terms that nobody could misunderstand.

BY ROY W. HOWARD

General Manager of the United Press

LONDON, September 28 (UP) *There is no end of the war in sight. Any*

steps at this time by the United States, the Vatican or any other neutral in
the direction of world peace would be construed by England as an unneu-
tral, pro-German move.

The United Press is able to make these statements on no less authority
than that of the British man of the hour, Right Hon. David Lloyd George,
Secretary of State for War.

"Britain has only begun to fight," was the Welsh statesman's size-up of
the situation. "The fight must be to a finish—to a knockout."

There were many great stories in the course of World War I, but it can
be doubted that any was as sensational or as significant as Howard's interview with Lloyd George. As news, the story was of great importance in every
country. Editorial comment on the interview appeared in practically every
newspaper in Britain, France, and other European countries, including
Germany, where the Frankfurter *Zeitung* was "scandalized" by the British
cabinet minister's use of sports terms in reference to the war. Howard, incidentally, had immediately gone to Berlin in an effort to persuade the German Chancellor to give him a similar interview or to reply to Lloyd George,
but his trip was unsuccessful.

In addition to its immediate importance, however, the Lloyd George interview was regarded by many observers as a significant sign post on the
road away from the old shabby methods and the secret deals of international diplomacy. Never before had there been such frank speaking from
the high seats of a world power at a time of great crisis. It was a break with
the past—something to send a tingle and a chill down the backbone of the
average man everywhere. And perhaps it took the son of a Welsh coal miner
and a brash young man from Indiana to bring it off.

2.

After the United States declared war on Germany in 1917, one of the most
important stories was the first draft drawing in Washington in September,
generally described as the "greatest lottery of all time." The government arranged to start the draft of men for the Army with a great deal of publicity
and with the Secretary of War, Newton D. Baker, selecting the first number
from a bowl in the caucus room at the Senate Office Building. Each man
eligible for the draft had a number, and the numbers drawn by lot at the
capitol designated certain lists of men to be called for service.

There was a tremendous jam of newspapermen, officials, and just plain
curious visitors around the caucus room and it was almost impossible to get
in or out by the time Baker arrived for the ceremony. Present in behalf of
the United Press were Bob Bender, Carl D. Groat, Charles McCann, Tony
Demma, a fleet-footed office boy, and Robert K. MacCormac, the best telegrapher in the office. They had arrived early and laid their plans, which
hinged on the fact that Groat was probably the tallest reporter in Wash-

ington. He was stationed beside the big bowl that was used for the lottery. Bender stood on a chair just outside the door of the room. Demma was down the corridor at a turn that led to the telegraph desk, where McCann and MacCormac waited.

Before the drawing started there was a good deal of banter among the wire service men as to which would be first with the first number. Finally, somebody designated George Hudson of the A.T.&T. as referee of the contest. Meanwhile, Baker appeared in the caucus room, police elbowed a way for him to the big bowl, the newsreel klieg lights were turned on, and the ceremony started. The Secretary reached into the bowl and drew a number. He read it off slowly: "Number Two five eight." There was a wild scramble among the reporters to get out of the room—except for Groat. He stood perfectly still, but raised his arms above the crowd so that Bender, standing on a chair by the door, could see that he was holding up two fingers. Then he signaled with five fingers, and finally with eight. Bender passed each signal along to Demma, who wrote the numbers down on a sheet of copy paper as he ran toward the telegraph desk. He arrived all alone, and McCann and MacCormac did the rest.

FLASH WASHINGTON FIRST NUMBER 258

The flash cleared before any other reporters had appeared. MacCormac began sending the bulletin that McCann had written:

ROOM 226, SENATE OFFICE BUILDING, WASHINGTON July 20 (By United Press) *Number 258 was picked today in America's human gamble whereby the United States will raise its anti-autocracy army. At 11:31 A.M., Secretary of War Baker drew the first number.*

MacCormac's telegraph sounder clicked away, but other instruments in the crowded room were silent. McCann began to wonder what was wrong. Had there been a mistake? By that time Demma had run back to the caucus room where he found the door jammed with reporters vainly attempting to fight their way out through the crowd. He grabbed one man by the belt, braced himself, and yanked. The whole crowd plunged across the hall, and the reporters ran for the telegraph room. Demma went inside and picked up the next nine numbers, which Groat had copied off, and returned with them to the telegraph room where there was such turmoil that nobody could hear Hudson shout: "The UP wins!"

3.

In 1917, Lowell Mellett was perhaps the least cheerful character in London.

"I came over here to be a war correspondent," he complained repeatedly to Ed Keen, "and you keep me working on a desk in London. How about sending me to France?"

Toward the end of the year Keen did give him orders to go to France but, as Mellett suspected, there was a catch in it.

"We've been having trouble for months getting the daily French war communiqué from Paris to New York," Keen said. "The Associated Press has been beating us from thirty minutes to almost two hours on most days. Doc Forrest [Wilbur Forrest] has been looking into the problem in Paris and he thinks we are being double-crossed somewhere along the line by some French telegraph company employee who is in a position to rush the AP dispatch and to hold ours back. What I want you to do is to go over there and get it straightened out."

"But I want to report the war," Mellett said for the hundredth time.

Mellett went to Paris where he and Jean DeGandt began studying what was probably the biggest and most confused communications tangle in the world, then or later. They soon became convinced that there was "dirty work at the crossroads" but had no luck in finding out which crossroads. But in studying the telegraph charts, DeGandt discovered that there were three leased wires running from Paris to French provincial newspapers and that one of them went to the offices of the Brest *Dépêche*. And Brest was the terminus of the French telegraph company's cable line to New York. Mellett arranged to meet Louis Coudurier, publisher of *La Dépêche,* and asked whether he would consider renting his leased wire to the United Press at certain hours each day—hours when it would not be crowded with dispatches to *La Dépêche*. Coudurier was agreeable and, for about fifty dollars a month, Mellett concluded the deal with an exchange of letters.

The next day about noon Mellett filed the French war communiqué on the leased wire from Paris into the Brest newspaper office. A messenger, provided by Coudurier, was standing by in Brest to carry the dispatch across the Place du President Wilson to the cable office, where it was turned over to the censor and filed to New York. That evening there was a message from New York:

BEAT ASSOCIATED PRESS TWO HOURS ON COMMUNIQUÉ

The second day there was a message saying that the United Press was thirty minutes ahead on the French communiqué, and on the third day it was two hours again. That was more than enough for Mellett. He wrote a message to Keen:

NOW KIN EYE GO TO FRONT?

Keen said all right, go to the front. Later the United Press began using the Brest leased wire for other important news at various times of day. Since these messages by-passed the crowded telegraph lines out of Paris, they frequently were several hours or more ahead of any other service. After taking many beatings due to this system, the Associated Press found out how the trick was being done and approached Coudurier with an offer to make a similar arrangement at a good price. The publisher said he would do it only if the United Press agreed. The United Press declined to agree and continued to use the Brest wire to great advantage until long after the war. Communiqués and other dispatches via the Brest wire rather consistently arrived in New York an hour or more ahead of cables sent by any other route. This represented a tremendous margin for afternoon newspapers, and it enabled Karl Bickel to sell service to many newspapers, especially in the Midwest and Southwest, that might not otherwise have subscribed to the United Press.

4.

Fred Ferguson, who had been manager of the New York bureau for a short time, arrived on the French war front in February of 1918 to take over coverage of General John J. Pershing's American Expeditionary Force, and luck was with him. Always looking for something different, Ferguson decided to do some stories on how the soldiers lived in the trenches. When other reporters returned to the rear-area press headquarters one night late in February, Ferguson remained to sleep in the trenches with the idea of writing a feature story. Early the next day, when most reporters were still far behind the lines, the Germans made their first big gas attack on the American lines. Ferguson had the story all to himself for a day.

Ferguson later scored one of the outstanding beats of the war on the first really big military operation planned and executed entirely by Americans—the battle of Saint-Mihiel. By that time the German threat to Paris on the Marne front had been relieved. The Allied forces had gathered strength, and Marshal Foch was launching the great offensive that would finally push the enemy back toward the Rhine River and bring an end to the war. The task of the Americans was to wipe out the Saint-Mihiel salient which the enemy had held since the beginning of the war.

As part of the effort to deceive the Germans, the American and other Allied correspondents were forced to remain on the Marne front until the day before the Saint-Mihiel attack was to begin. Then they were taken at intervals by automobile to Nancy, press headquarters for the American sector. Arriving late at night, they were ushered into a hotel where the blinds were drawn and where guards had been posted against possible German spies. Colonel Dennis Nolan, the American intelligence chief, then showed correspondents a detailed map of the sector and described exactly how the attack would be made—hour by hour—how the tanks, being used for the first time by Americans, would advance, how the aerial and artillery support would be organized, and how the infantry would move on a well-planned schedule.

Actually, the attack was almost a pushover. The German position was vulnerable and, since it was the first big all-American attack, every precaution was taken to make sure that it succeeded. This fact was never publicized in the United States, but it was well known to correspondents on the scene and it gave Ferguson an idea. When the great artillery barrage preceding the attack was started by the Americans at midnight, most of the correspondents went out to watch. But Ferguson sat down to write.

Drawing on Colonel Nolan's exhaustive lecture, he wrote the story of the attack in brief "takes" or sections, each one complete in itself and none longer than fifty words. These "takes" covered vital points such as the time the offensive started, the capture of the first objective, the capture of the second objective, and so on. In half an hour, Ferguson had written enough "takes" to cover each planned step of the first day's fighting. Then he went around to the censor's office. The chief censor was Captain Gerald Morgan, and Captain Morgan was a friend of Correspondent Ferguson.

"Captain," Ferguson began with his most winning smile, "would you like to do me a little favor?"

The captain thought he might.

"Well, I've got here a dozen pieces of copy addressed by way of several cable routes to New York," Ferguson went on, handing over his story. "On each telegram I have written a specific time of release. This one, for instance, is to be released when the troops capture their first objective. Here's one for capture of the second objective, and so on. Now Operations Headquarters will be sitting here getting a play-by-play official report over the field telephones. I wondered if you would be willing to file these messages for me as each of these designated objectives is reached?"

Captain Morgan looked over the little pile of messages and said he would do it. "You want them to go on the new American-manned telegraph line to the cable head?" he asked.

"No," Ferguson replied. "I think that line is going to be a muddle. It has new men on it and it is going to be overcrowded with official and press messages. I want these filed on the regular French telegraph lines, which may not be as jammed."

The captain nodded and Ferguson set off at dawn to follow the American offensive. He had his own automobile and a French driver, but he decided to go to the front with Major James, an intelligence officer, who was taking the correspondents of the Associated Press and the International News Service with him. Ferguson's chauffeur was instructed to follow them. At the front, they saw that the offensive was moving even faster than the timetable Colonel Nolan had outlined. For several hours they followed, picking up whatever information they could. Somewhere along the line, the three reporters shifted from Major James's automobile to Ferguson's car and took off on their own. About eleven o'clock Henry Wales, the International News Service correspondent, suggested that they return to press headquarters at Nancy to write their stories.

"Oh, what's the hurry?" Ferguson asked. They toured for a while longer.

Then both Wales and James Howe, the Associated Press man, began insisting that it was time to get back to Nancy. It was Ferguson's automobile and he took his time about returning, but they arrived at press headquarters shortly after noon. Captain Morgan looked up as they entered the censor's office.

"Some telegrams for you guys," he said. Ferguson's was from New York and it congratulated him on an exclusive story of the first all-American offensive of the war. Ferguson was still reading it when Wales came up, waving a telegram.

"Yeah," he said sourly, "I got a telegram from New York, too. I see it all now, you bastard."

Both Wales and Howe then filed their stories on the new American telegraph line. As Ferguson had guessed, it was so jammed with traffic that their dispatches didn't reach New York until late that night.

5.

Ferguson, Mellett, Frank J. Taylor, and Webb Miller had covered the front-line phases of the war with the American troops in 1918, while Simms accompanied the British Army and Henry Wood was with the French. The whole team followed step by step the progress of Marshal Foch's offensive that pushed the enemy back to the Vesle River in the final stages of the war.

As the war drew to an end, Ferguson returned to Paris to prepare for coverage of postwar diplomatic developments and Taylor went to Switzerland to be ready to dash into Germany the moment an armistice was signed. Miller was left alone on the Argonne sector to cover the end of the war on the front lines. Since it took hours to get from press headquarters at Bar-le-Duc to the front lines, he paid a call on Eddie Rickenbacker's famous squadron of American fliers and Rickenbacker helped arrange with Lieutenant James Meissner, an ace pilot, to fly Miller over the front lines immediately after the cessation of hostilities.

On the morning of November 11, Miller was at army headquarters at Souilly when news arrived that the armistice would be effective at 11 A.M. He telephoned Meissner who sadly told him that there was so much fog over the front that airplanes couldn't fly and that he wouldn't see anything if they did. Miller got in his car and drove to the village of Bras, from where he walked to the front-line trenches. A captain who met him at the door of a dugout didn't know anything about the armistice, and, in fact, both the American and German artillery were then engaged in a wild outburst of shooting their biggest field pieces. But at 10:50 A.M. the message to cease hostilities came over the field telephone in the dugout, and ten minutes later the front was silent.

The next day Meissner flew Miller up and down the front lines at a low altitude. He could see Germans and Americans playing games within a couple of hundred yards of each other. In German-held territory there were long lines of soldiers moving to the rear. They laughed and waved as the plane swooped over their heads. At other points, graves were being dug and bridges were being repaired. Miller returned with the first graphic story of the front lines at peace.

CHAPTER NINE

At this point in the story of the United Press Associations it is necessary to go back a few days in history. Roy Howard was in Europe as the war was drawing to an end. He left Paris on the night of Wednesday, November 6, 1918, for Brest to get passage on an Army transport to New York. It seemed certain that the fighting would end before he arrived home. Only three days earlier, Colonel House had said in Paris "it's all over," and had cabled the State Department that the "terms of the armistice to be offered Germany have been agreed to and signed by the Inter-Allied Conference unanimously."

When Howard arrived in Brest on November 7, he was met by an American intelligence officer who told him that the armistice had been signed but that there had been no official announcement. At headquarters of the American commander in Brest, the chief intelligence officer, Lieutenant Arthur Hornblow, Jr., suggested to Howard that they call on Admiral Henry B. Wilson, commanding officer of all United States naval forces in France, to see whether he had any new information. The admiral was not at his desk, but was expected back later in the afternoon. General George H. Harries, American commander in Brest, then assigned a member of his staff, Major C. Fred Cook, a former Washington newspaperman, to accompany Howard around Brest and on his visit to Admiral Wilson later in the day.

A few minutes after 4 P.M., Howard and Cook climbed five flights of stairs to Admiral Wilson's office overlooking the Place du President Wilson. It was a warm, sunny day. A U. S. Navy band was giving a concert in the square, surrounded by American soldiers and French civilians. Inside Admiral Wilson's office all was bustle and enthusiasm.

"By God, Major," Wilson said to Cook as they entered, "this is news, isn't it!"

He ruffled a handful of carbon copies of a telegram and handed one to an orderly. "Here, take this to the editor of La Dépêche and tell him that he can publish it—tell him to put it on his bulletin board. And here, take this copy to that bandmaster; tell him to read it to the crowd both in English and French and then tell him to put some jazz in that music!"

Wilson then shook hands with Howard, while Cook asked what the big news was.

"The armistice has been signed," Wilson replied, handing him a copy of the telegram.

"Is it official?"

"Official, hell," the admiral said. "I should say it *is* official. I just received this over my direct wire from the embassy. It's the official announcement."

At that moment there came a roar from the square below as the crowd heard the news. The navy band played "There'll Be a Hot Time in the Old Town Tonight."

Howard broke in. "I beg your pardon, Admiral," he said, "but if this is official and you've announced it to the base and have given it to the local paper for publication, do you have any objection if I file it to the United Press?"

"Hell, no. This is official. It is signed by Captain Jackson, our naval attaché at Paris. Here's a copy. Go to it."

Wilson then ordered Ensign Sellards, who spoke fluent French, to accompany Howard to the cable office and "see that he gets this message cleared through the censorship."

They stopped at the office of *La Dépêche* and had the leased wire telegraph operator there retype the message on tape which was pasted on a regular cable blank:

UNIPRESS NEWYORK
URGENT ARMISTICE ALLIES GERMANY SIGNED ELEVEN SMORNING HOSTILITIES CEASED TWO SAFTERNOON SEDAN TAKEN SMORNING BY AMERICANS
HOWARD SIMMS

It was necessary for Howard to sign the name of his Paris bureau manager, Simms, as well as his own, and the number of Simms's official press card, in order to send a collect message to New York. He knew that the great delay in telegraph messages over the land lines from Paris to the Brest cable head made it wise for him to send the armistice flash, but he assumed that the news was already out in Paris and that it had been filed to New York by the Paris bureau. He was merely "backstopping" from Brest on the chance that Paris messages were greatly delayed.

At the cable office, the censor's room was deserted when Howard and Sellards arrived with their message. The entire personnel had gone out into the streets where a mass celebration had started in the Place du President Wilson. Sellards suggested that Howard wait in the office while he went alone to the operations room at the cable head where he was well known to the telegraphers. He delivered the message to an operator who transmitted it

—unknown to Howard—without submitting it to the French censor. It arrived in New York at 11:20 A.M., November 7, bearing a Paris dateline, due probably to the fact that the cable operator regularly handled Simms's messages over the leased wire and assumed it had been sent from Paris.

The New York cable desk flashed the armistice on all wires and then turned out a story under a Paris dateline, weaving into it material previously received from the French capital:

PARIS, November 7 (United Press) *The war is over. Germany and the Allies signed an armistice at 11 A.M. today, hostilities ceasing three hours later. As Marshal Foch's terms are known to include provisions which will prevent resumption of hostilities, the greatest war of all time has come to an end.*

The news spread with incredible rapidity. In every city and village of America delirious citizens celebrated the end of the Great War. The trouble was that the war wasn't quite over. By the time Howard and Sellards had fought their way back through the cheering crowds in the Place du President Wilson, Admiral Wilson had left his office. Howard went to a restaurant a bit later for dinner, but before he could even get a drink an orderly arrived with a message from Admiral Wilson. It said that he had received a second message from Paris stating that the first dispatch was "unconfirmable." Howard dashed over to the office of *La Dépêche* and wrote another message to New York quoting Wilson's second message. It was filed approximately two hours after the armistice flash had been transmitted, but it did not reach the United Press office in New York until almost noon on the next day, November 8.

2.

W. W. Hawkins, the United Press general manager in New York, was a man with courage and strong nerves. He and Howard were a great deal more than business associates. They were companions. They planned together, they argued together, they accused each other of blockheadedness and shortsightedness. Hawkins was a kind of balance wheel, a steadying influence on Howard's mercurial temperament. If Howard came into the news room when things were going badly and perhaps kicked a couple of wastebaskets across the floor to show his displeasure, Hawkins could nonchalantly and patiently say what nobody else dared say: "Oh, for Pete's sake, Roy, take it easy."

He wasn't afraid to talk back when he felt Howard was wrong, and the two often fought bitterly, exchanging insults that sometimes convinced outsiders that they were on the point of a fist fight or, certainly, would never speak to each other again. One day an associate of E. W. Scripps was in Howard's office in New York during such an argument between the two. He left hurriedly, remarking to a friend in an adjoining office that he was sorry to have been present when the long association between Howard and Hawkins came to such a violent end.

"Just stick around a few minutes," the friend said. "It's almost lunch time."

Five minutes later Howard and Hawkins strolled out for luncheon, chatting happily about trivial matters.

When there was a crisis, when there was an attack from the outside, Howard and Hawkins knew how to stand together. And there was a crisis on November 7, 1918. It was Hawkins who had rejoiced when Howard's armistice flash went on the wires in New York—another "beat" on the biggest news of the war. It was Hawkins who stood firm when, as Carl D. Groat, the State Department correspondent, said, it began to look a few hours later as if the "exclusive" flash was "too damned exclusive." Washington had no official word on the signing of the armistice. Hawkins went to the front windows of the United Press offices overlooking New York's City Hall Plaza. A mad crowd of countless thousands milled through the streets, celebrating the end of the war. Newspaper confetti filled the air. Women threw their arms around complete strangers on the sidewalks. There was a kind of hysterical joy spreading over the city. Automobile horns raised a tremendous din. Army truck drivers in the streets added to the noise by backfiring their motors in a series of thunderous explosions.

There was not so much joy in the United Press offices by that time because—as the hours passed—nothing more than Howard's original flash had been received. There was growing tension among the staff, and worried frowns appeared on the brows of editors. Hugh Baillie, the New York manager, and Harold D. Jacobs, the cable editor, went down to the street to get a close view of the celebration, which was mounting in volume. As far as the public was concerned, the war was over. Jacobs, worried and silent, watched for a few minutes. Then he took his pipe out of his mouth and gestured at the hysterical throng.

"*By United Press,*" he said with discomfort.

In the news room above, Hawkins stood grimly by when, a little after two o'clock that afternoon, the Associated Press carried a bulletin from Washington saying "it was officially announced at the State Department that the Germans had not signed armistice terms." Within a short time the United Press bureau in New York was flooded with inquiries. Many newspapermen rushed to the office to find out what had happened. For all of them Hawkins had the same words. He had slipped the original cable from Brest under the glass on his desk, and he merely pointed to it and said: "This dispatch came from the president of the United Press and it is all we know. Roy Howard is not a faker. Until we receive some further word, there is the answer."

All attempts to reach Simms or Howard over the clogged cables had failed. Late in the afternoon Hawkins—his coat off, his necktie loosened—went over to stand beside F. A. Gribbon, the crack telegraph operator who handled cable messages. There was nothing he could do but wait. The United Press wires to afternoon newspapers closed down, but Hawkins still stood there. Messages of inquiry and telephone calls from United Press clients all over the country came into the office. Hawkins had them answered with messages stating the facts about receipt of Howard's flash.

At midnight, Karl Bickel, who was now business manager, got back to New York from a trip to Baltimore and went directly to the office. As he crossed the sidewalk in front of the New York *World* building he literally waded through torn and crumpled newspapers that were scattered far and wide around City Hall Park as a result of the day's unrestrained celebration. From what Bickel had learned in Baltimore he was worried that something had gone wrong, and when he reached the third floor his fears were quickly confirmed. Gribbon, tall and lank with a rugged face topped by a thick thatch of hair, sat beside his silent telegraph instrument, a pencil behind his ear, a cigarette dangling from his lips, and a cup of coffee at his elbow. Beside him, silent and grim, was Hawkins, the sleeves of his blue shirt rolled above the elbows, his hands smudged with carbon. As Bickel pushed through the door of the big, almost silent room, Hawkins turned slowly. He saw Bickel and shook his head.

"Not a thing," he said. "You go home for a few hours. Get back here early in the morning and tell the telephone girl to switch all long-distance calls to your office."

When Bickel started home, Hawkins was still standing beside Gribbon. When he returned before dawn, neither one of them appeared to have moved.

"Nothing new," Hawkins said. "Here's a copy of everything we've received. When the calls come in, just give them the facts."

Bickel hadn't been in his office ten minutes before the first call came in from an irate newspaper editor. After that there were so many calls that Bickel didn't put the telephone down all morning. Meantime, Hawkins had received an anonymous telephone call early in the day from a man who refused to identify himself, but whose voice Hawkins recognized as a former newspaperman who was now in the Navy censorship. The man said that within two hours after Howard's armistice flash had been received, a second message from Howard, quoting Admiral Wilson's words that the flash could not be confirmed, was received by the censor in New York but, on orders from Washington, was sent to the Secretary of the Navy instead of to the United Press office. The informant also said that just prior to the arrival of Howard's first armistice flash a similar message announcing the armistice had been delivered to the War Department.[1]

---

[1] This was confirmed by State Department records made public in 1933. Among the records was this message from Secretary of State Lansing to Colonel House in Paris: "Warburton (the American military attaché in Paris) informs War Department armistice signed. Please confirm and notify us when we may publish armistice."

Hawkins got the Washington bureau busy prying the second Howard message out of the Navy Department, but it was not until late in the morning, after the issue had been carried to the White House, that the second cable from Brest was delivered to the United Press. There was then no longer any doubt that the United Press had been the victim of an error compounded by American officials in Paris and Washington, and made possible only by an incredible series of coincidences connected with Howard's activities in Brest.

Howard did about the only thing possible under the circumstances. He told Admiral Wilson the facts and asked him to issue a statement setting forth the manner in which he had secured the armistice flash. "The statement of the United Press relative to the signing of the armistice was made public from my office on the basis of what appeared to be official and authoritative information," Wilson's statement said. "I am in a position to know that the United Press and its representative acted in perfect good faith, and the premature announcement was the result of an error for which the agency was in no wise responsible."

Still not fully aware of the tremendous bomb of excitement or the terrific morning-after hang-over that he had given America, Howard climbed aboard the troopship S.S. *Great Northern* at Brest two days later and sailed for New York.

3.

In keeping with the bitter and uncompromising newspaper rivalries of the day, the United Press took a drubbing in connection with the November 7 armistice report although, strangely enough, there were also a surprisingly large number of leaders in the newspaper world who reacted with a spirit of understanding when they learned the details of Howard's experience at Brest. It was a minority of Associated Press newspapers which were in stiff local competition with United Press newspapers that reacted with the greatest venom, perhaps because they were irritated by the competition that the United Press had provided throughout the war.

On November 8, the Associated Press carried what might be regarded in the circumstances as a restrained story:

NEW YORK, November 8 (Associated Press) *Millions of Americans realized today that they had been hoaxed into celebrating the end of the war by publication of the United Press dispatches declaring the armistice signed and fighting ended.*

But the Associated Press member newspapers were less restrained. The Brooklyn *Eagle* pointed out: "The *Eagle* is the only newspaper in Brooklyn having the service of the Associated Press. Consequently it was the only paper in Brooklyn that did not convey to its readers a palpably suspicious if not deliberately misleading dispatch from Paris declaring the armistice had been signed."

"Yesterday was a sad day for newspapermen who like to believe in the essential integrity of the great body of their profession," the New York *Globe* said editorially. "They saw profiteering newspapers, assisted by a great body of profiteering newspaper sellers, join in victimizing the public with probably the greatest fake in newspaper history."

The New York *Tribune* added: "The statement of Admiral Wilson is an amazing one. It only intensifies the mystery of what must now rank as one of the greatest hoaxes in newspaper history."

But it was smaller newspapers engaged in local wars that really made the most of the occasion. "For several months past," said the Dayton *Daily News*, which was in bitter competition with the Dayton *Herald*, a United Press client, "an afternoon paper published on Jefferson Street, this city, has been taking a daily emetic and besmearing Dayton with nauseous claims concerning its superior achievements. Not until yesterday have its boasts about itself or its superior 'news' been taken seriously; but when it issued its fake extra announcing the signing of the armistice . . . the public fell for its impudent hoax and pandemonium broke loose. . . . Having fooled the people of Dayton, it insulted them by exulting over the manner in which they had been misled into engaging in a demonstration of thanksgiving while our army was still struggling under a rain of shot and shell upon the blood-soaked field of France."

There was a good deal more along the same line in various parts of the country, but *Collier's Weekly* later summed it all up in an article saying that, as far as the public was concerned, most people didn't care. "They felt that if the Germans didn't surrender today they would tomorrow." They had a big time on November 7, and when the real armistice came along on November 11 nobody paid much attention.

Howard never did find out exactly how the armistice report had originated, and later he remarked that "there are many people who still believe that an armistice of some sort actually was signed on November 7. They cite the never officially denied report that German emissaries crossed the French lines at daybreak on the morning of Thursday, November 7; that the terms of the armistice were already drawn at that hour; and that they had probably been agreed to in advance by the Germans. These people contend that this first delegation, headed by Herr Erzberger, came to Marshal Foch bearing credentials from the Kaiser's government. Their theory is that, after having signed at least a preliminary armistice with Erzberger, Foch learned of the Kaiser's abdication and the appointment of Prince Max of Baden as Chancellor; that, inasmuch as the first emissaries no longer represented the *de facto* government, Foch reconsidered, questioned their authority, and sent them back to Berlin to obtain credentials from the new provisional government. It is contended that neither side has been willing to admit that hostilities might have been terminated on November 7 because none of the leaders has dared to assume responsibility for the casualties (in such a situation, needless casualties) that resulted between November 7 and 11."

Howard, however, did not accept this theory and was later inclined to agree with Colonel House, who informed the Secretary of State that he had investigated the matter, and that "It is perfectly clear that the United Press was not at fault, and that the fault, if any, lies with [the naval attaché] or the French official who started the rumor."

Nobody ever discovered the identity of the "French official," although there was no question that a telephone call over a private and official channel from the French foreign office to the United States Embassy on November 7 had announced the signing of the armistice and asked that the information be communicated to the ambassador.

There was reason to believe, however, that no French official ever made the call, which may well have been the work of a German secret agent in Paris. The Germans feared that the French were going to be ruthless in their terms for ending the war and they wanted an armistice quickly. They may have decided to give the negotiations a shove, if possible, by a false report that would arouse great enthusiasm for peace.

The tumult, the recriminations, the denunciations, and the confusion that followed might well have wrecked not only Howard's career but the future of the United Press. It didn't. Howard arrived in New York to learn that he had touched off an earthquake in the newspaper world. He could not perhaps quite realize how great an earthquake it had been, but regardless of its size it wasn't going to lick him or the United Press. He came up fighting, refusing to be put on the defensive.

Once when Karl Bickel sent around to his desk a letter from a Philadelphia publisher calling the armistice story a "fake" and saying that he desired to cancel his contract with the United Press, Howard charged into Bickel's office like a prize fighter coming out of his corner.

"No, he doesn't!" he shouted. "Don't you let him cancel. He's got two years to go on that contract and he's going to keep it for two years."

The tumult died down. The United Press rode out the storm. Amazingly, it lost only one client on the basis of the November 7 armistice story—the Burlington *News* in Vermont. In the next few years the organization was bigger and better and flourishing as it had never flourished before.

CHAPTER TEN

Roy Howard's farfetched dream of a world-wide news distributing agency began to be something more than a dream before the end of World War I. Until 1916 the only client the United Press had in the Far East was Nippon Dempo Tsushin Sha (Japanese telegraph news agency), which served some of the most influential Japanese newspapers. In Paris the United Press began serving Agence Radio as well as two newspapers—*Le Matin* and *Le Journal*—in 1916. The Exchange Telegraph news agency in London also was a client, and an arrangement was made in 1916 for an exchange of news with the Australian Press Association, which served newspapers in Australia, Tasmania, and New Zealand.

This meager foreign service—that is, the dispatches sent from this country to newspapers abroad—underwent a sudden change in 1916 because of the great interest of certain South American newspapers in coverage of the European war. Here again the United Press benefited by its struggle against the European news agency cartel, which had allotted South America exclusively to the Havas Agency of France. After the war started the Havas Agency, presumably for patriotic reasons, refused to carry the daily official German military communiqué. Since Havas alone supplied news reports to South America, newspapers there could not get satisfactory reports from Berlin unless they sent their own correspondents to Europe.

In Buenos Aires there were two influential and fiercely competitive newspapers, *La Prensa* and *La Nación,* whose readers included many German immigrants to Argentina. Don Jorge Mitre, the director of *La Nación,* vainly tried to get Havas to supply the German communiqué. Then in 1915 he sent a cable to the Associated Press in New York asking whether that agency would supply him with official statements from Berlin. The Associated Press never answered the inquiry because Melville Stone, under terms of his alliance with the European cartel, could not send news into the territory of any of the cartel agencies.

Mitre didn't get a reply but he didn't believe it was impossible to get the

German communiqués. He later sent a similar inquiry to the United Press. "Will you sell to *Nación* the product of the United Press war correspondents and the official communiqués?" Mitre asked. Howard didn't much like the idea of selling war coverage instead of the entire news report, but after talking it over with Hawkins he agreed to Mitre's request and completed the deal by cable. Howard transferred Charles P. Stewart to Buenos Aires to handle the service to *La Nación*.

In the summer of 1916, Howard went to Buenos Aires and worked out a ten-year deal with Mitre to pool the dispatches of United Press and *La Nación* correspondents and to sell this combined service to South American newspapers. Thus *La Nación* received a world-wide service from the United Press and its own foreign correspondents, and Howard, traveling along the west coast of South America, sold this service to what he regarded as the strongest newspaper in each large city. The profit from this arrangement later mounted to around $75,000 a year each to Mitre and to the United Press. Suddenly but impressively the United Press was a big news-distributing agency in foreign lands.

On his South American trip, Howard had been disturbed by the slanted dispatches that were being distributed there by Havas. When he returned to New York he saw Kent Cooper, now with the Associated Press, and suggested that the Associated Press also should go into the Latin American field so that the two American agencies might counteract the Havas influence. Cooper was interested, but Stone regarded the Associated Press's alliance with the European cartel—which was handicapped but not broken up by the war—as more important.

The United Press arrangement with *La Nación* was highly successful for more than two years. In fact, it was so successful that Mitre began to get restless. He was a slight, dark, and temperamental man, always full of ideas and fierce ambitions. By 1918 he had decided to spread out in an effort to establish his own South American news agency and to squeeze out the United Press.

In the winter of 1917–18, Howard became concerned that his arrangement with Mitre was falling apart despite his ten-year contract. He decided to return to Argentina, but the day before he left New York he received a surprise message from his manager, Stewart, in Buenos Aires.

Stewart had decided to quit and began looking around for someone to take over his job. The gathering place for newspapermen in Buenos Aires was the Helvetica Bar, a pleasant, unpretentious establishment with polished mahogany furnishings and sawdust on the floor. It was also handy to the newspaper offices and the cable company. One afternoon at the Helvetica, Stewart met a young man from Stanford University named James I. Miller.

"You a newspaperman?" Stewart asked hopefully.

"No," Miller replied.

Stewart kept the conversation going.

"Look," he finally said to Miller, "you're not busy at the moment. I want to quit my job and I'd like to have you take it over at least until the New York office can send a replacement."

Miller grinned. "I don't know much about newspapers."

"It's a cinch. You can learn to handle this job in a few days and I'll break you in. It pays seventy-five dollars a week."

Miller liked Buenos Aires, then a bustling, rapidly growing city with its harbor full of big ships from Europe. He decided to take the job. Stewart was delighted. He promptly wrote a cable to Howard:

AM RESIGNING IMMEDIATELY TO TAKE OVER POTATO FARM. SECURED RE-PLACEMENT OLD CALIFORNIA NEWSPAPERMAN JIMILLER

Howard worried all the way to Buenos Aires about operating in Argentina with an "old" Californian at the helm, but when he arrived he was greeted by a tall and handsome young man with a firm jaw and steely eyes. In no time at all he was satisfied with his new manager but not at all satisfied with the maneuvers of Mitre as his partner in a profitable South American service. He was convinced that Mitre was planning to squeeze the United Press out, and there wasn't much hope that the publisher could be legally held to the contract he and Howard had signed. But when they discussed the future, Mitre assured him that all was well and that their partnership would continue—assurances that did not ring true to Howard.

There were two newspaper prospects in Rio de Janeiro, and Howard went there late in the spring to try to sell them United Press service, which could be relayed from Buenos Aires. One was *O Imparcial*, which was run by Macedo Soares, and the other was *O País*, whose director was João Lage. The two newspapers were lively competitors and neither could afford to permit the other to provide readers with exclusive services. Howard signed them to three-year contracts, each at $1500 a week. This made it possible to establish a major United Press bureau in Rio de Janeiro, with Harry Robertson in charge. Mitre was just then starting a trip to New York, and he arrived in Rio de Janeiro at about the end of May. Mitre had been there only a few days when Robertson called Howard one afternoon and asked him to hurry to the bureau.

"I was just talking to Lage, of *O País*," Robertson reported. "He said Mitre had visited him and announced that he was breaking his contract with the United Press. He's going to try to take over all of our joint clients in South America, and he gave Lage until seven o'clock this evening to decide whether he will go along with Mitre or stay with the United Press. He's already persuaded Soares to leave the United Press and join his new service."

This was what Howard had feared. He hurried to confer with Lage, who had been friendly toward the United Press. The *O País* director said that he didn't want to take Mitre's offer and would stay with the United Press if he could be assured of good service. Howard returned to the United Press office to make sure that the day's cable report was furnished to *O País*.

Robertson met him at the door with horrifying news. "Mitre has seized our duplicate copies of all of the incoming cables!" he exclaimed. "He took everything. We haven't got a word of cable news for *O País!*"

Both Robertson, a slow-spoken but stubborn man, and Howard were fighting mad. They called the Western Cable Company office to demand another copy of the day's report from abroad. They had no luck. Mitre and Soares were ahead of them, had taken all copies of the cables, and had told the company manager not to turn anything over to the United Press. Mitre was an important client of the company as well as an influential man in South America, and Howard's angry demands on the manager were of no avail. He and Robertson then hurried to the cable office, where they saw Mitre and Soares.

"There they are!" Robertson exclaimed. "Look! Can you handle Mitre if necessary? He's got a reputation as a toughie and probably carries a gun. I'll take care of Soares."

Howard nodded. "Hell, we've got to do something."

They hurried across the room to intercept Mitre and Soares.

"I think you've pinched our copies of the cables," Howard said, planting himself in front of Mitre. "I want them."

Robertson edged himself in between Mitre and Soares, keeping one eye on Soares and looming up over the suave little publisher of *La Nación*.

"They belong to me," Mitre replied.

"No they don't," Howard said. "One copy belongs to us."

"Suppose I don't give it to you."

Robertson doubled up his fists and shoved himself a bit closer to Mitre. The latter turned to Soares, asking: "Should we?" Soares shrugged. "Oh, let's give them a copy." Mitre then made a quick motion toward his pocket and Robertson tensed, suspecting he was reaching for a gun. But Mitre tugged at his pocket and produced a thick, folded sheaf of carbon copies of the day's cable report. He handed the cables to Robertson and walked away with Soares.

The service to *O País* continued, but Mitre had dealt the United Press a body blow. Instead of going home, Howard returned to Buenos Aires. Everything seemed to be going wrong, even the weather. On the day that he arrived in Buenos Aires wearing a light summer suit the city experienced one of its rare snowstorms. Shivering and unhappy, Howard and Miller surveyed the situation. Newspapers in Chile, Peru, and other countries were dropping the United Press service to join Mitre's new agency. Miller had signed two or three small newspapers in Buenos Aires but not enough to keep a healthy news report going, and it wasn't difficult to see the end of the South American venture. He and Howard concluded that their only hope was to persuade Don Ezequiel Paz, the distinguished proprietor of *La Prensa* of Buenos Aires, to buy the United Press service.

La Prensa was one of the great newspapers of the world, not only as a journalistic enterprise but as a civic institution and as a money-maker. But Don Ezequiel Paz did not have a very high opinion of press associations in the United States. He took the Havas service but he depended primarily on his own correspondents abroad and regarded the United Press as too much inclined to "featurize" the news. *La Prensa* wanted all the news and it wanted it in the old-fashioned style. Howard and Miller sweated over the problem of getting Paz interested, but they made no progress as the weeks wore on.

Meantime, still another threat to Howard's hopes of world distribution of news developed. Mitre had gone to New York in an effort to secure membership for *La Nación* in the Associated Press. This posed a vital question for the Associated Press in regard to the European cartel and Havas' exclusive rights in South America, but after some weeks of negotiation an agreement was worked out. It provided that the Associated Press would go into South America but that it would reimburse Havas if the latter lost any income as a result of newspapers in Brazil, Uruguay, Paraguay, and Argentina being taken into the Associated Press. It also provided that Havas could continue to use Associated Press news from the United States for its own service in South America, thus using Associated Press dispatches to compete with the Associated Press itself in that field.

This may have been a strange arrangement, but the fact remained that the Associated Press decided to enter the South American field. Kent Cooper arrived in Buenos Aires in July of 1918 to see what could be done about establishing Associated Press service. As it turned out, a great deal could be done. He visited a number of countries and later—just as the European war was drawing to a close—he almost swept the board clean, signing up no less than twenty-five large and small papers in Argentina, Brazil, Peru, and elsewhere.

But the heaviest blow was struck at Buenos Aires. In that city, Cooper not only brought *La Nación* into the Associated Press fold but began negotiating with Don Ezequiel Paz of *La Prensa*. Throughout the last months of 1918, Miller also kept closely in touch with Don Ezequiel and attempted to impress him with the advantages of the United Press service. But when he picked up his newspapers on the morning of January 1, 1919, he got a shock. *La Prensa* had become a member of the Associated Press, and that agency's credit lines were scattered through the newspaper.

2.

When Howard left South America in 1918 the United Press was all but cleaned out on that continent. He told Miller that his salary would have to be cut to fifty dollars a week until something was done to revive the service. Miller not only saw a challenge in the situation, but he saw an opportunity for a man who could play his cards right. Don Ezequiel Paz was not likely to be content with having merely the same news service that his biggest competitor, Mitre, had in *La Nación*. It would not be long until he would be demanding something bigger and better, and when that happened Miller intended to be on hand. There was a certain amount of business that he could and did pick up among small newspapers in South America, but he had no intention of working his way up from the bottom. He intended to start at the top. Miller appeared often at Don Ezequiel's office, becoming well acquainted with the operations of *La Prensa* and taking frequent opportunities to point out to the publisher how his news service might be improved through the United Press. It was slow, discouraging work, but Miller had expected that. He kept at it. Finally, starting on June 1, 1919, *La Prensa* agreed to take a special service from the United Press.

Miller advised New York and London of the circumstances and warned them that the United Press, especially the European bureaus, would have to excel every other service if they expected to satisfy *La Prensa*. Miller himself stood by in the Buenos Aires office as the service opened. There was no wire into the offices of *La Prensa,* and dispatches received in English had to be translated into Spanish by the United Press and sent by messenger to the newspaper. The first cable that morning was a dispatch from Paris, sent at the urgent rate, announcing the signing of the Versailles treaty between the representatives of Germany and the representatives of the Allied Powers.

Miller grabbed it from the typewriter of the translator, thrust it in the hand of a messenger, and started him running up the Calle San Martín to the big *Prensa* building. The boy dashed inside and handed the flash to a receptionist, who trotted back to the desk of an editor. A little later Miller checked with the editor and was told that the United Press flash arrived twenty minutes before the news was received from any other agency. The service was off to a good start.

Foreign Editor Barney Furay in New York, with the assistance of Lawrence S. Haas in Buenos Aires and European Manager Keen in London watched over the report to *La Prensa* every hour of the day and most of the night. Anything that might be of even minor interest in Buenos Aires was tracked down with great care and covered in detail. It was an anxious, demanding period of intense labor. One day Furay was summoned to Bill Hawkins' office. Hawkins motioned him to sit down and then, mysteriously, poker-faced, locked the door.

"Barney," he said solemnly, "I've got a long message here from J. I. Miller." He paused and looked over his glasses at Furay. Then he beamed. "Miller says Paz is satisfied and has signed a contract for our full service!"

Hawkins tossed the cable into the air with a whoop. Furay fell back with a sigh of relief. They talked excitedly for a few minutes and then Hawkins looked at the foreign editor and said: "Well?" Furay was puzzled. "Well, what?" he asked.

"Well," Hawkins said, "why in hell don't you ask for a raise?"

Furay's face brightened.

"Mr. Hawkins, sir," he said, "I want a raise."

"Nothing doing," Hawkins replied abruptly.

For a moment Furay was stunned. Then for one of the few times in his life he became furiously angry, berated Hawkins, and shouted that he'd get a raise or the United Press could find a new foreign editor.

"Okay," Hawkins said. "If you've got the guts to speak up for yourself you get a raise. I just wanted to know how you really felt about it. Ten dollars more a week starting Monday."

3.

In later years it would be difficult to overestimate the importance of *La Prensa* on the growth and development of the United Press. Just to start with, Don Ezequiel Paz decided that as long as he was going to pay for the United Press report he might as well go all the way and have that news agency handle his entire foreign service. Miller had more or less promised him that anything he wanted to pay for would be provided, and gradually the United Press took on the job of covering in great detail areas of Europe that were of special interest in Argentina, where there were many immigrants newly arrived from such countries as Spain and Italy.

Don Ezequiel wanted as much news from large and small towns in Spain, for example, as normally would be printed in newspapers in Madrid. He published column after column of such items—fire in a country church, an autobus accident that injured six persons, the announcement of an appointment to fill a provincial office. And on important political or economic developments in Europe, where Argentina sold her meat and grain, he wanted complete and detailed coverage. To provide this news, the United Press expanded its staff of reporters and stringers throughout the continent and transmitted at least 5000 words—often far more—a day by cable. Whatever news *La Prensa* required outside of the normal field of a press association in the United States was provided as special service and charged to *La Prensa*. In time, *La Prensa's* payments mounted to as much as $10,000 or $14,000 a week—or $550,000 a year—probably the largest sum that any newspaper in the world paid to any news-gathering organization.

All of the news that was gathered for *La Prensa* was the property of the United Press and available for its general service elsewhere. This meant that the coverage in Europe soon became far more complete than any other news agency in America, that the United Press had scores of regular and stringer correspondents in provincial towns who could be called upon at a moment's notice, and that there was a huge volume—far more than the North American market could absorb—of European news flowing through the London and New York bureaus every day en route to Buenos Aires. This news coverage also was available for sale to other South American clients of the United Press. On this basis—plus the prestige gained by the decision of Don Ezequiel Paz to cast his lot with the United Press—Miller was soon able to start regaining the business that had been lost. Lawrence S. Haas had been sent to Buenos Aires as Miller's assistant, and in the next few years Joshua B. Powers, Miles W. Vaughn, A. L. Bradford, Ricardo Díaz Herrera, Grant Keener, Gesford Fine and Rafael Fusoni became bureau managers in Miller's expanding division. Never having been a reporter himself, Miller was the kind of newsman who frequently demanded that correspondents in Europe and the United States perform "impossible" journalistic feats for the benefit of his clients in South America. If a bureau replied that his request—say, for an interview with the Pope—could not be filled, Miller simply amplified his demands. More times than not he finally got what he wanted by refusing to accept the excuse that it could not be done. Over the years, this persistence was responsible for countless headaches among United Press correspondents around the world, but it also greatly improved the agency's news report. Within a comparatively short time, the United Press was serving more clients than ever in South America. The European cartel's news monopoly, which once was absolute on the continent, had been broken. Henceforth there would be robust competition, but on balance the United Press was the dominant agency.

Another benefit accrued to the United Press from its association with *La Prensa*. The Buenos Aires newspaper required a comprehensive type of news coverage which was not yet popular among United Press clients in the U.S.A. Thus *La Prensa* gave the service its first major outlet for dispatches treating vital international problems in a thorough and detailed manner, which had not always been typical of the United Press coverage. The acquisition of a large and important client always had an impact on the reporting and writing of the men who produced the United Press news report. Now the service had to adjust its approach by putting more emphasis on solid "think stuff" in order to hold its contract with Don Ezequiel Páz. *La Prensa* was a hard, if well-paying taskmaster. It never relaxed. The United Press had to earn its big fees from Buenos Aires, and in doing so it became a far more substantial and comprehensive press association in North America and, eventually, throughout the world.

4.

When the United Press first began serving *La Prensa,* there was very little interest in boxing in South America. Miller, however, was a good amateur boxer and worked out regularly at the Jockey Club with a former British professional fighter, Willie Farrell, to keep in physical trim. As a result of this interest in boxing, Miller may well have been responsible for building enthusiasm in South America for the sport.

One day in July of 1919, he was en route on a business trip to Chile and took the train to Puente del Inca, which is on the Argentine side of the 13,000-foot pass through the Andes Mountains. From Puente del Inca the traveler had to leave the train and go through the pass by muleback and then down to the Chilean railhead at Juncal. Unhappily, Miller mounted a mule and swayed up the mountainside past the Cristo de los Andes. There were other passengers making the trip on mules, but there was also one burly, black-haired giant of a man who disdained the saddle and, instead, trotted along the steep trail at a smooth, effortless pace.

"Why don't you ride?" Miller asked as the man loped along beside his mule.

"Doing my road work," the big fellow replied, smiling.

"You a fighter?"

The man nodded. "Got a match in Santiago."

Miller watched him with interest. He was big, strong, and apparently enthusiastic. "What's your name?" Miller called.

"Firpo," the fighter replied. "Luis Angel Firpo."

Miller talked to Firpo en route to Santiago and later kept a close watch on his boxing career. When Miller went to New York in 1921, he told his friend Tex Rickard, the boxing promoter, about the big Argentine fighter and said he believed Firpo could be shaped into a good drawing card in the United States. On the strength of Miller's recommendation, Rickard offered Firpo $10,000 to come to New York with the idea of building him up to fight Bill Brennan, and perhaps working his way up to become a challenger of heavyweight champion Jack Dempsey.

Firpo arrived in 1922, a great, awkward man who carried a terrific punch in his right hand but knew comparatively little about the business of professional fighting. New York sports writers took one look at him in training and wrote him off as a third-rater to be ignored. In Buenos Aires, however, the afternoon newspaper *Crítica* had taken a great fancy to Firpo and made a considerable fuss about his journey to the United States. *Crítica* was served by the Associated Press. The other big afternoon newspaper was *La Razón,* which subscribed to the United Press. As soon as Firpo became a newsworthy subject in the columns of *Crítica,* the United Press began receiving requests from *La Razón* for coverage of the fighter's activities, and it was typical of Miller that he demanded daily, detailed stories.

By the time Firpo was matched against his first opponent, a strictly third-rate fighter, he had become a kind of national hero in Buenos Aires in the eyes of almost everyone except the editors of *La Prensa.* They virtually ignored him, regarding prize fighting as a ridiculous and rather barbaric North American sport. In Buenos Aires, all newspapers had huge bulletin boards in front of their offices and posted the day's news dispatches on them at regular intervals. For the first Firpo fight, *La Razón* posted bulletins after each round, and in a short time there were 50,000 shrieking fans in the street in front of the newspaper office. Attracted by the noise, Alberto Gainza Paz, nephew of the director of *La Prensa,* observed that there were only a few persons in front of the bulletin board at his own office, where a French cabinet crisis was the big news of the hour. He went back to his desk and, after due deliberation, decided that it was time for *La Prensa* to pay attention to prize fighting, which it did thereafter with great enthusiasm.

In 1923 Firpo defeated a fading Jess Willard and was pitted against Jack Dempsey the following year with the world title at stake. As the date for the match approached, Argentina was ablaze with excitement and Firpo's countrymen bet huge sums that he would be the next champion. Both *La Prensa* and *La Nación* arranged to announce the fight blow by blow over loud-speakers in front of their offices, with the former using the United Press report and the latter using the Associated Press. Huge crowds gathered to listen to progress of the fight, which was a slam-bang affair from the opening gong. In an early round, Firpo reached the zenith of his career with a mighty swing that knocked Dempsey through the ropes and into the laps of sports writers at ringside. Both the United Press and Associated Press flashed: "FIRPO KNOCKED DEMPSEY OUT OF RING." But by a strange twist of fate, an excited cable operator someway managed to drop the last two words of the Associated Press flash.

Moments later *La Nación's* loud-speakers announced that Firpo had knocked out Dempsey and was champion of the world. The crowds went wild. So did Miller, but for different reasons. Then it gradually became apparent that the fight was still going on. Dempsey climbed back into the ring and soon had the Argentine fighter on the floor for a count of ten, saving Miller's sanity and permitting Firpo to return to the Pampas—beaten but happy—with a considerable fortune in North American box-office receipts.

CHAPTER ELEVEN

The war and the immediate postwar years brought many new faces into the United Press, some of them for brief appearances. War Correspondent Frank J. Taylor, who was at the Swiss border when the war ended, made his way to Berlin. Taylor was lucky. Shortly after he got across the frontier the Germans closed the border and, except for two British correspondents who also beat the deadline, Taylor was the only foreign reporter in Berlin during a period of turmoil, revolution, and counterrevolution that made news for the next two weeks. A small group of American and Allied army officers had arrived in Berlin, and the Americans managed to send a courier to Paris with their diplomatic pouch at regular intervals. It always contained at least one story by Taylor which was turned over to the United Press bureau in Paris.

Early in 1919 New York told Taylor that the United Press had to get a correspondent into Russia. At that time German forces were still occupying a large area in Russia, American troops were fighting the Communists in the Archangel area, and other Allied soldiers were harassing the Red Army on several fronts. Nobody had any very good idea of what was going on in Moscow. Taylor agreed to try to get to Moscow through the German lines in Lithuania, where both sides were observing a kind of undeclared armistice.

When he reached Lithuania, however, he was stalemated. There seemed to be no way to get to Moscow unless he walked through the lines, and that appeared to be highly dangerous. Finally, near Kovno, Taylor explained his problem to a German general who immediately picked up a telephone and asked to be connected with the Russian general at his headquarters on the other side of the "front." The call went through immediately and there was a long conversation in Russian, which Taylor could not understand. Shortly afterward, however, he was directed to a droshky in which two German officers drove him across the snow to the front lines. Just as they arrived another droshky came out of a thick forest, carrying two Russian officers. They met and exchanged greetings, and Taylor was directed to get into the Russian droshky, which carried him behind the Russian lines. Nobody there seemed to know just what to do with him, but after a few days he was put into a box-car load of Russian prisoners returning from Germany and sent to Moscow.

In the Soviet capital, Taylor was informed that he was under "house arrest" at the old Metropole Hotel. This, he soon discovered, meant that he could go almost anywhere he pleased during daylight hours but in the company of an armed soldier—who turned out to be a woman. Taylor took advantage of this to call at the offices of the top Communist officials and demand interviews with them for distribution by the United Press. His approach seemed to please the Russian bureaucrats, who couldn't quite decide whether the Americans were enemies or potential friends at that time. Maxim Litvinov, who later became Foreign Minister, took an interest in Taylor, partly because he wanted to brush up on his English, and occasionally took the correspondent to a performance of the ballet. Taylor also visited the editors of the official news service, Rosta, and persuaded them that they should buy the United Press report.

After a couple of weeks, a surge of anti-American feeling swept Moscow because United States troops were fighting the Red Army in Archangel and a dozen or so American soldiers captured there had been brought to the Russian capital. One morning about 3 A.M. there was a heavy knock on Taylor's door and a Red Army soldier motioned him to get dressed. The soldier then led him away so solemnly that Taylor was pretty sure they had decided to solve his problems by shooting him without further ceremony. They went down an underground stairway, and Taylor was unceremoniously propelled into a dimly lighted room. Inside there was an old man with a shawl around his shoulders. He had a feather duster and was busy dusting off a large, cluttered desk. He greeted Taylor in English and went on dusting so industriously that the reporter hesitated to ask him if he expected to be shot, too. At last, however, he worked the conversation around to the subject of the underground office and asked why his companion was there.

"Why, I'm the Foreign Minister," replied Grigori Chicherin, "and this is my office. I understood you wanted to interview me."

Taylor gulped and got down to the business of an interview. A week later the Russians decided to get rid of the captured American soldiers and Taylor as well. They were deported into Finland but only after the border guards had "confiscated" all of Taylor's equipment, including his camera. The Finnish border guards promptly demanded Taylor's credentials and, when he could not produce any, tossed him into an internment camp. That night the reporter climbed over a fence, went into the nearest town, and telephoned the American consul at Helsingfors.

"Where are you now?" the consul asked after hearing his story.

"In the middle of town."

"Well, get the hell back in that internment camp in a hurry so I can get you out tomorrow," the consul commanded.

Taylor "broke into" the camp later that night and the next morning was summoned by a delegation of Finnish officials. They greeted him as "a representative of the Hoover relief commission," apologized profusely for the regrettable error that had been made in sending him to the camp, and put him into a first class railroad carriage for Helsingfors.

Among the men Taylor had hired to act as string correspondents for the United Press in Central European cities was Edward J. Bing, an athletic former army officer and a scholar, who was editing a small journal in Budapest. Bing displayed a remarkable ability to adapt himself to American methods of covering the news. In the early postwar period, the Communist government at Moscow was almost entirely isolated. There was, however, a small wireless station on the Danube island of Csepel, at Budapest, which was in regular communication with the Moscow wireless station.

Bing composed a long radiogram in German to Soviet Foreign Minister Grigori Chicherin and dispatched it over the Csepel station, asking whether Leon Trotsky, head of the Red Army, would reply to a series of questions by wireless. This was a novel idea in journalism—interviewing by radio—and it struck a responsive note in the Moscow foreign office. After several days Bing received a message of approval. He then filed a series of questions by the same route and said he would be in the Csepel station at three o'clock the next afternoon to receive the answers. They came through at exactly three o'clock, and Bing's radio interview—perhaps the first of its kind—was prominently displayed two days later by United Press newspapers in England, the United States, and elsewhere. The kernel of Trotsky's remarks was: "We shall fight on until we are left alone."

This interview proved so successful that, shortly thereafter, Bing got a similar series of answers from Lenin himself, who outlined his general policies and warned the Western world that "capitalism . . . has outlived itself . . . and the victory of the International Soviet Republic is sure." It was the first direct word from Lenin in months.

Ralph Couch, who had been sent to London late in the war, started back for New York via Plymouth, but decided to spend a weekend in Dublin before sailing. He had a contact with the Sinn Feiners, who were then in rebellion in Ireland, and while talking to them about the uprising against British rule suggested that it would be a good thing for him to take back to New York a newsworthy statement from Eamon DeValera, the rebel leader who was in hiding with a price on his head.

"I can carry the message personally," he said, "and there won't be any problem of British censorship. They won't know about it. And a message from DeValera at this time could do a lot for your cause among the Irish in America."

The next day Couch's Sinn Feiner friend appeared with a horse and buggy and a blindfold. "If you still want a statement," he said, "you can have it if you follow instructions exactly."

Couch agreed. The blindfold was placed over his eyes and he was led to the closed carriage. They drove for what seemed like several hours over what appeared to be bumpy country roads but actually may have been a deceptive circuitous route in or near the city. Still blindfolded, he was helped out of the carriage and led into a building. When the blindfold was removed, he was in a room with blinds drawn, but DeValera was there too. They talked for an hour about the rebellion, its aims, and its progress. Then Couch was blindfolded again and taken back to the carriage, which jolted him around for a couple of hours before depositing him back in the city.

Couch's story was widely displayed by American newspapers and bitterly denounced by the British censor in Ireland. In London the United Press bureau was threatened with all kinds of reprisals by minor officials of the government, but they were restrained by Lloyd George, who treated the episode with good humor.

2.

In Washington, Bob Bender fully appreciated the service's basic theory of providing fast, concise coverage for afternoon newspapers, which were often close to a deadline when important news was breaking. After he was made manager of the Washington bureau in 1917 he continued to cover a great deal of White House and other news and, as the war drew to a close, personally handled such important stories as President Wilson's famous fourteen-point statement of conditions on which a peace settlement would be acceptable and, later, the terms of the armistice agreement.

On both of these stories the text of official statements was made available to reporters an hour or so in advance, but with firm instructions that nothing could be carried on the wires until the official release hour. On each occasion Bender swiftly studied the documents and then sent out a note to editors that a series of flashes containing the highlights of the statements would be carried on the wire at the hour of release—noon. This gave editors an opportunity to prepare the front page for a big story. Then, on the stroke of noon, Bender dictated:

FLASH WASHINGTON WILSON'S TERMS FOR PEACE SETTLEMENT FOLLOW:

This was followed by fourteen flash sentences setting forth the highlights of the statement. Some newspapers that were close to a deadline merely cleaned out a two- or three-column space on the front page, set up the Fourteen Points in large type, wrote a headline, and went to press. Bender's system gave them perhaps fifteen or twenty minutes' advantage over any story that could be written to cover the same information.

When President Wilson decided to make his historic journey to Paris for the Versailles peace conference, Bender was assigned to accompany him, and Fred Ferguson was directed to delay his return to New York long enough to help cover the conference. The Big Four leaders—Wilson, Lloyd George, Georges Clemenceau of France, and Vittorio Orlando of Italy—had agreed that all provisions of the peace treaty would be kept secret until the entire text could be made public. This led to many rumors as to what the treaty contained, but the greatest excitement, particularly in the United States, revolved around Article Ten, which attempted to guarantee the territorial status quo against aggression and, in the minds of some experts, raised questions as to the national sovereignty of the nations which were to become members of the League of Nations.

Some members of the United States Senate feared that Article Ten infringed on the sovereign rights of this country. But, since there were only rumors as to its contents, the political foes of President Wilson—particularly Senator Borah of Idaho and Senator Lodge of Massachusetts—were continually demanding: "What is Article Ten? Will it destroy the sovereignty of the United States?"

Ferguson moved in on Colonel House, who was President Wilson's confidant, in an effort to find out about Article Ten, but he got nowhere. He then switched his efforts to a friend who was a minor official of the delegation. This friend would say nothing for some days, but finally he loosened up.

"Look, I'm not going to tell you a thing about it," he said, "but you know where the little workroom is on the sixth floor of the Crillon Hotel. [The Crillon was the meeting place of the delegates.] Why don't you drop around there about two o'clock tomorrow morning when the regular guard has gone? You might even have to walk up to the sixth floor instead of taking the elevator. There's a guard who remains at the elevator. If you get to the workroom I doubt that the door will be locked."

A little before two o'clock the next morning, Ferguson wandered into the Crillon, stalled around briefly in the lobby, and then started up the stairs. He puffed his way up to the sixth floor, which appeared to be deserted, and went to the workroom. The doorknob turned easily under his hand. Inside there was a single small light bulb burning over a table. And on the table was a thick volume entitled *The Covenant of the League of Nations*.

Ferguson had assured his friend that he was interested only in Article Ten. He leafed quickly through the book to that section, which he copied swiftly, and departed. He didn't even write a story about it but scribbled a sentence to the effect that "here is the text of Article Ten" and turned it over to the cable office. The story that went out on the United Press wires the same day created a sensation in America and consternation in Paris. Members of the United States delegation stormed at the United Press for days, but nobody ever found out how the text of Article Ten had been revealed.

3.

The course of the United Press seldom ran smoothly. One day an opposition news agency carried a story, originating in London, that Field Marshal Paul von Hindenburg, the famous German war leader, had died in Berlin. Many newspapers in America published the dispatch under banner headlines, and some issued extra editions. The United Press newspapers sent frantic queries to New York, and New York sent them on at urgent rate to London and Berlin. A few hours later the United Press correspondent in Berlin, Carl Groat, had established that the report was false and that Hindenburg was in good health. Just to make sure, he got in touch with the marshal's doctor and got a statement from him that included a reading of Hindenburg's temperature that morning (it was normal) and what he had for breakfast. This information he forwarded to New York.

The next day the editor of a Pennsylvania newspaper came into the New York office demanding to see Bill Hawkins. Since he had already received several indignant messages from the editor, Hawkins guessed what had prompted the visit and was properly prepared.

"I pay the United Press a good price for service," the editor began, "and I expect to get something for it! Why were you scooped on the death of Hindenburg?"

Hawkins didn't say anything. He just laid out on his desk the United Press reports from Berlin showing that Hindenburg was doing fine and had had two eggs for breakfast. The editor looked them over carefully, but his indignation did not lose its keen edge. He stood up and pointed an accusing finger at Hawkins.

"I don't give a damn about this stuff you've got here," he cried. "What I know is that my opposition newspaper sold 50,000 extras yesterday with a headline saying that Hindenburg was dead. I'm going to buy the service that provided them with that headline!" And he did.

CHAPTER TWELVE

In 1919 the United Press was a highly profitable news service for 745 clients
—mostly afternoon and Sunday-morning newspapers in the United States,
Canada, and Latin America. But that was not enough.

The company had started in 1907 as a spot news service trying to compete
with the far more comprehensive Associated Press report, trying to cover
up its shortcomings with a liberal dash of verve and enthusiasm. There were
limits, however, to what could be done with such methods, and an interesting change soon occurred. In order to expand and to secure additional
clients, Howard exploited the feature story, the exclusive interview, sparkling
sports coverage, and the Red Letter mail service as a means of attracting
editors who wanted something different. This approach did prove attractive,
and many large newspapers purchased the United Press as a supplementary
service.

The war period opened up the South American field and showed what
might be done in other foreign countries. But this also created some grave
new problems. The largest United Press clients in South America were morning newspapers. In Europe or elsewhere that the agency might sell its service
there would be not only morning newspapers but a great difference in dead-
lines in various time zones around the world. If the United Press was going
to be a world-wide news distributor it had to be a twenty-four-hour service.

By 1918 the idea of starting a service for morning newspapers in the
United States began to emerge as the next logical step in the company's
growth. The best approach would be to reverse the process by which the
afternoon service was built up. Instead of starting a straight news report for
morning editions, the morning papers would be offered a leased wire service
that would specialize in well-written features, exclusive interviews, and lively
sports stories. On this basis it could hardly be called United Press. Something like United News would be better.

The plan for a night wire service had been kicked around so much it was
almost in tatters on January 1, 1919, when Karl Bickel wandered into his

office in the *World* building in midafternoon with the idea of getting a jump on the New Year. Bickel had been enthusiastic about the proposed night service, but nothing had happened to bring it to a head. In a quiet, gloomy office he sat down and pulled out his portable typewriter and began pecking out a letter to the editor of the Atlanta *Constitution.*

The United Press, he wrote, was considering the inauguration of a night wire service. He described the kind of service he had in mind and he asked a question: Are you interested? Then he typed out the names of editors of about a score of other morning newspapers, including the Chicago *Tribune,* and left a note for his secretary to send the letter to all of them the next day. Ten days later he went around to General Manager Hawkins with half a dozen letters.

"Look, Bill," he exclaimed, "here are some newspapers that want to buy a night wire service from us."

Hawkins wasn't much impressed. "You can't run a night wire for six papers," he rumbled.

Then one afternoon a visitor whose name seemed familiar to Bickel came to his office and was ushered inside. Bickel did not recognize him.

"I got your letter," the visitor said, "and thought I'd come by to talk to you."

"Who are you?" Bickel finally exclaimed in perplexity.

"I'm William Field, business manager of the Chicago *Tribune.*"

Bickel, a tall, impressive man with sharp blue eyes and a high Bavarian forehead, blushed to the roots of the fuzzy hair on his balding dome.

"We would be glad to serve the *Tribune,*" he said, "if we start a night service."

"Well, we are interested, but not entirely for the benefit of the *Tribune.* I would like to ask you to come to Holland House at seven forty-five this evening."

By this time a cloak-and-dagger air of mystery had swirled around the whole business and Bickel was becoming curious. He appeared at Holland House and gave the desk clerk his name. The clerk motioned to a man standing nearby, a man with a dead-pan face and the air of an undertaker. This solemn character led Bickel to a private elevator, they soared up to the top floor and went through several unoccupied rooms. The guide tapped on the door of a fourth room and they entered. There was a smell of fragrant cigar smoke in the handsomely furnished room. There was a bottle of champagne in a bucket of ice, and there were two men—Colonel Robert McCormick, editor of the Chicago *Tribune,* and his cousin and partner, Captain Joseph Medill Patterson. Patterson told Bickel that they had been talking about the progress of tabloid newspapers that had recently proved so successful in England.

"I'm preparing to start one in New York and want to know what the United Press can do for us," he added.

This was the kind of break Bickel had been praying for in connection with starting a morning service, but he couldn't have imagined that it would be so favorable. McCormick and Patterson were among the most successful publishers in the country. If they started a newspaper in New York it would have almost unlimited resources and it would have maximum skill and talent to make a success of the venture. About the only thing it wouldn't have would be an Associated Press franchise. Once again the Associated Press co-operative system, which limited the number of franchises available in any area by agreement of member newspapers, had played into the hands of the United Press at an important turning point. Patterson, who was the spark plug of the new tabloid, had no immediate hope of securing membership in the Associated Press, but he could afford to make a heavy contribution to inauguration of a new night wire service by the United Press.

Bickel was eloquent on the subject of what the United Press could do for Patterson's proposed New York *Daily News.* Soon thereafter he took off at high speed on a swing across the United States and made deals for delivering a night report to the Atlanta *Constitution,* the New Orleans *Item,* the Dallas *News,* the Portland *Oregon Journal* (which started a morning edition), the Montreal *Star,* and a few other newspapers. The Chicago *Tribune,* which had previously received the Saturday-night report, came on the new wire setup in combination with the *Daily News.*

In June of 1919 the United News started operations with less than a dozen clients and with Robert J. Bender in charge in New York. Later, Fred Ferguson returned from Europe and became general manager of the new service with Bender as United News manager in Washington. The service was staffed then and later by some of the United Press's best writers—Westbrook Pegler and Sidney B. Whipple in New York; Ralph H. Turner in London; Raymond Clapper and John M. Gleissner in Washington; Alexander F. Jones and Earl J. Johnson in Chicago; Rodney F. Dutcher in Boston; and William Slavens McNutt, who had made a reputation as a brilliant writer in France, on general assignment. But in addition the United News carried articles on politics, world affairs, sports, and other subjects by a stable of famous names that included William Allen White, J. M. Keynes, Robert T. Jones, Major General Leonard Wood, Edna Ferber, Sir Arthur Conan Doyle, and Nina Wilcox Putnam. The new service struggled along, gaining a few clients, losing others, and gaining still others for eight years. By that time its staff had grown, too, and the news report was improved sufficiently to drop the name United News and become the night service of the United Press Associations, which thus became an around-the-clock news agency.

2.

The United News was not the only new baby brought into the organization in 1919. That year witnessed the beginning of the United Feature Syndicate, although it started out as a very limited service briefly known as Union

Syndicate. And it started casually, almost without advance planning, with the assistance of Frank Vanderlip.

Vanderlip was president of the National City Bank in New York and one of the best-known figures in the financial district, but he had once dabbled in journalism and still had a yen for writing. As the war drew to an end, he made a tour of Europe and wrote a short book on the financial outlook abroad. The theme of his story was that syndicalism—basically trade-union direct action by general strikes and organization of workers to control production—was growing rapidly in European countries and that the value of American loans there might be damaged or destroyed as a result. The board of directors of the National City Bank held an emergency meeting, took issue with the conclusions that Vanderlip had reached in his book, and fired him as president of the institution.

All of this led Bickel to furious thought and he sought out Vanderlip, whom he knew slightly, and asked him if he had a few minutes to talk. The banker was in a great rush and explained that he had to catch a train that afternoon for Washington. Bickel arranged to see him at Pennsylvania Station for a few minutes at train time. They met on the platform and went into Vanderlip's compartment.

"I've read your book," Bickel said, "and I think you've written a warning that should be read by everybody in the country. My idea is that you should syndicate the book so that it could be published in installments by newspapers everywhere."

The ousted banker seemed to be interested in the idea, and Bickel stayed aboard as the train pulled out for Washington. They talked about what kind of arrangements could be made for sale of the articles. Finally Bickel said, "Well, do you want dough or do you want to get your message to as many people as possible?"

Vanderlip smiled. "I don't really need dough," he said.

Bickel then explained in detail what he could do about distribution of the articles and Vanderlip agreed. The train was just pulling into the Trenton, New Jersey, station. Bickel got off and took the next train back to New York, where he began writing telegrams to editors who might be interested in the Vanderlip series. Many of them were, and the book was quickly edited into 1500-word installments and distributed for publication. It was highly successful. Vanderlip got nothing at all from the syndicate, but the United Press made a net profit of $7000, which became the foundation stone of United Features.

Many world-famous figures wrote for United Features over the years, but the syndicate's rapid early growth was largely due to the attention attracted by a series of articles under the signature of the former Crown Prince of Germany. The Prince was living in exile on an island off the Dutch coast in the winter of 1921–22 when Bickel cabled a suggestion to Ed Keen that he try to purchase the memoirs of the Kaiser's son for syndication. Keen went from London to Holland to see what could be done, but his luck was poor. The coast was cluttered with ice, and boats could not get out to the island on which the Prince was living. He cabled Bickel:

PRESS BICKEL UNIPRESS NEWYORK
    CAN SEE ISLAND EXCOAST BUT IMPASSABLE FOR BOATS DUE THICK ICE STOP WHAT SHOULD EYE DO

KEEN

Bickel was not a man to be intimidated by the weather. He cabled right back:

PRESS   KEEN   UNIPRESS   AMSTERDAM
WALK

BICKEL

Keen again tried to hire a boat but without success. Then he buttoned up his new overcoat, tightened his muffler around his neck, and started walking across the ice. It was difficult going, but an hour later he was knocking at the door of the modest cottage in which the Crown Prince lived. Keen wasn't his usual impressive self when the door opened. His new overcoat was covered with muddy slush from a couple of falls and he was red-faced from the cold, but he introduced himself formally and was soon seated close to the stove in the company of His Royal Highness. They had little trouble reaching a decision to syndicate the Prince's memoirs in a series of twelve articles of about 1000 words each.

"Now as to payment?" the Crown Prince inquired.

"We thought we could pay you about $5000," Keen replied.

"I had a larger figure in mind," His Royal Highness remarked.

They spent another hour over figures, but Keen could not get a price of less than $12,000 for the series. Finally, he paid $1000 for an option to buy at $12,000 and returned to Amsterdam. He then cabled the details to Bickel and added that he believed $12,000 was highway robbery because, at the current rate of exchange for German marks, the Crown Prince could live in luxury for the rest of his life on that many dollars.

Bickel received the message about ten o'clock in the morning. He picked up his telephone and put in calls for editors in Boston, Detroit, Washington, and other cities. A few hours later he had sold the Crown Prince's memoirs to enough newspapers at around $750 each to be assured of getting $25,000, and the field had been hardly touched. He cabled Keen to buy.

The Crown Prince's memoirs represented the first big profits for United Features, and made it clear that there was gold in the words of a number of world-famous figures who might want to turn author. Quite a number did, with the encouragement of United Features and with large profits to both. In the later years United Features not only offered for sale the flapper-girl drawings of John Held, Jr., and the "how to play tennis" advice of Helen Wills, but the opinions on world affairs of Premier Benito Mussolini of Italy, former Premier Raymond Poincaré of France, and others. Poincaré was a brilliant scholar and mathematician, who was extremely methodical in everything he did. When he signed his contract in Paris after a talk with Bill Hawkins, he assured Hawkins that he would get his copy in on schedule each fortnight because he had a pencil and a pad of paper hanging on a string in his bathroom and would write a few hundred words regularly each morning.

3.

After David Lloyd George was ousted as Prime Minister of Great Britain in 1922, Bickel arrived in London with a proposal that the statesman write regular articles for United Features on world political questions. Keen was doubtful that such a deal could be arranged.

"You don't know these Britishers," he told Bickel. "No member of Parliament [Lloyd George was still leader of the Liberal Party] has ever written articles on current affairs. It just isn't done."

Keen arranged for a mutual friend to introduce Bickel to the former Prime Minister, but the friend insisted that it would be impossible for Lloyd George to write such articles. "In fact," he added, "I don't want you to even bring up the subject. This will have to be just a brief social call."

He took Bickel around to a small, middle-class house in London. It was a surprisingly modest establishment for a man who had just stepped out of one of the world's most powerful political offices. Bickel waited until several political callers had finished a conference with the Liberal leader and then was ushered into a rather shabby office. He made no effort to talk business and, after a few minutes, shook hands and departed. But as he was walking down the narrow hall a hand reached out from behind some glass bead portieres over a coat closet and plucked at his sleeve. He stopped and saw a small, blondish woman in a tweed suit.

"Are you the man who wants Mr. Lloyd George to do some writing for the American press?" she asked.

When Bickel replied in the affirmative, she continued. "I'm Florence Stevenson. What did Mr. Lloyd George say?"

"He didn't say anything because I was told not to ask him."

"I keep the books here," Miss Stevenson said. "Mr. Bickel, I don't know how much you know about such things, but I can tell you that this family needs money. He's been in government service since 1911 and has never had a bank account in his life. If he is going to make that trip he's planning to France, he'll need to buy a new suit. All he has to live on now is his $2000 salary as a member of the House of Commons and about the same amount from other sources. What were you going to offer him?"

"About $800 for a weekly article of 1200 words."

She shook her head. "That's not enough. We can't go on living here like this."

Bickel said that he was leaving London for the continent but would return in mid-November. As he went out Miss Stevenson said: "I'll do what I can."

Upon his return to London there was a message waiting for Bickel to telephone her. She asked him to come at five o'clock to the Liberal Party headquarters.

"But don't come with any $800 ideas," she warned him.

Keen and Bickel went to the headquarters at dusk, but Keen said he would wait in the reception room. "If you've got any fantastic idea that you can get him to write on current subjects, I don't want to be in on it," he said.

Lloyd George was waiting in a large room with a blood-red carpet on the floor. He stood behind a heavy, black walnut desk, wearing a Prince Albert coat, a stiff collar, and flowing tie. His hair was a white halo and his eyes two gleaming blue marbles.

"I understand you think I might write for the press," he began abruptly. "Think anyone would be interested?"

"Everyone," Bickel said promptly.

Lloyd George seemed immediately to forget the whole subject and launched into a ten-minute discussion of the English climate and the benefits of Scotch whisky. "I never drink, myself," he ended up, "but I'm told it's beneficial drink in England. It's hard to prove it is harmful here, but it has killed some of my best friends in the United States. I tell them it's not the drink, it's the climate over there. . . . Now about this article writing. Let me think it over for twenty-four hours."

As Bickel was leaving Miss Stevenson intercepted him again. "What did he say about money?" she asked.

"Not a thing."

"Well," she said severely, "it will be $1200 for each article."

"Are you speaking for him?"

"I will be in a few minutes."

"All right. We'll pay $1200."

"Also," she added quickly, "a pound each time for a messenger."

Bickel nodded and left. The next day she telephoned to tell him that everything was fixed except that the price would be $1200 per article or 50 per cent of the net profits, whichever was greater.

Bickel went back to New York with a two-year contract for world rights to the Lloyd George articles. They were a major success in many countries, and the former Prime Minister collected many thousands of dollars as his share of the profits over a period of seven years in which he wrote for United Features.

4.

Signed articles by famous personages were part of the selling talk for United News as well as United Features in the 1920s, but the night wire "special signers" were usually short pieces on subjects that were in the day's news. Sports were very prominent in the news in the Golden Twenties, and George Herman Ruth was the greatest figure in baseball. Fred Ferguson decided that it would be a good idea for the United News to carry a story of about 200 words signed by Babe Ruth every time he hit a home run. The story would tell what kind of a ball—a curve or spitter or fast ball—the pitcher threw to Ruth, how it came over the plate, and where the Babe knocked it. With Ruth then holding the record of twenty-nine home runs in a season this seemed likely to be a sure-fire feature.

Ferguson went over to Philadelphia, where the Yankees were playing, to talk to Ruth about the idea. He called at Ruth's hotel but was told that the player was in conference. He tried all morning to get through on the telephone but repeatedly was informed that Ruth was busy. At last he went up to the room and knocked. Somebody yelled, "Come in," and Ferguson opened the door. There were a half dozen men inside and the Babe was rolling the dice in a crap game. When he lost the dice Ferguson approached him, but Ruth growled: "If you want to talk business with me you got to wait till I'm not so busy."

The game finally broke up and Ferguson presented his idea, telling Ruth he would pay him ten dollars for every home run he hit. "All you have to do," he added, "is to give us a telephone call or send us a telegram after the game describing the kind of pitch and where you hit the ball and how you felt about it."

"Ten dollars?" Ruth said. "Okay, it's a deal."

For a week or two, Ruth telephoned faithfully after each home run and described it to the United News sports editor who then wrote a story under the Babe's signature for the wires. But when the team went on the road the Babe was erratic in reporting by telegram, and the sports editor sometimes had to call him. Even when Ruth remembered to send a telegram it was usually short on information. His complete story from St. Louis on one occasion read:

> FERGUSON   UNITEDPRESS   NEWYORK
> LOW OUTSIDE
>
> BABE

On another occasion the telephone rang on Ferguson's desk and it was the Babe calling from Chicago.

"This is Babe. You owe me twenty dollars."

"What are you talking about?" Ferguson protested. "We've paid you every time and you know it."

"Yeah—but today I hit *two!*"

5.

One of the men who moved rapidly toward the top of the United Press hierarchy in the decade after World War I was an energetic, competitive fellow from the Pacific coast. Hugh Baillie had been a pistol-packing police reporter—he sometimes wrote underworld exposé stories under the name of John Danger—in Los Angeles before joining the United Press. After working in various Western bureaus, he was shifted to New York as manager and, in 1919, took over as manager of the Washington bureau. Baillie was the kind of newsman who liked to be on the firing line instead of at a desk. He had a highly aggressive attitude toward covering the news and did not intend to be hampered by long-established and sometimes outdated traditions of correspondents in the nation's capital. When the press corps moved to Chicago to cover the 1920 Republican national convention, Baillie created consternation by appearing in the press box with a typewriter. Nobody had ever used a typewriter adjacent to the speakers' platform, and there were loud cries of protest from other reporters. But Baillie demonstrated that his machine was one of the new, noiseless typewriters and would not disturb the speakers. He kept it, too—the first typewriter to be used in the press section at a political convention.

A little later in the convention Baillie attracted still greater attention. One sweltering morning several Republican leaders were called to the center of the platform for a conference on procedure with the presiding officer, Senator Henry Cabot Lodge of Massachusetts. Some important decision obviously was being made, and Baillie climbed up from the press section and joined the huddle on the platform. Seeing him there, a correspondent of the International News Service and one from the Associated Press also climbed up to the platform. One of them made so much noise, however, that the austere, gray-bearded Lodge looked up and spotted Baillie, who was wearing a brightly striped shirt. He correctly ordered Baillie to leave. The reporter started back to his seat but stopped when he saw the other two reporters were remaining. Lodge pursued him.

"I said get off the platform, sir!" the slight, graying senator cried, his whiskers trembling as he shook his gavel in Baillie's face. "Sergeant at arms! Put this man off the platform!"

Baillie was seized from behind. He twisted his broad shoulders and broke free, instinctively doubling up his fists. When he looked around, however, he discovered that the man who had tried to seize him was almost as small as Lodge. By that time the two other reporters were leaving the platform and Baillie, too, climbed down through a rope railing that had been broken in the scuffle. The Connecticut delegation seated adjacent to the press box stood up to give him a jovial cheer. Arthur Brisbane, noted columnist for the Hearst newspapers, dashed over to interview him and next day wrote a column in praise of aggressive reporting. Senator Lodge pounded with his gavel and announced that the convention stood in recess.

The United News crack political reporter at the convention was Raymond Clapper, a persistent, hurrying young man from Kansas. Clapper was quickly convinced that neither of the two leading candidates for the Republican presidential nomination—Governor Frank Lowden of Illinois and General Leonard Wood—could rally enough votes to win. Harry M. Daugherty of Ohio had previously toured the country trying to line up delegates for Senator Warren G. Harding and, when the convention became deadlocked, he remarked to reporters that the nominee was less likely to be selected on the floor of the convention than in a hotel room where the party leaders could get together privately and agree on a compromise candidate.

Clapper took this suggestion to heart. When it became evident that neither Lowden nor Wood could muster enough support, he began prowling the hotel corridors late in the evening. One midnight he found what he had been seeking, a hotel suite in which a group of political leaders was gathered, furiously smoking cigars and furiously debating what could be done to break the deadlock. Clapper took up a strategic position outside the door.

Some time later Daugherty emerged smiling but would make no comment. A little later a plump, round-faced man came out, the cigar smoke swirling around his bald head. He was Senator Charles Curtis of Kansas, with whom Clapper was well acquainted.

"Senator," Clapper asked, "what's the verdict?"

"Well, they are going to go for Senator Harding," Curtis replied. "They can all agree on him."

Clapper hurried to the United Press wire room and wrote a story that put a new phrase—"the smoke-filled room"—into the language of American politics.

6.

In 1920 the United Press was thirteen years old and the most profitable enterprise that had ever been developed as a completely independent venture in gathering and selling news. Howard was enjoying every minute of his career—he once felt that he had almost been insulted when a newspaper article suggested that he might give up his job in order to become an ambassador—but for some time E. W. Scripps had been urging him to join Robert P. Scripps in the Scripps newspapers with the idea that the two would become controlling partners.

In June, Howard resigned as president of the United Press and became general business director of the Scripps-McRae League. Hawkins succeeded him. But those closely associated with Howard and Hawkins were doubtful whether these changes in leadership were to be considered as final. The relationship between Howard and Hawkins was so close that it seemed unlikely it would really be broken up at this stage. And it wasn't long before there were signs that Howard missed Hawkins in his new job—and that he was likely to do something about it. This became more evident when Hawkins began making a number of top echelon changes in the United Press to prepare for the future.

Bickel went to Europe in 1922, and when he got back to New York Hawkins called him into his office and said abruptly: "Karl, I'm going to break it off sharp for you."

Bickel's pink cheeks paled a little because his first reaction was that he was about to be eased out.

"I'm resigning before very long," Hawkins went on. "You're going to quit being business manager now and become general news manager. You know, E. W. Scripps always wants to put newsmen in top posts rather than men from the business side. Then, later, you're going to be president."

"What does Roy say?" Bickel asked, getting the color back in his cheeks.

"He says okay," Hawkins replied.

"Well, that's good but I want to hear him say it," Bickel remarked. Howard later assured him that Hawkins' plan had his full support, and Bickel took over the general news managership. Larry Earnist succeeded him as business manager, and Hugh Baillie, who had made several lightning shifts as manager of the New York and Washington bureaus, was appointed assistant general news manager.

In January of 1923 Hawkins resigned to join Howard in the Scripps newspapers and Bickel became president of the United Press.

CHAPTER THIRTEEN

In 1923, when Hawkins was resigning and Bickel was becoming president, the United Press was in a kind of frenetic period of growth and change. The organization had become too large for the intimate, personal relationships that had existed during most of Howard's leadership. Nobody could know all of the employees in the early 1920s. A financial department, for example, was added in 1922 to supply newspapers with the latest information from Wall Street. The sports department was expanded under the direction of Sports Editor Henry Farrell. The foreign department in New York had grown rapidly under the direction of Joseph L. Jones, who became foreign editor in 1924. Sale of United Press service in Central Europe was started in 1923 by Edward J. Bing, who had become an energetic salesman-reporter. The British United Press was launched by Charles F. Crandall in the same year. In the Far East, where Clarence du Bose was manager at Tokyo, the growth of Japanese newspapers after the war led to expansion of United Press cables to Nippon Dempo, which was serving some 230 journals.

All around the world United Press correspondents were having their triumphs and their troubles. One August evening in 1921 the London bureau was all but silent. The reason was well known to all. Ed Keen had received a cable from Karl Bickel in New York containing two words: "Downhold imperativest." The word "downhold"—then and later—was an ominous but familiar cablese term in the organization. It meant that, for one reason or another, the company had been exceeding its budget and the management wanted to cut down on expenses of all kinds. One of the simplest ways to economize was to cut down on cable tolls. When the word "downhold" came over the cables it meant that news coverage should be shaved to an absolute minimum and that very few cables should be sent until the budget was brought back into balance.

On that August evening the only story of much importance in England, so far as Americans were concerned, centered on the new dirigible R-38, which the British had built for the United States Navy and which was about to be turned over to American officials at a Royal Air Force base near Hull. The United Press had been invited to send a correspondent to the RAF base to witness the final trials of the R-38 (which the U. S. Navy had renamed the ZR-2), and Charles McCann of the London bureau had been selected to make the trip. Keen, however, was highly conscious of Bickel's "downhold" message and he told McCann not to leave London until the day of the flight, thus keeping expenses for the trip at a minimum. McCann was late reaching Hull and failed to see the R-38 take to the air, carrying American and British personnel.

Arriving at the RAF base, McCann discovered that other American reporters had watched the take-off and then gone to a base in southern England, where the dirigible was supposed to land. A question had arisen, however, as to whether the ship would actually continue to the base or return to Hull, and McCann couldn't make up his mind whether to remain there or go back to London. Finally he decided to return to London but he bought a railroad ticket only to the first station outside of Hull. There he got off the train and telephoned the RAF base to ask for the latest word from the dirigible.

"She's returning to Hull," a communications officer told him. "You'd better come on back."

McCann caught the next train back to Hull and again called the base. The communications officer stuttered out the news: "The R-38 has just blown up over the Humber River!"

A few minutes later the telephone rang in the London office of the United Press. The only reporter there was Al West, who had been asked to do an extra trick because the regular night-desk man was missing and presumably had consumed too much beer at a nearby pub. He picked up the telephone and said "Hello." A voice crackled back at him over a wire that was making a great deal of noise. He couldn't understand anything except the words "Charley McCann."

"That you, Charley?" he shouted. "Can't understand you."

The connection cleared up a little and McCann rasped, "The R-38 has just blown up and crashed. Get a flash going, dammit!"

West cabled a flash to New York and took a brief cable from McCann, who then hung up the telephone to try to get to the scene of the disaster. He hired an old automobile but had gone only a few miles when it broke down. He "thumbed" a ride on the running board of a small car and then hitched another lift from an RAF car carrying British and American naval officers to the scene. One of the officers was a paymaster who had the names and addresses of all the American naval men aboard the R-38. When they arrived on the scene, they found that sixty-two persons, including seventeen Americans, had been killed in the disaster. McCann telephoned the facts to his London office. He then visited the hospital where survivors had been taken and again telephoned the office. There was not another American reporter closer than London, and McCann virtually had the story to himself.

West had been frantically trying to telephone Ed Keen, meanwhile, to ask him what to do about Bickel's "downhold" orders, but he never reached the boss. When McCann called back with all the details he took them down, shuddered, and handed them to the cable operator for transmission to New York. By midnight in London when the story was pretty well cleaned up, he checked the file and discovered that he had sent several thousand words to New York—several times more than London would have filed in twenty-four hours under the "downhold" order.

"Well, I guess I better start looking for a new job," he told the cable operator. "I've busted the budget wide open. They'll fire me before dawn."

He was debating whether he could afford to send out for a cup of coffee when a message started coming in from New York. A little pale, West looked over the shoulder of the operator who copied it:

> PRESS UNIPRESS LONDON
> CONGRATULATIONS THATS WAY TO COVER BIG BREAKS
> BICKEL

West sighed and relaxed. We never would have done it, he thought, if Ed Keen hadn't been trying to save a couple of dollars by holding McCann in London until the last minute.

2.

President Harding fell ill in the summer of 1923 while returning from a visit to Alaska. He was confined to bed in San Francisco, where Bureau Manager Morris DeHaven Tracy turned out his staff to help Lawrence Martin, who had accompanied the presidential party from Washington, cover the story. After a brief period of grave concern, Mr. Harding's physicians reported that he seemed to be on the road to recovery. He was able to sit up in bed and frequently asked his wife to read to him. She was reading an article from the current issue of *The Saturday Evening Post* early in the evening of August 2, when the President suddenly suffered a stroke. Shortly before eight o'clock Tracy flashed the word across the nation that Mr. Harding was dead.

That night the San Francisco staff gathered the details of the President's last hours, and Martin wrote the story that opened the wires the next morning. It was so well put together that it was never changed throughout that day of black headlines across the nation.

BY LAWRENCE MARTIN
United Press Staff Correspondent
PALACE HOTEL, San Francisco, August 3—*The President is dead. Death,*

apparently balked by medical science, struck suddenly and with no warning at 7:20 last night.

The President was definitely on the road to recovery from ptomaine poisoning, acute indigestion and a pneumonic infection which followed them. But death found a way through the armor—it struck into the brain with apoplexy, and without a struggle or word, and only a shudder of his weakened frame, and the raising of one hand, the nation's head passed beyond.

Tonight they will take Warren G. Harding's body home—back to the White House where he lived and worked as the chief magistrate of the people who today, shocked beyond expression by his death, mourn for him and his wife. . . .

Calvin Coolidge of Massachusetts, the vice president, today wore upon his shoulders the mantle of authority and tremendous responsibility which slipped last night from Mr. Harding when he passed beyond the ken and power of mortal things.

The President passed with the sunset. The last rays of California's golden sunshine were pouring into his room, where Mrs. Harding, the wife who had been by his side since he was stricken seriously last Saturday, sat reading to him from a magazine. . . .

In the following year another President died. Woodrow Wilson had been stricken in 1919 while on a nationwide speaking tour attempting to rally support for his League of Nations plan.

Wilson never fully recovered and, as 1923 drew to a close, he began failing rapidly at his home on S Street in Washington. A "death watch" was established there in January of 1924, with A. L. Bradford in charge. Herbert Hoover lived a few doors away and he permitted the installation of a telegraph wire and an operator in a small room off the front entrance of his home. All reporters had about the same facilities, however, and Bradford wasn't satisfied. He finally made an arrangement with a real-estate dealer who lived directly across the street from the Wilson home to install a telephone in his cellar, where a window looked out toward the Wilson front door. This was done secretly, and a relay of United Press reporters was secretly assigned to man the telephone day and night.

The death watch went on. News of Mr. Wilson's condition was received from Admiral Grayson, his physician, who met reporters at intervals on the front porch of the Wilson home. He would give them a medical bulletin and the reporters would scatter and run up or down the street to their wires or telephones to relay the information to their Washington offices. Bradford followed this procedure, and the man in the cellar across the street just sat at his telephone and watched. But one morning Admiral Grayson appeared about eleven o'clock and announced that the former President was dead. The reporters asked for details before they made a wild dash off the porch

—except for Bradford. As soon as Grayson started speaking, Bradford—a tall man—engineered a beat for the United Press by simply raising his arms above his head and clasping his hands together. The man at the cellar telephone saw Bradford's signal and dictated the flash to his office. The desk man relayed the flash on Wilson's death to the telegraph operator and then began dictating a story. Ten minutes later the United Press had moved 400 words of copy on Wilson's death by Morse wire but didn't have a word written down in the Washington office. Eventually the Baltimore bureau operator had to send back to Washington the first two pages of the story to make the Washington file complete.

3.

In 1922 Ferdinand C. M. Jahn was sent from the Berlin bureau to Doorn, Holland, to cover the wedding of the exiled Kaiser to Princess Hermine von Schoenaich-Carolath. Jahn, who spoke Dutch fluently, previously had secretly arranged for a friend attached to the former Kaiser's household to provide him with an eyewitness account of the wedding. But when he reached Doorn he found that exiled monarch had ordered all reporters barred from the grounds of the castle where he lived. There would be no exceptions.

Jahn decided not to accept this dictate and wandered around the castle wall until he found the captain of guards, who had been posted to keep reporters out.

"Captain," he said in a humble voice, "I am a theological student who was promised aid by the Kaiser. I was instructed to call and talk to one of his representatives, who will assist me."

He looked so doleful that the captain slapped him on the back and led him inside. Jahn thought that he would at least get a chance to see the scene of the wedding before being tossed out. But, once inside, he got a break. Almost the first person he saw was the friend who had promised to give him information about the wedding.

"There's the man I am to see," he exclaimed, and walked away from the captain. He then explained the circumstances to his friend and through him arranged not only to get details of the wedding but to secure a signed article by the Reverend Vogel, who performed the ceremony.

In Rio de Janeiro, Bureau Manager U. Grant Keener had an assistant, Charles M. Kinsolving, who suffered severe frustrations in trying to cover a revolutionary movement in 1924 in the state of São Paulo. Kinsolving filed a story on the uprising against the government of President Bernardes, but it was killed by a censor installed at the cable office with orders not to pass a word. Kinsolving protested in vain. By afternoon, reports indicating that the revolution was gaining ground were received and Kinsolving was more than ever determined to send his dispatches. He told Keener that he might try something, went to his home, and wrote a personal telegram to J. B. Powers, the United Press manager in Buenos Aires. In the telegram he described a sick woman in Rio de Janeiro who was about to undergo an operation for acute appendicitis. He said that infection from the "rupture" was spreading swiftly. When Powers received the message he had no difficulty in understanding what Kinsolving had written and, after decoding it, transmitted it to New York, where the United Press carried an exclusive story on the revolution in Brazil.

This had worked so well that Kinsolving tried it again the next day, adding details of the spread of "infection" in the weakening body of the old woman. Again the censor paid no attention to the message and the United Press continued to be the only agency with direct on-the-scene news of the Brazilian uprising. This went on for three days, at the end of which Bickel sent Kinsolving a glowing message of congratulations and suggested that he offer the government an opportunity to issue an official statement which would be carried by the United Press. Strangely enough, with the help of Dr. Regis de Oliviera, a Brazilian diplomat, Kinsolving persuaded President Bernardes' secretary to prepare such a statement with permission to transmit it to New York.

But when Kinsolving arrived at the cable office the censor advised him that this permission had been rescinded by telephone and that nothing could be transmitted. This "double cross" so irritated Kinsolving that he pressed his luck a step too far. He wrote another telegram to Powers about the old woman's operation and included in it the sense of the official statement. It sailed through smoothly, but a few hours later the Brazilian foreign office began to wake up to the fact that there was a leak through the censorship. They examined cables sent from the capital, and then an official called Kinsolving on the telephone.

"Who is the old woman with a ruptured appendix?" he asked.

Kinsolving thought for a few moments but couldn't find any answer that would postpone the inevitable.

"I don't know," he replied. A little later two detectives arrested him and placed him in solitary confinement in the municipal jail. A day or so later, after strenuous intervention by members of the United States Embassy staff, he was released on condition that he send no more telegrams. But the next day a government decree was published disqualifying both the United Press and the Associated Press from operating in Brazil. It took three days of negotiations to get the order rescinded and service re-established. A week later, Kinsolving sailed for New York.

4.

The most important part of a reporter's work is often done before he starts out to cover a story. In 1925 William J. McEvoy was assigned to cover the court-martial of Colonel Billy Mitchell in Washington. Mitchell had defied the army brass by vigorously campaigning for establishment of a United States Air Force, and his case had stirred great controversy throughout the

country. McEvoy was thoroughly familiar with details of the Mitchell crusade, as was every other reporter in Washington, but he decided before the
trial opened that it would be a good idea to bone up on court-martial procedure. He read a couple of books and went around to talk with the judge
advocate who would preside. He discovered among other things that the
trial was conducted according to iron-clad rules and that it was mandatory
for the jury to ask the defendant a certain question before it could declare
him guilty.

The testimony came to an end and, on December 17, the crowded courtroom, as well as the nation, was awaiting the decision of the jury. The wait
was interrupted by a brief appearance of the jury of generals, who asked
Colonel Mitchell to stand.

"Have you ever before been convicted by court-martial?"

"No, sir," Mitchell replied.

As soon as the question was uttered, McEvoy quietly slipped out to flash
the word that Mitchell had been found guilty. Due to his pre-trial studies,
McEvoy knew that question would have to be asked if Mitchell had been
found guilty and only if he were found guilty. McEvoy's news beat hummed
along the wires while everybody inside the courtroom waited for the jury
to go through the remaining rigid formalities of court-martial procedure before declaring the defendant guilty.

CHAPTER FOURTEEN

Karl Bickel had a knack of looking at the news of the day—the big stories and the little ones—from the long-range viewpoint of a historian fitting together a jigsaw puzzle. He was imaginative; his mind raced through the broad current of news flowing over the wires and cables from every part of the world, picking out what was significant and seeking clues to the trend of world affairs. A paragraph telling of a sudden increase in the flow of gold from Hong Kong to New York was indicative of an economic trend. The sudden switch of Paris couturiers from short to long skirts was not just a fashion note but an important dollars-and-cents story to manufacturers throughout the United States, and, on one occasion, he soundly berated his top New York editors for "muffing" an announcement that big hats were coming back into style. Bickel was always selling the United Press on his ramblings around the country, but he was also infecting many of the editors he saw with something of his boundless enthusiasm for seeing the daily news report in the broad framework of history. He never lost a kind of evangelistic fervor about what the news of the day meant in the political and economic history of the world; and he never lost his firm conviction that any interference with the free flow of news throughout the world was a deadly blow to the progress of society.

Bickel had been intensely interested in Russia since the Bolshevik revolution of 1917. The idea of communism was abhorrent to him, but the idea of change, of building something new on the ruins of the Czarist empire fascinated him as a reporter-historian. At Stanford University, he had studied under an English professor who was a Fabian socialist, and had learned something of the European socialist movement. When the Reds took over in Russia, Bickel was highly skeptical of the opinion of British, French, and United States foreign-office experts that the new government wouldn't last long.

He also felt that the world should know a great deal more about Russia than was available to Western newspapers in the early 1920s. The Moscow government regarded virtually all foreign reporters as hostile. Their activities were strictly limited, and eventually many of them were expelled. The United States Department of State was not doing anything to improve the flow of news between the two countries and, at times, acted to discourage it. American and British correspondents stationed in Finland or at cities like Riga, Latvia, near the Russian frontier wrote more words about what was going on in Russia than the correspondents at Moscow. And the result was that many newspapers published a mixture of rumor, propaganda, gossip, and fact about the Communist government.

In 1922 Bickel attempted to secure a visa to visit Russia with the idea of making some new arrangement for exchange of news, but the Moscow government turned him down. In the same year a Russian representative in New York approached him with a proposal to buy a service from the United Press. He wanted 1200 words a day sent to Moscow and offered to pay $1200 a week, but the State Department heard of the proposal and informally opposed it. Nothing was done then, but after Bickel became president in 1923 negotiations were renewed. The Russian official news agency, Rosta, made a deal by which the United Press sent correspondent John Graudenz to Moscow, where he was given access to the official agency's reports. In return, the United Press cabled to Rosta a news report of about five hundred words a day.

Late in May, Bickel received a message from Jacob Doletzky, head of the Rosta agency. Doletzky, later purged by Stalin, was a gentle, soft-spoken man who knew little about running a news agency but was willing to learn. He asked Bickel to visit Moscow to advise him on improving Rosta service, and the United Press president arrived there in mid-July of 1923, planning to remain for ten days. There was so much to be done, however, that he remained until September. He spent much of this time giving Doletzky the benefit of American news-agency ideas, explaining how telephone circuits could be set up for transmission of daily reports to several newspapers simultaneously, drawing designs for copy desks and other news-room equipment, and helping the Russians order a number of new teleprinter machines —some of which were still in use in Moscow thirty years later.

As Bickel was about ready to leave Moscow in 1923, word was received that a tremendous earthquake had shaken Tokyo and other Japanese cities, causing vast loss of life. Most communications were wrecked, American correspondents in Tokyo were isolated for days, and about the only news of the disaster was being received by wireless from Osaka.

Fortunately, the Osaka *Mainichi* was one of the powerful newspapers of Japan and a client of the United Press by way of the Nippon Dempo agency. In 1921 the *Mainichi* correspondent in New York was Moto Takata, who worked closely with the United Press bureau. When Takata returned to Japan in 1922, Barney Furay arranged with him to cover the agency on any outstanding news that occurred at Osaka. When the earthquake story broke, communications between Osaka and Tokyo were severed, but *Mainichi* chartered several airplanes and established a kind of taxi service by air to Tokyo. They sent their own reporters and photographers to the capital and had the planes bring back members of their staff in Tokyo. For several days this was virtually the only method of communication with the stricken zone.

The United Press had sent a cable to Takata asking him to forward any information available, and he responded with a message of more than a thousand words—costing three dollars and sixty cents a word at the urgent rate—that gave the first graphic report of what had happened in Tokyo. Furay later figured out that it was the most expensive single message ever received by the United Press up to 1923. It was well worth it. The first American correspondent to send out a detailed story on the devastation in Tokyo—an estimated 100,000 were dead in the earthquake zone—was Duke Parry of the International News Service. He had walked along the railroad tracks from Tokyo until he managed to get a ride on the cowcatcher of a locomotive on the last stage of a thirty-six-hour trek to the wireless station at Osaka.

Bickel decided to return to New York by way of Japan. When he arrived there he found devastation that was worse than war. Baron Motoyama was head of a family that owned both the Osaka *Mainichi* and the Tokyo *Nichi Nichi*. His Tokyo property had been all but wiped out, and the Japanese generally faced a great economic crisis, but everybody was looking forward to rebuilding instead of weeping in the ruins. The baron entertained Bickel as if he were riding a wave of prosperity and, after three weeks, decided that his newspapers would henceforth buy a special report from the United Press on world economic affairs. He paid $1000 a month for the service, which was the beginning of United Press expansion into a profitable news-distributing venture in the Far East.

2.

The postwar expansion of United Press coverage and news distribution in Europe encountered many difficulties, especially in countries such as Spain and Portugal, in which South American newspapers were greatly interested but from which United States editors wanted only the most important news developments. The European news-agency cartel had been long established in those countries and the Associated Press benefited from that fact, but the United Press had to build up an extensive coverage almost from scratch. This proved slow and often tortuous, but eventually it was to mean destruction of the cartel's monopoly grip on the press of Europe.

One of the early United Press setbacks was in Lisbon where Eugene Pilgrims had been hired as bureau manager. There was a great deal of tension in Portugal at the time, and Pilgrims made a conscientious effort to report political developments, including what the opposition to the government was doing and saying in 1920. Unhappily he included in his dispatches one day the comment of two left-wing radical newspapers which were engaged in bitter controversy with the government. The dispatches were confiscated by the censors, and Pilgrims was picked up by the police and put in prison. Apologies by the United Press, the intervention of the United States minister, and appointment of a new bureau manager—Adolfo DaRosa—were necessary before the prison gates opened for Pilgrims about two weeks later. He was escorted to the frontier and put aboard a train for Paris.

The United Press had some grave difficulties with official censors in France, too, but its correspondents didn't knuckle under easily. Webb Miller, manager of the Paris bureau in 1921, wrote a series of stories about French occupation of the Ruhr, a rich coal and industrial district seized from Germany. Miller told what he saw, which was that the French policy of "digging coal with bayonets"—that is, by military direction—was not a success. The French foreign office was incensed when these stories were published in the United States and elsewhere, and Count Charles de Chambrun, who was head of the foreign office press department, summoned Miller to his office for some severe criticism.

Miller tried to explain that he was reporting the situation as objectively as possible, but De Chambrun merely replied: "You can't be neutral about France. Either you are with us or you are against us." Miller refused to accept this idea and was consigned to the foreign office "doghouse."

A few years later, when the exchange rate of the French franc was fluctuating wildly, De Chambrun again called Miller to his office and, with great anger, said: "I have you! You are hostile to France, and I have the evidence. I'm going to have you deported."

"Why?" Miller asked.

"You telegraphed a false quotation of the franc, a quotation that was lower than the franc was at the moment. Our legation at Rio de Janeiro reported that when your false quotation was published in South America it precipitated a further fall of the franc, which spread all over the world. Also you said there was a panic on the Paris Bourse. That was false."

Miller insisted that he should have an opportunity to produce evidence that his dispatches were accurate. He then obtained an official copy of the fluctuations of the franc on the day in question and, with certified copies of his messages, showed that he had cabled the correct quotation to South America. He also obtained clippings from the semiofficial French newspaper Le Temps, which referred editorially to a panic on the Bourse. He delivered these to De Chambrun.

The foreign office official studied them and said he would drop his request for deportation. But, he added, "I know your organization is hostile to France. I have just read a dispatch sent from one of your offices, not from France, and it says: 'If France is out to cause trouble in Europe she is going about it the right way.' That clearly shows hostility to France."

"That's impossible," Miller replied. "That is an expression of opinion, and none of the men in our agency would dare to start a message that way. Where was it published?"

De Chambrun refused to tell. But Miller checked with London and discovered the sentence had been lifted from an article written by former Prime Minister David Lloyd George for United Feature Syndicate. Lloyd George, of course, was expressing his personal opinion. Such United Feature articles were wirelessed to New York several days prior to publication, and Lloyd George's name was not mentioned in the message, his authorship being indicated by a code word. Furthermore, the article had not been published in any newspaper at the time De Chambrun read the sentence to Miller. Armed with a copy of the article and the text of the International Telegraphic convention, Miller returned to the office of De Chambrun.

"This message has never been published," he told the foreign office official. "It is still confidential between the man who wrote it, our London office, and our New York office. Anyone else who has possession of it has obtained it by illegal means. Furthermore, it is not a United Press dispatch. It belongs to the United Feature Syndicate and is not due to be released until day after tomorrow. It was transmitted from London by wireless. Now, how did the French foreign office get a copy? I think I have a mystery story here of France spying on international wireless communications between England and America. It will make a good story in the American newspapers."

De Chambrun was visibly upset. He finally acknowledged that the message had been picked out of the air "by chance" by the French government wireless station and turned over to the foreign office. He suggested that the entire matter be dropped because "it is a regrettable misunderstanding." Miller rejected the suggestion and reported the incident to U. S. Ambassador Myron T. Herrick, but the ambassador urged that it would be wise to let the matter drop, and Miller's superiors in New York agreed. It was, however, the last time that De Chambrun ever called Miller "on the carpet."

When General News Manager Ferguson was on a European inspection tour in middle 1920s, the Rome bureau suddenly became a trouble spot. A New York newspaper had carried a story about plans for dedication of a new athletic field adjoining the Vatican, on land that had been given the church by an American millionaire. The report said that the Pope would dedicate the field and that during the ceremony he would step on Italian soil for the first time since he became a "prisoner" in the Vatican in 1871.

This was a big news break, especially for South America, and was played up there under black headlines. But the United Press had nothing. Frantic cables were sent to the Rome bureau. No reply was received. Finally Bickel told Ferguson, who was in Paris, to hurry to Rome and find out what was wrong. Henry Wood, who had been Rome manager at one time, was then in

Geneva, covering the League of Nations. Ferguson wired Wood to drop everything and join him en route to Rome.

When they reached the Italian capital they hurried to the United Press office. Ferguson found on the news desk a spike loaded with messages from London, New York, and Buenos Aires demanding some reply about the New York newspaper's story on the Pope. He shook the spike at the bureau manager and asked him why he had not answered the queries.

"There's nothing to answer," was the reply. "I know that the Pope will not step on Italian soil. There isn't any story."

"How do you know?"

"I know it."

"Are you planning to attend?"

"No. I know what the ceremony will be and I'll write something about it."

Ferguson angrily said that this was an important story in the United States. Then he went around to call on the American donor and asked for tickets to the ceremony but was informed there were none left. Ferguson and Wood later walked beneath the high wall around the Vatican gardens, adjacent to the new athletic field. "There must be some way we can get in," Ferguson muttered, looking for a high tree or a telephone pole as if he were a knothole gang kid trying to see into a baseball park at game time.

About that time an elderly monk in brown robes approached a small door in the wall, pulled out a key ring, unlocked the door, and entered. Ferguson took two quick steps forward and stuck his foot in the door so that it would not quite close behind the monk. After waiting a minute or two, he pushed the door open and he and Wood went down a narrow path that led to the new field. The crowd was arriving and the American sponsor was standing near seats that had been placed for the dedication ceremonies. He was wearing a white tie and tails, and when he saw Ferguson and Wood in wrinkled business suits he was horrified.

"Gentlemen," he exclaimed, "you are not properly dressed. At least, I hope you will keep in the background so no one will mistakenly think you are my guests."

Not wishing to press his luck, Ferguson dragged Wood back a dozen yards where they could stand almost concealed behind a fence. Being rather short in stature, he found a box to stand on so he could see the ceremony, got out his pencil and paper, and began asking questions. Wood, who was familiar with Vatican affairs, identified the various groups and personages who paraded around the field as the dedication ceremonies began. There was a group of students from the United States. Then came monks from a certain order, followed by a group of dignitaries from the diplomatic corps. At last there emerged a group of cardinals, walking slowly across the field—but then Wood gasped in surprise.

"All of those stories were wrong," he said. "The Pope is not here!"

Ferguson at the moment was still taking notes.

"Who are those two near the end of the procession?" he asked.

Wood peered over the fence. "That's the Papal Secretary of State and one of the other cardinals," he said, giving their names.

"Okay. Now that guy walking between them—the fellow wearing a cutaway and striped trousers? Who's he?"

Wood peered again. "Why, that's Tom Morgan of the Associated Press!"

Ferguson almost fell off his box. He jammed his notes and his pencil into his pocket and stepped down to the ground, facing Wood. "Henry," he said, "we have just one thing to do before we leave—hire Morgan to be the United Press manager in Rome." He swung around and trudged down the little path to the door that led out through the Vatican wall.

A day or so later Ferguson did hire Morgan, who ably managed the Rome bureau for almost a decade.

3.

One of the busiest men in the United Press in the middle 1920s and later was Harry W. Frantz, who had started out on the New York foreign desk but moved to Washington after two years to supply stories of special interest to Latin America. This specialized report had grown steadily since 1919 as a result of expansion of the service in South America. Both Frederick Kuh and Ferdinand Jahn had been assigned to it before they were transferred to European bureaus. In 1922 Frantz and in 1924 Louis J. Heath became the stalwarts of what was known as the foreign department of the Washington bureau.

In 1925 Frantz was assigned to cover a plebiscite on the Tacna-Arica border dispute which had threatened to bring on a full-fledged war between Chile and Peru. Diplomatic negotiations, assisted by the United States and other American powers, led to an agreement to hold a plebiscite to determine where the border should be drawn, and General John J. Pershing was appointed chairman of the Plebiscitary Commission. A shy, soft-spoken, and studious man, Frantz bought a cutaway coat and silk hat, packed his bags, and departed with General Pershing's official party for Arica, aboard the U.S.S. *Rochester*. He didn't get back for a year.

The Tacna-Arica plebiscite was a strictly secondary story in the United States, but in South America it was big news. It was also a tough, tedious story to cover. The Pershing commission met daily, and the reporters had a long walk to the Cuartel, where the sessions were held, several times a day. Chilean officials were close at hand but, to keep in touch with the Peruvian officials, reporters had to go to sea every day on a visit to the steamship *Ucayali,* the Peruvian headquarters three miles offshore. This daily grind was exhausting when added to the strain of covering developments on a competitive basis and might have been unbearable except for the fact that the All America Cables office closed down at ten o'clock each evening, giving the correspondents a respite at least until the next day.

Newspapers in Santiago, Lima, and Buenos Aires demanded such detailed coverage that Frantz kept the cable office crowded week after week with a heavy file and on one occasion filed a Peruvian report of 40,000 words that required all of one evening and most of the next morning to transmit. It took up almost three pages in *La Prensa* of Buenos Aires the next day. In point of volume over a long period, the Tacna-Arica dispute was without precedent, and there have been few, if any, comparable assignments in the United Press history.

There was more to Frantz's job, however, than just covering news developments. His stories were transmitted simultaneously to United Press newspapers in Chile and Peru, which were on opposite sides of the bitter dispute. These were important clients and it was important to keep their good will. It is usually a sign of objective reporting if a correspondent gets complaints from both of the opposing sides in any controversy. But in a year of daily coverage, Frantz received no complaints at all. Instead, when he finally finished his assignment, he was complimented by both Chilean and Peruvian newspapers for his factual reporting.

Frank H. Bartholomew planned his vacation with care in the late spring of 1925. Bartholomew had joined the United Press as bureau manager in Portland, Oregon, in 1921, and had been on the move ever since. He had been shifted to Los Angeles to report on the affairs of the motion-picture colony, he had covered revolutionary activities on the Mexican border, and he had roamed through Oklahoma, Arkansas, and Texas as a highly successful salesman. When he was appointed San Francisco manager in 1925 he decided he would take a good rest before starting the new job and that he would take it in some quiet spot where he could lie in the sun and do nothing. He picked his spot near the California resort town of Santa Barbara and settled down on his backside to relax on June 28.

At twenty minutes of seven o'clock on the morning of June 29 Santa Barbara was shaken by the worst earthquake in many years. Several persons were killed, many were hurt, and damage in the downtown area amounted to $6,000,000. An hour or so later Bartholomew and a telegrapher, Tom Kelly, were driving by automobile into the devastated city, the first outside reporters on the scene. They soon had plenty of news to report but no way to get it to the outside world. All power lines were down and telephone communications were disrupted. Kelly found a telegraph line that seemed to be all right, but they had to have some kind of power. They hooked a line to the battery of Bartholomew's car, used it as a booster, and soon had sole possession of the only usable telegraph circuit out of Santa Barbara. Setting up an "office" on the loading platform of a wrecked warehouse, Bartholomew wrote the story and Kelly sent it out over a line that was hooked into the United Press main circuit for the Pacific coast. As darkness closed in they secured lanterns and continued at work until midnight, when the wires normally closed.

At that point, however, New York instructed Bart to keep the wire open to serve a couple of West Coast clients that had asked for extra service from the quake and to move (to New York alone) a completely new story for use in afternoon newspapers the next day. Tired but willing, he drew back and wrote a flowery, slow-paced story about the devastation wrought by an earthquake in the wonderland of California's orchards and gardens. Kelly had sent three paragraphs of the new story when he got a "break" by the telegrapher of the Klamath *Morning News* in Oregon, who had a terse message from his editor, Jack McDonald:

BARTHOLOMEW WE PAYING FOR THIS WIRE TO GET LATE NEWS, NOT A LESSON IN BOTANY

MCDONALD

Bart had just read the message when another and more severe tremor hit Santa Barbara. The walls of the warehouse collapsed around him, dust rose in a great cloud, and his automobile slid downhill with a crash. He and Kelly dug themselves out of the wreckage and patched up their telegraph wire. Bart dictated:

FLASH SANTA BARBARA ANOTHER STRONG QUAKE HITS

Then he dictated a bulletin on what he could see of the damage caused by the new tremor. He had hardly finished when the Klamath Falls operator came on the wire with another message:

BARTHOLOMEW OKAY . . . OKAY . . . THATS FINE BUT DONT OVERDO IT

MCDONALD

Bartholomew and Kelly remained on the job from Monday until Friday, being reinforced during the week by reporters from the Los Angeles bureau. There were about a hundred tremors in the area that week, and for several days they had the only direct wire out of Santa Barbara.

CHAPTER FIFTEEN

In January of 1926 President Karl Bickel perched his portable typewriter on his desk and began pecking out an important memorandum to all United Press bureau managers and business representatives. Bickel had recently made an extensive business trip through Latin America and had been busy since his return surveying what was going on at home. He was, as the new year started, feeling pretty good about the company's progress.

Important gains had been achieved in 1925. The number of newspapers served throughout the world had passed the 1000 mark, and the company had spent $3,000,000 during the year to collect and distribute news. The United Press main wires were "double-trunked"—that is, a second 3500-mile trunk wire was established—in the summer of 1925. The new wire was a telegraph-printer circuit, but the old Morse wire also was continued and, in fact, was preferred by many telegraph editors because they could always get the operator to request various bureaus to speed up stories that they wanted. They couldn't make such requests of a printer machine. With increased wire space available, a promising young man in the Columbus, Ohio, bureau—Earl J. Johnson—was shifted to Chicago to work up special features for the printer circuit. Shortly afterward he became Chicago manager of the United News.

These signs of rapid change and growth were in Bickel's mind as he tapped at the keys of his portable typewriter:

The United Press closed 1925 with the best record in every department of its business that it has ever made. The United Press, the United News, United Financial and various subsidiary services closed the year with 1032 client newspapers. The United Press serves its report directly to newspapers in 36 countries.

We are, without any possibility of dispute, America's greatest world-wide distributor of news, and I believe we can match country for country with Reuters and have plenty of counters to spare . . .

In South America, the United Press now serves over 95 per cent of all the business available on that continent . . . The Associated Press has but five clients in the entire continent, as far as we can ascertain, and of those five clients the United Press would not serve two if it had the opportunity. Recently La Razón, *principal afternoon paper of the entire continent, which had been taking both the United Press and the Associated Press, threw out the Associated Press . . . despite the fact that the Associated Press offered to serve them for a figure about one tenth of what the United Press rate was and still is. . . .*

The United Press has developed one of the strongest news collection and distribution machines in the world . . . It should be our determination to pass the 1200 line [in number of clients] *before December 31, 1926 . . . I understand, from casual conversations with certain of the boys along the line, that there is a feeling the opposition has bucked up somewhat during the last few months. Fine. The stronger the better. The United Press always thrives on competition, and the harder the competition the faster we grow and the stronger we thrive.*

K.A.B.

Bickel's pep talk to bureau managers and business representatives may have been a bit exaggerated in spots, but it was by no means idle boasting. The United Press already was expanding its news-distributing service in Europe and starting to spread out in the Far East, although it still required an imaginative point of view to compare its world-wide service with the government-assisted service of Reuters. The difference perhaps lay in the fact that the European news agency cartel agreements barred Reuters from certain areas of the world where the United Press was prospering.

Since 1923, for example, Ed Bing had been selling United Press service in Central Europe and by 1926 he was continental business manager with a list of approximately fifty clients. The British United Press organized by Charles F. Crandall in Canada in 1923 had extended operations to London and was serving clients in the United Kingdom. In 1924 Herbert Bailey was made managing editor of the British organization and began setting up coverage of British news from many cities in the Commonwealth. Eventually, after Frank Fisher had succeeded Bailey, the British United Press introduced into England many features of American newspapers. Although the service made use of the dispatches of United Press correspondents from all over the world, it also had its own reporters scattered throughout the Commonwealth and on duty at various war fronts in later years.

In 1926 Pacific Coast Manager Frank H. Bartholomew persuaded the Honolulu *Advertiser* to drop the Associated Press service in favor of United Press. He then sent H. R. Ekins to Honolulu to handle the news report, which consisted of about 500 words a day by wireless from San Francisco. Radio Corporation of America was the main commercial service across the

Pacific, but the United States Navy also had extensive wireless communications there, and Bartholomew saw in the Navy a chance to transmit more news for less money. The Navy sent daily by wireless a kind of news report to its personnel on ships at sea and at isolated Pacific bases in order to keep them abreast of developments at home. Bartholomew arranged for the United Press to prepare this service, and in return the Navy communications system agreed to hand over a copy to the United Press offices in Honolulu and elsewhere.

The United Press news report broadcast by the Navy could be picked up in Manila as well as Honolulu. In 1925 William B. Kuhns went there as bureau manager, and in the next year or so the UP was serving more than a dozen Manila newspapers. These included the struggling English-language *Philippines Herald* edited by Carlos P. Romulo, who later became the Philippine ambassador to the United Nations. The Manila newspapers were, for the most part, small and sometimes slow to pay for service delivered, but they gave the United Press another foothold toward Hong Kong and China.

Breaking into the news-distribution field in the Far East was slow work. In the mid-twenties Ray Marshall had started selling a brief United Press news report to newspapers at Peking and had hired a former Minneapolis *Tribune* reporter, Demaree Bess, then working on the Shanghai *Times,* as a string correspondent. After Miles W. Vaughn became Far Eastern manager with headquarters at Tokyo in 1925 he added Bert L. Kuhn, Henry F. Misselwitz, and Randall Gould to the China staff and made a 10,000-mile tour to arrange for string correspondents in cities of China, the Federated Malay States, Singapore, the East Indies, and elsewhere. In many instances American missionaries served as stringers—and often very good ones, too— but there were also young businessmen and even a few American newspapermen in cities like Hankow who covered for the United Press. In addition, an important duty of correspondents in the Far East was to make friends with American naval and State Department officers in remote stations, in the hope, often justified, that they would tip off the Shanghai or Peking bureau when important news broke. Vaughn also began selling service to both Chinese and English-language newspapers in Shanghai, Hankow, Peking, and Tientsin, but it would be several years before important progress could be made in opposition to the powerful Reuters agency.

In the middle 1920s there were two meetings of international press representatives under auspices of the League of Nations at Geneva. These sessions brought together the heads of news agencies from all over the world, both independent agencies such as the United Press and official or semiofficial agencies such as Havas, to discuss mutual problems and to make recommendations to the various governments through the League of Nations.

The long fight the United Press had waged against any kind of news monopoly and especially against the European combination of official and quasi-official news agencies had borne fruit in South America with the breaking of the grip of Havas on that continent. Sale of United Press service in European states had begun to achieve similar results, but the favored status of the cartel agencies with government officials in their own countries was still a major deterrent to the free flow of news as well as to the gathering of news on the basis of equal rights for all agencies.

The second international press meeting at Geneva was attended by Bickel and Robert P. Scripps. Bickel was eager to get before the conference a resolution in favor of freedom of the press and of unbiased international reporting. "I think it's important," he told Scripps, "that we try to force such a resolution to a vote. It will show whether some of the delegates are here merely to sabotage any efforts toward guaranteeing a free press or whether they mean to co-operate."

Ed Bing also was attending the sessions and he suggested that Bickel's purpose might be achieved by a little parliamentary maneuvering. "If the resolution is submitted in the ordinary course of events," he said, "it will be put to a voice vote. Then it will be quashed because most of the delegates represent government press departments or subsidized agencies and they want to keep their jobs. They'll just shout it down, with nothing on the record to show how each one voted. But if we can force a roll call, each one will have to stand up before the sixty-three other delegates and vote. And that will make them see it in quite a different light."

He and Bickel then consulted with Lord Burnham, publisher of the London *Daily Telegraph,* who was presiding over the conference. Burnham looked up the rules and assured them that if anyone asked for a roll call he would order it. The next day Bickel moved adoption of the resolution and asked for a roll call. One by one, sixty-three delegates stood up before press representatives from all over the world and blandly voted "aye" on the freedom of the press resolution. The sixty-fourth delegate, representing Turkey, voted "no." He doubtless had in mind that, only a few months previously, President Kemal Ataturk of the Turkish Republic had hanged all members of the parliamentary opposition he could get his hands on. It was thereafter considered unhealthy to speak of freedom of any kind in Turkey, and none of the Geneva delegates blamed their Turkish colleagues for declining to go along with the Bickel resolution.

There was no means of enforcing the action of the conference. But the repeated references of Bickel and others to the "official" and "semiofficial" status of the cartel agencies was having an effect, and representatives of the cartel were becoming more and more indignant at these public implications as to their governmental connections. At last one of them made a heated protest and the conference thereupon adopted a resolution that such government-subsidized agencies should be referred to as the "Allied Agencies."

Perhaps nothing could have better illustrated the change that had taken place in a decade or so in the attitude of editors, especially in the United States, toward the cartel. Monopolistic methods were being outdated. By persistently and impatiently fighting for a free flow of news, by unceasingly pressing in the court of world opinion for elimination of bias the United Press had made progress in a struggle of vital importance to every reader in every country of the world. It was a struggle for the principles on which E. W. Scripps had founded the United Press. It was a struggle in which officers of the United Press had been—and would continue to be—pioneers both at home and throughout the world.

2.

There was a traffic jam on the English Channel in 1926 when a score of ambitious long-distance swimmers gathered at Cape Gris-Nez on the French coast and at small towns on the English coast in a bid to break into the headlines. One of the swimmers on the French coast was a plump, smiling American girl named Gertrude Ederle, who applied a liberal coating of grease to her body and plunged into the water near Cape Gris-Nez with a fanfare of publicity that echoed across the United States.

The United Press expert on channel swimmers at that time was Sidney J. Williams of the London bureau. Over the years, Williams used everything from pigeons to a wireless transmitter to cover channel swimmers, but for the Ederle effort he decided to charter a fast motorboat. Other newspapermen assigned to the story got aboard a press tug which accompanied the swimmer. Williams' plan, as the rival reporters soon realized, was to accompany Miss Ederle to a point near the end of her swim and then to speed on ahead of the tug to the shore, where he would be able to cover the arrival of the American girl over the nearest telephone to London. Such tactics, he figured, would give him perhaps a half-hour edge over the reporters in the tug.

As Miss Ederle neared the English shore, Williams' pilot had to maneuver the motorboat close to the tug. Several other reporters had been waiting for just such a chance, and they immediately jumped from the tug into the boat, somewhat like a pirate boarding party. Williams said nothing but whispered instructions to his pilot. When the motorboat arrived about a hundred yards from the beach, the pilot made a quick turn and headed back out into the Channel. At the moment the turn began, Williams leaped fully clothed into the water and began swimming ashore. By the time the other reporters realized what had happened they were being carried rapidly out to sea, where the motorboat cruised lazily around for half an hour. Meantime Williams staggered into a house near Dover, exhausted and dripping gallons of salt water, asked a startled homeowner if he could use the telephone, and quickly relayed his story to the London bureau thirty-two minutes ahead of rival stories on the first woman ever to swim the English Channel.

Aviators kept trying to fly the Atlantic Ocean, but with little success. When a Swiss crew arrived in Portugal, bound for South America, they posed a difficult problem for Adolfo DaRosa, the United Press manager at Lisbon, by deciding to take off from a barren pasturage about twenty-five miles from the capital. There were no communications facilities in the vicinity, and there was no time to make arrangements for anything except a telephone at the village of Villa Franca, several miles from the take-off field. Furthermore the Swiss suddenly decided to depart on Sunday morning when the Villa Franca telephone exchange was closed down.

DaRosa dashed around to the telephone company offices at Lisbon and arranged for the exchange to stay open until the fliers had taken off. Then, after posting a man at the telephone, he roamed along the road to the airfield-pasture with half a dozen shotguns in his automobile. At intervals he stopped and hired farmers to take up positions on the hills, each armed with a shotgun. Then he rushed on to the take-off point and stood by with the last of his shotguns. When the airplane bounced across the pasture and roared into the air, DaRosa fired his shotgun. A mile or so away, one of the farmers he had hired heard the gun and immediately fired. . . . And so on, until DaRosa's assistant at the telephone in Villa Franca got the signal and flashed the news of the departure to New York.

3.

On the twentieth anniversary of the United Press in 1927, Bickel decided to have some guests in for a celebration dinner. Eleven hundred and seventy, including the President of the United States, showed up.

Bickel began working on the idea of an anniversary dinner early in the year, and his big objective was to persuade President Coolidge to be the speaker. The President was reluctant when the subject was first broached but reserved decision. Dashing down to the capital, Bickel arranged to see Mr. Coolidge late in the afternoon. The President was still reserved. He pulled a box of cigars out of a drawer of his desk, selected one, and put the box back without asking whether Bickel smoked. He got his cigar going and then said: "I've decided I'm going to do it. You can make the announcement."

"Oh no," Bickel replied. "You should make the announcement."

That evening the White House announced that the President would speak at the United Press anniversary dinner.

Later Mr. Coolidge proposed that the dinner be moved to Washington to save the expense—several thousand dollars—of his special train and entourage going to New York. He eventually gave up this idea and sent Starling, the White House secret service chief, to New York to make arrangements for the visit. Starling instructed Bickel to reserve the three top floors of the Biltmore Hotel, where the dinner was to be held, and to have twenty limousines waiting at Pennsylvania Station for the presidential party. One elevator in the hotel was to be reserved for the exclusive use of the President and his party.

"Something also will have to be done about entertaining Mrs. Coolidge that evening," Starling added. "Your wife should have some ladies in for a dinner for her. About thirty, I would say."

Bickel nodded and nodded and went about arranging things according to Starling's instructions. The West Point band had been invited to play at the dinner, but they badly needed some new uniforms. Bickel chipped in $1000 on the cost of new uniforms.

The publicity preceding the dinner irritated the Associated Press, and that agency's high command finally issued word that its officers were not to attend the dinner. Kent Cooper called Bickel to explain the decision. "That's the way it is," he concluded. "But, Karl, keep my seat warm. I'll be there." Several directors of the Associated Press sent similar messages.

After the Coolidges arrived at the hotel, Mr. and Mrs. Bickel paid a formal call on them. Then they rushed back to their own suite and the Coolidges paid a formal call on the Bickels. Then Mrs. Bickel went down to inspect the dining room where she was to entertain Mrs. Coolidge at dinner. Starling was there, frowning disapproval.

"There's a gold service on the table!" he exclaimed. "You can't have a gold service for the President's wife. It's undemocratic."

The gold service was removed.

The anniversary dinner was a success. Bickel sounded the keynote briefly: "Believing that nonexclusive collection and dissemination of news is the cornerstone of journalistic independence, seeking no special privileges and granting none, the United Press for twenty years has stood as a bulwark against every threat of news monopoly."

Mr. Coolidge delivered the principal speech. When he had finished, Starling touched Bickel on the shoulder. "I'll take over now," he said, as the President withdrew. Bickel sighed with relief, wiped the perspiration from his forehead, and sank back in his chair. Just then there was another touch on his shoulder and a uniformed waiter shoved a slip of paper in front of him.

"Sign here," he said severely.

Bickel signed. Then he did a second take.

"Just a moment," he exclaimed, reaching to recover the paper. "Let me see what this is!"

He recovered the paper and put on his spectacles. His name was boldly scrawled across a check that totaled $17,989.

CHAPTER SIXTEEN

The late 1920s in America were a zany, irresponsible era, but, strangely enough, an era in which the United Press gained strength and stature and maturity. The foundations for the agency's growth had been strongly built as a result of the management's aggressive search for wider and more varied horizons in the distribution of news. Howard had a sense of empire building, of spreading out, of crashing through barriers into unexplored territory. Hawkins was able to keep him from pushing too far too fast and to consolidate the gains that had been made. By the time Bickel became president, the ground had been prepared for a solid, growing organization that could hold the lead in what would inevitably be a long struggle for the free flow of news around the world.

Bickel had started his career as a reporter, and he had been strongly infected by Howard's sense of empire building, but he had spent more than a decade as a salesman and business representative under Hawkins' rigorous tutelage. He hadn't wanted to be a salesman, and at first he had been doubtful of his ability to sell. Riding around and around the Middle West in jolting, coal-dust-covered day coaches, he had collected and read dozens of books on "how to be a salesman." He had studied the needs of editors of large and small newspapers, and as he learned he also acquired enthusiasm. Once he knew the problems involved, his enthusiasm and his easy eloquence made him a highly effective business representative. The late 1920s were a time of tremendous growth and often reckless expansion, but Bickel emphasized both fiscal responsibility and integrity in the United Press.

Hugh Baillie had switched to the business office and had proved an able organizer. By the time he became business manager in 1926 he had coaxed so many newspapers away from the Associated Press that the older agency changed its rules to require editors to give two years' instead of six months' notice if they desired to relinquish their membership. Baillie was sometimes described as a "slugger" who kept up a steady assault on the opposition, and the United Press client list continued a steady growth, particularly in southern and far western states.

The United Press Red Letter mail service also was expanded in 1926 and sent to editors every other day, frequently carrying special features such as a full-page article by Queen Marie of Roumania, who had just completed a grand tour of the United States. The Saturday night wire, under direction of Dale Van Every, was expanded to double trunk in September of that year. Growing interest in Wall Street led to expansion of the financial department now headed by Elmer C. Walzer. All Morse telegraph transmission was replaced by high-speed teletype printers in the financial department by 1929, when stock-market sales were running to as much as 7,000,000 shares a day. Gradually, high-speed printers sending sixty words a minute were being installed on state and regional news circuits throughout the country, moving the wire report to clients faster and in greater volume.

Thus, in an era when Americans often seemed less responsible than ever before, when the Jazz Age was at its climax and Wall Street was the center of get-rich-quick hysteria, the United Press Associations were in a period of unusually solid and substantial growth that sharply lifted the agency's prestige throughout the world. Throughout the organization the emphasis was on responsibility and integrity. Yet the very nature of the times demanded, too, the exercise of initiative, speed, and imagination to keep ahead of the swift and often fantastic pace of world events.

2.

The most sensational criminal trial of the 1920s was that of Mrs. Ruth Snyder, a handsome, blond housewife, and Henry Judd Gray, a corset salesman, who, in 1927, murdered Mrs. Snyder's husband and tried to cover up the crime as the work of a burglar. Mrs. Snyder claimed the burglar tied her to a bed and killed her husband, a tale that was soon proved false. For many weeks the crime dominated headlines in American newspapers, and for many weeks a slight, prematurely gray reporter named Sam Love labored to put the story of a sordid love affair and murder into words that would explain the two criminals to newspaper readers. When the Snyder-Gray trial reached its climax, with both defendants desperately trying to put the blame on the other, the proceedings became a kind of Greek tragedy in modern dress and Love translated it with care:

BY SAM LOVE
United Press Staff Correspondent
NEW YORK, May 4—*Seven lines of spontaneous blank verse from the lips of Henry Judd Gray, telling of the murder of his mistress' husband, climaxed one of the most curious and dramatic days in the history of American murder trials.*

Tears streaming down his face, otherwise as expressionless as a ventrilo-

quist's dummy, the corset salesman told every detail of the murder of Albert Snyder and the burning love affair which preceded it.

Every detail seemed an additional strap binding dreadfully, but surely, his co-defendant, the blond Mrs. Ruth Brown Snyder, in the electric chair, where the state is determined she must die. Each was no less binding upon the small, crinkly-haired, bespectacled Gray.

But his story of his plight would have stirred laughter in an audience at a French farce and pity in the heart of a wooden Indian. At its completion —the murder done—the unsuspecting husband cold in death—the foolish plans for deceiving the police accomplished—the bloodstained garments of the conspirators consumed odoriferously in the furnace—Gray told of his leave-taking from the mistress who had brought his ruin.

Said he:

> *"I tied her feet and I tied her hands.*
> *I told her it might be two months—*
> *It might be a year—*
> *It might be never,*
> *Before she saw me again.*
> *I left her lying on her mother's bed*
> *And I went out."*

Gray spoke no more words on this day. He had spoken enough—far too many for his former mistress who was weeping, perhaps in terror, for she is no simpleton. Far too much even for his own palpitating lawyer, whose plump body was bathed in the perspiration of excitement.

3.

There was never anything to compare to the excitement aroused in the summer of 1927 by the so-called airplane "race" across the Atlantic Ocean between New York and Paris for a prize of $25,000 offered by Raymond Orteig. Lieutenant Commander Richard E. Byrd, fresh from North Pole triumphs, gathered a crew of skilled aviators to enter the race with the airplane *America*. Another entry was the *Columbia*, with Clarence Chamberlin as pilot. A third was the French team of Nungesser and Coli, who were off first in a great black plane that vanished somewhere over the ocean.

The *America* and the *Columbia* were at Roosevelt Field, on Long Island, making final preparations for the flight and awaiting a break in the weather in the middle of May. Then, flying alone from California, came a belated entry in the transocean "derby"—a tall, thin boy with tousled hair who was known to air-mail pilots as "Slim" Lindbergh. The arrival of Captain Charles A. Lindbergh in a little silver monoplane, *The Spirit of St. Louis,* was timely. Mechanical troubles and the weather had repeatedly delayed the *Columbia* and the *America,* and the public was beginning to wonder whether the planes would ever get started. But Lindbergh caught America's fancy. There was little fuss about his preparations. When, on the night of May 20, the weather reports indicated favorable conditions over the Atlantic, he went to Roosevelt Field, crawled into his single-motored plane, from which even a wireless transmitter had been eliminated to save weight, and took off shortly after dawn for Paris.

As he flew northeastward through a murky sky, carrying five sandwiches and a letter of introduction to the American Ambassador to France, his countrymen watched and waited in almost breathless suspense. There were brief reports of his progress over New England and then over Newfoundland as the silvery plane drifted across the horizon, dipped down between two hills, and headed out to sea.

There was nothing more as the hours rolled by. Darkness closed over the Atlantic and the suspense mounted. Morris DeHaven Tracy wrote the night wire story on a single, poignant theme—"Flying alone . . ." Flying alone, Slim Lindbergh was somewhere over the Atlantic Ocean with 120,000,000 Americans pulling for him to make it to Paris. Dawn brought no news, and it was midday before the welcome flash came via London that *The Spirit of St. Louis* had been sighted on the Irish coast.

As he flew on to the coast of France that afternoon, crowds began swarming to Paris' Le Bourget flying field. So did American correspondents. Nothing like this had ever happened before. Ralph Heinzen, of the United Press Paris bureau, foresaw trouble in the growing confusion. He arranged for use of a telephone in an office at one side of the field and stationed a staff member there to keep a line open to the bureau, awaiting positive identification of Lindbergh's plane. At dusk, *The Spirit of St. Louis* was not in sight. Searchlights were turned on. Crowds still filled the roads, streaming toward the field, when the little monoplane was finally caught in the glare of a searchlight. Swiftly, as if weary of flight, the plane turned and drifted down to the runway where the searchlights made positive identification possible. Heinzen passed the word to the correspondent at the telephone, who broke off his description of the scene on the field and said: "Flash—Lindbergh landed." In the Paris office Manager A. L. Bradford had held open a direct cable line to New York for the final minutes of the flight, and seconds later the flash was being transmitted.

In New York a telegraph operator rumbled the word "flash" and General News Manager Bob Bender repeated it in a shout that silenced every machine in the big news room.

FLASH PARIS LINDBERGH LANDS AT LE BOURGET

Hysteria gripped France as well as the United States. Except for the newspapermen covering a story. In the New York office, Cable Editor Lyle C. Wilson pounded out a bulletin and tossed it to Tracy for the late day wires. Night Editor Dale Van Every had a similar bulletin moving on the wires to morning newspapers. The flash on Lindbergh's safe landing was in every newspaper office on the United Press circuits within five minutes after his plane touched down at Le Bourget.

There were several thrilling transatlantic flights in the summer of 1927 and they provided a severe test for news-agency reporters. Each one was a headline story that the world followed with intense excitement. To be a few minutes ahead on the arrival of a plane in Europe was of utmost importance to the press association; to lag behind was a humiliating failure. The flight of Clarence Chamberlin and Charles Levine in the *Columbia* to Germany early in June was timed to arrive at Berlin early Monday morning. Throughout the United States, morning newspapers held their last editions for news of the *Columbia,* and it was late Sunday night in America when the Associated Press flashed the word that the plane had reached Berlin.

Many newspapers immediately went to press with a brief bulletin under eight-column banner lines announcing the arrival. Shortly afterward, however, the Associated Press killed the story. For the next couple of hours there was confusion. In all, the Associated Press carried three flashes or bulletins reporting the arrival of the *Columbia* and subsequently killed each of them. Meanwhile the United Press announced—correctly—that the *Columbia* had made a safe forced landing at Eisleben, in Saxony.

The following month when Commander Richard E. Byrd's monoplane *America* flew from New York to France, the Associated Press carried a bulletin from Paris on July 6 stating that the plane "landed at Issy-les-Moulineaux, near Paris, early this morning." Actually the *America* had made a forced landing in the surf near Ver-sur-Mer on the French coast, where a United Press provincial correspondent was first with the news of the safe but hazardous ending of the flight. Because of the tremendous public interest in these early aerial adventures, the steadiness and accuracy of United Press coverage was of very real importance to the agency's prestige.

4.

Such words as "flash" and "bulletin" were part of news-agency technique from the beginning of the United Press. They were originally intended as a means of speeding up transmission of important news over the wires. A desk man or a wire filer would sing out the word "flash" in a loud voice, thus giving the telegraphers notice that they were to break off whatever copy they were sending and be ready to send a news item of great importance. Then the desk man would dictate a brief "flash"—a few words in the form of a headline. A few moments later a "bulletin," which was the first paragraph of the important story, would be written and handed to the telegraphers for transmission on the wire. But these key words also developed another purpose over the years: to call the attention of editors and relay points to stories which the United Press regarded as of particular importance. In other words, the "flash" and "bulletin" slugs on stories became a kind of advertisement of something unusual and presumably worthy of being played up on page one.

This technique was often abused and overworked in the 1920s and early 1930s. But it was true that a "bulletin" slug brought dispatches to the attention of editors and frequently influenced their decision as to how to display the story.

"You sometimes have to hammer a story home to a busy, overworked newspaper editor," Bob Bender told his staff again and again. "If it's an unusual story—something they're not accustomed to handling—you may have to hammer it for several days. Some stories just don't catch on until the third day."

One morning in 1929 a long cable arrived in the New York office of the United Press from Thomas B. Morgan in Rome. It started with the word "authoritativest," which meant that, while it was not official, it came from an unquestionable but unnamed source. The story that Morgan wrote concerned an agreement between Papal Secretary of State Cardinal Gasparri and Italian Premier Benito Mussolini to settle the fifty-eight-year-old alienation of the Vatican and the state, and thus to end the self-imposed "imprisonment" of the Pope.

Cable Editor Louis F. Keemle recognized the significance of Morgan's report as he transcribed some 800 words of copy. There was no official statement, however, and Keemle decided not to put a "bulletin" slug on the story when it was passed along to the news desk. It was a busy morning, with important news breaking in Washington and elsewhere. The news desk cut the story slightly because of the crowded wires and passed it along to the wire editors. There was early action on the stock market that day, and the Wall Street story tumbled more and more words across the news desk. The wire editors were swamped with copy. After considerable delay, Morgan's story of the Vatican agreement managed to get on some wires, but in abbreviated form, and it was all but lost in the rush.

It wasn't lost in South America, however. Newspapers throughout that continent and elsewhere played it up under black headlines, a United Press exclusive that was of great interest in every Latin city. The next day the Rome correspondents of other news agencies began receiving urgent messages of complaint—known as "callbacks" or, later, as "rockets"—from clients in South America, demanding information on the concordat to be signed by Mussolini and Cardinal Gasparri. They started digging furiously for the story but Morgan had it so neatly tied up that it was not until several days later that they were able to confirm the facts. When these facts were cabled to New York the Associated Press promptly carried on its wires a comprehensive story and, within a short time, messages from United Press newspapers began buzzing over the wires, demanding coverage on the big story breaking from Rome.

"But we carried the story four days ago!" Keemle exclaimed. The news editor checked and found the original story, but when he looked further to see how much of it actually got on the wires he found nothing or only a paragraph buried among the day's fast-breaking news stories. In one way or another everybody except Morgan had muffed the ball. In disgust Keemle dug out a copy of the original story, changed the date line, and handed it over to be filed ahead of everything else on the wires. What should have been a major scoop for the United Press had fizzled out as a dud.

One of the customs of the Senate in the late 1920s was the "executive session" for approval of presidential nominations of persons to fill federal offices. This meant that the Senate frequently ordered all spectators and reporters to leave the chamber late in the afternoon while nominations were considered in secret. Usually this was of no importance to reporters because there was no controversy over the appointments. But occasionally it led to bitter complaints because, if there was a controversial nominee for a federal job, the senators could avoid putting their votes on the record by going into executive session.

Paul R. Mallon, chief of the United Press Senate staff, didn't take such secrecy complacently. In the United Press tradition, he and his assistant, Kenneth Crawford, began digging out the facts on how each senator voted on important executive session roll calls. This was not too difficult for a man who knew the Senate as Mallon did, and at first the reaction of the senators was not particularly strong. But after several "secret" roll-call votes had been published in full by the United Press the legislators began to be concerned about preservation of their device for keeping votes secret. And when President Hoover's controversial nomination of Senator Irvine L. Lenroot of Wisconsin to be a federal judge came before the Senate, extreme precautions were taken to assure that the vote would not be disclosed—particularly since a number of senators feared their stand on Lenroot would be used against them in the 1930 election campaign.

But the next day Mallon again came up with a complete record of the roll call, showing that some senators had talked one way and voted another way. The cries of outrage from many distinguished legislators echoed sadly through the august chamber that afternoon. The traditions of the Senate had been flaunted. There were traitorous elements at large in the chamber. An investigation was ordered to bare the details of the betrayal, and Mallon was subpoenaed as a witness. It seemed likely that a member of the Senate, tired of seeing his colleagues evade their responsibility of voting publicly, had assisted the reporter by tabulating the roll calls, but Mallon never revealed the source of his information.

The United Press and most of the Washington press corps strongly backed Mallon's stand, and the only revenge that the Senate could think of was to cancel a long-standing arrangement under which one reporter from each of the three press associations had been permitted to go on the floor of the Senate when it was in regular session. Mallon had been the United Press correspondent with that privilege. But the press associations bore up bravely under this punishment, especially when newspapers and some senators expressed such indignation that the whole system of executive sessions was abolished and thereafter the votes of senators on nominees were publicly recorded—thanks to the endeavors of a United Press reporter.

5.

The most sensational news of 1929 for the United Press as well as everybody else originated in the financial department, which usually had been relegated to the back pages of newspapers. Not many years before, the agency might have been hard put to cover the news from Wall Street. Some market quotations had always been carried on the news wire, but they were regarded as necessary evils until 1922, when Karl Bickel decided that financial and business news deserved better treatment. He was encouraged in this decision by William H. Grimes, a desk man who had had so much trouble getting the markets filed on the news wire that he suggested establishment of a separate financial wire. Bickel agreed and appointed Grimes as the first financial editor.

The new wire, established on April 17, 1922, carried a daily stock-market story that was telephoned from Dow, Jones & Co., publishers of the *Wall Street Journal*. It carried the grain markets, the livestock markets, and stock quotations. It carried business stories and information from brokerage letters. It also carried horse-racing results. After Grimes left the organization in 1923 it was run in haphazard fashion until, one day in March of 1925, there came an afternoon when there wasn't anybody in the New York office who knew how to prepare the stock list for filing. Bureau Manager Morris DeHaven Tracy was vainly trying to decipher the stock-exchange symbols when one of his wire filers, Elmer C. Walzer, volunteered to help.

"Do you know what these abbreviations mean?" Tracy asked him.

"I know them all," Walzer answered.

"Sit down right here and get going," Tracy ordered.

Walzer took over and made a career of it. Not long afterward he developed the first news-agency compilation of stock tables and began to develop his own market and business stories. Eventually the department compiled all New York and Chicago markets and acquired a staff of seventeen tabulators and twelve writers, who provided quotations and business articles for a full-time double-trunk circuit carrying market news to all parts of the nation.

The financial department was hard pressed, nevertheless, to keep up with the great bull market of 1929. Walzer's financial stories were front-page news almost every day as the market soared to record heights and then collapsed. On Black Thursday, October 24, almost 13,000,000 shares changed hands. By the time Walzer's staff had cleaned up the story late that night the Wall Street boom was over.

CHAPTER SEVENTEEN

The strength and resiliency of the United Press were demonstrated during the economic depression that followed the Wall Street crash. By 1930 the agency had 1317 client newspapers—a gain of 220 over 1929—of which 1000 were in the United States and the remainder in 44 other countries. The actual number of newspapers in the United States had been decreasing for some years due to mergers or failures. But United Press leased-wire circuits, three quarters of which were for teleprinters, had gradually expanded to 140,000 miles in North America.

Perhaps even more significant than the agency's world-wide growth in this period was the fact that the United Press made more and more progress in getting its news report into the pages of the largest and most important newspapers in the country. "In the history of the Associated Press the year 1929 will surely rank with 1914 as one of the darkest of all," wrote Oswald Garrison Villard in *The Nation*, referring back to United Press reportorial successes at the start of World War I. "For it was during this period [1929] that a dreadful blow descended. Incredible as it seems, the New York *Herald Tribune* and the Chicago *Daily News* subscribed to the news service of the United Press. If Mr. Hoover were to hoist the red flag on the White House some morning and Secretary Mellon were to denounce the right to hold private property, the Associated Press would surely not be more startled."

Such solid gains obviously were of great psychological as well as financial importance to the news agency at the end of the razzle-dazzle 1920s. And, instead of drastically pulling in its horns as the economic depression deepened in the 1930s, the United Press continued a solid expansion of both news-gathering and news-distributing services and, after some fumbling, opened up a vast new communications field by service to radio stations. There were, of course, concessions to the downward economic trend, particularly in the early 1930s. The revenue of many client newspapers dropped sharply, and there were constant requests from publishers for a reduction of news-agency rates. The company made sizable reductions in business sales travel, bureau, and correspondents' tolls, and other flexible expenses in America and abroad. New men were hired at prevailing wage rates, which were low. Some leased wires were consolidated and cable budgets were curtailed where possible. There was one ten per cent cut in all salaries. But, speaking broadly, the agency proved structurally able and willing to buck the economic tide, and its personnel generally felt the effect of troubled times less severely perhaps than most comparable business corporations.

Nor was the strength of the organization demonstrated merely in its financial position. The 1930s brought a far keener realization in American newspaper offices of the need for thorough and thoughtful reporting of the news of the day. This challenge was one that Bickel was quick to foresee and one for which he was well prepared. His attitude was indicated in a letter he wrote to Bob Bender in 1930 after reading the previously mentioned article by Oswald Garrison Villard, who had made a study of American news agencies. Villard was critical of many of the practices of the United Press, expressed belief that the agency's stories were directed too much toward the poorly educated masses, deplored overemphasis on sports and human-interest dispatches, and indicated various weaknesses in news coverage.

The critical review [by Villard] *cannot but be exceedingly interesting and extremely valuable and important to us* [Bickel's letter said]. *The United Press . . . has literally grown on the constructive and sometimes bitter and excoriating criticism of its "friends." I say friends, for while often enough the men offering criticism were doing it in far from a friendly spirit, the fact they were doing it and the fact that the organization was intelligent enough to appreciate the value of the comment and discount the bitterness in which it was delivered made all of these critics really our best friends.*

Much has happened in the internal organization of the United Press in the last four or five years—much that you have been so responsible for— and it is very difficult to get a really up-to-date and sound criticism of our present-day news service.

Villard . . . tried to get honest, independent critical comment. What he secured was fair and honest enough but it was from five to eight years old . . . Except for the airplane, I can think of nothing that has changed so fundamentally and so definitely in the last five years as the product of the news department of the United Press—and of the Associated Press, for that matter.

Today we know it is the spirit and aim of the United Press to produce the "quality" news report of the world. We know that in 1925 we were— to a degree we did not then appreciate—still under the curse of the "milkman in Omaha" theory and the bad, and I hope forever outworn, idea that news—important and significant news—had to be "written down" and popularized to "get over." . . . [But] we have not today anywhere nearly acquired the unvarying standard of quality production that . . . we must

*acquire to secure dominance in leadership in the American field. . . . That
is ours to have if we only demonstrate that we have the brains and capacity
and the understanding to move in and fill it.*

*We have not "sold" ourselves to the news observer or to the discriminat-
ing news consumer as yet as always [being] the producer of the best copy
on the most important and significant news stories of the day. The element
of "thoughtful preparation"; of a broader, more certain and more accurate
grasp of complicated foreign and domestic stories . . . is not always consistently evident. We must attain that consistency and regularity to deserve
leadership. . . . There is no question that there is an exceedingly lot more
of that element in our report today than there was five years ago, and nothing . . . is more to your credit than the big job you have done in raising
our basic editorial standards, and your steady fight against the flip, the spe-
cious, and the cheap.*

*That doesn't mean I feel we must enter into a ponderous regime of sol-
emn journalism. But it does mean that the dumb editor—even if in a majority and even if stridently vocal—is not going to set the standards of the
United Press—never again, I hope. We must never be stuffy; we need never
be dull; we must always be intelligent, and we always can, I trust, be smart.
With honesty, which I take for granted, these are the essentials. . . .*

Early one morning in May of 1930 a buzzing telephone got Webb Miller
out of bed in his London apartment. It was, as he had expected, the overnight man in the London bureau.

"Message from New York," he said. "Thought you'd want to know about
it. They want you to go to India by the first available airplane to cover
the Gandhi salt march. The next Imperial Airways plane leaves tomorrow
morning."

Miller was accustomed to such messages and to moving about the world
on short notice. When there was trouble brewing he was likely to get a hurry
call to action, and in May there was plenty of trouble brewing in India.
Mahatma Gandhi, a 104-pound Hindu lawyer, had become the leader of
India's campaign for self-government by nonviolent resistance. His basic
idea was that a campaign of civil disobedience could so complicate and
hamper the mechanics of government for the British that they would eventually give up and submit to the demands of the rebellious Indian masses,
and he was fundamentally correct.

As a major avenue of attack Gandhi declared that the tax on salt, which
affected every one of the nation's 350,000,000 population, was unfair and
iniquitous and should be abolished because the millions of poor required
just as much salt to live as did the prosperous few. He led a party that
marched to the coast to make salt from sea water illegally as a gesture of
rebellion, and it was this demonstration that prompted Miller's orders to
fly to India. Miller arrived in India too late to see Gandhi, who had been

arrested on his salt march to the sea and was held incommunicado in jail. But a Gandhi sympathizer told him that the biggest demonstration of the civil resistance movement would be held soon at Dharasana, about 150 miles north of Bombay, under direction of Sarojini Naidu, a famous Indian poetess. There was a train to Dungri, but no regular transportation over the remaining half dozen miles to Dharasana. Miller sent a telegram to Madame Naidu asking if she could have somebody meet him at Dungri.

British officials made a great point at that time of the fact that there was no official censorship of news from India. But Miller immediately began to encounter a kind of indirect censorship that was far more insidious because the reporter never knew just what steps were being taken to interfere with news coverage. British officials, for example, confiscated Miller's message to Madame Naidu. Then, while he was en route to Dungri, they ordered the train crew to eliminate that town from its scheduled stop. As a result, Miller was put off at a small town called Bulsar, despite his protests that he had been sold a ticket to Dungri, with little hope of reaching the scene of the demonstration in time. He managed, however, to make friends with the stationmaster, who persuaded the crew of a freight train to carry him on to Dungri. There was, of course, no one to meet him, and he had to walk six miles across country under a broiling sun to the assembly place of several thousand Gandhi followers.

When he arrived the demonstration—a raid on local salt pans—was ready to start. Madame Naidu demanded that the demonstrators avoid all violence, that they should not even raise their hands to ward off possible attacks by police. Then at a signal the throng started walking slowly toward a barbed-wire barricade that surrounded the salt pans. They were accompanied by a score of stretcher-bearers. Four hundred Surat police, carrying five-foot-long clubs tipped with steel, and half a dozen British officials surrounded the salt pans.

A hundred yards from the stockade the main body of marchers stopped but a picked column continued to advance, waded several ditches, and walked toward the police line, ignoring an order to disperse. As the column reached the stockade, scores of police ran at them, striking out with their clubs. Not one of the marchers raised a finger to defend himself, and soon the ground was covered with the injured. After all of them had been knocked to the ground the stretcher-bearers carried off those most seriously hurt. But at the same time another column had formed and advanced, heads up but silent, toward the salt pans. They met the same fate. There was no fighting. The police simply knocked them down, breaking their heads and inflicting other injuries that frequently covered the victims with blood. Later Miller counted 320 injured in a temporary hospital erected by the demonstrators, but found only two dead. He was talking to Madame Naidu when a British official approached, touched her on the arm, and said: "You are under arrest."

"Don't touch me!" she exclaimed haughtily, shaking off his hand. "I'll come with you."

The throng cheered loudly as she was taken to the barbed-wire stockade. Gandhi's son, Manilal, also was arrested.

Miller was the only foreign correspondent to witness the demonstration —a classic example of "satyagraha" or nonviolent civil disobedience. But the amazing story that he had gathered was worthless until he could get it transmitted to London and New York. He found a Gandhi follower with a ramshackle automobile to drive him to Bulsar. There he wrote five telegrams of about 100 words each and filed them with the telegraph operator at the railroad. They would be slow, but he knew that sometimes telegrams from a small town would be transmitted directly to the cable office in Bombay and, with luck, might not be noticed by British officials there. On the train he wrote another 2000 words which he filed as soon as he reached Bombay.

A few hours later a messenger brought him a crumpled piece of paper on which was written in pencil: "Mr. Miller, the messages you deposited about Dharasana have not been telegraphed." Presumably the unsigned note came from a Gandhi sympathizer in the cable office. Miller went to the office and asked why his messages had not been transmitted to London. Officials there would not admit that his dispatches were being delayed. At government headquarters of the Bombay presidency, where he went to protest, Miller was passed from one official to another in a traditional delaying maneuver. At last he talked to the Secretary for Ecclesiastical Affairs, who acknowledged that he had been appointed to act as censor and that the messages had been held up.

"Very well," Miller said, "I'm flying to Persia tomorrow and I will file the whole story from there, including a complete story on the stupidity of British censorship."

After further argument the censor agreed to approve the dispatches but made several eliminations regarding the police action. The story was started on its way to London. Meantime, it turned out that three of the five telegrams Miller had sent from Bulsar had slipped through the censorship, as he had hoped, and were already in London and New York. After they had been delivered the London cable office called the United Press and said that the government of India had issued orders for the messages to be canceled because they had been "transmitted by error." The order naturally was ignored.

Gandhi was a figure of intense interest in the United States at the time, and Miller's vivid story of the Dharasana demonstration was little short of sensational in American newspapers. It was read into the *Congressional Record* the next day and later reprinted in several hundred thousand leaflets distributed by representatives of the Gandhi movement in the United States.

2.

Young reporters sometimes get a rough initiation in the news-agency business. At New Haven in the summer of 1930 Manager Boyd Lewis sent a bustling recruit, Ernest Barcella, to check on a telephoned report that "a maniac is throwing people off West Rock"—a high precipice near the Connecticut city. Barcella leaped into a taxicab and raced to the base of West Rock. As he ran up a footpath toward the cliff top he came on the bodies of a small girl and a boy and then the body of a woman. The reporter ran back to a nearby drugstore and telephoned his office, but his story was incomplete.

"Who are they, Ernie?" Lewis demanded. "Get their names. You've only got part of the story."

Barcella ran to the cliff top. Firemen and police were already there, but they knew only that a man had brought his wife and four children to the scene for a picnic and then, in maniacal fashion, thrown them over the 400-foot-high precipice. All were dead except the man, who had jumped or fallen from the cliff but had been caught in a thick, scrubby tree growing out of the face of the rock, about forty feet from the top. A fireman tied an inch-thick rope around his waist, and his comrades lowered him down the face of the cliff until he was close to the maniac.

"Don't come any nearer or I'll jump," the man shouted at the fireman. "Stay away."

From the cliff top Barcella urged the fireman to find out who the man was, but with no success. The maniac merely mumbled wildly. Finally Barcella crawled to the edge of the precipice, grabbed the taut rope, and slid down until he was a few feet above the fireman.

"Who are you?" he shouted at the man. "Where do you come from?"

For a few minutes there were only mumbled replies, but at last the man gave his name.

Perched perilously almost 400 feet above the rocks below the cliff, Barcella sweated and asked another question: "Who are those people down below?"

The man muttered that they were his wife and children and then began raving incoherently. Barcella painfully pulled himself back up the rope to the cliff top and ran down the footpath to the telephone. His trembling fingers pushed a nickel into the telephone box. He called the office and spelled out the name of the tragic family.

"Okay," Lewis snapped. "Now get the rest of it."

Barcella hung up the telephone receiver and ran. Just as he reached the footpath once more there was a wild scream from the top of West Rock and, an instant later, the body of the maniac was impaled on jagged rocks less than twenty feet in front of the exhausted reporter. Barcella had the final fact.

He trudged back to the telephone. By risking his life dangling from a cliff top, by running his lungs out, and by witnessing a shocking tragedy, Barcella had made it possible for the United Press to be ahead of everybody else with a dispatch that would appear in newspapers across the country that afternoon—and would be forgotten tomorrow.

3.

The Spanish elections on April 12, 1931, resulted in a big majority for the Republicans and touched off demonstrations in Madrid and other cities against King Alfonso. Manager Jean DeGandt and his staff in Madrid had prepared well for such a political crisis and were in close touch not only with members of the monarch's household but with leaders of the Republican movement. On the morning of April 14, Alfonso's advisors told him that his retirement was becoming inevitable. The King himself acknowledged this fact to his staff but decided to seek some kind of delay. A high government official passed this decision along to a United Press correspondent a few minutes later, and half a dozen staff members, including Emilio Herrera and Pedro La Grava, fanned out to strategic points to cover the story.

At noon the King's representative, Count Romanones, called on Republican leader Niceto Alcalá Zamora. A United Press reporter followed in his wake. Romanones proposed a "truce" to last until a constitutional convention could be held to decide on the future of the nation. Alcalá Zamora refused and said that, in view of the mass demonstrations, it was impossible to guarantee the safety of the King if he remained in Madrid for another day. By the time Romanones was able to return to Alfonso these developments had been reported exclusively by urgent cable and telephone to the United Press bureaus in New York and Buenos Aires.

A rather remarkable situation had now arisen. The people of Madrid had no information as to developments in the crisis, but readers of United Press newspapers in New York, Buenos Aires, and other cities around the world were getting a play-by-play account and were aware that at any moment Alfonso must decide whether to go peacefully into exile or to attempt to rally the pro-monarchist Civil Guard for a fight. While Madrid demonstrators roamed happily through the streets, many other capitals were waiting anxiously for the climax.

The tip-off came when a Republican flag was raised over the Madrid post office. Republican flags had been raised occasionally in the city but they had always been promptly torn down by the Civil Guards. When a reporter telephoned the news that another flag was flying over the post office, William H. Lander was on the news desk. Lander had made a careful study of the Civil Guard in relation to the monarchy and he had only one question: "What is the Civil Guard doing about it?"

"Nothing," was the reply. "The flag is still flying."

"Then that means it's all over," Lander exclaimed, reaching for another

telephone to put in an urgent call to London. He dictated to the London
bureau a report on the flag and added that the failure of the Civil Guard
to remove it meant that the last vestige of armed support for the monarchy
had vanished.

Shortly afterward Count Romanones informed a United Press reporter at
the palace that he had advised the King to leave at once. Alfonso summoned
an emergency cabinet meeting for midafternoon, and at the same hour the
United Press carried a story that he would announce, not his abdication, but
his retirement as soon as the Cabinet could be assembled. DeGandt set up
an open telephone line to the United Press bureau in London and another
to the United Press bureau in Buenos Aires. So great was the interest of
South American newspapers that—despite prohibitive tolls at that time—the
Buenos Aires telephone connection was held open for seven hours until it
was made official that the King, while not signing a formal abdication, would
leave Spain.

The Madrid bureau and a dozen provincial correspondents followed every step of the departing monarch as he climbed into his powerful racing
car and drove at high speed to a Mediterranean port, where he boarded a
warship for France. At Marseilles the local United Press correspondent
boarded the train with him for the journey to Paris. The Queen meanwhile
had left Madrid for Hendaye, on the French border. There she was met by
a single newspaperman, Stewart Brown, of the United Press Paris bureau,
who rode with her far enough to secure an exclusive interview and then
dropped off to telephone his story to Paris. At Paris, Richard D. McMillan
succeeded in evading a cordon of police to greet the Queen as she stepped
from the train, and she walked to a waiting automobile with Jean Chiappe,
the prefect of Paris police, on one side, and McMillan on the other.

4.

In the spring of 1931 the economic depression in the United States was
deepening. There were long lines of unemployed in search of jobs. Others
were selling apples on the street corners. Wall Street was like a city of the
dead. On April 27 the United Press headquarters was moved from the old
New York *World* building in downtown New York to the newly constructed
Daily News building in mid-town Manhattan.

It was not easy to move so complicated a telegraphic establishment without interruption of service to newspapers, and preparations had been started
six weeks in advance under the direction of William F. Lynch, superintendent of telegraph, and his assistant, H. M. Schultz. Harry Breuer and James
Morris of the maintenance department were in direct charge of the transfer
of 164 leased-wire loops as well as the wires of Western Union, Postal Telegraph Co., A.T.&T., Commercial Cables, Radio Corporation of America,
and All America Cables.

"The vital part of the move was accomplished on the morning of Sunday, when the news room was switched over without a moment's service being lost," reported *The Hellbox*. "Complete equipment had been set up at the new uptown location, news and telegraph staffs were on duty at both places, and when all was ready the switch was made without interruption. Other departments were moved later in the week as the finishing and fitting of the offices was completed . . . The new quarters give the United Press the most modern and complete press association plant it was possible to devise."

The entire twelfth floor of the *News* building was occupied by the United Press, with business offices and the Special Service Bureau, headed by Tom W. Gerber, on the eleventh floor. It seemed as if there was plenty of room for expansion at the time, but within a few years the offices would overflow the entire eleventh, twelfth, and thirteenth floors. Just before the move to the *News* building, President Bickel announced the election of Hugh Baillie as executive vice-president of the United Press. Clem J. Randau became general business manager.

CHAPTER EIGHTEEN

One of the most difficult scenes of the United Press drive to establish a free flow of news around the world was the Far East in the 1920s, a period in which Generalissimo Chiang Kai-shek was struggling to unify China and in which the Japanese were eager to expand their influence in the Orient. When Chiang began his campaign there was comparatively little news from China reaching the average newspaper in America and even less from the United States was disseminated to Oriental newspapers. This was partly due to lack of public interest, but an important factor also was the great expense of cable dispatches from faraway countries.

Cable rates on ordinary press dispatches were as much as twenty-five cents a word from China and thirty-nine cents a word from Japan to New York or San Francisco. Karl Bickel, with the active aid of General James G. Harbord, president of Radio Corporation of America, campaigned earnestly for reduction of these rates to further the flow of news, particularly to and from Japan, but it was not until 1927 that the Japanese Ministry of Communications agreed to cut the press rate in half, and it was only in 1929 that the rate was further reduced to ten cents a word.

In this period the European cartel agencies such as Reuters had almost a clear field in the Far East because of government subsidies or special rates over government cable routes. But after Miles Vaughn became Far Eastern manager and Demaree Bess was made a full-time correspondent at Peking, a couple of incidents gave the United Press a boost. At that time, service to Chinese newspapers was based on a cable budget of skeletonized news reports that could be expanded into brief dispatches, but it was a meager report as compared to Reuters. Then one day Bess met an American telegrapher who, happily, suffered from severe insomnia.

"I can't get to sleep at night," the telegrapher remarked, "so I stay up until all hours fooling with my wireless set. I can pick up wireless stuff from all over this part of the world late at night when atmospheric conditions are good. I listen to a lot of United Press news being sent to Manila or to navy stations in the Pacific."

Bess had an inspiration. "How would you like to copy down the United Press dispatches you can pick up and turn them over to me?" he asked. "I'd be glad to pay you for your trouble."

"Sure," the telegrapher agreed. "That'll give me something to do when I can't sleep."

Thereafter Bess received from the telegrapher every morning a long roll of copy paper on which had been transcribed United Press dispatches being transmitted by wireless. With this additional material Bess was able to blossom out suddenly with a handsome news report for United Press newspapers in China—often more voluminous even than the Reuters report.

For weeks the Reuters representative in Peking tried to find out the secret of the improvement in United Press dispatches. He convinced himself that the news was not coming in by cable or through the local wireless office, but he never did find out about Bess's telegrapher who suffered from insomnia.

Another factor that boosted the United Press prestige in China in 1928 was a long-standing friendship between Bess's wife, Dorothy, also a United Press correspondent, and Madame Chiang Kai-shek. When Generalissimo and Madame Chiang Kai-shek first arrived in Peking after the conquest of North China, they invited Demaree and Dorothy Bess to dinner at the city's most fashionable restaurant even before the general had received members of the diplomatic corps. As a result the United Press correspondent was well acquainted with members of the generalissimo's entourage, and it was no surprise when a telephone call from W. H. Donald, an Australian who was advisor to Chiang Kai-shek, roused Bess from bed before dawn on the morning of September 18, 1931.

"The Japanese are seizing Mukden," Donald exclaimed, "and I wanted to tell you that we are appealing to the League of Nations."

Bess was suddenly wide awake. "Who is 'we'?" he asked. "Are you speaking for the government at Nanking?"

"No, but I assure you we are appealing to the League. Be sure and make that clear in your story."

Bess didn't have the story at that point, but he knew that Donald was fully trusted by Chiang Kai-shek and he quickly set about rounding up details of what had happened. What had happened was that the Japanese had seized strategic points around Mukden, the capital of Manchuria, and then occupied the city as the Chinese troops of Marshal Chang Hsueh-liang retreated in the general direction of Peking.

After filing such news as was available in Peking, Bess sent Martin Sommers, a New York newspaperman living temporarily in Peking, to Mukden for the United Press, enabling Bess to remain at Chinese headquarters. Sommers and several other correspondents traveled on a special train that took three days to make the customary twenty-four-hour run to Mukden because the railroad was jammed with troop and refugee trains. In the Manchurian capital the military passes issued by Japanese army headquarters at the Yamato Hotel were virtually worthless because soldiers on sentry duty couldn't read them. Japanese soldiers were still shooting stragglers and threatening occasionally to shoot a newspaper correspondent. There was only fragmentary information available about the fighting front which in fact appeared to have disintegrated.

After the first day or so, the Mukden "incident" had lost its importance in the opinion of most United States editors, and the New York bureau advised Vaughn that Peking and Tokyo were filing too much wordage on the story. Vaughn acknowledged the instructions, explaining that the staff had filed heavily because it appeared that the story would only last a few days and they wanted to make the most of it while it was news.

As events demonstrated, the story that began in Mukden would last longer than a few days. Japan had started the first of a series of undeclared wars that would shake almost every nation on earth and end only in the holocaust of World War II.

2.

Bickel had been in Europe when the Mukden incident began, but when he arrived back in New York it was obvious that the Japanese were out to seize all of Manchuria and that they were warning Soviet Russia to offer no interference. So far as news dispatches indicated, the Russians were not going to interfere. All was quiet in Siberia.

Bickel, however, was not satisfied. He believed there would be trouble between Japan and Russia. He talked with a number of friends who were in a position to guess what Moscow had in mind and then, one evening, strode across the news room in New York waving a cable message that he wanted sent to Berlin without delay. It directed Frederick Kuh, in Berlin, to proceed as quickly as possible to Moscow and thence on the Trans-Siberian Railroad to the Manchurian frontier. Bickel offered no explanation for these instructions, which caused considerable perplexity among the staff.

Kuh paused in Moscow only long enough to buy a fur cap and then was off on the week-long railroad trip across Siberia, where, so far as could be foreseen, there was nothing to report except the price of reindeer meat. But by the time he arrived on the Manchurian frontier there was news aplenty. A character named General Ma Chan-shan had suddenly captured the attention of newspapers everywhere by putting up a battle against the Japanese seizure of Manchuria and, at the moment, had some 13,000 troops entrenched near the railroad which ran from Harbin to the Soviet frontier—the road on which Kuh traveled into Manchuria. The railroad service was only temporarily interrupted by General Ma's hit-and-run guerrilla tactics, and Kuh was able to continue to Harbin with the first front-line reports.

Then he made his way by train and automobile to Tsitsihar, where the Chinese general had established his headquarters in a little stucco house that was well hidden in a heavily wooded area. It was a desolate and primitive countryside, but General Ma welcomed Kuh and Reginald Sweetland of the Chicago *Daily News,* the only reporter who had reached Harbin from the south, with considerable formality. He served champagne and talked boldly of resistance to the Japanese conquest.

Kuh filed his story of the interview from Anangchi to Harbin and London via the Great Northern telegraph lines, but when he arrived in Harbin later he discovered that the local censor, a collaborator with the Japanese, had rewritten the dispatch to give it a distinctly pro-Japanese flavor. The correspondent was able to get the dispatch "killed" and to make a secret arrangement with Russian officials of the Chinese Eastern Railroad to send uncensored dispatches over their wires to Vladivostok and London. Thereafter he covered the Japanese struggle against General Ma without benefit of censorship. Bickel's original hunch that there would be trouble on the frontier between Japan and Russia vanished in the smoke of a guerrilla war, but Kuh's dispatches kept the world informed of the Chinese resistance until the Japanese brought up heavy reinforcements and scattered General Ma's little army.

The Japanese attack on Shanghai in 1932 was started in January. With little regard for treaties, the Japanese landed marines from their warships in the Whangpoo River, took over the predominantly Japanese Hongkew sector of the International Settlement, and began shelling Chinese troops that resisted in the native part of the city. H. R. Ekins, United Press manager at Shanghai, lived in the French concession about a mile from the battlefront. The war was plainly audible but there were no official communiqués and no way of getting information except to walk to the scene of action. Ekins walked to a point near a racecourse held by the Chinese. It was reasonably safe in Hongkew in daylight because the Japanese were in control and the Chinese mortar fire usually fell far short of its target. Ekins was dressed for the occasion in a fedora hat and a black ulster, and carried a gold-headed walking stick. The Japanese paid no attention to him as he watched them firing howitzers at the racecourse. He walked on to where an infantry company was stationed. Everything was quiet. He kept on walking until suddenly there was a rifle firing in front of him—and then behind him. Without realizing what had happened, Ekins found himself between the Chinese and Japanese troops, crawling on his belly in a deep ditch and wishing it were deeper. He huddled in a culvert until the shooting died down, then saw a group of Chinese soldiers entrenched nearby.

"Mei kuo hsin wan ch'i cha," he yelled, meaning—he hoped—that he was an American newspaperman. He got up and started toward the soldiers. They shot at him but not very seriously and later assured him there was nothing personal about their shooting—they just didn't like to see anybody

coming from the direction of the Japanese lines. One of the soldiers took him to headquarters where a Chinese general served tea. He collected a few bits of information there and took a roundabout way back to the United Press office in the International Settlement, still carrying his gold-headed walking stick. It was an odd war in which a reporter could crawl down a ditch from one front line to the other, but it was none the less serious. The Chinese fought off the Japanese marines so bitterly that the Japanese Army finally had to be moved in for a major assault behind a heavy bombardment. The native city burned for many days.

This was merely the start of the long Japanese conflict in China. There were recurrent periods of fighting, there were months of stalemate, there were truces. The scene of fighting changed and the United Press personnel in the Far East changed, but the conflict went on. By 1933 John R. Morris, who had joined the United Press in Washington and later been manager in Mexico City, was Far Eastern manager, Vaughn having returned to New York. Harold O. Thompson, recently of the Washington bureau, became Tokyo manager in 1936. The following summer Thompson accompanied Japanese forces when they began an all-out campaign against China in the north, where Peiping (formerly Peking) was seized early in August of 1937.

War tension immediately enveloped Shanghai. Chinese regular troops entered the city. Thirty-two Japanese warships concentrated in the port, disembarking heavy military reinforcements for the Japanese settlement. There were minor clashes and a growing threat of major military action.

A few days later—August 13—Robert Bellaire finished a long trick at the United Press bureau on the ground floor of the Cathay Hotel and went directly to his room on the sixth floor of the hotel. He had just climbed into bed when Japanese warships in the Whangpoo River close to the hotel began a heavy antiaircraft barrage. Bellaire jumped to the window. Three Chinese planes were overhead and bombs were already falling—aimed at the Japanese flagship *Idzumo,* but obviously more likely to hit the Cathay Hotel. He ran into the corridor and crouched against the wall. There was a tremendous explosion as one bomb hit near the Cathay and another struck the Palace Hotel across the street. Windows shattered into a million slivers of glass and debris from the Palace Hotel landed on the bed Bellaire had just vacated, cutting it to shreds.

Morris and Bud Ekins were in the Palace Hotel, grabbing a late lunch after a busy day. The blast shattered windows and jammed doors in the restaurant, but they were able to climb through a window into Nanking Road, which was crowded with frightened and wounded civilians and a number of dead. Weldon James, a new staff member, and Paul Feng, an experienced member of the bureau, had been looking from the windows of a nearby office building which was badly damaged by a bomb. Still another staff member, John Goodbody, was near the Cathay Hotel.

Morris, Ekins, Bellaire (still in pajamas), James, Feng, and Goodbody converged on the United Press bureau on the run, but Robert T. Berkov, who had been on duty, already had filed a flash and several bulletins by wireless to the United States. It is not likely that so many United Press reporters ever before or afterward were literally caught in the middle of a big, quick-breaking story. Even as they were filing the story of what they had seen from their scattered vantage points, another bomb from a crippled Chinese plane fell on a crowded square a few blocks away. James, who had been rushing from one trouble spot to another since dawn, dashed to the scene of the explosion in the French concession. Approximately a thousand persons, including several Americans, had been killed, and the final death toll on Shanghai's "Bloody Saturday" was placed at around 1600.

The United Press staff worked without a break that night, except for thirty minutes when two smartly dressed officers from the Shanghai Volunteer Corps, an organization of foreign residents who had the city under virtual martial law, arrived at the bureau. There had been a telephoned message from the seat of government at Nanking, they said, indicating that eighty planes of the Chinese Air Force would resume attack on the Japanese warships at dawn. It had been decided to evacuate everyone from the Cathay Hotel and adjacent buildings, the officers announced, and that included the United Press staff.

"If we leave here we will have no communications," Morris replied. "This office is going to remain open."

"We have our orders," one of the officers said, "and we'll move you out by force if necessary."

There followed a hot argument, a bit of table pounding, and a number of telephone calls to higher authorities. In the end the United Press staff remained in the bureau and the cable and radio staff continued to operate in their office a few doors down the hall—on the understanding that the Shanghai authorities were not to be blamed for the consequences. Early in the morning, bombers were heard above Shanghai but no explosives were dropped. Just at dawn Generalissimo Chiang Kai-shek announced that the Japanese would be fought to the bitter end, but he ordered his air force to discontinue flying over the foreign settlements in Shanghai. A few hours later the story of "Bloody Saturday" had been wrapped up. Almost 50,000 words of copy had been filed by the Shanghai staff on the story, which won the annual award of the National Headliners Club for 1937.

During the following period of active warfare in which the Japanese extended their power in China, the United Press enlarged its services throughout the Far East. New bureaus were opened at Hankow and Canton. Staffs were enlarged to cover several fighting fronts. Jack Belden, John Snipes, Earl H. Leaf, Ed Beattie, and others reinforced the China bureaus. Belden traveled approximately 10,000 miles with Chinese troops, sometimes using couriers to send his copy long distances to a telegraph office and sometimes using a portable wireless transmitter to keep in direct touch with the Shanghai and Hong Kong bureaus.

In November, Morris sent Weldon James to Nanking, where the government was preparing for a Japanese attack. James had to slip secretly out of territory held by the Japanese and circle back into Chinese-held areas. He traveled by canal boat, river boat, and by land with a huge suitcase as his only luggage. The suitcase contained very little except a radio transmitter with which James was able to maintain direct touch with the Shanghai bureau even after the advancing Japanese had knocked out or closed all other means of communication except by way of the United States gunboat *Panay*, anchored in the river near Nanking. Later, as the Japanese closed in on Nanking, James went aboard the *Panay* and was the only news-agency man on the scene when Japanese airplanes bombed and sank the gunboat. His eyewitness story was a major scoop of the war in China.

In the decade prior to World War II the United Press made a great deal of progress in competition with Reuters in the Far East. As compared to a single staff correspondent in Peking, in 1924, the agency had spread out over China, Japan, Manchukuo, Hong Kong, the Philippines, Indo-China, Siam, and the Malay Peninsula with an organization that both collected and distributed news. Harold Guard was instrumental in breaking through the Reuters monopoly in Hong Kong, Singapore, and India after the United Press began radio newscasts in 1935 from San Francisco to Far Eastern points. The United Press receiving station at Hong Kong was under direction of George Baxter, a wizard at juggling direction aerials and improving equipment, and the prestige of the agency was greatly increased by his ability to pick up dispatches from remote relay points or from correspondents such as Jack Belden and Weldon James, who were using portable wireless transmitters to cover the war in China. Sometimes these dispatches were printed in United Press newspapers days ahead of other agency news from the fighting fronts. The daily news report mounted to around 10,000 words. Shanghai radio stations broadcast United Press dispatches throughout China. The agency had moved a long way toward opening the Orient to a free exchange of news.

But while the United Press had been spreading out in the Far East, it had run into troublesome times in Soviet Russia. The Russians were both suspicious and uncertain in all of their foreign relations, and as early as 1924 they began to indicate dissatisfaction with the arrangement that Bickel had made only a year earlier for exchange of news with Rosta. A sloppy job on a London story that involved forged Russian documents gave the Russians an excuse to charge the United Press with anti-Soviet bias, and Jacob Doletzky, head of Rosta, even ordered the Russian agency's New

York office moved from the third floor of the *World* building where it had been adjacent to the United Press office.

"One thing that I don't understand," Bickel wrote to Frederick Kuh, who was in Moscow at the time, "is the apparent conviction on the part of every-body in Moscow . . . that the United Press has suddenly sold out to the opposition or the reactionary influences or whatever you might term them. Russia has been persistently and consistently and everlastingly lied about by the Reuters agency and Havas agency . . . since 1917. The United Press is neither pro- nor anti-Soviet. We are tremendously interested in getting the truth and the facts out of Russia and in distributing around the world the truth and the facts."

There was more to the picture, however, than the Russians wanted to acknowledge. The Moscow government was negotiating for diplomatic recognition by Great Britain and France, and one of the conditions appeared to involve the cancellation of the United Press service to Rosta, if not the actual banning of the American agency from Russia. In 1925 Doletzky again asked Bickel to come to Moscow. When he arrived, Bickel learned that Rosta was canceling its contract with the United Press, joining the European news cartel and making an exclusive contract with the Associated Press. The United Press, however, was permitted to keep its Moscow bureau, and Eugene Lyons was sent there as manager in 1927. This arrangement in Russia lasted until 1934.

Meantime a number of important developments elsewhere in Europe tended to aid the United Press in breaking down the domination of the official news cartel. Premier Benito Mussolini of Italy was a former journalist who fully recognized the importance of propaganda, and he often privately denounced the cartel agencies because he believed their dispatches presented primarily the ideas of the British and French governments. There was great interest in Mussolini during the 1920s and Bickel, who had persuaded him to write two articles a month for United Features, made a number of trips to Rome, where he usually visited for several hours with the Italian Premier. After they became acquainted the two men often sat on the Fascist dictator's big desk in his huge office, swung their heels, and talked about all manner of things.

Mussolini frequently expressed to Bickel the idea that he would like to visit the United States and would welcome an invitation—hints that Bickel sometimes passed on to the State Department without comment. He questioned Bickel closely on what he had learned in Russia and Germany, and on one occasion described Adolf Hitler as "dumb, crude, and thieving." But most frequently he complained that Reuters distorted what he said in speeches and presented his views through the eyes of the British Foreign Office.

This was an attitude with which Bickel could sympathize, but he also realized that Mussolini was primarily interested in finding some way to combat the news cartel with another combination that would be sympathetic toward his Fascist government. Inevitably the subject of forming a news-agency combination with the United Press was broached by the Italians, but Bickel rapidly backed away with the explanation that his agency had no official connections with any government, including that of the United States. In fact, he added, he sometimes had serious trouble with State Department representatives, particularly in South America, who vainly tried to censor the news distributed by the United Press, or to inject propaganda into dispatches.

After Adolf Hitler came into power in Germany there were also complaints in Berlin that the cartel agencies were hostile to the German state and were dominated by the French foreign office. But perhaps the most important change in the early 1930s was the growth of suspicion in Moscow. The Russians were appalled by the success of Nazi and Fascist propaganda, by the skill with which both Hitler and Mussolini used news as a weapon of war. Since Tass, formerly Rosta, was entirely a government-operated agency, the Russians were inclined to regard all other news agencies as creatures of their governments and to blame Reuters and the British Foreign Office for much of the success of Fascist propaganda. As a result they began to look with suspicion on Tass's alliance with the Reuter-dominated cartel, and in 1933 approached the United Press with a view to resuming contractual relations.

Meantime the cartel had suffered still another blow. The Associated Press was no longer basically dependent on Reuters and Havas and other official or quasi-official agencies for its world coverage, having increased the number of its own bureaus abroad. The organization's general manager, Kent Cooper, had been eager to break out of the fetters which the cartel imposed on expansion of Associated Press service abroad. With the agreement of the board of directors Cooper finally advised Reuters that the Associated Press was terminating its alliance with the cartel in 1934 and desired to make separate agreements with the various cartel agencies for exchange of news, on the understanding that the Associated Press would be free to sell its service in any country.

The managing director of Reuters, Sir Roderick Jones, promptly communicated with the United Press, presumably with a view to arranging for it to replace the Associated Press in the cartel's scheme of world coverage. Bickel was not interested in assuming the fetters that Cooper had dropped. On the contrary he accepted a suggestion made by Cooper for an agreement between the United Press and the Associated Press that neither would assist "the practice of European agencies which at the dictation of one or more of them hinders international news exchange by making exclusive arrangements for the availability of their news." This agreement, signed in New York in 1934, provided that neither American agency would make exclusive agreements with any European agency or accept any advantage in coverage of news in European countries. (The contract, incidentally, was terminated five years later by the Associated Press.)

The Associated Press's decision to join the United Press struggle for free interchange of news around the world was followed by completion of negotiations in Moscow to end Tass's alliance with the cartel. Doletzky had asked both Bickel and Cooper to visit Moscow, and they arrived in March. The Tass Agency withdrew from the European combine and rewrote the United Press contract that had been canceled in 1925. A similar Tass contract was made with the Associated Press.

Thus, after more than a quarter of a century of effort led by the United Press, the cartel's attempts to maintain a news monopoly around the world were shattered, although the battle for free exchange of news everywhere was still far from won. Bickel went home by way of Rome, where he talked briefly with Mussolini. The dictator was greatly interested in the Russian withdrawal from the cartel.

"So they did it, eh?" he said thoughtfully. "Well, I've had much the same thing in mind in regard to Stefani [the Italian official agency]. I thought I would make a deal with the United Press in regard to distribution of news in South America."

Bickel was appalled by the Premier's bland assumption that the United Press, which had been fighting against monopoly by official agencies for years, would turn around and agree to such collaboration with Stefani. But by this time he knew Mussolini well enough to speak his mind.

"Like hell you will!" he said firmly, and took his leave.

CHAPTER NINETEEN

The state of the United Press in the early 1930s was summed up in an article by Stephen Vincent Benét appearing in the May 1933 issue of the magazine *Fortune*, but more accurately applicable to the year 1932. The income of the company, Benét estimated, was around $8,500,000 in a good year, collected principally from hundreds of small-town newspapers that paid between $18 and $40 a week, and a smaller number of large newspapers that might pay as much as $2500 a week for as many as seven news, financial, regional, and sports wires. The company had about 1200 client newspapers at that time as compared to some 1300 newspapers served by the Associated Press. It spent close to $8,000,000 a year to cover the world and distribute its news reports. Its dispatches from abroad totaled around ten million words a year.

The United Press is neither a charity nor a philanthropy [Benét wrote]. *It is a business concern and its members work for profit. But there is another motive which drives them quite as strongly. You can call it pride of profession or professional zest or enthusiasm or self-hypnosis. But whatever you call it, it is as common to the stockholding executives as to the lunch-money copy boy—it is indeed the strongest of the bonds that holds the UP together. And what it boils down to, when the sentiment and the wisecracks are both skimmed off, is an actual and genuine love of the game. Unipressers are bound in an unusual* esprit de corps, *hard to define but nonetheless real. No doubt it has something to do with the UP's fearless independence.*

The *Fortune* article suggested that the United Press was prepared to cope with almost anything that could happen around the world—and in the next few years the agency had a chance to prove that it could.

In the spring of 1932 jobless veterans of World War I marched on Washington, demanding a bonus payment by the government. They camped in tents and shacks on government property along Pennsylvania Avenue, in a ramshackle camp in the southwestern part of the city, and on the Anacostia flats. Late one afternoon Morris DeHaven Tracy, who was then news editor of the Washington bureau under Manager Ray Clapper, received a tip that United States marshals had been ordered to evict the bonus marchers the following morning, starting at ten o'clock. Knowing that his information was exclusive, Tracy decided not to carry a story that would merely tip off other agencies. The staff was mobilized in the office early the next morning and quietly sent to strategic positions around the bonus army's camps. In one way or another most of the reporters in the bureau were pressed into service, and even a couple of office boys were stationed at telephones along Pennsylvania Avenue with instructions to call the office if they saw any fighting.

Shortly before ten o'clock, but not soon enough to give other reporters time to get to the scene, Tracy moved a story on the wire disclosing that an attempt would be made to evict the bonus army. The attempt was made promptly at ten o'clock—and the result was a riot that lasted until almost dawn the following day. As the disorder increased, the White House called on Chief of Staff Douglas MacArthur to move troops from Fort Myer into the capital during the afternoon.

Joseph Baird was on guard for the United Press at the War Department, and when he saw MacArthur departing he asked if he could go along. "Sure," MacArthur replied, "but you'll have to ride home with me first." Most army officers at that time wore civilian clothes, but after he had been notified to direct the operations of the troops the general had to stop at home to change into uniform. Baird rode with him. Later, when the big, black army car drew up at the point where the troops were being formed, it was recognized by a score of reporters, who rushed over to question MacArthur. The door swung open and Unipresser Joe Baird stepped out to wave a cheery greeting to his colleagues. A few minutes later the grim, unhappy struggle to clear the bonus army from government property was in progress.

By that time Tracy had almost stripped the regular capital runs of reporters in order to cover the disorders in which close to 10,000 bonus marchers were directly or indirectly involved. Thomas L. Stokes, who had remained on his regular job in the House of Representatives, was one of the few who had no specific assignment, but he chanced to go along Pennsylvania Avenue that afternoon just after a clash in which two veterans were fatally wounded by gunfire from police who had been showered with bricks. He stopped to investigate as the troops arrived to clear the area. A cavalryman struck Stokes with his saber and then led a charge of soldiers into the crowd. The camping places of veterans along lower Pennsylvania Avenue were cleared that afternoon by cavalrymen and infantrymen with tear-gas bombs. Reporters and veterans alike were forced to run before the advance of the armed forces.

Late in the afternoon, when some of the secondary wires had closed, Tracy sent an experienced printer operator, Granville Stagg, to cover a new outbreak of trouble at the so-called southwest camp. The troops made a running charge through this area, driving the veterans before them and setting fire to their shacks. Stagg later went across the river to the Anacostia flats where there was a large encampment of bonus marchers, many of them with wives and children. Lyle Wilson, Stokes, and several other staff members were on the scene when the troops, accompanied by fire-department trucks and six tanks, arrived and ordered the bonus marchers to evacuate. Reporters who attempted to question officers in charge of the troops were brushed aside, and Stagg was almost run down by a cavalryman flourishing his saber. The troops moved into the camp with tear-gas bombs and torches, setting fire to the shacks and forcing the veterans to leave at bayonet point.

It was almost dawn before the story was cleaned up and the veterans' camp was in ashes.

Washington Manager Ray Clapper was a serious, friendly, tenacious reporter, always digging for a story. In the late spring of 1932 he came up with a whole series of stories that attracted great attention throughout the country—a report on nepotism in connection with the congressional payroll. There was nothing illegal about members of Congress putting relatives on their official payroll. Some of the relatives worked hard and proved of great value to the congressmen. But there were many instances where relatives who were on the payroll seldom showed up on the job. These congressmen and their relatives were obviously working a racket at the expense of the taxpayers.

In April, Clapper began writing a series of articles exposing the nepotism racket in Congress. As the names of more and more members of the House and the Senate appeared in his stories, the series created a sensation—particularly in the home states of the congressmen named. Within a few weeks hundreds of letters were pouring into the United Press bureau offering leads on additional cases of racketeering. Editorial writers everywhere had a big day when Clapper got around to congressmen from their localities. By election day in November, Clapper had named 169 members of Congress, including a number of the House and Senate leaders, who had relatives on their payrolls. He was not, in that period, very popular in some offices on Capitol Hill, but neither were some congressmen very popular back home. A large number removed relatives from their payrolls after Clapper had written about them, but sixty of those named were defeated in the November election. There were, of course, various reasons for these defeats, but Clapper's series was one of the most highly praised reportorial feats of the year.

2.

In the winter of 1933 the feel of momentous events was building up like a thundercloud. Franklin D. Roosevelt had been elected President of the United States and would take office in March. Everywhere the prolonged economic maladjustment was being illuminated by flashes of great political and social upheaval, by forces that were difficult to comprehend but that foretold revolutionary change. On the morning of February 14 Governor W. A. Comstock of Michigan issued an order closing all of the state's banks for a period of eight days.

There had been numerous bank failures in the United States, but there had also been a tendency on the part of the nation's press to handle such stories with great circumspection—sometimes such great circumspection that the news was all but left uncovered. "Don't rock the boat," was the theme of many publishers. "Don't play up bank failures—you might cause a panic." Such blindness toward the nation's economic misery obviously was doing nothing to bring about a cure. On the contrary it was undermining confidence because the people were not always getting the facts. At 7 A.M., on the morning of February 14, News Manager Earl Johnson took off the kid gloves. He telephoned United Press Manager Joseph Hearst in Detroit and told him to go all out on the Michigan bank-closing story.

"This is news and big news," Johnson said. "It's bad news, sure, but it's better to know everything. Give it the works."

Washington and New York financial and economic experts followed up on the story that the Detroit bureau laid down with all of the trimmings that day. There was no more evasion or side-stepping of bank closings by the United Press. By the time Mr. Roosevelt was inaugurated, the nation was well informed on the economic and financial state of the nation. The President's order for a bank holiday throughout the country brought relief rather than panic.

Late in February, Johnson had telephoned Merton T. Akers, manager of the Chicago bureau. "There's a problem in Washington," he said. "We need somebody to take over the news desk. Can you get moving in a hurry?"

Akers, who joined the United Press in Chicago in 1928 and became bureau manager in 1930, said he guessed he could. He arrived in the capital late one night, a few days before Mr. Roosevelt was inaugurated. He arose the next morning about dawn and arrived in the office at seven o'clock. Julius Frandsen, who was alone on the overnight shift, was amazed. Nobody ever got to work in Washington at that hour. When the staff began showing up around nine o'clock, Akers said he would like to get some idea of the various assignments. Lyle Wilson took him to Capitol Hill and gave him a quick look at the press-room establishment. E. W. Lewis and William Kerbey steered him through the gallery at the House of Representatives. John Reichmann took him on a brief survey of the Supreme Court, and then sent him to the White House, where Frederick C. Othman gave him a quick greeting and turned him over to Joseph Baird at the State Department, who passed him on to Virgil Pinkley, covering the Treasury Department. Shortly after noon Akers got back to the office for a short chat with Bureau Manager Ray Clapper. The Washington manager was a brilliant reporter and the bureau he ran had always put a major emphasis on reporting. The job of running the desk was not a popular assignment among members of the staff, but at the moment it was being performed by one of the bureau's top reporters, Harold O. Thompson, who hated every minute of it. That afternoon Thompson happily gave up his chair and Akers sat down. He almost literally didn't get up again, except to go home to sleep at night, for the next three months. The "One Hundred Days"—the first frantic, unbelievable months of the Roosevelt administration—were beginning. Washington became the news center of the world, providing the great bulk of the United Press daily report. Akers, with a highly developed talent for running a desk, had arrived at the right place at the right time.

There were a dozen hot stories breaking every day in all parts of the capital from the beginning of the Roosevelt administration and many new faces—Richard L. Harkness, Hobart Montee, Mack Johnson, Harrison E. Salisbury—were soon added to the Washington staff. One big story that had started breaking earlier was the so-called Wall Street investigation by a subcommittee of the Senate Banking and Currency Committee, directed by Ferdinand Pecora. Lyle Wilson, head of the Senate staff, directed coverage of the committee hearings which, coming soon after the Wall Street collapse of 1929, were headline news everywhere.

Many of the subcommittee meetings were held behind closed doors when some of the big Wall Street banking houses such as J. P. Morgan and Kuhn Loeb were questioned about how their earnings were split among the various partners. This was a closely guarded secret, and lawyers for the banking houses tried to avoid giving the information to the subcommittee on the grounds that it would be "leaked" to newspapermen later. Their argument was ignored by the committee but their judgment proved to be sound. Before the details of the Kuhn-Loeb partnership arrangement were presented, Wilson called on a member of the committee.

"I want to get the terms of the partnership agreement immediately after the meeting," Wilson said. "Will you have the information for me?"

"If I take notes during the hearing," the senator replied, "it will make it obvious that I leaked the information. However, I have a good memory and I'll see what can be done."

When the committee session broke up that afternoon the senators were questioned by a crowd of reporters. Wilson maneuvered his friend to one side and asked him for the details. "I'll have to talk fast before I forget," the senator said, "and don't take any notes or somebody will know that it came from me." He rattled off all of the details he could remember and Wilson dashed to the Senate press gallery and put them down before *he* forgot. When the story later appeared on the United Press wires it proved that both the senator and Wilson had good memories.

Still another major headline during the investigation fell into Wilson's hands by accident, but it was the kind of accident that occurs only when a reporter keeps digging for the facts. Late every afternoon, when the hearings had ended, Wilson made a regular canvass of members of the committee in an effort to pick up a few details of what had happened. One evening he was talking to Senator James Couzens who complained about the "preferred lists" of the big banking houses. These were lists of persons who were let in on the ground floor when the banking house brought out stocks that were sure—before the Wall Street crash—to go up sharply and net a quick profit for the owner.

"Why, it turns out that even Calvin Coolidge is on that damn preferred list of the Morgans!" Couzens finally exclaimed indignantly. Wilson asked a few more casual questions and departed with another banner-line story.

Wilson became manager of the Washington bureau in December of 1933 and directed its destinies during a period of tremendous expansion, particularly in the 1930s and the years of World War II. The great expansion of federal powers during the Roosevelt administration made Washington the news capital of the country and, often, of the world. The staff was steadily increased to provide newspapers with coverage of daily developments that directly affected the lives of almost every citizen. Day after day and month after month the Washington bureau was responsible for by far the greatest share of the world's news, and the approach of another world war in the late 1930s served merely to increase the load carried by Wilson's staff.

The first frenetic cycle of the New Deal administration might be said to have ended with the first major decisions by the United States Supreme Court on the constitutionality of a number of revolutionary acts that Mr. Roosevelt steered through Congress. The five gold cases involved the authority of the federal government to confiscate gold, to declare all gold debts payable in currency, and to refuse to pay government bonds in gold. One of these cases, which challenged the right of the government to pay off gold bonds (such as Liberty bonds) in currency, had reached the Supreme Court in the form of two tricky questions on appeal from the Court of Claims:

1. Was the holder of a Liberty bond entitled to receive an amount in legal tender currency in excess of the face amount of the bond?
2. Was the United States liable to a damage suit in the Court of Claims by a holder of such a bond due to abrogation of the gold clause in all obligations?

For weeks after the issue came before the court the technical aspects of the gold cases were studied by John A. Reichmann, the United Press expert on Supreme Court affairs, and Richard Gridley, who covered the Treasury Department. In preparation for the decisions, a direct telephone line to the United Press office was installed in the Capitol corridor about fifty yards from the doors of the old senate chamber, where the Court then met. Duane Wilson, Arthur DeGreve, Carl Skinner, and Russell Turner were assigned to assist Reichmann. On the day the decisions were expected, Reichmann wrote in advance a number of flashes designed to cover the decision whether it held that refusal to pay in gold was constitutional or unconstitutional. In addition, the reporters covering the Court had persuaded Chief Justice Charles Evans Hughes to vary the usual procedure by preparing a brief statement to be read at the opening of the Court showing how each of the five cases had been decided. This would enable them to flash the news at once rather than wait until the long decisions were read in each case. Such was the importance of the Court's ruling in its effect on markets all over the world that the news would be spread without a second's unnecessary delay.

With twenty different flashes clutched in his hand, Reichmann took his seat in the Court feeling that he was prepared to cover any possible decision in the five gold cases. No reporter would be permitted to leave his seat until all of the opinions had been read, but they were permitted to write their stories in the courtroom and hand them to attendants who carried them to the door. Turner stood just outside the door to grab whichever flash Reichmann sent out and run for the telephone.

After the Court convened at noon, the Chief Justice read—for the first and last time—a brief summary of the decisions. Reichmann jotted down the Court's decisions. Then he began thumbing hurriedly through his previously prepared flashes to select the proper one. He didn't find it. A court attendant came down the aisle and picked up a flash written by the Associated Press correspondent and carried it to the door. Reichmann went through his prepared flashes again but this merely confirmed that he had not written one to cover the decisions. He began scribbling furiously. Then he realized why he had no prepared flash to cover the situation. The government had actually won the Liberty bond case but, at the same time, the Court had declared its action was unconstitutional. The decision not only had been difficult to foresee—it was difficult to understand.

In the office, meantime, a message had been received from New York that the Associated Press was carrying the story—a story saying that the government's action had been declared unconstitutional and that the Treasury would be required to pay the equivalent of the market price of gold on its gold bonds; that is, about $1.69 for every gold-bond dollar. By that time Turner was on the telephone reading Reichmann's flash to Julius Frandsen on the desk:

FLASH
SUPREME COURT THROWS OUT LIBERTY BOND GOLD CASE

BULLETIN
WASHINGTON, February 18 (UP) *The Supreme Court today threw the Liberty bond case out of court but ruled that the action of the government in refusing to pay gold was unconstitutional.*

For the next couple of hours confusion took over. Editors all over the country bombarded Washington with demands for an explanation. Was the United Press story correct or was the Associated Press story correct? And, anyway, what did it mean? Frandsen could only pass inquiries along to Reichmann at the Capitol. But Reichmann could only repeat what the Court had said. The explanation would have to wait until the formal decision was read. It was getting on toward two o'clock before the suspense was finally ended. The Court had decided that the government's action was unconstitutional in regard to government obligations but that, since the plaintiff had actually suffered no monetary loss, he could not collect in the Court of Claims. Reichmann had avoided jumping at any conclusions and his story was right.

The Associated Press story conveyed a misleading impression that the government would have to pay the high market price of gold in its gold bonds and had thrown world markets into a wild state of confusion. The fact that the United Press had handled the story in a steady, conservative fashion—at the risk of being beaten on the most important flash in many months—made a strong impression on the minds of editors all over the world.

3.

Early on the morning of March 2, 1932, the telephone awakened Bickel at his New York apartment. He answered sleepily and then popped wide awake.

"Mr. Bickel," a voice said in his ear, "this is Colonel Lindbergh. We are in very serious trouble. My son has been kidnaped. Major Charley Schoeffel of the state police is here, and he believes that the presence of reporters near my home may make it difficult to make contact with the kidnapers. Since I knew you, I thought I would ask whether you could come here and advise us how best to handle the problem."

Bickel, after checking with the office, telephoned Business Manager Clem Randau and asked him to drive to Hopewell. They met on a New York street corner before dawn and took off across New Jersey to the Sourland Mountains home of the Lindberghs.

Lindbergh and his advisor, Colonel Henry C. Breckinridge, asked Bickel for suggestions on how to handle the problem of reporters, whose numbers grew rapidly during the morning. The police felt there was little hope of making contact with the kidnapers unless Lindbergh could be permitted to move about freely and without being followed. Would the newspapers agree to co-operate? Bickel felt sure they would. He pointed out that the reporters had to be protected on any news breaks but that they undoubtedly would agree to arrangements that would facilitate recovery of the child. He suggested that regular daily press conferences should be arranged at which a spokesman would inform the reporters of developments, and that an experienced newsman should be brought in as an advisor. That afternoon Lindbergh met with reporters and explained the problem. His request for help was respected and the reporters withdrew from the estate. Bickel also sent telegrams to about a hundred newspaper editors asking them to co-operate. There were scores of reporters scurrying over the countryside for the next few weeks, but in general the press did everything possible to aid the Lindberghs.

Bickel said nothing to the United Press staff about what he had seen or heard at Hopewell. He had gone to Hopewell in a personal and confidential capacity. He was in contact with Lindbergh during the next few weeks. Several times the famous flier, wearing dark glasses and a cap, came unrecognized to Bickel's office at the United Press for conferences. A copy of the symbol with which the kidnap letter had been signed was locked away in Bickel's safe. But nothing that was exchanged between the two men then or later was ever mentioned to any person in the United Press organization as even a "tip" on what was happening.

The search for the kidnapers went on day and night. Unipresser Delos Smith, covering the Lindbergh home near Hopewell, had had no sleep for the first three days of the search. Bates Raney was stationed in Trenton. Robert L. Frey of New York and Paul French of the Philadelphia bureau were sent to Hopewell, as was Harry Breuer. Smith later managed to get a single room in the rambling old hotel at Hopewell, but on some occasions he had seven United Press reporters sleeping there in the course of twenty-four hours. The search for the baby went on, with many alarms but no results.

Then, early in April, Lindbergh telephoned Bickel. "Can I see you late tonight?" he asked.

"Certainly," Bickel replied. "Why?"

"We are going to make contact tonight. I have the $50,000 ransom with me now. I would like to come by your house later."

It was two o'clock in the morning when Lindbergh arrived. In response to a message from the kidnaper, delivered through Dr. John F. Condon, an educator and lecturer in the Bronx section of New York City, the ransom money of $50,000 had been delivered to a man who identified himself as "John" at a meeting in St. Raymond's cemetery in the Bronx. In return Dr. Condon was handed a note saying that the baby was on a boat, the *Nelly*, between Horseneck Beach and Gay Head, (presumably Martha's Vineyard) near the Elizabeth Islands. Lindbergh secretly flew to the Rhode Island coast the next day and spent forty-eight hours looking for the *Nelly*. There was no such boat.

On the afternoon of May 12, two truck drivers with a load of lumber stopped by the side of the Mount Rose-Hopewell road, less than five miles from the Lindbergh home. There, in a thicket only a few yards from the road, they stumbled on the body of the Lindbergh baby. When officials were satisfied with the identification, Colonel H. Norman Schwarzkopf, head of the state police, called a press conference at the Lindbergh home. The reporters arrived, the doors were locked, and no one was permitted to leave until Schwarzkopf had finished reading a statement announcing the discovery of the body. There was only one man in the crowd who was in no hurry to leave—Frank Jamieson of the Associated Press, who had delayed his arrival long enough to make a telephone call to New Jersey's Governor A. Harry Moore. The governor didn't know why Schwarzkopf had called the press conference, but while Jamieson waited he made a telephone call and found out. Jamieson then flashed the news that the body of the baby had been discovered. The next hour or so, while the Associated Press spread the story across the nation and while the press conference was in progress behind locked doors at Hopewell, the United Press suffered untold agonies and took a beating.

The Lindbergh case did not end until three years later. On September 15, 1934, a man with a German accent paid for ninety-eight cents' worth of gasoline with a ten-dollar gold note at a service station far up on Lexington Avenue in New York City. The attendant thought "something was screwy" about the man, took his automobile license number, and turned the note over to his bank. For many weary months, as the ransom notes had been cautiously cashed, the Federal Bureau of Investigation had slowly narrowed the field of search for the kidnaper. Now they had him.

Sidney Whipple, Harry Ferguson, James C. Austin, and Jane Dixon covered the trial of Bruno Richard Hauptmann, with the able assistance of Norma Saunders, daughter of the county sheriff, who was hired as a messenger. Judge Thomas W. Trenchard had barred all mechanical contrivances in the courtroom, including silent typewriters, and he had announced that when it came time for him to charge the jury the doors would be locked and reporters would be required to remain in their seats until his instructions were completed. The same procedure would be followed, he said, when the jury reported its verdict. Thus, at the most important period of the trial, the reporters theoretically would not be able to send out any information until formalities were completed and the doors unlocked.

The United Press staff had discussed in great detail the manner in which the verdict could be handled but, in the end, decided on the simplest possible method. Sandor S. Klein, who had been sent down from the New York bureau, was stationed at a rear door in the gallery—a door that opened just across the hall from a small room in which the United Press teleprinter was located. Whipple and Austin sat in the courtroom. Ferguson manned a desk beside the teletype. Other organizations had made more elaborate preparations. One newspaper was persistently reported to have arranged with a court attendant to smuggle out word of the verdict even before it was announced to the court, and later there was reason to believe that they did get the verdict some fifteen minutes in advance and attempted to get it out of the courtroom over a small, concealed radio transmitter. The Associated Press staff at Flemington also went in for electronics, stationing a telegrapher in the courtroom with a small radio transmitter concealed under his coat and a code signal for each of several possible verdicts. A receiving set was secretly set up in another room in the courthouse attic.

The Hauptmann case went to the jury at 11:23 A.M. on February 13. At ten o'clock that night the sheriff was summoned for a conference with constables guarding the jury and then went to Justice Trenchard's chambers. Apparently a verdict had been reached. Reporters rushed to their seats but at that instant all lights in the courthouse were extinguished. Matches were lighted all over the room as reporters tried to write in the darkness. There were shouts and laughter and confusion for a few moments until the lights came on again. A few of the reporters speculated that the flashing off of lights was a signal by some court attaché to a newspaperman that a certain verdict had been reached. Attorney General David Wilentz roared orders to state police and deputy sheriffs to lock the doors and pull down the window blinds —thus blocking the plans of several reporters to signal the verdict to colleagues outside.

At 10:28 P.M. the bell on the courthouse was tolled to announce that a verdict had been reached. At almost the same moment there came an angry buzz of bells on the United Press printer on the second floor of the courthouse. Operator Edward Bungue and Ferguson leaned over the printer as it spit out a message:

HF

OPPOSITION FLASHING HAUPTMANN GUILTY WITH LIFE SENTENCE

EJJ NX

Ferguson tore off the message with a nervous hand and dashed downstairs to the door of the courtroom. Before he was halfway there the Associated Press bulletin on the verdict had reached every member newspaper in the country. In many cities, editors worked frantically to close their front-page forms, to get the presses rolling with the word that had been so tensely awaited. Within a few minutes the word had been repeated thousands of times in restaurants, theaters, and public gathering places.

At the door to the courtroom a burly deputy sheriff barred Ferguson's way. But there was—despite the judge's orders—a heavy traffic in notes and news copy being slipped through a crack in the door. Ferguson sighted his girl messenger inside the door, pushed the message through to her, and she carried it to Whipple. She was soon back with an answer:

HF

THE JURY IS STILL OUTSIDE COURTROOM. IF AP IS RIGHT IT IS NICE TO HAVE WORKED WITH YOU.

SBW

Ferguson got back upstairs and advised Johnson that the jury was still out. Meantime, telephone calls and messages were flooding the New York office from client newspapers everywhere. For the longest fifteen minutes of his life Ferguson just sat. Then at 10:46 P.M. a thin piece of paper was pushed over the top of the gallery door at which Sandy Klein had been stationed. Harry Breuer grabbed it and handed it to Ferguson. Bungue tapped out the flash that Hauptmann had been found guilty of murder in the first degree. The death sentence was mandatory.

On the first floor the Associated Press got the same message in about the same way—but too late to keep some of its clients from issuing extra editions with the wrong verdict. Later the agency's officers said that they never were able to find out just what had gone wrong with the signal system, except that the receiving operator picked up or thought he picked up a radio signal which the operator in the courtroom said he never sent. Anyway, it was added, the use of such tricky transmission systems was strictly against the "rigorous rules" of the Associated Press and none of the officers had been aware of what the Flemington staff was doing.

The steadiness of the United Press in handling the Hauptmann verdict, coming within a week of the Liberty-bond case in Washington, was of incalculable importance in boosting the prestige of the agency and reinforcing its reputation for accuracy and reliability.

4.

Very few United Press correspondents wrote their stories while sitting naked on a rock, but H. Allen Smith was different. Smith was an expert on screwballs, unusual social trends, cockeyed fads and—perhaps because he didn't play cards—bridge tournaments.

Sitting naked on a rock with a portable typewriter perched on his knees one August day in 1933, he was writing about a nudist colony near Highland, New York, but he didn't have any hope for the story. It wasn't the kind of story a press association normally carried on the wires. There was a long-standing prejudice in the newspaper world against writing frankly about such things as "nakedness." Instead, it was customary to substitute more refined words such as "nudity" or "disrobed" and to use these words only if absolutely necessary. This practice, a hang-over from Victorian days, irritated Smith. He didn't think he could do anything about it, but he could always try. He pecked at the typewriter.

HIGHLAND, N.Y., August 17 (UP) *All arguments to the contrary, it is very embarrassing to have a young woman walk up to you stark naked and tell you that nudism is going to sweep the nation.*

The shed-your-pants apostles at this particular nudist camp are serious about it. . . .

This is your correspondent's first visit to a nudist camp and this one, operated by Miss Jan Gay, who apparently cuts her own hair, is a little dandy. . . .

Miss Gronlin . . . came around the corner of the dining hall, very blonde and very handsome. And she didn't even have shoes on. Your correspondent, a bird lover, became intensely interested in a thrush which was going into a power dive over Bear Mountain. Miss Gronlin . . . came right up and said: "Are you Mr. Smith?"

Your correspondent never tells a lie.

"I am Miss Gronlin," she said, and laid a hand on my arm. "Please come and go swimming. The lake is wonderful."

"Miss Gronlin," your correspondent told her firmly, "I am not used to this business."

"Oh, that's all right," she burst forth, "the water isn't so deep in places."

Smith finished his story, put on his clothes, and took his copy around to the nearest telegraph office in a dour mood. The story, he told a friend, would not get to first base. It was too frank to end up anywhere except in the wastebasket. He went back to New York expecting to be taken to task by the night service editor, but when he walked into the office he was almost greeted with cheers. The story had gone on the wires unchanged. So many commendatory messages had been received that Smith was asked to go through his notes and turn out another story about the nudist camp. The reporter began to feel that he had struck a blow for frankness in reporting. Maybe he had. When Dean Frank Luther Mott of the State University of Iowa School of Journalism later compiled in book form "a representative selection from the best news and feature writing in American newspapers in 1933," he included Smith's nudist-camp story, sandwiched between a story on the inauguration of President Roosevelt by J. Frederick Essary and a story about Premier Stalin by Walter Duranty.

CHAPTER TWENTY

One of the most important factors in growth and development of the United Press since its foundation was the eagerness of its leadership to expand facilities for dissemination of news in the United States and throughout the world. Basically this was a kind of crusade to get more and more information to more and more readers in less and less time. In the 1920s and early 1930s another tremendous advance in the communications field—the development of radio broadcasting—opened an unparalleled era in the dissemination of news at a speed that would have seemed impossible a decade earlier. Strangely enough, it also opened up a long period of confusion, controversy, and frustration for the United Press. In retrospect the controversy would be difficult to understand. But for almost a decade the broadcasting of news by radio stations was a burning and bitter issue among newspaper publishers, many of whom feared that the new medium might destroy their properties. And for some years they were inclined to fight rather than make the best of it.

The possibilities of radio, both for collecting and distributing news, fascinated Karl Bickel. He tried out a kind of primitive walkie-talkie set for covering an important golf match. It didn't work very well. But, as soon as there were enough radio stations operating to make it profitable, the United Press started a special service that provided newspapers with weekly programs of the leading stations across the country. This service was quickly sold to more than 200 client newspapers whose readers were listening regularly to radio entertainment programs.

Such a service, however, was a mere side line that would soon be outdated. What fascinated Bickel was the impact of radio on the nation, and the fact that a word spoken in a broadcasting studio was heard instantly in thousands of living rooms over a vast area. He began thinking up ways to get the words "United Press" mentioned as often as possible in broadcasting studios. In 1924, at the suggestion of an editor on the Pittsburgh *Post-Gazette,* he worked out an arrangement for broadcasting United Press bulletins on the general election returns over a dozen of the best-known radio stations in the country. In a crude way this was the first news hookup of radio stations, comparable to later network broadcasting. A news room was set up at station WEAF in New York, with two United Press wires installed to carry election returns. The United Press client newspapers in New York, Detroit, Boston, Chicago, Dallas, Pittsburgh, and half a dozen other cities made deals with their local radio stations to join the "network" on election night.

Hugh Baillie manned the news desk in the WEAF studio, where Graham McNamee was assigned to direct a program of entertainment and, at regular intervals, read the latest election returns. An orchestra, a number of singers, and Will Rogers provided the entertainment. But about every fifteen minutes Baillie would give McNamee a couple of bulletins on election returns. The announcer would beat on the orchestra's triangle to interrupt the musical program and then in breathless fashion read the latest returns—by United Press—from Illinois or Florida or Nevada.

The election broadcast was a sensational success as far as the news agency was concerned. That night Bickel stood in front of the New York *World* building on Park Row and looked up at the huge bulletin board on which the newspaper posted election returns. Then he looked at the crowd of probably 500 or 600 persons assembled in front of the building. "The difference between that bulletin board and radio," he thought, "is that one gives the news to 500 persons in a hurry and the other gives it to 5,000,000—hell, it will soon be many times 5,000,000! It's inevitable. Even if the newspapers wanted to do anything to stop it they would be helpless. But why try to stop it? Radio news will just make more people interested in reading the newspapers."

By now Bickel was convinced that radio had opened a tremendous era of change in news distribution, in which the press association would be a major factor. Some publishers agreed with him. A majority of others, including Roy Howard, did not. The majority saw radio stations as competitors for newspaper advertising revenues. They saw, too, that no newspaper could compete with radio in speedy delivery of the news. But there was more to their argument. News delivered to homes by word of mouth was far different than news printed on paper and delivered to homes. A newspaper had vast responsibilities, trained reporters, and a public position. It stood behind the printed word. But radio seemed little better than street-corner gossip. The spoken word vanished into thin air. Who assumed responsibility for it? Words could be twisted or tainted with propaganda. Many publishers were honestly fearful and disturbed by the possibilities of anything more than entertainment on radio, and they were also conscious of the competitive situation created by the new medium.

In more than a score of cities there were newspapers that owned or were affiliated with local radio stations. In most instances they soon recognized the value of broadcasting news bulletins at regular intervals. An editor of the

Brooklyn *Eagle,* H. V. Kaltenborn, also broadcast over station WOR a weekly résumé of the news. It became a popular feature. These developments soon raised the question of whether it was proper for news agencies to permit the use of their services for broadcasting purposes. The question was not easy to answer because radio was untried and because the press associations depended on newspapers for their existence. The trade journal *Editor & Publisher* made a survey of leading editors on the issue in 1928. It reported that editors voted two to one against making press-association news available to radio stations.

As a result of this trend of opinion, the United Press was unable to do much about developing the new field of radio. When Kaltenborn, for example, left the *Eagle* and started a regular radio news program, he wanted the benefit of some kind of world news service. He discussed the problem with Bickel, who pointed out that the United Press did not sell any kind of service for news broadcasting.

"There's nothing I can do about that," Bickel added, "but any time you want to come into my office I want you to know that you will not disturb me."

For months thereafter Kaltenborn appeared in the United Press news room late every afternoon. He would wander quietly over to a printer machine in one corner and gather up yards of copy that had run into a big basket. After half an hour or so he had a thorough knowledge of the day's news and returned to his studio to broadcast a report on the day's developments.

The controversy over selling news to radio reached a climax when the New York publishers discussed a rather remarkable compromise proposal —they would permit radio stations to broadcast news twenty-four hours after it had appeared in the local newspapers. Bickel protested this suggestion as ridiculous, but one newspaper executive asked: "Well, what can they do about it? Where are the radio stations going to get the news?" There wasn't any question in Bickel's mind that they would get the news in one way or another, and by that time his purpose was to sell it to them if he could overcome the objections of certain United Press clients, including some of the Scripps-Howard newspapers. But it was slow work.

In 1931 the agency's news reports were being broadcast by certain radio stations affiliated with client newspapers. In addition, Frank Bartholomew sold a special service to KNX in Los Angeles. Under this deal KNX had access to the United Press report for four daily dramatizations of current news. These programs were not sponsored and thus did not cut into newspaper advertising revenues.

2.

Bickel's belief that radio stations would refuse to be deprived of access to a satisfactory news report was soon confirmed by various preparations to organize special services. "We have information that the Consolidated Press is now discussing the organization of a radio press association," Baillie wrote to Bickel in December of 1932. "Some of the big broadcasters, in addition, are talking of organizing a mutual press association.

"If news broadcasting [of press service news] is limited to stations affiliated with newspapers, approximately 80 per cent of the stations in this country will be cut off from any source of news. Included will be a powerful group of stations, which will be in the market for a news report. . . . Within the span of a year or two, I can see a new press association operating in the field, one geared to serve both radio and newspapers."

The conclusions that Baillie reached in his memorandum were not news to Bickel. He had not, however, won the agreement of the company's board of directors for any feasible approach to the problem. Like many other publishers, Howard was opposed to handing over to competitive radio stations the right to broadcast news collected by a news agency that derived its major revenue from the newspapers. Nor was the United Press alone affected. Both the Associated Press and the International News Service faced the same difficult problem.

The publishers, however, had to do something. The American Newspaper Publishers Association created a Press-Radio Committee and, in March of 1934, it established a Press-Radio Bureau, which was intended to control and limit news broadcasts. The bureau had the co-operation, however reluctant, of the United Press, International News Service, Associated Press, CBS, and NBC. The broadcasting networks dropped their own newsgathering plans and the news services agreed to provide material for two daily broadcasts of five minutes each, plus bulletins on important news breaks. It was agreed that radio news commentators would confine themselves to "background" material, and the daily news broadcasts were so arranged that they would contain only information already published in the daily newspapers. No news broadcasts could be sponsored.

This arrangement, which later would appear so incredible, was continued by more than 200 of the nation's 600 radio stations for more than a year, despite the fact that many independent stations and the Yankee Network declined to co-operate. In fact, these stations promptly began organizing their own news service. Confusion and controversy were compounded.

3.

Bickel had vainly argued at every opportunity for delivery of news to radio stations. Once, at a meeting of the ANPA radio committee, he angrily remarked that even if publishers had set out to buy something to bolster newspapers in the depression years they couldn't have invented anything better than radio, which created greater interest in news and increased newspaper circulation. This was regarded as little short of blasphemous. Roy Howard spoke in an opposite vein at the same meeting and, for several weeks thereafter, didn't speak to Bickel.

The controversy was a severe strain on Bickel. His health had been none too good for several years, and his doctor told him that he had to slow down. He made several vacation trips on which he was able to pay little attention to office affairs. He had begun to think about resigning. Then one morning late in 1934 Howard telephoned him.

"Haven't seen you for a while," Howard said. "I just bought a new car and thought you might like to go for a ride."

They went for a ride up the Saw Mill River Parkway in Westchester County. It was a fair, crisp day.

"You going to quit?" Howard asked.

Bickel said he didn't know but that it was hardly worth while to go on butting his head against a stone wall in connection with the mess over service to radio stations. Howard drove on in silence. He had been under pressure, too. Both Bill Hawkins and Howard's son, Jack, had been convinced that the best solution was for the regular agencies to sell service to radio stations. They had made their view clear to Howard.

"I don't like this whole idea of selling to radio," Howard finally said to Bickel. "But you and Hawkins and Jack think I'm wrong." He paused and shrugged his shoulders. "So go ahead and try it. If you fall on your face, it's your face."

The log jam was breaking. Bickel returned to his office and told Baillie to put the machinery into motion. Business Manager Clem Randau and Sales Manager Edwin Moss Williams had previously worked out a procedure whereby stations affiliated with client newspapers could broadcast four fifteen-minute news periods a day with credit to the news agency and the affiliated newspaper but still without a sponsor. Now they drew up another plan under which the stations affiliated with United Press client newspapers could broadcast the news report at any time during the regular hours of service by payment of 15 per cent of the basic cost of service to the newspaper. Such broadcasts could be sponsored only on agreement between the United Press and the newspaper. As for independent stations, the company decided that service would be sold only in communities where the local client newspaper consented to such sale.

At the next meeting of the Press-Radio Committee in the spring of 1935, Baillie stated his belief that it was only reasonable for the established press associations to sell service to radio stations instead of giving it to them through the Press-Radio Bureau. "I think it is time," he said, "for radio to be stopped from getting a free lunch off the newspapers. Radio ought to be and is willing to pay its own way. The Press-Radio agreement, after more than a year, has shown that it cannot control news broadcasting to the extent originally intended because many stations will not co-operate. They broadcast as they please. Therefore, we are relaxing restrictions on United Press clients so they can meet their broadcasting requirements without having to go out and buy a non-newspaper service for that purpose. We will, of course, continue to make our news report available to the Press-Radio Bureau."

The Associated Press did not attempt—until some years later—to sell service to radio stations. On the contrary, its employees paid for a double-page advertisement in *Editor & Publisher* stating that the agency was not selling service to radio stations and thus was "the only exclusively newspaper press association" in America. Across the top of the advertisement was a dramatic heading that described the Associated Press:

IN THIS CHANGING WORLD—ONE THING AS YET UNCHANGED

This inflexibility of the Associated Press was something that United Press salesmen had been talking about for several decades, but not so effectively.

4.

Bickel had spent a long time trying to regain his health. He went to Canada for a short time, but his nerves were still bothering him. He went to Ireland, but after four straight days of rain decided to try the French Riviera. It was better. He sat in the sun and thought. For a quarter of a century he had been moving at the rapid pace that makes a news agency click, and he had loved almost every minute of it. When he became president of the United Press in 1923 it had 867 client newspapers; now it had 1300 in 49 different countries; its bureaus had increased from 50 to 81 in the past dozen years. But the strain of the last few years had taken some of the joy out of the job. His doctor's warnings did the rest. Bickel made up his mind to resign. Then he went back home.

There had been a lot of work to do before the United Press could start selling service for broadcasting, but Baillie had done it in whirlwind fashion with the assistance of Randau, Williams, and A. F. Harrison, who later set up the first special news wires to radio stations. Webb Artz, as radio news manager, designed a news style suitable for reading on the air. The final step was up to the board of directors. In April of 1935 the board met in New York and approved a resolution for sale of the news report to broadcasting stations. The board also accepted Bickel's resignation and named his heir apparent, Baillie, to the presidency.

Bickel packed up his personal belongings to catch a train for Florida. "The press association business is a young man's business," he said. "An old man shouldn't be the head of the United Press." He was fifty-three years old.

Bickel's last official act before leaving his big, baroque, Spanish-style corner office on the twelfth floor of the *Daily News* building was to sign the authorization for sales to radio. Baillie had brought it to his desk.

"Here, Karl," he said. "Sign this and next year it will earn us $150,000."

This was an error of judgment on Baillie's part. The next year contracts with radio stations earned the United Press close to $300,000.

CHAPTER TWENTY-ONE

Hugh Baillie was forty-four years old when he became president of the United Press Associations. He was a tall, square-shouldered man who had an erect military bearing and, despite his Scots ancestry, rather resembled the Hollywood version of a Prussian officer. His hair was closely trimmed in a bristling pompadour, his voice was strong and penetrating even above the chatter of a room full of printer machines, and his bearing was deliberately aggressive. There had been no doubt in Baillie's mind for years—perhaps never—that he could run a news agency better than anybody else, and he may have been right. In any event the new president had the thorough knowledge of operations, the inexhaustible energy, the dramatic showmanship in news coverage, and the self-confidence that would be so vital to success in perhaps the most frenzied and difficult twenty-year period ever to face a press association.

Baillie was well prepared for his job. After switching from the news to the business department of the company in 1924 he had been instrumental in reorganizing the sales department and establishing semiautonomous divisions of control that encouraged more efficient operation in both news and business matters. He had supervised establishment of additional state and sectional wire circuits in the late 1920s to "tailor" the news report to the needs of regional papers. He had organized in 1930 a Special Service Bureau to handle a dozen miscellaneous services for clients other than newspapers. In addition, particularly after he became executive vice-president, Baillie was active in the news department and frequently turned up outstanding news stories of his own. One of these was an exclusive interview with Chancellor Franz von Papen of Germany, who frankly heralded the rise of Nazism by declaring that the Versailles treaty must be "rectified" and that the Reich must be restored to her "place in the sun." This was one of a series of interviews with European leaders—from Joseph Stalin to Neville Chamberlain—with which Baillie made headlines during the critical 1930s.

Nobody ever mistook Baillie for what would later be described as an egghead. He approached the news—and most other affairs—dramatically, by action, by prodding, and by striking out in many places where he could be reasonably sure of stirring a good story out of the bushes. If the United Press report was handled in lackadaisical fashion on one day or another, Baillie was capable of expressing his feelings by kicking a wastebasket across the news-room floor or jerking his desk telephone out by the roots. But he was more likely to broadcast scorching telegrams to a score of his bureau managers in the United States and abroad demanding that they do something about it in a hurry. This system he sometimes described as scattering "a few red ants" around to wake up the staff. Eventually, the "red ants" file in Baillie's office was thick with messages like this one to London:

EITHER ASSOCIATED PRESS IS TRYING HARDER THAN EVER BEFORE OR WE ARENT TRYING AS HARD AS WE USED TO STOP LETS BURN OPPOSITIONS POSTERIOR THREE OR FOUR GOOD STORIES THIS WEEK

BAILLIE

Baillie's "red ants" messages, especially when he sent duplicate telegrams to a score of key bureau managers demanding that they get off their backsides and pep up the news report, usually brought quick responsive telegrams agreeing with the voice of authority. But not always. On one occasion the manager of the Los Angeles bureau received his copy of a broadcast "red ants" message, studied it with mounting irritation, and sat down at his typewriter to knock out a reply:

BAILLIE UNITEDPRESS NEWYORK

COMPLETELY AT LOSS UNDERSTAND WHAT YOU TALKING ABOUT STOP WE BEEN OUTTURNING LONG LIST EXCLUSIVES AND SHARP FEATURES FROM THIS AREA STOP WE HAVE BEEN AND WILL CONTINUE KICK HELL OUT OF ASSOCIATED PRESS ALL DEPARTMENTS STOP REGARDS

BILL PAYETTE

Baillie was no armchair brass hat. He had the experience, the craftsmanship, and the drive of the good reporter, and as president he demonstrated a remarkable ability to turn up at the scene of action. If the world was enthralled by a king's decision to give up his throne for love, Baillie might be found collecting comment in the crowd outside the palace gates. If there was a war on, Baillie studied the problems of reporters by putting on a tin hat and going to the front.

There was an important point to be noted at the beginning of Baillie's tenure as president. The United Press decision to sell news to radio stations soon began bringing in substantial new revenue. Still somewhat concerned about the reaction of the agency's newspaper clients to the broadcasting of news, Baillie repeatedly emphasized that this money would go to improve and strengthen the general news report so that the newspapers would get better news coverage. He immediately began putting this principle into practice. When a big story broke, United Press correspondents converged on the scene from all directions. European bureaus were strengthened and communications improved. When Hitler sent German troops into the demilitarized Rhineland, when Italy began threatening the kingdom of Ethiopia—wherever news breaks occurred, Baillie emphasized that the staff must go "all out" to get the jump on everybody.

2.

One of the early tests of Baillie's policy of "outswarming" the opposition on big news stories occurred in September of 1935 when Senator Huey P. Long, the "Kingfish" of Louisiana, was shot at Baton Rouge. In the past it would have been more or less expected that the United Press correspondents on the story would be outnumbered two or perhaps three to one by Associated Press reporters. But Earl J. Johnson had been building up mobile, flying units of experienced reporters who could move swiftly to any main scene of action in an emergency. When Long, one of the most colorful and powerful political figures in the United States, was shot by a young political foe in the corridor of the state capitol on the evening of September 8, the only United Press correspondent in Baton Rouge was J. Alan Coogan. He was sitting at his desk about eighty feet from the scene of the shooting, having been delayed in leaving the state house because Long had stopped to chat with him a few minutes earlier. Coogan, the only reporter on the floor, looked out into the corridor, saw Long wounded on the floor, saw his bodyguards pumping bullets into the body of the assassin, and then grabbed the telephone. Earl B. Steele, on the night desk at New Orleans, handled the flash from Coogan. Then, almost before the doctors could get the wounded senator to the operating table, Earl Johnson had a squadron of top reporters on the move by air. I. I. Femrite, manager of the New Orleans bureau, Harold O. Thompson, who was in Florida covering a hurricane story, Harry Ferguson from the New York bureau, Harrison E. Salisbury from Washington, Valco Lyle from Memphis, and recruits from several other nearby bureaus were rushed to Baton Rouge.

When Femrite and Thompson arrived there was virtually no hope that Long could survive. The big job ahead, therefore, was to prepare for a fast break on medical bulletins and to be ready for news of the senator's death. This was not easy for two reasons. First, the Associated Press correspondent at Baton Rouge had already been designated as a kind of unofficial liaison man between officials at the hospital and the press. Physicians turned over to him their bulletins on Long's condition and he gave them to other reporters. Second, Long's bodyguards were highly suspicious of everybody and especially of reporters. The state police ordered all reporters to remain in the hospital lobby and made it clear that they were prepared to shoot first and ask questions afterward if there were any untoward incidents. Furthermore, they admitted reporters to the lobby of the hospital but, once they were inside, refused to permit them to leave.

Upon learning of the police orders, Coogan wisely refused to go inside the hospital until his reinforcements arrived. When Femrite reached Baton Rouge he went to see a friend who was very close to Long and who was well known to Long's bodyguards.

"Huey's going to die," Femrite said, "and I've got to be first with the news. You're the only person I know who can help me. The bodyguards and police know you and you can go to his room on the second floor. They don't know me and, if you say so, they'll let me go with you."

"He's not going to die," the man replied. "He just can't die!"

Femrite argued and his friend finally agreed to accompany him to the hospital. They arrived about three o'clock in the morning on September 10, walked past the guards and to the second floor. For a while they stood outside Long's door, asking questions of the nurses and doctors. When the door opened, Femrite could see Long under an oxygen tent. A little later a doctor came out and said: "He's dead."

Femrite moved casually to the back stairway and walked down to the basement where he knew there was a telephone. He called Coogan in the press room at the state house and dictated the flash. Coogan wrote it down and then handed the telephone to Harold Thompson so that he could confirm it. Thompson listened and nodded. Coogan looked around the press room, which was full of reporters and telegraphers. Casually he picked up the flash and drifted over to the United Press wire, where he removed the tobacco can that the operator used as a sounder. Then he tossed the flash in front of the operator and, for the benefit of others in the room, remarked that "here's some more malarkey for you." The operator assumed a bored expression as he sent the flash. By that time Thompson had jotted down the details from Femrite and, with a similar bored expression, was typing the story. Nobody in the press room paid any attention to them.

Meanwhile Long's bodyguards at the hospital had learned there was a newspaperman loose on the premises and were searching for Femrite. He managed to drift back upstairs to the lobby, however, without being seen. He mingled with other reporters and borrowed a match from the Associated Press correspondent to light his cigarette.

"Do you think Huey's going to die tonight?" the Associated Press man asked. Femrite never got a chance to reply. At that moment there was a stir of excitement on the stairway. The official word that Long was dead was being passed along to the press, and everybody—except Femrite—scurried to get the news. All over the country, morning newspapers had been holding their final editions for the last word on Long's condition. Femrite had already given it to them.

3.

Accuracy and speed were two fundamentals for news-agency reporting, but after Earl Johnson became general news manager in 1936 he also expended a great deal of time and effort on the problem of writing—the presentation of a story in the form that was going to be most satisfactory to newspaper editors and readers.

"News stories on a press wire are like firecrackers," he advised all correspondents. "The tighter you roll them the more noise they make when they go off. Too many of our stories don't go off because the editor doesn't have time to compr ss them to fit a tight paper. The biggest single service we can render our clients is to give them more news in fewer words."

Again he pointed out that "stories that take you by the hand and lead you right into the scene are in big demand. Richard L. Harkness drove down a country road in Missouri, visited a drought-stricken farmer, listened to his woeful tale. Then, in one story, Harkness gave you a better idea of what the drought was doing to people, livestock, and crops than you could get by reading columns of sweeping generalities and statistics."

There had been a time when a strike was usually reported in terms of the number of heads broken in disorders, and not infrequently with incomplete information about one side or the other. But Johnson emphasized that times had changed. "Every strike lead must be made to reflect a serious and sincere effort to tell both sides," he hammered at reporters in a series of memoranda. "If one group refuses to be quoted, show plainly in the body of the story that an effort was made to obtain that group's version. Every strike story must contain prominently a clear explanation of the reasons for the strike. When a labor dispute is settled don't make the mistake of 'picking a winner.' Give the terms of settlement and the original demands of the union and let the terms speak for themselves. Beware of inside dope on what employers or labor unions plan to do at some future time."

Frankness in writing also was a subject of some of Johnson's memoranda. On one occasion a correspondent in a southern city telephoned to New York late at night the story of a triangle love affair and shooting involving a high state official who, just before he pulled the trigger, exclaimed: "I'll kill the son of a bitch." Delos Smith, editor of the overnight desk in New York, put the quotation on the wire the next morning with some trepidation, but Johnson backed Smith's judgment although he doubted that many newspapers would use the quote. He also backed up another news story in which a federal judge, questioning a witness in an important trial, used the phrase "whore houses."

"This raises the question," Johnson wrote in his weekly memorandum, "of how far we can go under our policy of frank reporting. What we must avoid (and this is the crux of what I have to say on the subject) is creating an impression of trying to be daring or flippant in the use of such terms . . .

We must employ our new freedom with discretion, restraint, and good taste always."

For the most part Johnson avoided the "needling" method of getting results from his news staff or, if he used the needle, it was subtly. In a way not easy to define he acted as a kind of shock absorber for Baillie's high-octane personality. It was not unusual for people to remark that Baillie was such a dominant personality that he overshadowed everybody else in the organization; that others had little chance to emerge because Baillie ran the works in unchallenged fashion. This was an exaggeration. Baillie was the boss, but Johnson knew how to make the most of his good ideas. Not infrequently, Baillie snapped at him: "You're watering me down! You're holding down my ideas." On some occasions this may have been true.

4.

Joseph L. Jones became general foreign manager of the United Press in 1937. A slender, quiet man, Jones had joined the company even before he was graduated from Columbia University, and had literally grown up with the expanding service to newspapers outside the United States, serving in South America and Europe as well as at New York headquarters.

In the 1930s Jones and Assistant European Manager Harry Flory began development of transmission over improved wireless communications facilities that, over the years, would make a tremendous change in distribution of news around the world. Lester Ziffren of the United Press bureau in Madrid had worked out a deal in 1934 for a brief voice broadcast each night from Spain to New York and Buenos Aires. This broadcast was something like the United Press system of telephonic "pony" news service to client newspapers in the United States. A member of the Madrid bureau read the report rapidly, it was recorded at the receiving points and then transcribed by running the recording machine at a lower speed. It was, of course, seldom useful for spot news and, for the most part, the dispatches transmitted in this manner were supplementary or secondary material.

In 1934 a similar method of transmission—slow but at a low cost—was started from the Pontoise wireless station near Paris, but it was in Morse code rather than voice. It started as a thirty-minute transmission but soon was extended to two hours daily. A similar broadcast was later started from Rome. This supplementary service proved successful enough to prompt Flory and A. L. Bradford, general manager for South America, to establish a more effective wireless transmission from Amsterdam in 1936. London, Berlin, and other bureaus could quickly get in touch with Amsterdam by telex—leased-wire printer paid for according to the time it was used—or by telephone. H. C. Buurman, the Amsterdam manager, and three assistants recorded and relayed these dispatches by telex to the government wireless station. There they were transmitted on separate channels to New York and Buenos Aires over regular circuits at speeds as high as 100 words a minute.

It was the beginning of a tremendous change in the distribution of news around the world. Greater and greater volume of words was giving the peoples of almost every country a better understanding of each other. And the steady improvement of wireless facilities was opening the way toward a day when news agencies could get news from or transmit news to a newspaper halfway around the world as easily and as economically as to a client twenty miles away.

5.

The spotlight on news developments shifted back and forth erratically from day to day and week to week, and a world news agency had to be prepared to shift a little ahead of the spotlight. In the spring of 1935 Webb Miller thought he saw signs that the spotlight was going to shift again, this time to the remote and almost inaccessible frontier between the African kingdom of Ethiopia and the Italian colony of Eritrea. On the surface there wasn't much reason for Miller to pick the Eritrea frontier despite the fact that there had been reports of minor clashes between Italian and Ethiopian troops. Premier Mussolini, to be sure, had rattled his sword occasionally in speeches directed against the Ethiopian government, but that was more or less normal for Il Duce. Most observers decided Mussolini was bluffing. The British Foreign Office refused to be worried. But Miller's information from Rome indicated that grave trouble was coming. In addition, the United Press had a string correspondent, Dan Sanford, in Addis Ababa, capital of Haile Selassie's kingdom, and his reports left no doubt that the government there was worried.

By the end of May, Miller was convinced that Mussolini intended to act. He sent Edward W. Beattie from the Berlin bureau on the long trek to Addis Ababa. Beattie was the first American correspondent to arrive in Ethiopia and the first to get an interview with Emperor Haile Selassie regarding the League of Nations' efforts to prevent an Italo-Ethiopian war. Sanford, who had been acting as United Press correspondent, was a trusted friend of the Emperor, but he resigned shortly after Beattie's arrival and T. J. Rohrbaugh was hired to replace him. The government had established a kind of press office with a couple of young European-educated Ethiopians in charge, and there was a radio station with a cluttered little office across from the Imperial Hotel. The Ethiopian armed forces were not modernized and did not appear likely to withstand an assault by Fascist troops. Beattie reported that the small Imperial Guard was the only unit with uniforms and modern weapons, and that the air force consisted of four old biplanes. The army was made up of tribesmen with swords, shields, spears, and in some instances guns with a few rounds of ammunition. Most of the guns were the French *fusil gras*—breech loaders made around 1874. Others ranged from blunderbusses to modern sports guns.

One of Beattie's expense accounts sent to Charles E. Campbell, the company's European comptroller, eloquently suggested the life of a war correspondent in Ethiopia:

	(35¢ per thaler)
Canvas bag for camping	48 thalers
Provisions in field	201 thalers
Mule	240 thalers
Boy's wages	60 thalers
Feed for mule	9 thalers
Mauser rifle and ammunition	280 thalers
Canvas for tent	135 thalers
High boots	45 thalers
3 pack & riding mules & feed	210 thalers

In August the British Foreign Office was still insisting that Mussolini would not dare defy Britain, the League of Nations, and world opinion by starting a war. A lot of other experts were insisting in much the same vein. General Manager Kent Cooper of the Associated Press was asked about the danger of military action by a reporter from the *Times-Union,* at Rochester, New York, when he arrived there for a sailing trip with the newspaper's publisher, Frank E. Gannett. Cooper was quoted in his host's newspaper as saying that war would remain just a threat.

Hugh Baillie, however, was still receiving ominous predictions from Stewart Brown, the United Press manager in Rome, and he decided to take no chances. He told Bud Ekins, then in New York, to get started for Harar, which was not far from the southern frontier of Ethiopia facing Italian Somaliland. Later, when he was in Paris, Baillie was still unsatisfied. He called in Reynolds and Eleanor Packard. "Can you catch a boat from Marseilles the day after tomorrow for Djibouti?" he asked.

"Isn't there anything sooner?" Eleanor quipped. The Packards caught the boat.

Meantime, Baillie had sent a message to London suggesting that Webb Miller cover the Italian armed forces assembled on the northern frontier of Ethiopia. Miller, the war correspondent who hated wars, bought himself a tropical outfit including woolen "cholera belts" to protect the abdomen from sudden chills, got himself inoculated against cholera, plague, typhoid, and paratyphoid, laid in a supply of quinine, and flew down to Rome to be enrolled as an accredited correspondent.

It took him almost a month to get his press card. By then the war scare had grown and the Italian Press Ministry had announced that fourteen foreign correspondents would be taken to Eritrea in a group on the S.S. *Vulcania* within a short time. Miller refused to wait and finally persuaded Count di Minerbi, assistant to the Press Minister, to give him press credentials—but without any official arrangements for his transportation to Eritrea. As a matter of fact, the crush of travel was so great that Di Minerbi assured Miller it was impossible to buy a ship or plane ticket to Egypt and that there was no possible way he could get to Eritrea prior to the official press trip. He was almost right. That night Miller, without a ticket, bluffed his way on to the crowded Italian liner *Esperia* at Naples. He bribed the purser to provide him a pallet in the tiny, hot quarters of a crew member, and arrived in Alexandria only a few hours before the twice-a-week Imperial Airways plane left for Khartoum.

All commercial planes out of Alexandria were overcrowded and there were no tickets for sale at any price. The Imperial Airways agent even showed Miller his manifest to prove that the plane for Khartoum was loaded to the last ounce permitted by Air Ministry regulations. Miller argued for an hour, and the agent eventually agreed to order other passengers to leave behind one piece of baggage each in order to get the correspondent aboard. Miller climbed on the plane at dawn, complaining as bitterly as other passengers about the last-moment arbitrary order to leave one bag behind. Actually his own baggage included a folding cot, blankets, a medical kit, water canteen, candles, flashlight, toilet paper, a Flit gun, and a large package of writing materials.

Flying from Khartoum the next day in an Italian plane, Miller landed at Italian army headquarters at Asmara on September 26. Floyd Gibbons of International News Service, who had wangled permission for a special flight from Rome because Mussolini was then writing articles for the Hearst newspapers, had arrived twenty-four hours earlier and was the only other American or British correspondent in the soldier-jammed, mosquito-infested little town. The next day Miller sat in the copilot's seat of an Italian bomber while Count Galeazzo Ciano, son-in-law of Mussolini and commander of the Desperation Squadron, flew him over the frontier, where some 200,000 Italian troops were concentrated, awaiting orders to invade a grim wilderness of mountains and gorges in Ethiopia. Miller also drove by automobile in the next few days to the advance posts of the army above the valley of the Mareb, seeing at first hand the elaborate preparations for the attack and studying for the first time the novel little whippet tanks manned by Mussolini's Black Shirts. The tanks hardly reached to a man's shoulder but they carried a driver and a machine gunner, could move at thirty miles an hour and climb almost anywhere on the rugged terrain.

By the time he returned to Asmara on October 1 Miller had notebooks filled with details of the preparations. He balanced his portable typewriter on a suitcase in his crowded, steaming headquarters and began writing a 2000-word description of the Italian and native forces assembled on the frontier, their modern equipment, the methods of fighting employed by native soldiers, and the manner in which the Fascists had blended ancient and modern methods of warfare for the invasion. Repeatedly he made it clear in his cable that "the most important developments" were at hand and that there should soon be "big news here or in Rome." To his surprise the censor passed the dispatch without a change. There was a great congestion of wireless communications from Asmara, but Miller's story reached New York, via Rome, in time for afternoon newspapers of October 2.

At one o'clock on the morning of October 3, Miller climbed into an automobile with Count di Bosdari, the Italian press officer, and drove in comfort from Asmara to the brow of Coatit Mountain to watch a Fascist dictator start a war. Never in history, he thought, had any war been so conveniently arranged on a fixed schedule for a correspondent. Not only had he had a full preview of the men and material assembled for the invasion, but he had a knowledge of the terrain over which the advance would move and the exact hour—5 A.M.—at which it would start.

Miller had not wasted the hours prior to his departure from Asmara. He had written a series of cable dispatches describing the scene of invasion, the equipment, and the troops involved. These he had taken to the censor, with whom he had a long talk. "You can't send these dispatches now," the correspondent pointed out, "but at five o'clock the official dispatches from the front will announce that the invasion has started. Then you will be able to put your stamp of approval on a dispatch carrying that announcement." Miller wanted to file his dispatches with the understanding that the censor would approve them and turn them over to the wireless operators as soon as possible—that is, upon official word that the invasion had started. The censor accepted the dispatches and Miller left for Coatit Mountain.

Dawn came shortly before five o'clock. A press officer notified the correspondents—there were still no American or British reporters present except Miller and Gibbons—that they could send five messages of twenty words each over the army telegraph lines that had been extended from Asmara to the front. All other copy had to be sent sixty miles by motorcycle to Asmara. Just before five o'clock Miller typed out his first message:

FLASH ITALIAN ADVANCE INTO ETHIOPIA STARTED FIVE A.M.

Holding the message in his hand, he watched through field glasses as gray-clad Italian soldiers waded the shallow Belesa River into Ethiopia. He could even see the rifles they held high above their heads as they crossed. He brushed a swarm of flies off his face and hurried to file his flash on the army telegraph to Asmara. The message reached New York at 4:27 A.M. (EST)—more than five hours before the Associated Press received its first news of the invasion from Rome. Three hours later Italian bombers attacked the Ethiopian town of Adowa, forty miles inside the frontier. By nightfall Miller had sent a number of brief messages by telegraph to Asmara and additional copy by courier. By then the Italians had occupied 2000 square miles of Ethiopian territory.

By nightfall, too, Miller had scooped the world, including the Italian foreign office. His foresight in turning over his background copy to the censor before leaving Asmara and his knowledge of transmission routes had enabled him to lay down a comprehensive, colorful story in every capital of the world. A message arriving from Rome Manager Stewart Brown late that night informed him that his first bulletins had reached Rome even before the Army's official dispatch advising the Italian government that the invasion had started. As Ed Keen had so often told his staff, a story was no good until it was laid down on the desk of the telegraph editors. Miller laid it down as few other war correspondents ever had.

The magazine *Newsweek* in its mid-October issue devoted a couple of columns to reporters covering the Ethiopian war. Its review included the following:

Had they had Jerusalem's Wailing Wall last week, Associated Press directors—in New York for their annual fall business session—could have poured out before it the multitude of woes that beset them.

Newspaper readers were eating up the Italo-Ethiopian war in large chunks. But Associated Press credit lines on battlefront stories were conspicuously lacking.

Weren't any of AP's 2,000 full-time employes on hand to watch Mussolini's son-in-law, Count Galeazzo Ciano, lead his bombing squadron over the Eritrean frontier? Was the world's biggest news service trying to cover history's best-advertised war from Addis Ababa, 350 miles from the front?

The Ethiopian war dragged on through the spring of 1936. The conquest proved much more difficult and expensive for Italy than Mussolini had anticipated. Covering the story was costly for the United Press, too. When the bills were added up, they totaled a quarter of a million dollars.

CHAPTER TWENTY-TWO

The great tide of news events that had begun breaking over the world in 1933 did not recede; on the contrary it gained momentum in the middle years of the decade and at times seemed to put an unbearable strain on news-gathering facilities almost everywhere.

Late on the morning of July 17, 1936, an unusual message was laid on the news desk at the United Press bureau in London. It was from Lester Ziffren in the Madrid bureau and it began something like this:

MOTHERS EVERLASTINGLY LINGERING ILLNESS LIKELY LARYNGITIS AUNT FLORA OUGHT RETURN EVEN IF GOES NORTH LATER EQUALLY GOOD IF ONLY NIGHT. . . .

There was more, much more, of the same. The desk man started to complain to the telegraph operator that the message was garbled. Then he had a second thought. He counted the words and checked the word count that appears on each telegraphic message. They tallied. This was the way Ziffren had filed the message. Bureau Manager Clifford L. Day was summoned for consultation. Harry Flory stopped by the desk and examined the message. They all agreed that Ziffren had sent the message for a good reason and the only reason would be that it contained a code. Everybody took a copy and started working. It didn't take long. The first letter of each word spelled out a message:

MELILLA FOREIGN LEGION REVOLTED MARTIAL LAW DECLARED

The Spanish civil war had started. Ziffren's message was the first word to come through Spanish censorship about the uprising of foreign legionnaires at Melilla, in Morocco, under the leadership of a group of monarchist generals and admirals. One of the longest and bloodiest struggles of Spanish history was under way.

The United Press corps of reporters—Irving P. Pflaum, Herbert Clark, Leon Kay, Eleanor and Reynolds Packard, Jan Yindrich, Everett Holles, Edward C. DePury, and others—covering the Spanish conflict soon discovered that it was not only difficult but often highly dangerous to collect and send out the news. There was a tendency on both sides to avoid taking prisoners. Mass executions were routine. Brother was pitted against brother and everyone, including correspondents, was likely to be suspect.

Henry T. Gorrell, who had been through a couple of South American revolutions, was sent from Italy to Madrid in September of 1936. The republican forces—led by the Spanish anarchist faction—were shooting first and asking questions later as they struggled to put down the insurgents. Watching the fighting outside the gates of Toledo in October, Gorrell observed that he was being viewed suspiciously by government soldiers because he spoke Spanish with an Italian accent and had recently been in Italy. A short time later he was approached by a soldier and told he was under arrest. He was so surprised and alarmed that he became even more confused when officers questioned him and replied in a mixture of Spanish and Italian. That was enough to convince his captors.

"You've been in Fascist Italy!" they accused him.

"Certainly," Gorrell replied, "but I am a neutral observer, a reporter. You have no right to arrest me."

Instead of replying, a soldier clipped a tag on Gorrell's arm and another on the arm of his Spanish chauffeur. Gorrell's number was 61. They were taken to a crowded dungeon in Madrid's central prison. There was not even room for everyone to sit on the floor at the same time. Gorrell saw a number of well dressed men and women—one of them wearing an expensive fur coat—as well as workers in dirty clothes. All of them wore tags. Occasionally a guard in blue denim overalls would call out a series of names and numbers. Nobody ever answered him because they knew that those led away were being taken to the execution grounds. The guard would then sort out the numbers called, tie the victims' wrists together and lead them away. Suddenly Gorrell was acutely aware of the numbers being called: " . . . thirty-nine . . . forty . . . forty-one . . ."

A group was sorted out and led away. Now the count was only a score short of his number—sixty-one. The count had gone up to forty-eight before colleagues from the Madrid bureau located Gorrell and his chauffeur and arranged for their release. So far as the correspondent could find out later, they were the only ones in the room who survived.

Two weeks later Gorrell discovered that the insurgents were operating in the same fashion. On October 25 he was driving on the Madrid-Valencia highway when a procession of vehicles was ambushed by Moorish troops which had been brought into Spain by the insurgents. Moorish soldiers surrounded Gorrell's automobile, motioning him to get out. While one pointed a gun at his stomach, others began relieving him of his possessions. Gorrell had been told that the Moors were being "paid" in loot but that they never robbed a corpse. This seemed at the moment to be no more than a technicality that would delay the shooting until after he had been robbed. As the last cuff link was being removed from his sleeves, however, an Italian tank rolled along the road and the driver recognized Gorrell as an American he had talked with not long before. He stopped, pointed out to the Moors that Gorrell had an American flag on his sleeve, and then led the correspondent back toward the field headquarters of the regimental commander. Along the road were the bodies—most of them stripped of even their underwear by the Moorish troops—of approximately 350 persons who had been killed in the ambush.

At field headquarters the commander looked at Gorrell without enthusiasm and said: "Congratulations. You are a prisoner of war—the only one we have taken today."

The tragedy of the Spanish war dragged on until the winter of 1939, when the exhausted republican government forces had fallen back on their last stronghold at Barcelona. Communist influence had mounted in government circles and Harold Peters, the United Press manager at Barcelona, was frequently in considerable jeopardy as he sought to send out news of the Franco advance. Despite the warnings of government officials about writing "pessimistic" dispatches, Peters managed on January 23 to give the impression that the end was near:

BY HAROLD PETERS

BARCELONA, January 23 (UP)—*The entire Spanish Republic was placed under a state of war, equivalent to martial law, today as Barcelona prepared to defend the city against General Franco's army of Spaniards, Moors, Italians and Germans. It was reported that the town of Martorell, ten miles to the west, had fallen.*

The next day he was talking by telephone to the London bureau. He had written a long and boring dispatch quoting official communiqués and the statements of government officials. It was so boring, he hoped, that the censor listening in on the telephone would be lulled to sleep. After dictating some 700 words in a monotonous tone, Peters interpolated in his dispatch a few words that he trusted would escape the ears of the censor: "big shots scrammed Franceward." Then, without changing his tone or interrupting the flow of words, he went on dictating his routine story. His interpolation was not missed when the recording was played back in London. A flash that the republican government had fled Barcelona in the direction of France was cabled around the world—and the end of the Spanish war was at hand.

2.

The flexibility of the United Press, the agency's willingness to move its best reporters and editors to any spot where news was breaking, was perhaps best demonstrated during the critical sit-down strikes of 1936 and 1937. Its two top correspondents in Detroit—James C. Austin and Wiley S. Maloney—had foreseen the conflict between labor and management and had spent many weeks building up close working relationships with officials of the big automobile companies and union leaders. After the United Automobile Workers joined John L. Lewis' Committee for Industrial Organization and began an organizing drive, Austin and Maloney kept in close touch with both sides, gave equal attention to news developments from management and labor, and, in return, received many advance tips that enabled them to prepare for important news breaks.

The sit-down strike, first practiced in France, was something new in America, but the UAW officials quickly adopted it as an effective weapon against the automobile companies. The basic pattern was established when the Inland Steel plant was struck in East Detroit. The workers simply took possession of the plant and refused to move. Women's auxiliaries cooked food for them and frequently demonstrated in front of the plant. Maloney got a pass from the union and was boosted into a window of the plant after dark. A guide was assigned to him because the strikers at that time were inclined to slug anybody they didn't know, and he made a tour of the dark, barnlike sheds. The workers were gathered around bonfires they had lighted in 50-gallon and 100-gallon steel barrels. The machinery was silent and the plant was unheated against the crisp fall weather, but the strikers were in high spirits. Maloney's story was the first vivid description of the manner in which the sit-down strikes were conducted under the firm disciplinary hand of union leaders.

At the same time Austin and Maloney maintained excellent contacts with representatives of management, and Harry Bennett, an ex-sailor and trouble shooter for Henry Ford, who had the best industrial spy system in the nation, gave them the terms of settlement of the Inland Steel strike hours before it was announced.

The UAW moved against the big companies on New Year's Day of 1937, seizing two Fisher Body plants at Flint that supplied Chevrolet, Buick, Oldsmobile, and Pontiac. Once the big show started, Earl Johnson moved his New York news editor, Mert Akers, and his top reporter, Harry Ferguson, to Detroit. He also began moving in a steady stream of reinforcements from other bureaus. In the following weeks the staff was expanded by the arrival of News Editor Boyd Lewis and Reporter William H. Lawrence from the Chicago bureau, C. L. Sulzberger of the Washington bureau, Ed Brant, Gene Pulliam, Robert LaBlonde, Don Pryor, Claude Markel, William McCall, and Harris Coates.

In Detroit and nearby industrial cities in this period there were as many as seventy-five strikes in progress at one time. General Motors eventually was granted an injunction that required the strikers to vacate, and Governor Frank Murphy made an arrangement with the union leaders to move the strikers out of the plants on the understanding that the company would bargain with the UAW. That day Bill Lawrence stopped at the headquarters of the Flint Alliance, a so-called company union, and was shown a statement that General Motors had agreed to bargain with them rather than with the UAW. Lawrence telephoned this development to the United Press office and then went around to see the UAW leaders who were preparing to hold a "victory banquet" before the sit-down strikers marched out of the plants. He told Wyndham Mortimer, a vice-president of the UAW, of what he had learned at the Flint Alliance headquarters.

"What!" Mortimer yelled. "We've been double-crossed! They are supposed to have agreed to bargain exclusively with us."

The UAW officials promptly called off their plans to vacate the plants and then called Lawrence into a meeting of officers to ask him for details of the announcement that had been made by the Flint Alliance. While he was still there, one of the officials telephoned Governor Murphy and told him that the whole deal was off. They then permitted Lawrence to use their telephone to relay these developments to his office before making an official announcement.

Several days later Murphy got the situation untangled, the strikers vacated the plants, and the UAW began negotiations that ended in a settlement, the terms of which Maloney had on the United Press wires just an hour before they were formally announced.

3.

In the autumn of 1936 romance almost crowded stories of war and threats of war off the front pages. On October 27, Mrs. Wallis Warfield Simpson, originally of Baltimore, was granted a divorce at Ipswich, England, from Ernest A. Simpson, an insurance salesman. No British newspaper took note of this event, but it was news in America and elsewhere because Mrs. Simpson had often been seen in the company of Britain's monarch, Edward VIII. The story of Mrs. Simpson's activities simmered along until November and then began to blossom out as a royal romance everywhere except in the British press.

When Hugh Baillie left New York for London the story was on every tongue and in most newspapers; but when he reached London on November 12 the newspapers there still had not even printed Mrs. Simpson's name. Furthermore, Baillie was sharply criticized by several London publishers because the United Press had carried stories linking the King with Mrs. Simpson. It was not, they insisted, in "good taste" and anyway it would all blow over.

This posed a highly difficult problem for the United Press bureau in London and, since he was there at the time, for Baillie. American newspapers were clamoring for information about the royal romance. Webb Miller was in daily contact with several persons, including Lord Beaverbrook, who were very close to Edward VIII. Beaverbrook was confident that the romance would not blow over, but might well lead to the most important decisions. Yet nobody could be sure. There was always the strong possibility that the King would bow to tradition and that the affair would never become public. Rumors of almost every kind were cheap in London; facts were scarce until December 4, when Prime Minister Stanley Baldwin announced in the House of Commons that Parliament would not be asked to pass a bill permitting a morganatic marriage between the King and Mrs. Simpson. There were mounting rumors that the King was planning to abdicate, and on December 6 the United Press carried a story saying that Queen Mary feared her son was planning to give up the crown for the American woman, who, by that time, had gone to France. The London *Daily Mirror* summed up the crisis by declaring that it was due to wild rumors circulated by the hooligans and gangsters of the American press.

On the following Monday, December 7, the Prime Minister declared that the government was waiting for Edward VIII to make up his mind. That afternoon Frederick Kuh came into the office with a story that the monarch had already decided—he was going to abdicate. Baillie had no doubt of Kuh's access to excellent diplomatic sources, but he decided against carrying the story. There was too great a chance that the King would be persuaded to change his mind. If that happened there would never be a chance to explain why the United Press had been right one day but wrong the next. The next day Webb Miller received practically the same story from Lord Beaverbrook, but there were so many rumors and counterrumors that again Baillie killed the story rather than take a chance.

Late that evening, however, a long-standing friendship paid off for the United Press. When Queen Victoria of Spain had been forced to flee from Madrid in 1931 she had been practically escorted by the agency's reporters all the way to Paris and London. During her exile in London, Henry Tosti Russell had called on her frequently, and occasionally she had given him information that he could use in a story. He called on her again on the evening of December 8 and they talked about the constitutional crisis that was shaking the country. The Queen was closely allied to Buckingham Palace and knew what had been happening inside the royal family. She disclosed that the King had made it clear to the family that he intended to abdicate in order to marry Mrs. Simpson and, emphatically, that his decision was "irrevocable." In other words, there was no longer any chance that he could be persuaded to change his mind.

Russell called the news desk not long after midnight and dictated the story, without naming the source of his information. As he finished, the desk editor got him on the telephone.

"This looks right," he said, "but in view of everything I have to have the boss's okay to send this to New York. Will you call Harry Flory and tell him the facts?"

Russell roused Flory from bed and repeated the story, explaining the source of his information. Baillie was asleep at his hotel and Flory decided not to call him. Instead he telephoned the news desk and said: "Go ahead and send Tosti's story. It's authentic."

Shortly after the cables had been filed, an urgent message reached the London desk. New York wanted reassurance:

WE READY GO TO TOWN ON TOSTIS STORY AND ASSUME THERE NO QUES-
TION AUTHENTICITY

JOHNSON

Flory replied that there was no question. Johnson went to town with the news of the King's "irrevocable" decision. The next day there was another message from Johnson:

PRESS UNIPRESS LONDON
WEBB FLORY CLIFF TOSTI KUH ETAL NEW YORK PAPERS SOLID UNIPRESS
STOP GREATEST CLEANUP EVER STOP HONEST GODWARD YOU NEVER SAW
ANYTHING LIKE IT COUNTRYWIDE STOP CHEERS INROLLING

JOHNSON

On December 11 Edward VIII abdicated to marry "the woman I love."

4.

There were oddities as well as crises in the swift current of news events during the late 1930s. One day in 1937 Boston Manager Henry Minott answered the telephone and heard the voice of his Portland, Maine, correspondent shouting: "Say, there's a guy being carried half a mile into the air by a bunch of toy balloons!"

Minott didn't believe a word of it. He began asking questions.

"Oh, the guy's all right," his correspondent said. "A priest just shot him down with a rifle."

This was almost enough to persuade Minott that he would have to hire a new correspondent in Portland, but gradually he established the facts. Phil Coolidge, a newsreel cameraman, had arranged to have one of his assistants, Al Mingalone, who was small and light, lifted into the air about 100 feet by a cluster of newly developed latex balloons used for weather studies. It was a stunt and Coolidge expected to get a good feature picture. Twenty-eight balloons were filled with gas, strapped to Mingalone's parachute harness, which in turn was attached to a rope. Mingalone was carried 100 feet into the air and was busy taking pictures of the countryside when the anchor rope snapped. Off he soared.

Father James J. Mullen of St. Margaret's Church at Old Orchard Beach happened to be watching. When the rope broke he ran to his rectory and got his rifle. He jumped into Coolidge's car and they started southward in pursuit of the frightened Mingalone. Just south of Biddeford they caught up with the unhappy balloonist, and near Wells Beach the priest fired several shots at the balloons, which were then high above the ground. His aim was good and the gas began leaking, slowly lowering Mingalone to the earth some thirteen miles from his starting point. He wasn't even scratched.

In a quarter of a century of service with the United Press, it was the strangest story Minott had ever handled.

There was trouble in Arizona in 1939. A notorious murderess, Winnie Ruth Judd, had escaped from the Arizona State Hospital for the Insane and was presumably roaming the countryside with homicide in her heart. Every law enforcement officer in the state was searching for her, and so was every newspaperman.

The United Press manager at Phoenix was a comparative newcomer, Roger Tatarian, who was badly outnumbered by opposition reporters and had little opportunity to sleep until the Los Angeles bureau sent Frederick C. Othman to give him a helping hand. After twelve days no trace of the escaped murderess had been found and both Tatarian and his wife, Eunice, who had been helping cover the story, were close to exhaustion. Othman took over the bureau that night while Tatarian covered the sheriff's office. There was no news and Othman, trying to keep awake, began pacing up and down the hallway, past the offices of the Phoenix *Republic's* radio station, KTAR, where a secretary was on late duty. As Othman passed the door the girl was talking excitedly on the telephone and exclaiming that she didn't know what to do. Othman offered to help.

"The governor is on the phone," she explained, holding the instrument out to Othman, "but I don't know what to tell him."

"I've been trying to get the city desk of the *Republic* for ten minutes," the governor exclaimed, "but all the lines are busy. I want to get a message to the city editor."

"Go right ahead, sir," Othman replied.

"Well, we've found Winnie Ruth Judd. She's been hiding in a cornfield and tonight she voluntarily returned to the hospital. She just got tired of hiding out."

"Thank you, Governor," Othman said. "Thank you."

He walked back down the hall to the United Press bureau and began sending out the story. A few minutes later the return of Mrs. Judd was announced exclusively by the United Press. Tatarian, meanwhile, had gone to the state hospital. There were two telephones there, one in the superintendent's office and one in an anteroom. Tatarian hid the phone in the ante-room under a table. He had already gotten the details of Mrs. Judd's return from the superintendent when the door burst open and a dozen reporters crashed into the room, demanded to know whether Mrs. Judd had returned and began fighting for the office telephone. Tatarian slipped out, crawled under the table in the anteroom, and began dictating the superintendent's story to his office.

5.

More than anything else in the late 1930s the threat of war in Europe domi-nated the news report. Month by month the angry voice of Adolph Hitler grew louder. Austria fell under Nazi domination. In 1938 Hitler demanded a plebiscite on the return of the Sudetenland, a part of Czechoslovakia, to Germany. Ed Beattie hurried to the Sudetenland and turned up a good story of preparations for Czech resistance to the Nazis. But when he went to the Eger post office to telephone Prague, the censor informed him that all toll calls would have to be made in the Czech language. Beattie protested bit-terly, and finally the censor agreed that he could talk to Prague in German. Beattie put his call through to the porter at the Ambassador Hotel, where most of the foreign correspondents stayed, and told the porter to look around the lobby for a German-speaking newspaperman.

"I see Mr. Shirer," the porter said.

"Put him on the phone," Beattie ordered.

William L. Shirer, one of the American reporters working out of Berlin, took Beattie's story in longhand and relayed it to London.

Meantime the Czechs were getting little support from the big democracies. Britain and France, allies of Czechoslovakia, vainly tried to bluff Hitler and then turned to compromise. In September, British Prime Minister Neville Chamberlain agreed to meet Hitler at the little Rhine town of Godesberg to discuss a general peace settlement with specific reference to Czechoslovakia. Some two hundred newspaper and press association correspondents as well as hundreds of tourists and German visitors descended on the Godesberger Hotel, which had just two ancient telephone lines to carry news of the con-ference to the world. Eight other lines were hurriedly rigged and a corps of telephone operators from Cologne rushed to the scene.

Beattie had arrived prior to the great influx and made such advance preparations as were possible, but it was obvious that there would be one of the greatest communications crushes of all time. Webb Miller accompa-nied Chamberlain to Godesberg and was quartered with the British dele-gation, at the Petersberg Hotel across the Rhine River. Telephone calls to any point were delayed by as much as five hours. By the time it became apparent that Hitler was likely to get the Sudetenland if Chamberlain could persuade the Czechs to give it up without war, Beattie was putting in si-multaneous lightning telephone calls at three times the usual cost to Berlin,

London, Paris, and Amsterdam and trying to hold his ground against fifty other correspondents who wanted to telephone at any given moment. One telephone girl was carried out in hysterics. Another kept her nerve only by taking regular sips from a glass of brandy at her elbow.

On one occasion when Miller, who could look out of his hotel window and see the Godesberger Hotel across the river, wanted to get a message to Beattie, the local telephone proved useless. He put in a lightning or triple-rate call to Paris and instructed the bureau there to send an urgent telegram to Beattie asking him if he could get across the river to the Petersberg Hotel. Later when Beattie wanted to exchange information with Miller he called Berlin, which opened a telephone line to the London bureau, which then telephoned Miller, and the two correspondents at Godesberg thus communicated through two relays over hundreds of miles.

The next day Reynolds Packard and Hans Thomas at Prague scored a beat of more than half an hour on announcement that the Czech government would accept the German demands for a plebiscite in the Sudetenland, but by that time Hitler was demanding outright cession of the territory. The process of yielding to Hitler to avoid war had begun. The fifteen-day international crisis reached a climax on September 29, when Hitler, Mussolini, Chamberlain, and French Premier Édouard Daladier met at Munich to seal the bargain at the expense of the Czechs. Miller, Beattie, Ralph Forte from Rome, Robert Best from Vienna, and Edward DePury from Paris converged on the Munich conference. By midafternoon they had the story—mostly from German sources—that the Sudetenland would be ceded to Germany in return for a four-power pact that Chamberlain later said would guarantee "peace in our time." The only question that remained was whether the Czechs would go it alone by fighting.

Packard provided the answer the next morning with a one-hour beat on an official announcement that Czechoslovakia had accepted the Munich agreement.

War had been averted—for a year.

The temporary end of the European war crisis was greeted with a mixture of relief and anger. Americans were officially neutral. Many were determined that this country would not again get into a foreign war. But there were many others who had watched the rise of the Italian and German dictatorships with alarm. President Roosevelt was among those feeling alarm. He sought to use his influence to strengthen Great Britain and France which had placed orders for hundreds of millions of dollars' worth of airplanes and other equipment from American manufacturers.

The United States Neutrality Act placed stern restrictions on the President's power to assist any nation at war. If war began in Europe it would be impossible under terms of the act to ship war materials to the democracies. The question was whether Hitler would strike again before Britain and

France were prepared. In March of 1939 a short urgent message from Hans Thomas, United Press correspondent at Prague, indicated the answer. There was trouble in Slovakia, where Hungarian Nazis were trying, with Hitler's encouragement, to break off another piece of Czechoslovakia. The Nazis were again denouncing Czechoslovakia. Ed Beattie flew to Prague just in time to turn out a story of German military occupation of the Czech capital amid tears and jeers of crowds lining the streets. On March 22 George Kidd of the Berlin bureau reported the details of Hitler's seizure of Memel, on the Baltic Sea, from Lithuania.

The swift sequence of events in March was followed by new Hitler propaganda attacks on Poland and left little doubt that German expansion would be pushed to the limit, that the policy of appeasement had failed. In Washington, President Roosevelt and Secretary of State Cordell Hull undertook a more vigorous role in behalf of the democracies. As a preliminary step, the President secretly sent a message urging peace to both Hitler and Mussolini. It didn't remain secret very long. On the morning of April 16 United Press Correspondent Pierre Salarnier met a French cabinet minister leaving his office in Paris. When Salarnier attempted to ask him a routine question, the minister explained that he did not have time to talk. He made a vague reference to a message from Washington. Salarnier began a systematic check of French government sources. Two hours later he called the office and talked to Manager Ralph Heinzen.

"It's a message from Roosevelt to Hitler and Mussolini," he said.

"Do you know what it says?" Heinzen asked.

"Well, I'll have to talk fast," Salarnier replied. "A friend lent me a copy of the text but I have to hand it back to him in just ten minutes."

Eleven minutes later the highlights of the President's message were on the cables to New York.

President Roosevelt did not put much faith, however, in messages appealing to the better instincts of the dictators. He began a drive in Congress for changes in the Neutrality Act that would relieve him of the necessity of declaring an embargo on arms shipments at the outbreak of war, and would thus increase the weight of his influence in European affairs. His first move in this direction failed. By a vote of twelve to eleven, the Senate Foreign Relations Committee decided not to propose the change in Congress. That afternoon, Ronald G. Van Tine, the United Press Senate chief, talked the situation over with a member of the committee.

"The President is hopping mad," the senator said. "He is talking about sending a rip-snorting message to Congress in hope of getting the changes made, but Hull is strongly opposed to trying to do it that way."

Van Tine advised Grattan F. McGroarty, covering the State Department, and asked him to do some investigating there. McGroarty called back later with similar information, and Van Tine wrote a story that the President and Hull "were reported in Administration quarters today to have disagreed on the language of a neutrality message the President plans to send to Congress." Mr. Roosevelt read the story in the antiadministration Washington *Times-Herald* under a screaming headline: "Neutrality Note Splits F.D.R. & Hull."

If Mr. Roosevelt was not in an angry mood earlier he certainly was after he had read the headline. He summoned Bureau Manager Lyle C. Wilson to the White House and bitterly denounced the story. Wilson said that Van Tine and McGroarty had every reason to believe their information was correct, that it came from highly responsible persons, and that he stood behind the story until it was proved wrong. The President then issued an unprecedented formal statement denying the story. "The headline is, of course, wholly false; so is the story," he said. "The United Press has been guilty of a falsification of the actual facts. If called upon to give the source of the information, they will decline to give it. . . . It represents a culmination of other false news stories. . . . This latest episode . . . represents the limit of any decent person's patience."

A little later the administration renewed its efforts to get action from Congress but, despite the fact that the President's feeling on the subject was known to be intense, the new neutrality message was moderate in tone and persuasive in the Hull manner rather than a Rooseveltian polemic. Hugh Baillie got in the last word with a statement calling attention to the fact that the tone of the message was in line with the controversial story written by Van Tine. "The information in the [United Press] story was obtained from government officials at both ends of Pennsylvania Avenue," Baillie added. "We regarded those sources as reliable and we regarded the information as news, and still so regard it."

In the early summer of 1939 Earl Johnson made a tour of European bureaus to prepare for the possibility of a war. Almost everything he saw and heard strengthened his belief that there was grave danger of a general conflict, and he supervised a number of important changes designed to improve news coverage and speed up communication among the principal European bureaus. Wallace Carroll was made London bureau manager and Frederick C. Oechsner, in Berlin, was made Central European manager. At this time and shortly thereafter a number of young reporters—Charles Collingwood, Eric Sevareid, Bill Downs, Clinton B. Conger, Alex Dreier, Dana Adams Schmidt, Richard C. Hottelet, Jack Fleischer, Peter C. Rhodes, Brydon Taves, Homer Jenks, and Hugo Speck—were added to the European staff.

By the time Johnson left for New York a great many kinks had been ironed out of United Press coverage in Europe, the number of string correspondents in smaller cities had been increased, and the bureaus had been geared to accuracy, speed, and conciseness as never before. In the next few months, the results of these changes began to pay off in a big way as Hitler's threats against Poland mounted to a harsh crescendo.

One day late in August, Wallace Carroll was standing outside the residence of the British Prime Minister in Downing Street, waiting for the breakup of a fateful cabinet meeting. The whole world wanted to know whether the British and French would stand by their alliance with Poland if that country were attacked by Germany or whether they would give in to the Nazis as they had done in the case of Czechoslovakia.

One by one the cabinet ministers emerged from the door of No. 10 Downing Street. One by one, they refused to answer the questions of reporters. But one of them, Carroll noticed, could hardly contain his feelings. There was about him a look of resolution, of confidence that bordered on exaltation. This was Walter Elliott, the Minister of Health, and the reporter followed him to his automobile.

"What did the Cabinet decide?" Carroll asked.

Elliott drew a deep breath. "We decided," he answered resolutely, "that if Poland is invaded we will fight."

At about the same time Frederick Kuh was turning in another story gleaned from the diplomatic run—the Germans had delivered what amounted to an ultimatum to the Poles. Neither Carroll nor Kuh believed that there was any longer hope of averting war: their stories, which were later confirmed almost word for word by official documents, reflected that belief so strongly that there were messages from New York warning them not to "get out on a limb." There was, too, a telephone call from the British Foreign Office suggesting, in an indirect fashion, that their reporting of diplomatic exchanges was becoming a bit too detailed for comfort.

"Do you wish to make any denials?" Carroll asked.

"No," was the reply. "There is nothing to deny."

In the United States it was difficult to believe that this war alarm—like others in recent years—would not be peacefully dissolved. There were so many rumors; there was such a flood of propaganda from the European capitals. Perhaps it was all bluff and bluster.

On Saturday, August 26, there was a moment of respite. An Associated Press dispatch from Berlin blossomed into headlines across America:

BERLIN, August 26 (AP) *A trustworthy and authoritative informant insisted today that a compromise in the German-Polish crisis is under way and declared that "the danger of world war is definitely averted."*

From half a dozen capitals urgent messages flooded into the Berlin bureau of the United Press. What had happened? Fred Oechsner had been writing and supervising the news report from Germany throughout the Nazi regime. He had an intimate knowledge of the skill with which Dr. Joseph Goebbels, the Nazi press chief, manipulated legitimate as well as illegitimate news in order to serve the purposes of his government and, at times, the purposes of himself or a faction of the Nazi party. Oechsner had been through the bloody purge of Nazi lieutenants, the hysterical propaganda campaigns and manufactured "border incidents" directed against the Czechs, the Poles, and others. He had spent half a dozen years patiently trying to separate fact from fiction as the Goebbels machine ground out the "news." There were times, of course, when correspondents had no choice but to accept and report, as such, the official Goebbels line. But there were many other times when Oechsner and his staff refused the proffered merchandise. On such occasions they sometimes received "call backs" from London or New York. Their refusal to go for the official line also built up a considerable reservoir of resentment against them at the Nazi press ministry.

On August 26, Oechsner was not buying any peace talk and particularly not from Nazi sources. There was then no question in his mind that Hitler was ready for war against Poland, regardless of the attitude of Britain and France. Oechsner stood his ground and there were no "war is averted" headlines over United Press dispatches that grim Saturday. Nor were there on later days. Before the next Saturday rolled around, Hitler had launched his dive bombers and armor across the parched plains of Poland.

CHAPTER TWENTY-THREE

Hugh Baillie remembered certain lessons of World War I. One was that communications was a major factor in successful war coverage. Another was a remark, made by Bill Hawkins, that the great test of reporting a war could make or break a news agency. The significance of Hawkins' remark was quickly demonstrated by the requests for United Press service that came from numerous newspapers, including the New York *Times,* immediately after Hitler invaded Poland. The agency had set a high standard for coverage of events leading up to the war. Now that hostilities had started it had to face the biggest test since 1914.

Baillie, accompanied by his assistant, Robert L. Frey, was in London when war was declared, and he promptly gave the word to "shoot the works" in setting up communications routes. The problem was complicated. Germany had cables via the Azores Islands to New York, but these were immediately cut by the British. Eventually virtually all cable routes to America were severed except those from London, but wireless more than made up for the lack of cable space. The immediate problem in September of 1939, however, was transmission of dispatches from Germany. These had been moving through London, and European News Manager Harry Flory believed that some arrangement to continue that system might be worked out.

First he expanded the Amsterdam relay bureau and one of the agency's most experienced men, Clifford L. Day, went there to take charge. Messages from Berlin, where there was no official censorship, reached Amsterdam quickly by teletype, and news from a dozen other European cities—Copenhagen, Stockholm, Rome, Budapest, Bucharest, and others—could be relayed through Amsterdam by telephone or teletype.

Then Flory approached the British Post Office with a plan for setting up a permanent United Press teleprinter line between Amsterdam and London for relay of European dispatches to London and on by cable to New York. The reply was prompt and emphatic: "That would be impossible because of the censorship." Flory then went around to call on Admiral Usborne, head of the censorship, and explained his idea. "That would be impossible," the admiral replied, "because the post office could not supply the cable."

Flory made several trips back and forth before he convinced both departments that the other had no objection. The important point was to arrange for news dispatches available at Amsterdam—including those from Berlin—to be sent to London and then forwarded to New York without passing through the British censorship. Actually it was obvious that the British could not censor such news as was available in Amsterdam. It could be sent more slowly by wireless direct to New York if necessary. But Flory wanted such dispatches, labeled as "transit" messages, to be permitted to flow through London without the delay that would be caused by submitting them to the censor.

"That means that we would have to trust you not to slip anything past the British censor by falsely labeling it as in transit," Usborne said.

"Yes," Flory answered, "but we've been trusted before."

Eventually the agreement was made and faithfully kept by both sides. Once the system was in operation, the London bureau was almost as closely in touch with the Berlin bureau and other European points as before the war. The London-Amsterdam wire was the first such circuit ever leased by any news organization between Great Britain and Holland, and it proved comparable to the Paris-Brest leased wire that gave the United Press many news beats during World War I.

News dispatches sent from Amsterdam on this circuit were slugged AMTRANS when received on the London desk. This code word signified that such messages did not have to be submitted to the British censor before being sent on to New York or elsewhere. The great value of the AMTRANS circuit to United Press clients was illustrated by the handling of a speech by Soviet Foreign Minister Vyacheslav Molotov in Moscow. The speech was delivered at the Kremlin, where Bureau Manager Henry Shapiro stationed an assistant at a telephone just outside the door to the auditorium. Standing inside the auditorium, Shapiro wrote in English the highlights of Molotov's speech and handed his translations through the door to his assistant in short takes. The assistant had an open telephone line to Berlin. As he read Shapiro's copy over the telephone, the Berlin bureau typed it out word for word and relayed it by teletype to Amsterdam within a few seconds. The Amsterdam desk man kept it rolling almost instantaneously to London and then—without censorship—to New York. There was a loss of only a few minutes on the entire complicated relay circuit from Moscow to New York, and Shapiro's detailed story was on the desks of American telegraph editors exactly an hour and forty-five minutes before any other news service had carried a word on the Molotov speech.

Getting correspondents attached to the armies proved more difficult than had been expected. There were various special war trips for reporters, but both the British and French were opposed to sending correspondents to the front. Instead, they proposed that a single reporter should cover each front for all agencies and newspapers. Webb Miller carried on a protracted campaign to convince the British that they should drop this "pool" system, but had little luck until he called a protest meeting of correspondents at the Ministry of Information. Lord Perth, the Minister of Information, had agreed to discuss the matter at his office, but so many would-be correspondents showed up that he had to move the meeting to an auditorium. Miller and others spoke effectively. Later, when the Ministry gave in and agreed to accredit a number of correspondents, they were required to sign an agreement to remain for at least three months on the front to which they were assigned as a precaution against any foreign correspondents changing sides while in possession of military information.

A considerable percentage of news in the early war days came through official announcements over government radio stations. Even Prime Minister Chamberlain's announcement that Britain was at war was made during a broadcast to the Empire. German and Russian official communiqués were often read on the air at the same time they were released to correspondents. To handle such material and also to keep up on what the belligerents were saying about each other the United Press established a series of listening posts near New York, London, San Francisco, and elsewhere to monitor broadcasts day and night. Eventually about 100 linguists and technicians manned these posts and recorded an estimated 70,000 words a day. Most of the listening-post material was for the information of United Press editors. But frequently important news was received more quickly by the monitors than by any other communications route.

2.

The "phony war" of stalemate on the Western Front in 1939 provided little news for correspondents. But there were soon important developments on another front. The Russians and Germans obviously did not trust each other and the Soviets were doing whatever possible to strengthen their western frontier. In November the Red Army moved to wrest the Karelian Peninsula from Finland, after having charged the Finns with "aggressive" actions and intentions. The Finns fought back far more effectively than anyone, especially the Russians, had anticipated.

Norman Deuel had been in charge of the United Press bureau at Moscow, but he was en route home when the trouble began and he stopped off in Helsinki. On November 30 he was awakened by air-raid sirens and promptly put in a telephone call to the United Press relay bureau at Copenhagen. While he was waiting, a bomb shattered a nearby building. A big glass dome over Deuel's hotel lobby collapsed. Just then a plucky girl telephone operator, shaking the splinters of glass out of her hair, called out that Copenhagen was on the line for the United Press correspondent. Deuel got up from the floor where he had thrown himself when the bomb hit, looked out the window at Russian planes dropping high explosives on the city, grabbed the telephone, and began dictating a notable news beat on the first bombing of Helsinki.

Reinforcements quickly were dispatched to aid Deuel. Herbert Uexkuell, an expert skier, took over coverage on the snowy front in Lapland. Webb Miller flew to Finland to cover his seventh war. Wrapped in white camouflage garments, Miller lived on the Karelian front for two months, sending back a steady stream of reports on one of the most bizarre wars ever fought. The Russians had sent inferior troops against the Finns and expected a quick victory. They had not got it. The Finns' Mannerheim line was deep, well camouflaged, and manned by courageous fighters. Their snipers and raiding parties drifted like ghosts through the forests. Supplies and men were moved at night on narrow sledges, racing almost soundlessly over the snow-packed roads and trails. As winter deepened the cold was intense, and attacking Red Army soldiers soon died of exposure if wounded. Russian planes often were permitted to fly unmolested over the front lines because firing at them would reveal the Finnish positions, which were deeply dug, reinforced by huge logs rather than cement, and hidden by snow, forests, and clever camouflage.

Beattie and Ralph Forte arrived in Helsinki as the war wore on, and Forte performed the unlikely feat of penetrating the border of the Soviet Union. This occurred following a Finnish success on the snow-covered Northern Front where several correspondents on skis were taken on a conducted tour. Forte was not exactly an expert skier but he was willing to try and did well until the party came to a rugged hilltop near the enemy border. There his skis took off in several directions with little regard for the correspondent's personal intentions. Forte ended, skis uppermost, in a large snowdrift at the foot of the hill, where he was eventually picked up by a Finnish press official with a sense of humor.

"Let me congratulate you, Mr. Forte," he murmured, as he tugged the correspondent out of the snow. "You are the first to arrive on the soil of Soviet Russia."

By the time Forte got safely back to Helsinki, the Russians had brought up their most powerful artillery and some of their crack troops on the Karelian front.

A few weeks later the Red Army broke through to Viipuri and the Finns accepted Moscow's peace demands for surrender of Viipuri, Hango, and the Karelian Isthmus.

By that time Webb Miller was back in London, hating war more bitterly than ever. He did not doubt that Hitler would strike again with the coming of better weather. Three months later, with the signs of a German onslaught in Europe mounting daily, the man who had risked his life a score of times on the world's battlefronts fell from a suburban London train in the blackout and was killed. Webb Miller was the first of a long list of casualties among American correspondents in World War II.

3.

On the evening of Thursday, May 9, 1940, there was a spate of rumors and alarms from Europe. That afternoon General Henri Winkelman, commander in chief of the Netherlands army, had taken stringent measures "in the interest of national security." Large gatherings were prohibited in the region of the German frontier. All canal locks in the Amsterdam area were closed. Then, at 11 P.M., government authorities telephoned the United Press bureau and advised Robert Dowson, who was on the news desk, that thereafter the only means of communication with foreign countries would be by cable.

Dowson tried the AMTRANS teleprinter line to London and, surprisingly, discovered that it was working. A story by Manager Clifford Day had moved earlier. Dowson sent a brief bulletin "lead" that must have seemed contradictory to the London desk man:

1st LEAD

AMSTERDAM, May 9 (UP)—*The government tonight closed all canal locks in the Amsterdam area and completely cut off telephone and teletype communications with other capitals after a spread of new alarming rumors that Dutch neutrality might be violated.*

Dowson didn't bother to explain to editors how this bulletin reached the outside world, but let them assume it was transmitted by cable. He began adding details—many planes could be heard over Amsterdam—to the story, holding his breath for the moment when the teletype circuit would be cut and he would have to switch to the much slower—and censored—cable or newscast channels. Miraculously the AMTRANS teletype remained open into the London bureau.

Grattan McGroarty, who had been sent from London to reinforce the Amsterdam staff, and Art Watt, a teleprinter operator, were grabbing a sandwich at a restaurant near the office when German airplanes appeared in large numbers over the city. They could see the dive bombers swooping on Schiphol airport in the early dawn, could see the Dutch planes engaging them, and could see and hear explosions as the bombs hit the runways. A little later German transport planes began dropping parachute troops in the vicinity of the airport. McGroarty ran to the office and began pounding out the story.

Meanwhile Day had hurried to the office. Watt was sent to Schiphol airport, from where he telephoned a description of the attack. At 1:02 A.M. New York time there was another flash:

AMSTERDAM—REPORTED GERMANS CROSSED DUTCH FRONTIER

And, as the details poured in, a new lead:

2nd LEAD

AMSTERDAM, The Netherlands, Friday May 10 (UP) *Germany invaded Holland, Belgium and Luxembourg today in a lightning war—the dreaded Blitzkreig—by air and land. Queen Wilhelmina appealed to her people:*
"Do your duty everywhere and in all circumstances."

Throughout the night, the AMTRANS teletype circuit to London continued to click out news that the "phony war" on the Western Front had ended with a massive German blow at the Low Countries on the road into France. The Amsterdam staff was no more than three minutes or so from New York with the fast-breaking news, and on Friday morning newspapers throughout America and most of the rest of the world were blanketed with United Press coverage of the battle that would decide the fate of continental Europe for the next four years. British United Press dispatches dominated London newspapers, and the British Government was getting virtually all of its information about the German attack by watching the AMTRANS circuit printer in the censor's office. "Not only did the United Press thus achieve a noteworthy scoop," Chief Censor Admiral George P. Thomson wrote later, "but this early news of the invasion was of greatest value to our own military, naval and air authorities."

Not until 10:25 A.M. did the AMTRANS teletype printer go dead, having been cut off belatedly by Dutch officials.

The war developed rapidly. German parachutists in Dutch uniforms landed behind the lines in an effort to spread confusion. Heavy bombs fell on The Hague. The German planes began bombing railroad and channel shipping centers in France and were engaged by Allied fighters. Pat McGroarty had been told by Day to try to drive to the front. He managed to tour close to The Hague, Rotterdam, and Leyden before noon. Dutch officials arrested him five different times but he turned in an eyewitness account of fierce fighting in the air and along a road on which German infantry had advanced near the Maas River.

In Amsterdam, Leon Kay toured the city that same morning and got through to New York with a story that the city "went calmly to war. . . . Buses began taking children to the country. The youngsters, their few belongings in wicker baskets, peered out of the bus windows at their parents and others who watched them depart."

But two hours later a bulletin from McGroarty, near Rotterdam, reported the Germans had a foothold on the right bank of the Maas River and were attacking the city in a stubborn, bitter battle. From Berlin came a German report that Nazi forces had seized bridges across the Albert Canal on the Belgian border.

The battle would be hard fought, but it was the beginning of the gallant end. On May 12 Dowson and Watt—both British subjects—escaped on a boat carrying 800 refugees to England. Cliff Day and his wife, and other staff members, including Eddie Mueller, the bureau's American accountant, later watched the German motorized forces sweep into Amsterdam with Teutonic precision.

4.

The end of the Low Countries came rapidly; the fall of France was not long postponed after a massive German break-through at Sedan. Paris Bureau Manager Ralph Heinzen and several staff members, including Pierre Salarnier and Herbert King, retreated to Vichy with the French government of Marshal Henri Pétain.

In Rome, meantime, Eleanor Packard stood outside the Palazzo Venezia on June 10 when, at 6:01 P.M., Premier Mussolini popped out on his famous little balcony and told a cheering crowd that—with the Germans already rolling deep into the West—Italy had declared war on France and Great Britain. For the next week, Eleanor noted later, most of the fighting that resulted from Il Duce's declaration was done by foreign correspondents in Rome who battled for an advantage in getting telephone connections to Switzerland in order to transmit the daily war communiqué abroad. Even this proved almost futile because the Italian army made virtually no progress along the Riviera and gained virtually none of the territory Mussolini had demanded. Soon afterward the war ended in France.

This fiasco so angered Mussolini that he looked elsewhere for a military triumph. In October of 1940 the Fascists began to build up charges that the Greeks were giving surreptitious aid to Britain and were "terrorizing" the frontier areas of Albania, then under Italian "protection." At 3 A.M. on October 28 the Fascist Premier delivered a two-and-a-half-hour ultimatum to the Greeks, who rejected it. Italian troops, already massed in the Albanian hills, invaded Greece half an hour before the expiration of the ultimatum. Mussolini apparently was convinced the Greeks would not resist seriously.

For the next three days American correspondents in Rome argued with the Fascist press ministry for permission to go to the Greek front. Herbert Matthews of the New York *Times,* John Whitaker of the Chicago *Daily News,* Richard Massock of the Associated Press, and others were busily plotting how to get to Albania with or without official permission. United Press Manager Reynolds Packard was nervously afraid that one of them would succeed and turn out the first eyewitness story of the fighting. As for himself, Packard couldn't think of any practical way to circumvent the press ministry officials. Then, on the evening of the third day of war, Eleanor Packard said:

"Remember that old Albanian *lascia-passare* signed by Count Ciano?"
"Sure. Where is it?"

"It's still stuck away in a bureau drawer where you left it after your last trip to Albania."

She dug it out and studied it with an odd look in her eye. It was good for another three weeks except for the fact that all such passes had been canceled with the start of the war in Greece. "Maybe," Eleanor said, "we could doctor this up a bit."

At the United Press office Eleanor found some impressive-looking rubber stamps and a machine for printing dates. She went industriously to work, making good use of a couple of stamps saying *autorizzato* and *valido*. After a while she did a little work with the date-printing machine. When she finally handed the pass to Reynolds it was marked "Valid, October 31, 1940" and looked as good as new. The next day Reynolds dropped in at the air ministry and handed the pass to an official there.

"I need your stamp on this to buy my airplane ticket," he remarked nonchalantly. "Will you fix it up, please?"

The officer looked at Count Ciano's signature and muttered, "Very, very unusual," but he put his stamp on it and Packard caught a plane for Brindisi, en route to the Albanian capital of Tirana. He was questioned only once—by a veteran Black Shirt police officer at Brindisi who complained that the pass could not possibly be in order. "You'll be arrested for this," he exclaimed.

"And what will happen when Count Ciano hears what little respect you have for his signature?" Packard roared.

The police officer gave up and permitted him to continue to Tirana. There, luckily, he discovered that Lorusso, head of the Albanian Propaganda Ministry, had just left for the front with a group of Italian correspondents. Lorusso's assistant, Paolo Veronese, was apologetic that he had not been informed of Packard's impending arrival and didn't even ask to see his credentials. Instead, he hastened to get him a military pass, signed by Lieutenant General Jacomoni, with red seal and ribbon.

Later Packard set out with an Italian correspondent for the Janina front. They met General Sebastiano Visconte Prasca, in charge of operations, on the road and he spoke pessimistically. In the afternoon they were under Greek artillery fire, and a shell tore off the arm of an Italian soldier lying in a ditch beside Packard. An Italian correspondent offered to drive him to a point from which they could see the Greek defenses of Janina, but after traveling a short distance their automobile was disabled by a Greek machine-gun bullet. They crawled two miles back down the road to safety. Packard was now convinced that the Italian attack had been so poorly prepared that it had been stopped by a few machine guns and some light artillery fire. He estimated that there could not be more than 30,000 Italian soldiers on the entire front.

Packard wrote several dispatches which he sent to Eleanor in Rome by an Italian correspondent who was returning there by plane. They were the first eyewitness stories of the Greek front by other than Italian correspondents, who were strictly under control of the propaganda ministry. Packard's dispatches, when published abroad, brought a flood of protests from other correspondents in Rome, particularly the Germans, who had received angry call-backs from their home offices. The German ambassador even protested to Foreign Minister Count Ciano that correspondents of Italy's Axis partner had been seriously embarrassed. The next day the foreign office sent orders to Lorusso to expel Packard from Albania. Back in Rome, Packard was severely reprimanded by the press ministry but he declined to reveal how he had reached Albania. By December 6, the Fascist army had been knocked back on its heels by the Greeks, who seized a large part of eastern and southern Albania.

5.

Only a few stories in the summer of 1940 briefly stole the headlines from Europe. Leon Trotsky had found refuge in Mexico City after his expulsion from Russia in 1929, but as the war developed there were increasing signs that elements of the Communist party in America were not happy about his continued agitation against Joseph Stalin. Edward P. Morgan, the United Press manager in Mexico City, had several contacts among Trotsky's associates and occasionally got a story from them. Then, in May of 1940, he received a telephone call from one of the exiled Red Army leader's lieutenants.

"Mr. Morgan," the lieutenant said, "what would the United Press be willing to pay for an exclusive story of an attempt to assassinate Trotsky?"

When Morgan had recovered from his surprise and determined that the assassination attempt had already taken place rather than still being in the planning stage, he replied that he would have to consult his New York office. "Hold everything," he added, "until you hear from me."

He telephoned New York with enough details—a machine gunner had sprayed Trotsky's bedroom but miraculously had not hit him—to get an exclusive story on the wires. Trotsky did not escape for long. In August another assassin succeeded in fatally wounding the former Russian leader.

6.

While the Greeks were chewing up the Italian army along the Albanian frontier, Hitler was busy on a distant but important diplomatic front in the Far East. For months his emissaries had been attempting to persuade the Japanese government to expand the Rome-Berlin-Tokyo Axis against the Communists into an alliance against the Western democracies. Specifically he wanted Japan to agree to come to the aid of Germany and Italy if the United States entered the war on the side of the Allied Powers. On several occasions the Japanese Cabinet had declined the German suggestions, but in the early fall of 1940 official sentiment in Tokyo began to change.

Harold O. Thompson, the United Press manager in Tokyo, talked with persons close to the Cabinet and quickly sensed the change. He knew, however, that the government was highly suspicious of American correspondents at that time, and he made no effort to sound out officials on the subject of an Axis military agreement. On the contrary he made a point of pretending indifference to the almost daily meetings of the Cabinet while he quietly canvassed his contacts for information. It didn't come suddenly, but after several days of indirect inquiries Thompson received a hint that the Cabinet had agreed to strengthen the Axis by an agreement directed against American participation in the war. He tried another source, and then another. From each he got part of the picture. When all of the pieces of the picture fitted together he was convinced that the Cabinet had agreed to cast Japan's lot with the Axis.

It was a big story—but one he could not send through the Japanese censorship. The mails, however, were not censored. Thompson wrote a long letter to Shanghai Manager Robert Bellaire, giving the outline of the agreement. He divided the letter into several pieces and put each one in an envelope addressed to Bellaire, with a message instructing Bellaire to hold the story in Shanghai until he received a release. A few days later Thompson received unquestionable word that his story was correct. He put in a telephone call to Shanghai and talked to Bellaire, with a Japanese censor listening in on the line. They chatted briefly and then Thompson said that it was okay to send along those letters.

The line buzzed and the censor cut in: "You are trying to get out some kind of news!"

"Oh no," Thompson replied. "I was just trying to get some information about developments in Indo-China."

The censor cut the line. But it was too late. Bellaire filed the dispatch to New York and Thompson had a clean beat on the most fateful story from Japan in many months. Three days later it was officially announced that, in effect, the Axis had been strengthened to range Japan against the democracies as well as against the Comintern if the United States entered the war.

CHAPTER TWENTY-FOUR

The Battle of Britain—the first great war in the air—opened the second week in August of 1940. Like almost everybody else in the British Isles, the United Press staff worked for weeks on an unprecedented emergency basis. Veterans of the London bureau like Harry L. Percy, Sidney J. Williams, George Chandler, Laurence Meredith, and Charles Hallinan kept copy moving to the cables steadily throughout the bombing raids, sometimes when blasts were so close that their desks trembled violently. Dan Campbell, a veteran of several South American revolutions, seemed constantly to be seeking the most dangerous centers of destruction, tireless in his search for news—much of which the censor killed—and human-interest stories. One night he staggered into the office, black with dirt, wearing one shoe, and carrying a kitten. That night the bombs had come to Campbell, destroying the apartment house in which he lived less than a block from the office. He had picked up the cat as he ran but didn't have any idea what had happened to his other shoe.

Night after night high explosives fell near the office. Homer Jenks, on the late trick, frequently dived under the news desk, waited until that immediate series of bombs had boomed safely past, and then crawled out to resume his work. (The *News of the World* building, in which the bureau was located, did not suffer severe damage until the following May.) A special telephone line had been run from the news desk to a seven-story-high tower on top of the *News of the World* building, which offered a fine panoramic view of London. Whenever the air-raid sirens sounded a staff member dashed to the tower to dictate a play-by-play account of the raid. The tower was often a hot spot and the watcher on many occasions had to fall flat on the floor to escape flying debris. But, if the staff reporters were busy, it was not unusual for Miss Sheena Stronach, the determined office secretary, to ascend to the tower to dictate an account of the attack.

The battle went on until the end of October, when a total of 2375 German planes had been destroyed. By then Hitler knew that the British would not cave in. He gave up his invasion plans. But the terror was by no means ended. Just after Christmas the Luftwaffe struck a last blow in terrible frustration and anger, centering its fury on the city of London, a great part of which went up in flames:

BY WALLACE CARROLL

LONDON, December 30 (UP) *Some of the London that Americans learned about in school or read about in books met death tonight in the flaming fury of a German fire raid.*

Some of the London of Shakespeare and Dickens, of Oliver Goldsmith and Dr. Johnson, I have seen crashing around me. . . . I wish I could ask Americans to put or their tin hats and go with me as I went through the City of London. . . . Beyond the fire we could see St. Paul's cathedral. I had never seen it looking so serenely beautiful. As the smoke and flames whirled around its dome it seemed to rise higher above them. So far as we could tell no military objective was destroyed, but what the Germans destroyed during the night can never be restored—beauty, serenity, grandeur, history in stone.

2.

In the winter of 1940–41, Hitler found his Axis partnership more of a handicap than a help in the Mediterranean theater of war. Italian troops had been defeated by the Greeks in Albania. Italian troops, after an early advance from Libya against the British in Egypt, also had been routed by General Wavell's Army of the Nile which seized 133,000 prisoners and pushed the enemy back 600 miles across the desert. It was not until April, however, that Hitler moved to rescue Mussolini by a blitzkreig invasion of Yugoslavia and Greece.

Henry Gorrell had been sent from Hungary to Athens in anticipation of the German invasion. He discovered that the Greek countryside had an overabundance of German "visitors" in civilian clothes. They were busy taking notes on military preparations while Nazi war planes flew low overhead. Neither the "visitors" nor the planes were molested by the Greeks, who believed, until almost the last moment, that Hitler would not attack them. By the time Gorrell reached Athens, however, the Greek government had changed its mind and accepted military assistance from the British. New Zealand and Australian troops already were landing at Piraeus Harbor and moving toward the Macedonian frontier to meet the Nazi panzer columns that snaked down across the Balkans and attacked the Rupel forts on the Greek border on April 6. Richard D. McMillan, who had been covering the desert fighting in Libya, went to the Greek front with the British Expeditionary Force of 30,000 men.

The battle was impossible from the beginning. A mile outside Larissa, on the slopes of Mount Olympus, McMillan watched Nazi dive bombers drop sickeningly almost to the roof tops and pound the town to pulp. It was still worse at Thermopylae, where the dive bombing was almost continuous. On April 25 all correspondents were ordered back to Athens. From Athens, McMillan and Gorrell moved on with the retreating British to an evacuation point at the little port of Nauplion. Eleven thousand soldiers already were on the nearby beaches awaiting rescue by the Navy.

The two correspondents slept that night in an olive grove, only to be awakened at dawn by the bullets of low-flying German planes. They dived with two New Zealand soldiers into a shallow ditch and switched back and forth from one side to the other as the planes crisscrossed the fields. When the enemy had departed one of the soldiers shook Gorrell's hand. "I was at Dunkirk," he said, "but it wasn't this bad. If we came through this one I guess we'll make it."

Orders came to demolish all vehicles. Many were just pushed off the piers. Others were shot to pieces. That night a press officer addressed the correspondents: "Gentlemen, I am instructed to advise you that in event of an air raid while we are walking to embark we will not halt. You will walk three abreast. Anyone who steps from the ranks to seek cover from aircraft will be left behind. If any of you are wounded we shall do our best to see you aboard the transport. The dead, naturally, will be left behind."

The column started forward, marching through a lane flanked by bomb-battered sycamores and fields of scarlet poppies. A munitions ship afire in the harbor cast a bright glow over the beaches. The men started singing "It's a Long Way to Tipperary" and "Keep the Home Fires Burning." Of the 30,000 British troops sent into Greece, about a third were evacuated that night on transports and cruisers waiting off the beaches. They left almost all of Europe in the hands of Adolf Hitler.

3.

Shortly before dawn on the morning of March 15, 1941, the overnight man in the Berlin bureau, Howard K. Smith, was dozing at his desk. At exactly five o'clock he heard the door to the outer hall click open. He waited a moment but the door didn't close. Smith walked across the big news room overlooking the Unter den Linden to investigate, but at the doorway he was blocked by a short, heavy-set man in a brown overcoat. The man pulled a small metal disc attached to a brass chain from his pocket and flipped it toward Smith. It was stamped *Geheime Staatspolizei*—the Gestapo or notorious Nazi secret police. A moment later a dozen big, grim-faced men in gum boots and thick overcoats walked into the room and started going through the desks and files in a methodical fashion that indicated they already knew the office layout.

"What does this mean?" Smith finally asked. "I am an American citizen and I intend to report this to the American Embassy."

The head man lighted a cigar and put his feet up on the desk.

"You won't report anything to anybody," he replied firmly.

The raiders had found little in the bureau except news dispatches and copies of Nazi press ministry handouts. They made no comment, but at dawn the DNB (German news bureau) ticker began tapping out its first dispatch of the day and Smith read it with sinking heart.

BERLIN (DNB) BECAUSE OF SERIOUS SUSPICION OF ESPIONAGE IN FAVOR OF THE ENEMY, THE AMERICAN CITIZEN AND CORRESPONDENT IN BERLIN FOR THE UNITED PRESS OF AMERICA, RICHARD C. HOTTELET, HAS BEEN ARRESTED AND IMPRISONE┌

Some kind of retaliation against the United Press bureau had not been entirely out of the minds of Frederick Oechsner and his staff for months because of their rigid insistence on handling the news objectively and their frequent failures to take a "co-operative" attitude toward the Nazi propaganda ministry. But Oechsner had successfully insisted that the staff be "correct" in all dealings with the Nazis and he did not believe that it would be possible even to fake any charges against the bureau. The arrest of Hottelet —and on the grave charge of espionage—was a frightening shock.

Six Gestapo agents had knocked on the door of the apartment shared by Hottelet and Joseph W. Grigg, Jr., at the same moment Howard Smith heard the office door open. Hottelet answered the door and was instructed to dress and accompany the agents. They began a thorough search of the apartment, which awakened Grigg. Three hours later Grigg was told he was free to go about his business.

At the bureau Oechsner and the staff members were closely questioned as to their backgrounds, but the regular United Press service to the outside world went on without interruption. Later in the day Oechsner was officially informed that Hottelet's arrest was connected with his personal and private activities and had nothing to do with his journalistic work or with the United Press.

In Berlin, Washington, and anywhere else that action could be taken the United Press immediately began efforts in behalf of the imprisoned reporter. That afternoon President Roosevelt instructed the State Department to "take immediate action" to investigate and ascertain all of the details of the case. The Berlin embassy promptly moved to discover what lay behind the Gestapo action. There were various theories. One that seemed most reasonable was that Hottelet had been arrested in retaliation for the arrest in New York of Manfred Zapp, American manager of the German Trans-Ocean News Service, and Guenther Tonn, one of his assistants. A federal grand jury had charged them with violating the act which required agents of foreign powers to register with the State Department.

Neither Oechsner nor the United Press officials in New York ever believed for a moment that Hottelet had engaged in espionage in any way. He was, however, a young man inclined to speak his own mind. Oechsner knew that Hottelet had occasionally irritated various Nazi officials by his questions while in search of news. The bureau manager discussed the arrest two days later with a high Gestapo official who said that Hottelet, in letters sent abroad, had written certain things about the results of Royal Air Force raids on Berlin and that such information, in war time, might be interpreted as espionage.

By this time—with Hottelet sitting uncomfortably in a cell—it was becoming apparent that the Gestapo probably could present some kind of fake case if the government decided to make an example of a not too friendly neutral reporter. But, after keeping the correspondent in prison for four months, the decision was reached to exchange Hottelet and Correspondent Jay Allen of the North American Newspaper Alliance, who had been arrested in Paris, for four German news-agency men held in the United States. On July 17 Hottelet was released from prison in Berlin and left for Lisbon. Jay Allen joined him at Frankfurt and they continued the journey home. Undismayed, Hottelet paused in New York long enough to regain the weight he had lost and then headed back to the war zone—but this time on the other side of the front.

4.

One of the main sources of news as the war wore on was the White House in Washington. The United Press had had a number of White House correspondents over the years—Robert J. Bender, Henry Misselwitz, Frederick Othman, Tom Reynolds, Frederick Storm, and others on a long- or short-term basis—but in 1941 Merriman Smith moved into the job and made a career of it. He became, in time, the dean of White House correspondents, the man who set the pace at presidential press conferences and who ended them by saying: "Thank you, Mr. President"—and dashing for the telephone.

Generally speaking, the White House job is one of the most demanding in the press association business because the correspondent seldom has a chance to sit at a typewriter and compose a story. He must be able to look at the notes he took during a press conference—notes on perhaps a dozen different subjects—and instantly select the most important item. Then he must run to a telephone booth and dictate his stories from his notes. Sometimes he dictates a one-paragraph bulletin on each of three or four different stories that developed during the press conference. He must be able to switch back later to the first bulletin and dictate additional material on that subject. Then he must be capable of making still other switches to pick up the threads of thought in the second or third bulletin that he dictated fifteen or twenty minutes earlier. In other words, he often must handle three or four stories almost simultaneously.

But, in addition, the White House reporter has to judge carefully the temper of the Chief Executive in framing questions and in deciding just how to ask them. Unlike other Washington officials, the President must maintain the dignity of his office at all times. And the good correspondent must be able to draw a thin line between his obligation to seek answers to embarrassing questions and his apprehension that he will be offensive by acting like a prosecuting attorney.

Smith soon developed a knack for meeting such situations. Once when President Roosevelt was discussing inflationary trends, he described how a garage mechanic friend of his "just happened to drop in for a chat" and complained about the high price of strawberries in the market. It was February, the President went on, and he lectured his mechanic friend on the folly of buying strawberries out of season. Why didn't his "missus" buy more sensibly? Then Mr. Roosevelt explained that he told this story to show that too many people were spending money on unnecessary luxuries and, for that reason, they believed the cost of living was going up. Actually, he added, the price line for necessities was being firmly held.

There were some odd points in Mr. Roosevelt's story. Nobody could recall that any mechanics had dropped in at the White House and nobody seriously believed that the story was more than a fable to illustrate a point. But, of course, nobody had the bad manners to challenge it. A few months later the inflation problem again came up at a press conference and Mr. Roosevelt was asked whether the line was being held. He thought for a moment and then remarked that he had had an experience "the other day" which might illustrate what was happening. A master mechanic that he knew had "just happened to drop in to chat" with him, the President continued, and had said that his "missus" was complaining about the high price of asparagus. Then he went on with approximately the same story he had told before.

There was a moment of silence in the room as the President finished. Then Smith judged the situation with hairline accuracy and asked:

"Mr. President, is that the same mechanic who came in a few months back complaining about the price of strawberries?"

There was a roar of laughter from the reporters and, after a second of hesitation, Mr. Roosevelt joined in. "By God, Merriman," he shouted. "It's true. It was the same man."

5.

The German blitzkreig into Russia in 1941 provided a number of new problems for news agencies. Russian censorship was absolute. The Moscow government adamantly refused all requests for correspondents to go to the front. In fact, there was no "front" in the traditional sense during the first months of fighting in which German armor executed vast encircling movements to break up and separate the Russian armies. Such news as there was from Russia came mainly in official communiqués.

As a result of these circumstances, coverage of the war in Russia was highly unsatisfactory from the viewpoint of editors and correspondents.

Even the Russian communiqués were normally delayed many hours in transmission from Moscow to London. As an early move to overcome such handicaps the London bureau strengthened its radio "listening post" and, as the monitors gained experience and knowledge of Russian methods, began picking up the Moscow official news dispatches as much as twelve or even twenty-four hours before they reached London by cable. Henry Gris, who had started the monitoring system in his London apartment but was later installed in a suburban house at Barnet, discovered that at certain hours the Russian official communiqué was being transmitted by wireless telephone from Moscow over an unusual frequency. Gris, who had four receiving sets operating in one room and three others in the next room, picked up the voice transmission more or less by accident the first time. He recognized a sentence or two in the stilted language of the communiqué. Then the voice switched to another set of frequencies. Gris chased it with another receiver. He soon had the daily hour and the frequencies plotted and confirmed that the Russian communiqué was being transmitted every day several hours prior to its broadcast over Moscow radio. Thereafter, Gris tuned in every day to what he called his "Secret Source" and plucked the communiqué, as well as other official news, out of the air an hour or sometimes three hours before any other agency or newspaper had it. He also discovered that the "Secret Source" was a special wireless telephone transmission each evening from Moscow to newspapers in besieged Leningrad, where the difficulties of publication were so great that it was necessary to start the presses rolling much earlier than elsewhere in Russia.

For many weeks other news agencies and newspapers in London vainly attempted to discover Gris's "Secret Source" but they failed until one of them offered a high salary to one of the seventeen members of the United Press listening-post staff and from him learned of the special transmission. The information became generally known soon thereafter and the Russians changed the special transmission so that it could not be picked up by any monitor in London.

Shortly after the German invasion of Russia, Henry Shapiro and M. S. Handler in the Moscow bureau were reinforced by Wallace Carroll, who had spent more than four years as correspondent at the League of Nations in Geneva and who was well acquainted with Maxim Litvinov and other Soviet officials. Shapiro, Handler, and other American correspondents had been unable to persuade the head of the official press bureau, Nicolai Palgunov, to permit them to go to the front. Shortly after Carroll reached Moscow, however, the Russians turned back German offensives in the vicinity of Smolensk and near Bryansk. Thus, for the first time, the Red Army had a real victory to report. In addition, the Russians were eager for American war materials and wanted to convince Washington that they could hold the Germans. The official attitude toward foreign correspondents in Moscow began to change and, on September 14, Palgunov advised Carroll and several other reporters that they could go to the front the next day.

The trip was revealing. Near Vyazma, which the Germans claimed to have reached in July, they visited a well-concealed Russian air base and got the first glimpse of a new fighter plane called the MIG-3. The dispatches written after several days of touring the front area gave Americans a better impression of the Russian prowess. Carroll took issue with the idea that the Germans could crush the Red armies before Christmas. They would still be strongly in action, he said, the following spring.

That was an important prediction, and perhaps a little risky. In October the diplomatic corps and all foreign correspondents were moved to Kuibyshev because of the threat to Moscow. But the Red Army held and the following spring it was still fighting. By that time the ability of the Russians to fight on had become of vital importance to Americans because the United States, too, was fighting for its existence.

CHAPTER TWENTY-FIVE

Frank Tremaine, the United Press manager in Honolulu, woke up at eight o'clock on the morning of December 7, 1941, with a roaring in his ears. He and his wife had attended a dinner party the night before and stayed a little later than they had intended, but Tremaine didn't think the roaring was due to a hang-over. After a few moments he recognized the sound of antiaircraft guns—a considerable number of them. "Another practice session," he muttered, and pulled the sheet up over his head. A moment later he popped out of bed. This was Sunday morning—an unlikely time for the Army or Navy to be shooting guns just for practice. Tremaine ran into the living room, knocking his wife's party dress off the hanger on which it had been hung on the door. His house was on a high hill, and from the window he looked down at Pearl Harbor. The sky seemed to be full of unfamiliar bombing planes and the United States' greatest, most secure naval bastion seemed to be exploding in thick clouds of smoke in front of his eyes.

Tremaine ran back to the bedroom, trampling his wife's party dress into the carpet, and grabbed the telephone. In the next few minutes he did a great number of things. He put in long-distance calls for San Francisco and New York. He telephoned an officer at Navy Public Relations to confirm that an enemy attack was in progress. He dictated several brief flashes to the cable office, addressing them to both San Francisco and Manila. He called Army Public Relations at Fort Shafter and confirmed that the attacking planes were Japanese. He filed another flash that the Japanese were attacking Pearl Harbor. He called his assistant, William Tyree, and directed him to go to the office. He called Francis McCarthy, who was in Honolulu en route to Manila, and told him to go to Fort Shafter. He got dressed. He barked unkindly at his wife, who had awakened, seen her party dress in tatters on the floor, and expressed a certain degree of bitterness. About that time a few stray shells fell near the Tremaine house and Mrs. Tremaine suddenly was wide-awake.

"It's an attack by Jap planes," Tremaine said. "I've got to go. I put in a call for SX. If it comes through, you tell them everything you can see."

Only half an hour had elapsed from the time Tremaine woke up until he was out of the house, driving toward Fort Shafter. As he left, several wives of naval officers living nearby arrived at the Tremaine house to get a better view of the naval base. One of them carried a book entitled *A Woman Faces the War*. At 8:30 A.M. the telephone rang and Jim Sullivan of the San Francisco office was on the line. Mrs. Tremaine read him a copy of the cables her husband had sent and then, standing at the window, began describing a second wave of enemy planes that had come over. She described the great harbor, the black puffs of smoke, the mighty gray ships that were the backbone of a nation's armed might and the hornetlike Japanese aircraft diving again and again on their targets. She could see a warship under attack off the waterfront and called out to her naval guests to identify it. They correctly decided it was a destroyer but could not identify it as the *Ward*. Some of the luckier warships were under way, moving, maneuvering, trying to get out to sea where they would have a chance to defend themselves. Mrs. Tremaine kept on talking and answering questions as Sullivan, Dan Bowerman, and others in San Francisco pounded out the first eyewitness story of the Pacific war. One shell exploded so close to the Tremaine house that Sullivan, in San Francisco, heard the blast.

Tremaine and McCarthy had met at Fort Shafter, meanwhile, and McCarthy put through telephone calls to San Francisco and New York while Tremaine vainly tried to get on to Pearl Harbor. Half a mile from the base he could see some of the wreckage and at Hickam Field he could see the ruins of hangars and planes and living quarters. He telephoned descriptive material to the office several times but at eleven o'clock Tyree gave him some bad news.

"Everything's just been shut down, Frank," Tyree said. "Our telephone call to SX was cut off and the censorship is on. Nothing can go out or come in."

So drastic was the censorship, once it had been established, that there was not another direct word of news, except for official communiqués, from Honolulu until December 11. The only exception was a telephone call Frank Bartholomew was permitted to make to Tremaine on the understanding that he would ask nothing except whether the staff was safe. As a result of that call, Bartholomew was able to write a story that the United Press staff was safe and that the Honolulu newspapers were publishing, but otherwise dispatches from Hawaii were missing. The censorship on incoming cables was not so complete, but only because the United Press wireless receiving station was still able to pick up broadcasts from the mainland and thus continued to provide a news report for the Honolulu *Advertiser,* the *Star-Bulletin,* and radio station KGMB.

2.

In the Washington bureau of the United Press the Sunday trick had been drawn by Arthur F. DeGreve, a veteran reporter and desk man, Roger Tatarian, a newcomer from the Southwest, and Milton Magruder. The capital had been tense because there were mounting indications that the Japanese militarists planned some kind of move against the British and Dutch in Southwest Asia. And for approximately a week there had been an ominous flow of news from Robert Bellaire, the United Press manager at Tokyo. Every day Bellaire sent quotes from editorials in several influential Tokyo newspapers which were highly anti-American. There were two unusual things about Bellaire's method of filing. First, he sent the editorial extracts at the urgent rate. Second, he did not comment or elaborate on the quotations in any way. Normally, extracts from editorials would be sent at the cheaper press rate and would be merely a part of a general story. The conclusion drawn by the United Press cable editors in New York was that Bellaire was trying to get across a warning that the Japanese were threatening some action against the United States and that he was fearful of being arrested by the secret police if he sent abroad anything except direct quotations from the Tokyo newspapers.

There had also been another warning from the Shanghai bureau. On December 5 a code message from William H. McDougall at Shanghai was relayed to New York and Washington. Briefly the message said that a Japanese friend had told McDougall that in Washington and London and other capitals the Japanese diplomatic officials were receiving orders to destroy their code books and code machines in preparation for a crisis. This fitted neatly into the information available in the Washington bureau. In fact, Carroll Kenworthy, head of the bureau's foreign staff, had written a story—later cited by Secretary of War Henry L. Stimson before the Joint Congressional Committee investigating Pearl Harbor—saying that it was felt "that talks between Secretary Hull and the special Japanese envoy, Saburo Kurusu, are near collapse" and it was "believed that Japan may strike."

Official Washington, however, was not at all convinced that the Japanese were prepared for anything more than harassment of the British and Dutch and French in Southwest Asia. Two Japanese special envoys—Admiral Kichisaburo Nomura and Saburo Kurusu—were still in the capital, and the biggest news story on DeGreve's desk early Sunday afternoon was that they had made an appointment to see Secretary Hull again that day. Then the telephone rang.

"This is the White House," the voice of an operator said. "Stand by for a conference call."

When the three major press associations were all on the same line, the official announcement was made that Japanese planes were attacking the naval base on Oahu Island—Pearl Harbor. DeGreve scribbled the biggest news flash of his career on a piece of copy paper and glanced around the almost empty office in frustration. The wires had not yet been set up for the Sunday night report. He opened a telephone line to New York, got Phil Newsom, who was on the news desk, and shouted:

"This is DeGreve in Washington—Flash—White House announces Japanese bombing Wahoo."

"Bombing what?"

"Wahoo, dammit—Wahoo."

"Spell it, for pete's sake."

"O A H U—Wahoo! We've got a war on our hands."

The bombs dropped at Pearl Harbor echoed around the world within a few moments. In the next few hours, while the story of Pearl Harbor was still coming over the wires, Baillie, Johnson, and other top editors were tearing apart the company's world-wide organization and revamping it to meet the demands of the biggest news-reporting job in history.

Johnson laid down the broad lines for war coverage. "Every Unipresser is a war correspondent now, and all of us must be guided by the strict code of that always important and sometimes hazardous calling," he wrote in a general memorandum.

We must raise our guard uncommonly high against putting into circulation any rumors which might cause alarm; we must be especially careful not to mislead our editors by giving undue credence to stories containing enemy claims. . . .

News is a more explosive weapon now than ever before. An error in news judgment can put men's lives in jeopardy. Don't speculate. Stick to facts.

EJJ

In Singapore the telephone awakened Harold Guard about four-thirty o'clock in the morning, December 8, 1941.

GUARD: Hello.

VOICE: This is Arshad, the office boy, sir.

GUARD: What's wrong?

ARSHAD (in tears): The beautiful teleprinter is broken, sir.

GUARD: What broke it?

ARSHAD: It fell from the table.

GUARD: Why?

ARSHAD: Because the bomb came, sir.

GUARD: What bomb? Where did it come from?

ARSHAD: From the Japanese airplane, sir. The Japanese are bombing Singapore, sir.

The air-raid alarm sounded while Guard was pulling on his clothes. At the office on Battery Road a bomb had gutted a building two doors away and almost wrecked the United Press office. The teleprinter, however, was put back together again and was working at six o'clock when the day's news report started moving.

Joseph F. McDonald, Jr., son of the editor of the Nevada *State Journal*, had no experience with the United Press when he arrived on Wake Island as a part-time news-agency correspondent, but for a while he covered the most exciting story in America's newspapers. The Japanese descended in force on Wake Island, which was protected only by a few fighter planes, some artillery, and 400 Marines under command of Major James Devereux. The first blows were repulsed, and a Pan-American Clipper that had stopped for fuel was able to escape to Honolulu. It carried the only news story that the only war correspondent on Wake was ever able to write—McDonald's description of the first eleven bombing attacks and the brusk, determined manner in which Devereux's Marines hurled back the Japanese, destroying nine planes, four surface craft, and one submarine.

After that the only news from Wake were the official communiqués— "Wake continues to resist"—and a famous quotation issued in Washington but supposedly coming from Devereux: "Send us more Japs!" Day after day the Japanese hammered the little island and its defenders to pieces while Americans breathlessly applauded the heroic Devereux's refusal to surrender. It was not until Christmas Eve that they were overwhelmed and the survivors, including McDonald, vanished into Japanese prison camps. Three years later United Press Correspondent Murray Moler found Devereux in a prison camp at Chitose, in Japan, and informed him that he had long since been promoted to a colonelcy.

"I'm curious about one thing, Colonel," Moler added. "What were the circumstances on Wake Island when you dispatched that famous message to Washington: 'Send us more Japs!' Why did you say that?"

Devereux looked at Moler in amazement. "Hell, I never sent any message like that," he sputtered angrily. "We already had too damn many Japs."

Karl Eskelund left the United Press office in Shanghai in the early-morning darkness of December 8 and was walking along the Bund when two Japanese destroyers attacked the American gunboat *Wake* and the British gunboat *Peteral,* which was soon ablaze. Eskelund ran back to the office, sent an urgent wireless dispatch to New York, and called Robert Martin, the Shanghai manager, and William H. McDougall, who was a recent recruit to the bureau.

A little later Japanese Marines landed and began taking over the International Settlement. At 10:15 A.M. they closed the Press Wireless radio transmitters and at noon they informed Martin and his staff that as "enemy nationals" they would have to have Japanese passes to move about the city. A week later they arrested two American newspaper correspondents, and Martin and McDougall decided to try to escape from Shanghai.

A previous contact had been made with Chinese guerrillas by Francis Lee, a former United Press correspondent in Tientsin. On Christmas night, Lee summoned Martin and McDougall, who blandly walked past a Japanese sentry at the door of their hotel, borrowed $500—the Christmas collection —from a Catholic priest and, by pretending to be drunken foreigners, made their way through Japanese lines to a point where they were taken aboard a sampan by guerrillas and started on the underground route to the new seat of the Chinese government at Chungking. At Kinhwa, they found Eskelund who, as a neutral Dane, had been able to leave Shanghai with his Chinese wife, Chi-Yun.

In Bangkok, the capital of Thailand, Darrell Berrigan woke up on the morning of December 8, turned on the radio, and was greeted with a broadcast from Singapore that the Japanese had declared war and were landing in Thailand, with co-operation of some local officials.

There were Japanese observation planes overhead as Berrigan hurried to the American legation, where he found two young officials spreading a huge American flag on the lawn.

"What in hell are you doing?" he screamed.

"Why, we are putting the flag out to identify the legation so that planes won't bomb us by mistake," one replied.

"By mistake!" Berrigan yelled. "Look, this is no Oriental war. Haven't you heard? The Japs have bombed Pearl Harbor. They're at war with *us!*"

"Oh," the young men said in unison as they rolled up the flag.

With an American tobacco grower and an Australian newspaperman, Berrigan went to the Rajdhani Hotel, which adjoined the railroad station, and with the help of friends who worked on the railroad was smuggled into a third-class car while the Japanese, with the aid of Thai police, were searching the first-class coaches for foreigners. They traveled to Chiengrai and then walked into Burma. American army equipment scheduled to be moved northward over the Burma Road to China was piled high on the docks at Rangoon and everybody who could drive a jeep or a truck—from RAF pilots to reporters—was urged to take military vehicles northward as they evacuated the city. Every correspondent had a jeep, and Berrigan had a six-wheel truck on the 400-mile retreat to British headquarters at Maymyo.

Soon after the fall of Rangoon, General Joseph Stilwell arrived at Maymyo to take charge of the Chinese front protecting the vital Burma Road supply line to Chungking. That day Berrigan encountered Major Frank Merrill, later commander of Merrill's Marauders, who was accompanied by an aging man with cropped gray hair and a floppy campaign hat.

"Think I could see Stilwell?" Berrigan asked Merrill.

Merrill looked toward the headquarters office. "I doubt it. He's pretty busy. He's also a crabby old bastard. Why do you want to see him?"

"Oh, I just wanted to welcome him to Burma."

"He eats correspondents' heads off," Merrill said, grinning.

Berrigan finally caught on and turned to the old soldier in his undecorated bush jacket and floppy hat.

"I guess I didn't get your name, sir," he said, sticking out his hand. "I'm Berrigan of the United Press."

"I'm Stilwell," the old man replied, shaking hands.

From then on Berrigan went with Stilwell almost everywhere, trying to keep up with the fast pace he set on foot or in a jeep, trailing him—often nervously—along the front, and getting a story out occasionally over the worst communications lines of the war. Berrigan and Jack Belden were the only correspondents to witness the dramatic destruction of the Yenangyaung oil fields. They were surrounded for three days in the battle of Yenangyaung and escaped only with the aid of Chinese friends.

Eventually, as Burma was overrun, Berrigan, Daniel DeLuce of the Associated Press, William Monday, an Australian reporter, and a British officer drove two jeeps to India. At Kalewa they got across the Chindwin River by steamer and then followed elephant paths most of the way through the mountains into the midst of a tribe of head-hunters who were peacefully singing missionary songs in Naga dialect, and on to Calcutta—perhaps the first time motor vehicles had ever made the trip.

3.

The war began for Frank Hewlett in Manila with a telephone call about four o'clock in the morning. Hewlett wasn't sleeping well that night, anyway. An army officer friend had dropped by the day before to ask Hewlett to witness his will and had remarked that "everything is worse than you think." Then there had been a code message from the Shanghai bureau reporting that a fleet of Japanese transports had been seen headed in the direction of French Indochina. And, unluckily, Hewlett's boss, Richard Wilson, who was Philippines manager for the United Press, had gone to Hong Kong a few days earlier. When the telephone awakened him at four o'clock with a bulletin saying Pearl Harbor was under attack he felt himself very much alone with the biggest job of war coverage a reporter could face. The Philippines obviously would be the first objective of the Japanese Army.

Hewlett dashed to the United Press bureau in the Wilson building overlooking Manila Bay, telephoned the press officer at Admiral Hart's headquarters, and read the bulletin he had received about Pearl Harbor.

"Bunk," was the reply. "Tell your Pearl Harbor correspondent to go back to bed and sleep it off."

Within a short time details of the attack reached Hewlett's desk. Manila was an important relay point for the United Press, and the bureau had its own radio transmitter, as did the Shanghai bureau. The two offices maintained contact until midmorning, when a final message came through from Shanghai:

SIGNING OFF NOW. JAP GENDARMES COMING INTO OFFICE. GOOD LUCK
MARTIN & MCDOUGALL

Early in the afternoon all question of Japanese intentions toward the Philippines was ended when word reached Manila of bombing attacks on the American air base at Clark Field and on Baguio. In the early evening, bombs fell on Nichols Field on the outskirts of Manila. The Japanese began landing invasion troops in Luzon. There was no chance that Wilson could get back to his post (he was later interned at Hong Kong) and communications with New York were greatly delayed. Hewlett had to act on his own. He hired two reporters, Robert Crabb and Franz Weissblatt, and started Weissblatt for the front in northern Luzon. Bert Covit, a shorthand expert who monitored the incoming news report, turned to reporting, too, as new enemy forces landed southeast of Manila on December 24 and the pincers began to close on the Filipino capital. In the next week Manila was under steady attack by waves of Japanese bombers and MacArthur began withdrawing his forces to the Bataan Peninsula and the rocky fortress of Corregidor.

For a comparatively inexperienced news-agency reporter, Hewlett had struggled against heavy odds during the early phases of the war, but he had had one big break. His radio transmitter continued to function and, after several days of experimentation, it was discovered that the United Press bureau at Santiago, Chile, could receive the Manila newscasts at certain hours of the morning. With regular communications channels disrupted or jammed with official dispatches, Hewlett was able to shift a large part of his copy to the newscast at specified hours, assured that it would be picked up in Santiago and relayed to New York far ahead of any other news reports.

On the evening of December 31, with the Japanese threatening to cut off Manila at any hour, Hewlett said good-by to his wife, Virginia, who had a job in the office of the American High Commissioner and would be under diplomatic protection after the Japanese had entered Manila. He climbed into Dick Wilson's sporty automobile, driven by a daredevil little Filipino chauffeur, Julio Carpio, and started a race to beat the Japanese to the last road open to Bataan. As they crossed the bridges leading out of Manila, army engineers were placing explosives to destroy them. Hewlett's car made it across one bridge just before it was blown sky-high. He was the last correspondent out of Manila.

For the next three-and-a-half months Hewlett covered the heroic but hopeless fight against the Japanese armies on Bataan and Corregidor. At first, communications were erratic. He received none of the messages sent to him by the New York office, and he felt that he was being left without any guidance in covering the headline story of the war. He groused to his companions that he was cut off from the world, but he kept on roaming the fighting zone and crowding his cables with all the news that the censors would permit. Then one day he got a message from New York. By some freakish turn of luck, the one message that got through to him was from the accounting department and asked: "What shall we do with your pay check?"

Hewlett crumpled the paper in disgust and sat around for an hour thinking up the most sarcastic reply possible. He was fed up. He wanted to show New York that he was fed up. He began composing a message addressed to the accounting department. He wanted to say that he was tired and dirty and discouraged and hadn't received a word of encouragement or guidance from New York. He wanted to say that he was worried about his wife, who was a prisoner of the enemy. He wanted to say why doesn't any help come to Corregidor? Why can't I get any messages except one asking what to do with my pay check? But in the end he didn't say any of these things. Instead, he tried to sum up all of his bitterness in a single sarcastic line:

HELL WHY DON'T YOU BUY LIBERTY BONDS?

That, Hewlett decided as he turned his copy in to the censor, will fix them! It did. The next day the United Press carried a news story under a New York dateline. The reporter who had stuck with the army on Bataan, it said, had asked his office to turn his salary into government bonds to carry on the fight against Japan. It was the kind of human interest story that made the front pages of hundreds of newspapers throughout America. Hewlett himself remained in happy ignorance of the results of his flippancy until the communications tangle was partially cleared up and he began receiving regular messages from New York. One of the first ones made his eyes pop wide open:

02142 HEWLETT YOU GETTING EXCELLENT PLAY DESCRIPTIVE STORIES STOP YOUR REPORTING BEEN ONE OF WARS HIGHLIGHTS. . . . BUYING DEFENSE BONDS WITH YOUR SALARY AS REQUESTED STOP GOOD LUCK

JALEX[1]

The army on Bataan surrendered on April 9 after ninety-eight days of fighting against incredible odds. Franz Weissblatt had been captured by a Japanese patrol that fired on his automobile, wounded him in the leg, and forced him to travel for many hours without medical attention. He was interned near Manila, as were Robert Crabb and his family, Bert Covit, and Mrs. Hewlett. Dick Wilson and George Baxter of the Hong Kong bureau

---

[1] To avoid confusion of his messages with those of Far Eastern Manager John R. Morris, the cable signature JALEX was used by United Press Foreign Editor Joe Alex Morris.

were interned in Hong Kong. Only Hewlett was still not a prisoner of the Japanese, but he felt he might become one almost any day. MacArthur, on orders from Washington, had left Corregidor and, one by one, the American correspondents had managed to escape by air or boat, leaving only Hewlett and Dean Schedler, who had been hired on Bataan by the Associated Press.

In mid-April, General Wainwright advised Hewlett and Schedler to leave. By that time, there were only two small trainer planes operating from the little airstrip on The Rock, and it was arranged for the two correspondents to be flown in these planes to Mindanao, from where they might hitch an air ride to Australia. Hewlett and Schedler went to the airstrip at one o'clock on the morning of April 12, but discovered that one of the planes had already gone in disregard of Wainwright's orders. There were two pilots preparing to leave in the second plane.

"We can take only one of you," they informed the reporters. "In fact, we are in such bad shape that we can take only whichever one of you is smallest."

They looked at the two reporters. There wasn't much doubt which one was the smallest—Schedler. Hewlett trudged alone back to his quarters.

The next day Hewlett heard that there was still one other trainer plane on Corregidor. It was badly damaged but repairs were being made and one of the pilots was going to try to get it off the ground that night. Under Wainwright's orders the correspondent went to the airstrip again at one o'clock, carrying a bag filled with army intelligence records. The plane had once been used for aerial reconnaissance and a large hole had been cut in the bottom of the fuselage for a camera. Nevertheless it was running, and Hewlett and the pilot climbed aboard. As the little craft clattered down the bomb-pitted runway a Japanese searchlight on Bataan picked it out and held it for a few moments in a gleaming ray of light. Then the searchlight snapped off and there was nothing but a severe thunderstorm between Hewlett and safety. The patched-up plane survived the storm and flew on to the Panay airfield. It collapsed gently upon landing.

American bombing planes from Del Monte plantation airfield in Mindanao had been on a raid against Japanese positions on Bataan during the night and one of them, piloted by Major P. I. Gunn, had run short of fuel en route home. Gunn landed at the Panay airfield and offered to take Hewlett to Del Monte. Arriving at Del Monte, he found bombers commanded by Brigadier General Ralph Royce were just ready to leave for Australia. Hewlett climbed aboard one of the big ships and was off on the long over-water flight to freedom.

4.

The swiftness of the Japanese conquest in Southwest Asia, the dire plight of the United States Navy, and the blanket of censorship and propaganda that covered military operations made the first months of 1942 a nightmare of confusion for correspondents at the fronts and editors at home. Again and again Unipressers as well as many other correspondents risked becoming captives or casualties by remaining on the job until the last hour. Sometimes they waited too long.

Harold Guard, the Singapore manager, covered the Japanese advance down the Malay Peninsula and scored a news beat of seventy minutes on the enemy landing in Singapore itself. On February 10 the situation appeared so grave that the New York office emphasized to Guard that he should use his own discretion about getting away. Two days later, with Henry Keys, who later became editor of the United Press European service in London, Guard managed to get aboard a little ship called the *Pangkor*. The *Pangkor* made a dash for Java while Japanese artillery and airplanes were heavily attacking all vessels in the narrow sea lane that offered the only escape from Singapore. Then the *Pangkor's* course led straight through a fleet of Japanese landing craft heading for Pasir Panjang on the southernmost tip of Singapore Island. British artillery at Pasir Panjang opened fire on the landing craft, searchlights from the shore flooded the scene, and the Japanese artillery fired over the *Pangkor* at British positions. The *Pangkor* skipper kept going full steam ahead. In the confusion, the ship lunged through the scene of battle and Guard arrived at Batavia on February 15, the day Radio Tokyo announced the fall of Singapore.

By that time Java was in a position of deadly peril. Far Eastern Manager John Morris had flown from India to Java in January. Censorship and a tremendous load of official messages were delaying communications from Batavia for hours and sometimes for days, but Morris was able to set up daily wireless telephone calls to New York that gave the United Press a series of beats from Java during February. Late in the month, the Dutch-led Allied fleet met the Japanese in battle off Java and was all but destroyed. The fate of the Dutch East Indies was then just a matter of time—and not much time at that. Morris flew to Ceylon with the Allied land and air-force commanders. Guard "hitched" a ride later on a Flying Fortress to Australia. Bill McDougall, who had already escaped the enemy in China, had made arrangements to go with Guard on one of Colonel Eugene L. Eubank's planes, but a few hours before the take-off on the last day of February he changed his mind.

"I'm staying," he told Guard and Eubank. "I'm going to cover the final battle for Java."

"It's your funeral," the colonel said.

"You'll be no good to the United Press if you're trapped in Java," Guard said.

"I guess I'll stay," McDougall persisted. He watched the planes take off and then drove back to Bandoeng. When he walked into the censor's office it was all but deserted. The Japanese had landed on Java and all except six correspondents had left for the south coast in an effort to get transportation to Australia. By March 4 it was about over. McDougall made his last radio telephone call to New York the next morning and ended by telling Miles Vaughn: "I'll have to be scramming soon." With DeWitt Hancock of the Associated Press, who had been the last American reporter to get out of Singapore, he drove to Wijnkoops Bay, where the motor vessel *Poelau Bras* was loading for Ceylon. McDougall and Hancock got aboard.

The *Poelau Bras* made full speed southwestward all night in an effort to get beyond the range of Japanese bombers, but at 9:15 A.M. the ship was spotted by an enemy scouting plane. Two hours later nine bombers converged on the helpless vessel, blew her to pieces, and machine-gunned survivors in lifeboats. The ship was half under water when McDougall and Hancock, ready to leap into the sea, were forced to throw themselves on the deck to escape a new flurry of machine-gun bullets. When the plane had passed, McDougall leaped. He was a good swimmer and only a good swimmer could have survived. Most of the lifeboats had been shot full of holes by the Japanese machine gunners. He swam from one to another. All were sinking. All around him men and women were drowning or clinging desperately to rafts or pieces of wreckage. Looking back at the *Poelau Bras*, he saw the tall figure of Hancock braced against the rail near the forecastle. He may have been wounded.

"Jump! Jump!" McDougall shouted, but Hancock gave no indication that he heard. With a long sigh, the *Poelau Bras* slid under the waves. Hancock, too, disappeared into the sea, the first American correspondent to be killed in the Pacific theater of war.

Later, McDougall would remember like a vivid dream everything that happened to him in the water that afternoon, but even then it would seem incredible that he survived. He swam after a lifeboat that was rowing away, heavily loaded. The occupants looked the other way. With tremendous effort he caught up with the boat but was too weak to pull himself aboard. No one dared help him; no one believed the boat had more than a fighting chance to reach shore with its heavy load. At last the man at the tiller pointed over a wave.

"There's another boat there," he said. "We are full."

McDougall didn't believe him. He pleaded for help. He grabbed a rope trailing behind the boat but it was jerked from his hands. He was near complete exhaustion. The boat pulled away. He lay motionless in the water. Then the mast of another lifeboat appeared over the top of a wave. He swam desperately toward it but it was moving away too rapidly. McDougall prayed—and swam. Sometime later he saw the outline of a drifting boat in which the crew was attempting to raise a sail. He shouted but it was too far away for the occupants to hear him. He swam harder. The sail, almost up, collapsed, but the crew quickly began raising it again. He would be too late! Then the sail collapsed again. McDougall shouted and waved his arm. The crew ignored him and worked rapidly with the sail, but now the exhausted swimmer was alongside. Two men leaned over and pulled him, choking and gasping, into the boat. The sail was up now, and the lifeboat headed back toward Sumatra—and a Japanese prison camp.

CHAPTER TWENTY-SIX

In the summer of 1942 the war reached almost everywhere. The men responsible for directing United Press war coverage had to keep a constant stream of reporters flowing to Europe, to Africa, and to the Far East. "We do not have the least idea how many years this war will last," Earl Johnson wrote to all bureau managers, "but we would be less than smart if we did not prepare now for a long war. . . . The important thing from the standpoint of operations of the United Press is that we preserve our record for doing a good job for our clientele. . . . We are not going to cheapen our product but will continue to compete toe-to-toe on the big stories of the day with a view of keeping a dominant position on the front pages."

The United Press was keeping its dominant position because a lot of young men and some not so young never ceased to gravitate to the centers of news, the centers of war. Nobody will ever be able to write exactly what they did or how they did it; it would no more be possible than to write about all the servicemen who fought in many battles in many distant places. Some of the most exciting, the most desperate chapters are always missing from the story. But there are enough to give an idea.

2.

At dawn on August 7, 1942, American warships and transports lay off the Solomon Islands. For the first time the Allied Powers were trying to strike back at the Japanese, trying to get a toehold on Guadalcanal, on Tulagi, and on Florida Island at the end of the long chain of islands seized by the enemy north of Australia. Among the warships were the American heavy cruisers *Astoria, Vincennes,* and *Quincy* and, on the *Astoria,* United Press correspondent Joe James Custer was watching thousands of Marines storm the beaches—often under heavy Japanese fire.

Within a short time, enemy airplanes launched counterattacks on the warships. Dive bombers hurtled out of the clouds over Savo Island, but antiaircraft fire and American carrier-borne fighter planes held them off for the most part and brought down a score. The next two days brought more of the same, but in the darkness of early morning on August 9 Custer awakened to find that Japanese warships had slipped in among the fleet and caught the Americans unalerted. It was a short, savage battle. By the time the reporter got on deck huge balls of fire were shooting back and forth between the opposing fleets. He stepped out into the glare of a huge searchlight sweeping the *Astoria's* signal bridge. Shells whistled through the superstructure, dropping debris and fragments on the bridge. Scrambling to one side of the tilting vessel, Custer could see a fire amidships. As he went back to get his life belt, flaky burning debris showered him. The lights went off. A shell ripped completely through his cabin, and he crawled out through the jagged, still-warm hole it had made in the bulkhead.

The whole center of the ship was blazing, and columns of water were spouting on all sides. Custer climbed down a ladder and started edging forward when another explosion spun him around. His left eye was burning with pain, and blood streamed down his face. "Lean on me," somebody said. There was an order to move all wounded men to the forecastle and Custer, with the sight of one eye gone, was helped forward where, as the battle ended suddenly a little later, he and other wounded were transferred to a destroyer. In less than half an hour the Japanese had sunk the Australian cruiser *Canberra* and the American cruisers *Vincennes, Quincy,* and *Astoria,* torpedoed the *Chicago,* and damaged two destroyers.

3.

As the conflict spread, Frank Bartholomew roamed from New Guinea to the Aleutians to strengthen coverage in the Pacific and to report—often under fire—what was happening on the war fronts. A corps of United Press correspondents—Charles P. Arnot, George E. Jones, Brydon Taves, Robert C. Miller, Don Caswell, Bill Tyree, Francis McCarthy—fanned out to the Pacific fronts as rapidly as the armed forces would accept them. Reporters on the battlefronts were the key to successful war coverage, but it was equally important that their dispatches be properly processed at relay bureaus and at New York headquarters. Two basic factors were involved in processing the United Press news report: first, a vast mass of material had to be presented in a form satisfactory to both large and small newspapers; and, second, this news had to be edited intelligently so that the editors would be kept constantly informed of important trends and not be misled by undue emphasis on rumors or minor developments.

During the 1930s Earl Johnson had pushed the development of what news-agency men called "the undated lead." There were often stories that could not be covered satisfactorily from any single city or under any one dateline. In such cases Johnson turned a top rewrite man to the task of collating all phases of the story in a dispatch that carried no dateline but included the highlights and the essential information that had already been put on the wires in dispatches from two or three or half a dozen different cities. With the great crush of news in World War II, this system was adapted to a daily presentation of the war situation.

The United Press undated war leads, however, were considerably more than a mere technical solution of a problem that confronted newspapers. Often they presented a trend or a development or even a news break that could not be found in other dispatches because of censorship or because of problems of communications in wartime. The success of this system was based on what might be called the art of collaboration among United Press correspondents scattered around the world.

This distinguishing trait in the agency's coverage was not to be confused with speculation. Any editor with background information could look at the headlines and speculate, and a great many did with skill and accuracy. But the art of collaboration called for an entirely different approach. It depended partly on the daily accumulation of tens of thousands of words from all parts of the world. It depended partly on the ability to analyze this information intelligently. But most of all it depended on the fact that key editors of the United Press in scattered centers of war had enjoyed a long period of association and co-operation in the handling of important news. Many of them had worked across desks from one another for months and years in various bureaus before they were separated by the war. Each one knew how the others worked, how they thought, how they reacted to this or that development. With the coming of censorship they could not always inform each other fully as to the information they had gathered, but on many occasions important ideas were conveyed by an editor in London or Cairo or New Delhi to an editor in New York merely because two men separated by thousands of miles were intimately acquainted with each other's working habits.

So close were these associations that in mid-June of 1941 Harrison E. Salisbury, on the New York cable desk, had started writing almost daily undated leads emphasizing the possibility of a break between Russia and Germany, and of a Nazi attack on the Red Army. There were no dispatches coming through the censorship that more than hinted at such a possibility—yet from a variety of sources and from the words used or the phrases not used by correspondents in key spots, Salisbury was able to piece together what was happening. Johnson questioned whether he was going too far in these stories. But after going over the accumulation of messages from reporters they had both worked with for years, Johnson's doubts were removed. Salisbury wrote another story for Sunday morning newspapers of June 21 in which he went a step further with the idea that the Nazis would turn on Russia within a few days.

Late that night he was discussing the situation with several friends at his home. "Actually," he remarked, "I'm almost convinced the Germans will attack Russia this weekend. Hitler likes to start things on Sundays."

The telephone rang as he finished speaking. The office was calling with a flash that the Nazis had invaded the Soviet Union.

Our staff—World-wide—is the best that any news service ever had [Johnson wrote in a memorandum touching on the art of collaboration]. *If you will review our big beats and exclusives you will see that they are notable for a quality that cannot be ascribed, unfortunately, to all press service beats. . . . You will not find them stemming back to the currying or accepting of special favors from governments or government agents. . . .*

Our reporters and editors are men of maturity and experience. They do not allow desire to catch a headline to sway their fidelity to accuracy or their sense of responsibility. Any newspaper editor should recognize that much more than just hunches lay behind the United Press undated leads which hard-pedaled the prospects of a break between Germany and Russia ten days before the break occurred. The cable desk in New York was being fed by correspondents who were in a position to know and found ways to tell us where the emphasis belonged. The same is true of our beat on the story that Roosevelt and Churchill planned a conference . . . These things are rarely luck.

In the late summer of 1942, with the Pacific war still heavily weighted in favor of the Japanese and with the Germans deep in Russian territory, this art of collaboration was demonstrated again. The Russians had been vigorously demanding that their Western allies establish a second front against the Germans by invading Europe. This was much easier said than done. Rommel's Afrika Korps had pushed into Egypt during the summer, threatening to capture Alexandria, and only exhaustion had prevented them from breaking through at El Alamein before the British could rally for a new stand. The African desert warfare had drained British resources, the flow of American troops and material into the British Isles was just beginning to build up, and speculation on a second front in Europe was based on flimsy hopes rather than fact.

Yet something had to be done, and eventually the dispatches and messages pouring across the cable desk in New York began to show a faint pattern. A few messages were sent to London and Washington. The replies began to add substance to the pattern. Some kind of major move was in the making, and American forces would carry the brunt of the thrust. On October 23 General Sir Bernard L. Montgomery struck Rommel's fortified positions at El Alamein with an unparalleled barrage of artillery and sent the British Eighth Army slogging forward on a long road toward Tunis. In the next few days several familiar signatures were missing from the London dispatches arriving in New York. Inquiries as to the whereabouts of these staff members brought no definite replies.

By now the pattern was complete. That afternoon Salisbury wrote a message to Lyle Wilson, the Washington manager, saying that he believed the Allies were about to invade North Africa in the vicinity of Algiers or Casablanca or possibly Tunis and that he was worried about what kind of coverage would be possible. "Can't you take this up with the proper authorities in Washington so we will get assurance of some kind of communications?" he concluded.

Salisbury filed the message to Wilson on a private teleprinter wire between the New York and Washington bureaus. A little later his telephone rang and Wilson was screaming in his ear. "What in hell is the matter with you guys? Don't you know that wire is cut in to the censor's office? Why would you send me any such message anyway? I'm up to my ears in military intelligence officers already."

Military intelligence officers continued to bear down on the United Press for several days. Only after Salisbury had gone to Washington to talk to them did they let the matter drop. But apparently the Germans were never able to work out the pattern that had been visible on the New York cable desk. The invasion of North Africa on November 8 was a successful surprise on Adolf Hitler.

4.

About nine o'clock on the night of October 23, Dick McMillan slogged across the desert at El Alamein and peered into a big hole in the sand which, covered with sacking and camel's thorn, served as headquarters for a brigade of the 51st Highland Division. Here men spoke with a broad accent, men from Ross and Cromarty, from Caithness and Inverness. All around the headquarters were men and machines, monster new tanks, new tractored 105-mm. guns, batteries of six-pounders, and antitank guns with thick defensive armor.

"We want to go with you," McMillan told a brigadier who emerged from the underground headquarters. He showed his credentials, as did Christopher Buckley of the London *Daily Telegraph,* and Jack Hetherington, an Australian correspondent. The brigadier nodded.

"Keep close to my vehicle," he said.

Suddenly from across the desert came a wild skirl of bagpipes. It was a challenging, defiant cry that must have been clearly audible in the positions of the Afrika Korps a few hundred yards away. The music swelled madly and then—with one stupendous bang!—Allied guns flashed death along the desert front. For twenty minutes the barrage descended like fire on the surprised Germans. Then the infantry moved forward. By one o'clock they had covered three miles. The great drive was on.

Late in October several members of the London staff simply went out of circulation. They had been told to report with their field equipment at certain hours. After that they were in the hands of military authorities.

Chris Cunningham went with General Dwight D. Eisenhower's headquarters to Gibraltar. John Parris went into Africa with troops that landed at Arzeu, near Oran, where the French forces under command of the Vichy government resisted stubbornly. Ned Russell went ashore from a British troopship with a commando unit heading for Fort Sidi Ferruch, near Algiers. Three days later Russell was the only American correspondent to accompany General Kenneth Anderson's First Army—mostly British troops—eastward on a drive to seize the coastal cities and push toward the port of Tunis. Phil Ault landed at Oran and then flew to headquarters at Algiers. Donald Coe joined the Algiers headquarters staff shortly afterward and was sent eastward to cover the first big tank advance to Kasserine Pass in Tunisia.

The American and British had made extensive pre-invasion preparations in an effort to persuade the French forces in North Africa to come over to the United Nations side without resistance. But in some areas the French armed forces obeyed Marshal Henri Pétain's orders to resist any foreign invader. Leo Disher, a tall, dark, and eager United Press correspondent, stepped into the worst of the bloodshed in the harbor of Oran.

Disher was aboard a former U. S. Coast Guard cutter, the *Walney,* which was crowded with troops and depth charges to a point where she listed slightly. The craft had been assigned the unenviable task of breaking the chain or boom that the Vichy French had built to keep unfriendly vessels out of Oran harbor. En route from England, Disher slipped and fell heavily on the deck, breaking his ankle, which had to be put in a cast by the ship's doctor. The ship officers tried to put Disher off at Gibraltar, but he had found a pair of crutches on which he could move about slowly and he refused to disembark. As the *Walney* approached Oran on the night of November 7, Disher attached a life preserver to the cast on his leg—just in case he had to swim.

At midnight a report was received that there were eight French warships in the harbor. Disher strapped another life preserver around his chest, put on his helmet, and hobbled out on deck. He climbed a steel ladder to the bridge, squeezed into a narrow passage, and braced himself against the bulkhead so that he could see across the bridge. The *Walney* raced toward the harbor.

It was about three o'clock when flaming tracer bullets began arching out across the water, followed by the crashes of a heavy gun. Twice the *Walney* shuddered under direct hits.

"Lie flat for the crash," the bridge commanded over the loud-speaker. "We're approaching the boom."

Amid a shower of machine-gun bullets and shells, the cutter snapped the boom and, a moment later, collided with a launch and began drifting without power. From the bridge of the *Walney* a powerful loud-speaker addressed the French ships in the harbor: "Cease firing. We are your friends. We are Americans."

Then everything happened at once—all of it bad. The loud-speaker was drowned out in a burst of fire from the harbor guns. A shell hit a fuel drum on the cutter and spread liquid fire along the deck. A destroyer loomed ahead and the *Walney* was raked again and again by point-blank fire from the warship. A French cruiser joined in the attack. The *Walney's* bridge and decks were littered with dead and wounded. Disher fell as a shell hit the bridge. He was wounded in both legs. His crutches were gone. Depth charges carried aboard the cutter began exploding below decks.

"Everybody off!" the bridge officer shouted. "Get ashore."

Disher groped almost blindly among the bodies of his companions on the bridge. He touched the rail. Then the night exploded in a sheet of flame as a whole volley of shells and bullets ripped the bridge. So far as Disher could make out there was only one other man still alive on the bridge, and at the instant they spoke to each other another shell exploded. Then there was only Disher. He tumbled down two steel ladders to the main deck, took off his helmet, and lurched through a gap in the rail. In the water, the life preserver around his foot automatically inflated, but the one around his chest—punctured by shell fragments—did not. He was floating with his crippled foot out of the water and his head under. He pulled the tube off his ankle and began swimming through a red glare that was intensified by a great explosion that sank the *Walney*.

Disher swam between a merchant ship and the pier. By luck his fingers touched a rope and he hung on until strength came back into his arms. After a while he dragged himself up to the edge of the pier. But, even with his elbows over the pier rim, the cast on his ankle dragged him down. He knew he couldn't make it. Then out of the darkness a single hand groped down and held him. He swung his good foot over the edge and somebody pulled him, gasping and exhausted, over the edge. He could see a hazy, unreal figure swaying over him. Disher looked again. His rescuer had used only one hand because the other had been shot off. Before they could speak there was a new burst of machine-gun fire. One bullet hit Disher's broken ankle. Another hit a wall and bounced across his temple. He crawled on his belly behind a large piece of timber, squeezing himself into the dirt. Still another bullet ripped through the edge of the timber and through Disher's exposed buttocks.

A little later a French patrol came along the pier and collected Disher and others who had escaped from the *Walney*. A French soldier slung the correspondent over his shoulder and carried him to safety and an ambulance. In the hospital a doctor counted twenty-six assorted wounds. The next time Disher woke up the battle of Oran was over.

In Algiers, headquarters for the North African invasion, there was probably even more confusion than at the front. When Admiral Jean Darlan, the controversial Vichy French leader, was assassinated in Algiers on Christmas

Eve, Unipresser Walter Logan got the story almost immediately and ran to the censor's office to file a flash. He was a few moments too late. The censors had just received orders to pass nothing, and Logan's potential scoop was lost. Seven hours later, after American and British experts had studied the political repercussions of the assassination, an army officer told the correspondents what information would be passed by the censor in connection with the Darlan story. He also announced that since only one story could be sent at a time over the wireless to New York the three American press associations would have to draw lots to see which dispatch moved first.

Chris Cunningham drew for the United Press and lost. Phil Ault wrote the story for the agency and submitted it to the censor for approval—a process that required some time on such an important subject. However, Ault also had "submitted" a carbon copy to Cunningham who quietly strolled out of the censor's office. An argument arose as to how many words the lucky agency that had won the draw could send before the stories of the other agencies would be moved. This further delayed the flashes. Meantime Cunningham had gone into the wireless room and found an old friend—a sergeant —on duty. When the reporter slid his copy of the Darlan story across the desk the sergeant didn't even look to see whether it bore the censor's stamp. He sent it. A little later, when the officially censored and stamped dispatches reached the wireless room, Cunningham had disappeared. The International News Service and Associated Press dispatches were sent first because they had drawn the lucky numbers and their authors never could understand how Ault's story beat them to the wires in New York.

CHAPTER TWENTY-SEVEN

Over the years it had been more or less customary for the United Press top brass to show up wherever there was a war in progress. So far as is known, nobody ever tried to stop them except the United States Army, which failed in its only attempt. That was in 1944, when the Army Public Relations Department refused Hugh Baillie's request for press credentials to visit Europe on the grounds that he was not a working reporter in the field. Baillie promptly got in touch with a British cabinet minister, Lord Beaverbrook, and received an invitation to visit Britain, which he accepted. In 1943, however, neither Baillie nor Frank Bartholomew, who had become a vice-president of the company, had any difficulty in being accredited to the armed forces.

Baillie went to Great Britain in June as a war correspondent, but also to check on preparations for the inevitable day when the Allied Powers would invade Hitler's European fortress. While he was touring American air bases in England there were indications that General Eisenhower would soon launch from Africa an attack on Sicily. Baillie flew to Algiers just before the Sicilian invasion started.

Virgil Pinkley, European general manager, had gone from New York to Algiers some time earlier and used his extensive knowledge of communications routes to establish a comprehensive system of transmitting copy quickly to New York and London. Pinkley, Reynolds Packard, Dick McMillan and William Wilson of the British United Press gathered in North Africa to bolster the Algiers staff in preparation for the Sicilian invasion. Packard, a dashing if somewhat bulky figure in the khaki shirt and South Seas sarong he wore around the office in the Aletti Hotel, presumed that he was going to the front. Baillie, however, was acutely conscious of the need for experienced editors at the Algiers headquarters and relay center, and one of his first acts was to appoint Packard as United Press manager for Rome—still in enemy hands—and North Africa. Then he pointed out that the manager's place was at headquarters in Algiers until American troops entered Rome.

(When they did, incidentally, Packard was with them and reopened the Rome bureau on June 4, 1944.)

Baillie wasn't assigned to any outfit for the invasion of Sicily, and, in fact, General Eisenhower and his staff were inclined to take the position that there was no place at the front for civilian brass. Baillie, on the other hand, believed it was important for the president of the United Press to appear occasionally at the scene of action, to learn the problems of reporters at first hand, and to lend both moral and physical support to the staff. The staff generally agreed, although they sometimes joked about it. One day Baillie wandered into the cluttered office at the Aletti Hotel and picked up a message that had fallen on the floor. It was from a staffer at an advanced base, addressed to Packard:

WHAT IN HELL IS BAILLIE TRYING TO DO—WIN THE AFRICAN STAR?

Baillie wasn't discouraged by attempts to keep him at headquarters. Soon after the invasion of Sicily started on July 10 he went out to the airfield and hitched a ride on a Hudson bomber, usually known as a "flying coffin," that was carrying troops to the invaded island. With a tin hat and bed roll, Baillie toured the front from end to end, checked in with Ned Russell, Chris Cunningham, McMillan, Williams, and other correspondents living in the fighting zone, wrote a number of dispatches giving his own impressions of the conflict, and lost fifteen pounds in two weeks. He was under fire half a dozen times and proved that he could leap from a jeep to a ditch or dive into a slit trench with the best of the younger reporters when enemy strafing planes were overhead.

As usual, Baillie's approach to the story was different. Much of his copy was devoted to informing the Americans how men lived and fought under combat conditions, why Sicilian towns were as hard to capture as a fortress, and what kind of miracles were performed by such units as the engineers and sappers. He also made a study of why soldiers slogging along the roads didn't sing popular songs as they had done in World War I. He concluded that it was because this was a mechanized army and soldiers didn't march much except when close to the front. Then they were too busy to think of singing.

2.

Frank Bartholomew traveled to Pearl Harbor in a convoy—nine men to one cabin with the portholes sealed—and then hitched a ride on a cargo plane loaded with incendiary hand grenades to the South Pacific. Leaving Nandi, in the Fiji Islands, the cargo plane blew a tire as it took off, but it got into the air. A few minutes later the pilot walked through the plane and stopped beside Bartholomew, who was sitting as comfortably as possible on the hand grenades.

"I guess you can vote too," the pilot said. "I'm asking everybody whether they want to go on to New Caledonia with a flat tire or turn back."

Bart said he was pretty indifferent on such a technicality and the plane went on to New Caledonia, where the pilot skimmed down the runway and let the big craft slither around and around in a mud puddle until it came to a peaceful halt. Early in January of 1943 Bart flew to Brisbane and then to Port Moresby, where Frank Hewlett and Harold Guard were covering the battle to oust the Japanese from the Buna area on the north coast of New Guinea. If there had been any question in Bartholomew's mind about the problems faced by correspondents in the war zone they were soon removed. At Port Moresby public relations officers were reluctant to issue orders for him to get transportation to Buna. After a few inquiries, however, he discovered that planes left each night from a nearby airstrip, flying over the Owen Stanley mountain range just before dawn in order to escape enemy fighter craft.

"Why don't you just get on one of the cargo planes?" an officer suggested.

The next midnight Bart went to the airstrip and found a medical-supply plane with only one man aboard. He was given permission to climb in and they took off in the darkness, circling for half an hour to gain enough altitude to get over the mountains. As the plane leveled off, Bart went forward and sat in the copilot's seat.

"Hi," the pilot greeted him. "Are you a pilot?"

"No."

"Hell, that's bad. I'm not either. I was at the field to guard this plane but the crew didn't show up, so I had to take it off. See the exhaust of that plane ahead of us? . . . Well, I'm just trying to follow it through the mountain pass. If it goes all right we ought to be all right, but I don't know much about landing."

They landed, with some extra bumps, near General Eichelberger's headquarters and Bart later flew in a small plane to join a detachment of Australian troops in the jungle a few miles away. The pilot let him off at a deserted airstrip and then departed without telling him which direction to walk toward the Australian lines. Bart walked down a rough log road that had been built through the mucky jungle. After a few hundred yards he saw an ammunition dump where two men were at work, but it was a little way off the road and he decided not to try to talk to them. He waved and they waved back, and he wandered on a couple of miles until he met an Australian soldier who directed him to a tent where tea was being served. An officer looked at him in surprise.

"Where'd you come from?" he asked.

"That airstrip down the road," Bart replied. "I walked from there."

"Did you see an ammunition dump on your way here?"

"Yes. Couple of fellows working there but I just waved at them."

"H-m-m. You landed at the wrong airstrip. That was a Japanese ammunition dump you saw and those were Japanese soldiers you waved at."

3.

There were times when a war correspondent had to forget that he was being paid to get the news first. One of those times was in the South Pacific in 1943, when Francis McCarthy was covering operations of the United States Navy. The Navy, thanks to the disaster at Pearl Harbor, was still woefully weak and had only one task force—Number 18—in action. McCarthy, who had seen Pearl Harbor, Guadalcanal, and several other war scenes at their worst, was assigned to Task Force 18 during a period when the warships did not touch shore for a solid nine months. The force, consisting of light cruisers and destroyers, was assigned to a wide variety of duties in an effort to give the Japanese the impression that there was far greater American naval strength in the South Pacific than actually existed.

One night the task force would lay mines. The next night the ships would "run the slot" between Guadalcanal and Rabaul, trying to intercept enemy convoys. The following day they would shell Japanese shore installations. In general, Task Force 18 tried to act as if it were three or four separate squadrons in order to discourage enemy aggressiveness.

There was a flaw in this deception. If McCarthy, the only correspondent with the task force, reported all of these activities the Japanese would soon realize that a single naval force was involved and the deception would fail. The Navy put it up to McCarthy: would he share his exclusive stories with the other war correspondents so that it would appear that several task forces were in action? McCarthy did the hard and dangerous work, and then gave his stories to rival reporters.

In the fall of 1943 Richard Johnston arrived at Efate in the New Hebrides with the Eighth Marine regiment. He and other correspondents in the party were told when they reached Efate that they would be assigned to various combat waves in an assault on Tarawa Island. Johnston drew the combat group that was to land on Red Beach Three.

Navy guns and airplanes battered Tarawa for thirteen days. Then Johnston crawled into a Higgins boat with forty Marines at three o'clock in the morning of November 20. A naval gunnery commander had assured everybody that practically all enemy troops on the island were dead, but when the landing boats were 500 yards off the pier somebody very much alive began shooting a remarkable number of machine guns and artillery pieces from the shore. Johnston's boat was under a steady shower of fragments from aerial bursts when the coxswain let down the ramp and shouted: "Everybody out—this is as far as I go." The Marines, an Associated Press photographer, Frank Filan, and Johnston spilled out into shoulder-deep water that was being riffled by thousands of unfriendly machine-gun bullets.

"Can you swim?" Filan shouted at Johnston.

"No. If I could I'd swim out to sea."

"Neither can I," Filan answered. "Let's get ashore."

Marines on each side of Johnston were killed before they reached the beach, where the reporter and Filan collapsed behind a four-foot-high sea wall. The Marines' forward line was just twenty-five yards inland. Johnston worked along the wall until he found Dr. Clayton Uridil, the battalion doctor, and stuck with him all day. In the afternoon he got out his portable typewriter and began writing a story. About that time a new wave of landing boats began coming ashore, but they were literally shot out of the water by the Japanese artillery. One moment a boat would be heading for the beach. Then there ﹀ ould be a klang! from a Japanese battery and the next moment the boat would be gone.

That night Uridil and Johnston drank a toast in medicinal brandy and discussed whether they would prefer to be killed by a bullet or a bayonet. They felt that there was no real hope of surviving an expected enemy counterattack at dawn. The naval bombardment, however, had been more effective than they believed, and the counterattack never came. The second day Johnston made his way to Red Beach Two with several other correspondents, but they were still pinned down. On the third day there was some improvement, and they were advised that a navy seaplane would arrive on the following day to pick up the correspondents' dispatches. They decided to get back aboard one of the navy ships to write their stories and get something to eat. Johnston and two other reporters crept down the beach for a better look at the fighting and, while they were gone, the rest of the press party, including the Associated Press reporter, had a chance to go out to a command ship. They went.

A little later another landing boat took the three remaining correspondents to another ship. They ate and wrote their stories and then, about midnight, Japanese bombing planes began unloading on the beach. They rushed to the bridge, where the captain was shouting orders to watch out for torpedo bombers.

"What's your cargo?" Johnston asked him.

"Two-thousand-pound bombs and high octane gas," he replied. Despite the fact that his ship was a floating bomb, the captain stayed near the beach, but the command ship to which the other reporters had gone put out to sea and didn't get back until the following evening. By that time, the seaplane had arrived from Pearl Harbor and picked up Johnston's dispatches, as well as those of Robert Sherrod of *Time* and Henry Keys of the London *Daily Express*. When the plane returned to Pearl Harbor with only one dispatch from a news-agency correspondent, the censors summoned reporters to headquarters. Bill Tyree appeared for the United Press at about two o'clock in the morning.

"We have received dispatches from only one news-agency reporter," the head censor said. "We are going to pool that story for everybody if there are no objections."

Johnston's main story was pooled, but he had written two other stories that were turned over to the United Press exclusively.

When the Associated Press representative at Pearl Harbor discovered that the pooled story was by Johnston he demanded that he be given custody of the copy until the cable office opened at six o'clock. Tyree agreed, and the Associated Press man went home to bed, taking the copy with him. Tyree went to a telephone, called up a friend at the wireless station, and persuaded him to come to the office at four o'clock and send Johnston's two supplementary eyewitness stories of the invasion of Tarawa. The first editions of afternoon newspapers were just going to press in the United States as they received Johnston's descriptive dispatches on one of the bloodiest battles of the Pacific war.

Brydon Taves was a reporter who liked action, but throughout the Pacific war he had been forced to remain at MacArthur's headquarters to coordinate the activities of other correspondents at the fighting fronts. He frequently protested, but it was not until late in 1943 that he was able to persuade New York to permit him to go on a front-line mission with the Marines landing at Cape Gloucester on New Britain Island. He started for New Britain, but at Christmas time the B-17 bomber on which he was riding crashed at Port Moresby. Taves was killed.

4.

In 1943 the news-agency manpower problem mounted rapidly throughout the United States as reporters were called into the armed services. Prior to the war the United Press had hired comparatively few women, and those were usually assigned to cover a special, limited field of reporting. Back in 1914 Alice Rohe had been Rome correspondent. In the 1920s, Lucille Saunders worked in the Buenos Aires bureau, and in the 1930s, Ruby Black was a part-time member of the Washington staff. Corinne Hardesty was in the Chicago bureau. Mary Knight did feature stories from the Paris bureau. Later Mary H. Fentress was a member of the Paris staff. The first full-time woman reporter in New York was Joan Younger, who, on her first assignment, was so impressed by Mert Akers' stern instructions to "stick close" to Mrs. Eleanor Roosevelt at a national political convention that she accompanied the First Lady to the speaker's platform and sat beside her in defiance of the sergeant at arms.

Once the war started, however, there was a sudden influx of women correspondents in many bureaus. Some smaller bureau managers had a majority of feminine employees and Manager Gaylord Godwin had seven girls and no men on the payroll at Omaha, Nebraska. The Washington bureau at one time was rather desperately seeking dictation-takers by advertising in the newspapers for girls who "want to work five feet away from where the world's greatest news is breaking." A high percentage of the women staff members quickly demonstrated that they could do general reporting on equal terms with men, and not a few of them remained on the job after the men had come back from the wars.

5.

After the Big Three meeting of Roosevelt, Churchill, and Stalin at Teheran in 1943, Harrison E. Salisbury was ordered to Moscow as temporary relief for Manager Henry Shapiro, who left for a vacation after a long, difficult period of coverage. It was customary for newly arrived correspondents to put in requests for interviews with Stalin, Molotov, and other Soviet dignitaries, and Salisbury followed the usual procedure. He was at a party at the United States Embassy a few nights later when he was summoned to the telephone. An official of the foreign office press department asked him to come there at once. Elated by what appeared to be a favorable response to his request for interviews, Salisbury quietly put on his fur cap and heavy coat and vanished from the embassy party into a swirling snowstorm.

At the foreign office, the press department was cold, gloomy, and tense when Salisbury arrived. He was kept waiting an hour and then led through a labyrinth of corridors to the office of Vice Commissar of Foreign Affairs Dekanozov, a brusque and sharp-tongued man who sat behind a big green-topped table. Salisbury smiled at him hopefully, and began framing in his mind the questions he would ask Molotov—or possibly it would be Stalin himself. Dekanozov, however, wasn't smiling. He began to talk in an angry hard voice about the shameful conduct of the United Press in regard to the Soviet Union. This tirade was translated by a frightened girl interpreter for some time before Salisbury could make any sense out of what the commissar was saying. He knew, however, that he was on the spot for some reason—and obviously a very tough spot.

"The Soviet Union," Dekanozov said sternly, "cannot understand why the United Press would permit rude fabrication of news regarding Soviet officials. Either the United Press will apologize for this slander or the United Press will not have any possibility of operating in the Soviet Union. The United Press has insulted the head of the Soviet government."

Salisbury still had no idea what had happened until he got a chance to ask a few questions. The details as later filled in by the London bureau were as follows. About the second week in February a United Press correspondent was talking to a strongly anti-Communist diplomat in London. The diplomat told him a story about a speech made by Russian Marshal Semyon K. Timoshenko at a birthday party that Stalin gave for Churchill during the Teheran Conference. The reporter later wrote a story, which he attributed to "a neutral diplomat," and handed it to the desk editor with a remark that it would never go through the censorship. But, surprisingly, it did.

Timoshenko [the story said] *apparently drank innumerable vodka toasts and became indiscreet in his remarks. Finally Stalin got up, walked to where Timoshenko was speaking, picked up a bottle from the table and "bopped" the Marshal on the head. Timoshenko, somewhat dazed, sat down. Stalin sauntered back to his seat and, turning to Churchill, remarked: "It always happens at every party. I hope you don't have to do that with General Montgomery."*

The next thing that anybody knew about it, Salisbury was being threatened with expulsion from Moscow. The correspondent explained that he had never heard of the story and that obviously the Moscow staff had had nothing to do with it. He offered an on-the-spot apology, however, and assured Dekanozov that the company would never intentionally offend the head of the government.

"One would suppose that to be the case," Dekanozov snapped, "but facts are facts. We will expect a public apology."

Salisbury sent a report on his conversation to New York, and Baillie cabled an apology to Dekanozov. He also cabled the text of a correction that the United Press planned to carry on its news wires. Dekanozov approved the correction with a few minor changes, which were made. The matter seemed to be ended. But a week later Salisbury got another summons and found Dekanozov more angry than ever. The apology was "not satisfactory," he barked. As the conversation progressed, Salisbury became convinced that Stalin had personally taken charge of the matter. Dekanozov, for example, had in front of him a memorandum written in red pencil, as was Stalin's custom. Dekanozov obviously had caught hell from his superiors if not from Stalin himself. The Press Department staff was tense and would not talk to Salisbury, and the correspondent's invitation to a party honoring the Red Army was canceled.

A few days later Salisbury was again called to the foreign office and escorted into a reception room where Foreign Commissar Molotov gave him a long, schoolmaster's lecture on the evils of slandering government officials. Molotov was reasonably friendly, but said that the United Press should carry a second apology. Salisbury vainly tried to point out that this would merely spread the erroneous story more widely. By this time, however, the Moscow bureaucracy was running under a full head of steam and Molotov insisted on the second apology which he—or perhaps Stalin—believed was necessary to emphasize the erroneous nature of the original story. It was carried on March 6.

Stalin, however, apparently had been irritated to an extreme degree. The story stuck in his mind. On two later occasions, once when he was talking about free exchange of news with Harold Stassen in 1947, the Russian Premier brought up the United Press story about Timoshenko as an example of how he had "had a lot of trouble" with American newsmen in the past.

CHAPTER TWENTY-EIGHT

The tempo of the war changed swiftly in 1944. There had been a long period of discouraging defeats followed by a period in which the Allied nations' armed forces stood firm and matched their strength against the Axis. American soldiers had gained battle experience, and so had American war correspondents.

The big problem in the Pacific war was co-ordination and communications, especially the lack of communications. In the Southwest Pacific all copy had to be filed through MacArthur's main headquarters in Brisbane or his advanced headquarters in Port Moresby or, later, in Hollandia, Dutch New Guinea. This usually meant that the front-line reporter had to spend most of his time planning how to get his stories back a thousand miles or so to headquarters ahead of his competitors.

When William B. Dickinson took charge of coverage in the Southwest Pacific he solved this problem rather neatly on his first mission. MacArthur, struggling to get started back to the Philippines, had planned a landing in the Admiralty Islands at the north entrance to the Bismarck Sea. Dickinson accompanied the invasion force—some 800 men of the 1st Cavalry Division made the initial landing—when they went ashore on Los Negros Island on the morning of February 29, 1944. Being new to the Pacific war, however, he went ashore with the first wave of troops, while the more experienced correspondents remained on the various ships until the beachhead had been secured. Fortunately for Dickinson, the landing was a surprise to the enemy and very little resistance was encountered and, even more fortunate, General MacArthur made an unexpected trip to the island to witness the operation. Dickinson was the only correspondent ashore during MacArthur's tour and he took quick advantage of an opportunity to beat the communications log jam by "hitching" a ride with the general back to Port Moresby. They traveled on the cruiser *Phoenix* until they could shift to MacArthur's airplane, the *Bataan,* for the final leg of the trip to headquarters. Dickinson had his story in New York just forty-eight hours ahead of any other dispatches on the invasion of the Admiralty Islands.

Dickinson and Ralph Teatsorth later covered the American landing at Hollandia, where Teatsorth found a huge brief case stuffed with Japanese money in an abandoned paymaster's office. For a week he and Dickinson gave away large-denomination bills as souvenirs, sent them home in letters, used them to light their cigarettes, and finally tossed the rest into an incinerator. It seemed a lot of fun at the time, but about a year later they both arrived in Tokyo and discovered that the Japanese currency was still in use at a set figure of fifteen yen to the dollar—enough, they figured, to have made them small-time millionaires if they had saved their souvenirs.

American and British and Chinese troops hacked away at the edges of Japan's Southwest Asia Co-Prosperity Sphere throughout the spring and summer of 1944. General Stilwell's Chinese army in northern Burma captured Malakawng and closed in on Myitkyina in June in a drive co-ordinated with Merrill's Marauders.

The war was picking up speed on all fronts, but there was trouble in Chungking. Generalissimo Chiang Kai-shek had begun to frown on Stilwell's methods, and during the summer they engaged in a serious dispute. This was generally known to correspondents in Chungking, but Stilwell remained in command and the censorship prevented disclosure of the extent of cleavage in the top command in China. Walter Rundle had gone on a bomber mission from one of the Chinese air bases and had come down with malaria upon his return to Chungking. He was in bed one afternoon when a Chinese friend came in with the news that Chiang had demanded the dismissal of Stilwell and that Washington had reluctantly agreed.

Rundle checked with other sources and confirmed that Stilwell would be withdrawn. He wrote a story, which the censor promptly killed. Rundle went back to his office, running a high fever due to malaria aggravated by censorship. A few hours later he wrote a service message to his New York office:

INFORMATIVELY BERRIGANS OLD SIDEKICK BEEN FIRED BY HOME OFFICE. SUGGEST CHECK WITH LYLE

He sent the message to the wireless office. Since it was a service message without any mention of military affairs it was not submitted to the American army officers in the censorship department but was passed by a Chinese censor. Once it arrived in New York the cable desk had no difficulty in recalling Darrell Berrigans's close association with Stilwell in Burma and knew that "Lyle" could be only Lyle C. Wilson, manager of the Washington bureau. The message was promptly relayed to Washington and the bureau broke the story the next day, many hours before the official announcement by the White House that Stilwell had been relieved of his command in the China-Burma theater at the request of Chiang Kai-shek.

2.

In the early summer of 1944 everybody knew that General Eisenhower was preparing to invade Hitler's Fortress Europa. But nobody, especially Der Fuehrer, knew just where the blow would fall. The British Isles were jammed to capacity with American troops, airplanes, and war material. The ports were full of warships. There wasn't any doubt that D-day could not be long postponed, but first there was some unfinished business to be cleaned up in Italy.

On the night of May 23 Bob Vermillion worked his way up to the front lines in the Anzio beachhead. It was a dark, moonless night, but Vermillion stooped over as he walked because the German machine gunners were edgy and repeatedly fired at random across the American lines. It had been a long, discouraging siege at Anzio, with the American troops unable to do more than hold the ground they had won four months earlier after their unsuccessful attempt to make an end run by sea around the Hitler line below Rome. Vermillion reached a farmhouse which was advance company headquarters, but it was being spattered by enemy bullets at regular intervals. He pushed on forward to the shallow trenches in which soldiers crouched, their faces grim and pale. He stopped to talk to Private Francis Entwistle of Herkimer, N.Y., who had landed in the first wave on Anzio beachhead, had been wounded, and had recovered to fight again. "I can't say I'm anxious to start out over that 'bloody mile' this morning but we've got to get it over with," Entwistle said, motioning toward a flatland that separated him from the Germans. Almost all of the men Vermillion talked with that night were veterans, picked troops ready to lead an assault. Behind them, tanks churned through the muddy fields. A little later the enemy fire around company headquarters was intensified and Vermillion dropped back to an observation post on a slight rise behind the front lines.

At dawn he could see the advance trenches, the fields of waist-high weeds and blood-red poppies that stretched out to the German position. At dawn, too, he could see the American tanks moving forward, the infantry officers crawling out of the trenches and motioning to their men to follow. At dawn the attack began and the shock troops crawled in long rows across the "bloody mile" partly hidden from the enemy by a white smoke screen. The long-awaited breakout from the beachhead was launched in co-ordination with a drive by the Fifth and Eighth armies northward toward Anzio and Rome. By nightfall the Germans were in full retreat.

3.

On the night of June 5 Walter Cronkite was ready for bed in his London apartment when an Air Force public relations officer knocked on the door. "There's a pretty good story breaking," he said. "I think you better come with us." When they had climbed into a staff automobile, the officer explained: "The invasion is about to start. We're sending a B-17 bomber group over the coast at a low altitude as a spearhead and can take only one correspondent. We drew lots and you won. Of course, if you don't want to go just say so." At dawn Cronkite was over the French coast with the 303rd Bomber Group—looking down through holes in the clouds at the assault on Fortress Europa.

From an altitude of 5000 feet Collie Small also watched the invasion of Normandy. He had a grandstand seat in a Marauder plane that twisted and squirmed through German flak. On the beaches he could see the wink of German artillery. On the sea he observed an endless stream of Allied ships en route from England to France. As his Marauder unloaded fragmentation bombs on German gun emplacements and turned back toward England, three German ME-109s swept out of the clouds but almost immediately were challenged by American Thunderbolt fighters. The Messerschmidts turned swiftly and ducked back into the clouds.

Henry Gorrell was on an LCT carrying vehicles to the Normandy coast. An infantry colonel repeated a blow-by-blow description that came over the radio of the fighting on the beaches. As the LCT approached the coast there was an increasing noise of gunfire. All around were swarms of warships and invasion craft. Overhead, airplanes laid down a white smoke screen. German artillery shells began hitting the water around the LCT. Then the ship crept up to the "Utah" beach and began unloading.

One of General Eisenhower's biggest problems was to keep the supply lines open across the Channel from England to Normandy. United Press Correspondent Robert C. Miller watched that struggle from the flying bridge of an American supply ship during the night of June 10, when enemy airplanes, submarines, and torpedo boats tried to isolate the invasion bridgehead.

Time after time dazzling white lights burst over the Allied ships plying the Channel, outlining the corvettes, destroyers, and torpedo boats that scurried back and forth in search of enemy craft. They found some, missed others. A huge puffball of smoke and flame shot upward behind Miller's ship as a U-boat torpedo found its mark in the boiler room of a cargo ship. Star shells drifted into the sky. Guns were firing sporadically as the haphazard battle went on.

Miller was standing alongside the engine-room ventilators, seeking warmth from the night chill, when an enemy E-boat crept through the defense fleet and fired a torpedo. It exploded in the ship's entrails, causing her to leap like a bucking bronco pursued by a blinding flash of flame. Sea water covered the decks where Miller struggled to regain his feet in the midst of a mass of wreckage. There were dead and injured men on the decks, but the correspondent was merely jarred—not even his glasses were broken. The ship, however, was rapidly sinking in a black, slimy pool of fuel oil.

"There's a life raft here somewhere," a voice shouted. "Cut her loose." A man crawled past Miller on hands and knees, dragging an almost severed left leg. Somebody hacked at the bindings of the life raft and it floated on the oil-covered water sloshing up the slanting deck. Twisted ropes, debris, the bindings of the raft, and thick oil swept over the reporter. He dragged himself free, caught at a rope, and missed. The raft floated teasingly away. Miller kicked and clawed his way into the water, grabbed the rope again and pulled himself up out of a thick, syrup-like mixture of oil and water that clogged his nose and mouth and covered him from head to toe. Others were crawling on the raft. They lay there until dawn, when rescue boats picked them up.

Jim McGlincy had a struggle fighting his way off the news desk in London but he finally got to France and, once there, he had to get to Paris the hard way. He joined up with a band of French guerrilla fighters and lit out across country. By the time they reached Orsay, on the outskirts of Paris, on August 24 they had become known as "McGlincy's Marauders" and were so overloaded with flowers that the jeep made slow progress. McGlincy also had been wounded—a large bouquet tossed into their vehicle struck him in the right eye.

That night, with the first French and American vehicles, they drove into Paris, where resistance squads were fighting the Germans. French troops in armored cars led the advance. The column in which McGlincy was traveling reached the Seine at Sèvres and a few tanks and armored cars established a bridgehead across the Pont de Sèvres. It was then about ten o'clock in the evening, and several correspondents shifted to a sedan for a dash across the bridge. They made it without coming under fire, but on the other side of the river the French tanks controlled an area of only a few blocks. The next morning there was sporadic shooting that developed into violent street fighting during the day. But in the middle of the fighting there were thousands of persons who watched, scurried about the streets, and insisted on kissing the Allied soldiers. The firing died down later and the correspondents, accompanied by two automobiles filled with resistance fighters, drove on toward the center of the city. At the Passy police station McGlincy stopped to write a story of the entry into Paris. The police gave him a car and an armed escort to the offices of Radio Paris, which was in the hands of resistance fighters by then, although a small tank battle was in progress nearby.

McGlincy was the first correspondent to reach the radio station and the first to broadcast over it a dispatch—picked up by the United Press listening posts—describing the liberation of the French capital. Three British correspondents and two other Americans, including Larry Leseur, a former Unipresser who had joined the Columbia Broadcasting System, also made broadcasts from the station. All six were suspended for sixty days by Supreme Headquarters Allied Expeditionary Forces because they had not submitted their copy for censorship, but the suspension was later reduced to thirty days.

The German armies had been badly battered across France, but in September they rallied in front of the Siegfried Line and made it obvious that Eisenhower would have a difficult time ending the war in 1944. There was, however, still a chance, and some experts believed it lay in an airborne drop into Holland, co-ordinated with a drive by British armor from Belgium across the Dutch frontier. This was designed to open the port of Antwerp to Allied supply ships.

During the Battle of France there had been a dozen different plans for glider and parachute troops to drop ahead of the Allied armies, but the advance had been so swift that these had all been canceled. They had, however, given Walter Cronkite a lot of time to think about how a correspondent accompanying airborne troops would be able to communicate with his home office. Cronkite talked the problem over with communications officers of the 101st Airborne Division. The division had its own radio channel to send messages to its base at Reading, England, and Cronkite was able to make advance arrangements for limited use of those facilities. In the first six hours after landing, for example, it was agreed that he could send a total of 100 words to the Reading base. These messages would be turned over to a public-relations officer, with whom Cronkite made arrangements for having them relayed to the United Press bureau in London.

On the morning of September 17 Cronkite crawled into a glider occupied by fourteen soldiers carrying their equipment. The glider was jerked into the air by a tow plane, and the greatest aerial operation ever attempted was under way. Almost 500 gliders and more than 1000 troop carriers were in the aerial armada, carrying one British and two American divisions. Cronkite, who had never been in a glider before, was startled by the noise of canvas fluttering in the wind so violently that it seemed the light craft would be torn apart. He was even more startled when the plane was cut loose over Holland and went into a steep nose dive. Actually his glider pilot was following the best and safest tactics over a battle zone—dive almost straight down to avoid antiaircraft fire, level out abruptly close to the ground, and then crash-land the glider in order to stop quickly and give the men a chance to get out and scatter instead of becoming sitting ducks for enemy machine gunners. This process was completed almost perfectly up to and including the crash-landing. The soldiers tumbled out and helmets flew in all directions.

Cronkite crawled out of the wreckage into a potato field near the town of Zon, northeast of Eindhoven and south of Arnhem. He grabbed the first helmet he saw, put it on, and started crawling across the field. Other gliders were landing nearby without any immediate opposition. Cronkite hadn't crawled far and had no idea where he was going before he noticed that a dozen other men were crawling along behind him. He dropped down a bank into a big ditch, and the others clustered around.

"Are you sure we're going in the right direction, Major?" one of the men asked Cronkite. The reporter sat very quietly for a few seconds and let the question sink in. Then he pulled off his helmet and looked at the insignia on it. He had picked up the major's helmet instead of his own following the crash. By the time that mix-up was straightened out it was apparent that there were no Germans in the immediate vicinity. Cronkite got into Eindhoven, established contact with the communications officers, and sent out his first brief story of the landings. It was badly delayed but eventually arrived in London, as did one other story he sent later.

The over-all operation had started out smoothly enough. British tanks drove across the Dutch border and reached Eindhoven, and a push on to Nijmegen and Arnhem was started. Cronkite ran into Bill Downs, a former Unipresser now working for Columbia Broadcasting System, and they jeeped northward on a crowded road to spend the night at Nijmegen. There were, however, rumors that the Germans were counterattacking with a large armored force. About dusk the two correspondents decided to drive to division headquarters to find out what was happening, but before they got there a score of enemy bombers attacked an Allied convoy jammed into a bottleneck road ahead of them. They turned into a side street, drove several blocks, and came to a dead end just as the bombers unloaded high explosives all over the place.

There was a six-foot-high fence at the end of the street, but the two reporters cleared it in a single bound and ran into a park, where they became separated. When the attack ended, Cronkite yelled for Downs and searched through the woods for him with no results. He feared that Downs had left the park and been killed in the burning wreckage of buildings along the adjacent streets. Finally he hitched a ride to Brussels on an army truck and got off at the Métropole Hotel. His equipment was lost and he was black with soot, but he decided that his first stop would be for a drink.

Dead tired, he dragged himself to the bar and was immediately clasped in a bear hug.

"Hell, Walter, I thought they had got you," Downs exclaimed. "I couldn't find you anywhere."

Hugh Baillie was in London again in September—in time for a loud welcome by the first of Germany's new V-2 rocket bombs which dropped into the city on the afternoon of September 8. The first explosion was heavily felt at the hotel where Baillie was talking with several American war correspondents, but nobody knew just what had happened. Some time later, Frank Fisher, managing editor of the British United Press, called Baillie and told him that the bomb had fallen in Chiswick. Fisher and Baillie drove there to investigate and found Bill Higginbotham crawling around the bomb crater, where he salvaged part of the rocket nose for an intelligence officer. By that time a second bomb had struck in another section of London and Sam Hales was at the scene. Hales, Higginbotham, and Baillie turned in stories on the new terror weapon, but they were promptly killed by the censor. Incidentally, even after Baillie had returned to New York his pledge as a war correspondent not to break the censorship rules prevented him from writing or speaking about the V-2 terror until the embargo was lifted later. Then one day when he was sitting at his desk the story he had written weeks before in London began moving on the wires. It made Baillie feel like a baseball pitcher who had delivered a ball from the mound and then had time to run around behind home plate and catch it.

While he was in London, General Carl A. Spaatz invited Baillie to SHAEF headquarters in France and he later traveled about 400 miles by plane and jeep along the fighting front, conferring with all United Press correspondents in the field except one—Ed Beattie. Baillie arrived at General Patton's headquarters on September 12, the day that Beattie had set out for Châtillon-sur-Seine to watch the surrender of 20,000 Germans who had been cornered and beaten up by a mixed force of Americans and French on the left flank of the Third Army. He was in a jeep with Wright Bryan of the Atlanta *Journal;* John Mecklin, a former Unipresser who had joined the Chicago *Sun,* and driver Jimmy Schwab. They suddenly came on a German road block and two wrecked American jeeps.

Schwab tried to turn the jeep around quickly, but it was towing a trailer loaded with bedding and food, and before he could reverse his course they were under enemy fire. One bullet struck the jeep and everybody dived out to take shelter. Beattie found himself crouching under the vehicle. Wright Bryan was stretched out alongside, and Mecklin was in a roadside ditch. Schwab was perched on the tow bar between the jeep and the trailer. There was another volley of shots, and Bryan was wounded in the leg. The Germans were creeping through the adjacent fields to surround them. Another jeep roared down the road and was caught in the German fire, which killed three of its six occupants. All of the survivors of the two jeeps were taken prisoner. It was the end of the war for Ed Beattie.

4.

There was much more to Baillie's visit to Europe than the improvement of co-ordination between the New York bureau and the men in the field. His main objective was to further the tradition of United Press leadership in the fight for free exchange of news among all countries.

With this goal in mind, Baillie sought out the leaders of European governments for discussion of postwar development of freedom of the press on the basis of a four-point program designed to prevent future news monopoly:

1. News sources, particularly official sources, competitively open to all.
2. Transmission facilities competitively available to all.

3. A minimum of official regulations of the flow of news itself.
4. All newspapers throughout the world to have access to all possible sources of news.

After several weeks of negotiation, Baillie had received public assurances from the Belgian, Czechoslovak, Dutch, Norwegian, Australian, South African, Canadian, New Zealand, and Swedish governments that they would go along with these principles after the war. Antoine Delfosse, the Belgian Minister of Justice and Information, assured Baillie that the utmost liberty for all legitimate news agencies would prevail in Belgium. Eduard Beneš, president of Czechoslovakia, said that "definitely and positively" his nation would be a leader among countries insisting on a free press. Prime Minister P. S. Gerbrandy of Holland informed Baillie that his government would promote all measures to strengthen free exchange of news, and Trygve Lie, Norwegian Foreign Minister, said that there would not be a vestige of restriction in Norway.

An even more important development was the action by the provisional government of General De Gaulle in France, which modified a press decree that it had enacted while at Algiers. This decree had provided that for a limited time after the liberation of France a new national news agency, Agence Française de la Presse, would operate without competition from foreign agencies. André Laguerre, director of foreign press services in the Ministry of Information, announced, however, that the decree had been lifted and that the door was being opened to all agencies to operate in France.

Baillie made clear in a broadcast to European peoples that his purpose in pressing for free exchange of news was to provide "the surest guarantee of liberty. As the nations of the world are liberated, the press of these nations must also be liberated, so that there will be the freest interchange of news among all countries. The best and most practical basis upon which to establish such a situation is to make sure that there is complete freedom to gather news everywhere and freedom to compete in distributing that news to all who want it. That is the policy upon which the United Press of America was founded, and it is the policy to which it has adhered ever since."

CHAPTER TWENTY-NINE

General MacArthur's "island-hopping" drive back toward the Philippine Islands was making swift progress in the summer of 1944. MacArthur had promised the Filipino people that he would return, and he now appeared almost ready to make good his promise. One day when Bill Dickinson was absent from the general's advance headquarters at Hollandia, all correspondents were summoned to a preliminary meeting on plans for covering the first landing in the Philippines. A public-relations officer informed them that only one news-agency correspondent and one radio correspondent would be permitted to accompany MacArthur on the invasion. The officer pulled an Australian florin from his pocket and flipped it in the air.

"Tails!" called Ralph Teatsorth, who was attending the meeting in Dickinson's absence. Tails turned up and Dickinson was later assigned to accompany MacArthur and write a "pool" story which would be made available to all press services. He went aboard the cruiser *Nashville* with the general and they settled down in the captain's cabin with a couple of ice-cream sodas. MacArthur began explaining what he was going to do—how the landing would be accomplished, how the offensive against Manila would be conducted, and how, once the Philippines were in hand, he would launch the final assault against Japan. Dickinson listened in amazement. It was a surprise plan for landing on Leyte Island, quite contrary to the belief of most experts—including the Japanese—that MacArthur would first attack Mindanao.

On the morning of October 20 Dickinson watched from the cruiser as a great armada of ships came to a halt off Leyte and began landing with comparatively little immediate opposition. About four hours after the first wave hit the beaches, he boarded an LCVP with the general and then splashed through the shallow surf to the beach. MacArthur went immediately to a radio station that had been hastily set up in a coconut grove and broadcast to the Filipino people the message that he had brought through 2500 miles of island fighting: "I have returned."

The general then picked out the best house in the town of Tacloban and established his headquarters. Dickinson picked out the second-best house in Tacloban and put up a sign:

UNITED PRESS
LEYTE BUREAU

2.

George E. Jones, who had covered so many island invasions that he was becoming known—much to his own embarrassment—as "First Wave" Jones, had a grandstand seat aboard Vice-Admiral Marc A. Mitscher's flagship *Lexington* for the greatest naval battle ever fought by an American and perhaps by any fleet in history.

Jones went aboard the *Lexington* at Ulithi anchorage early in September and set out on a series of raids by carrier-based airplanes on the Philippines and Formosa leading up to the Leyte invasion. On October 23, when Mac-Arthur's forces had landed and were pressing inland past San Ricardo, Jones sat on the flag bridge of the *Lexington* with Mitscher and Commodore Arleigh Burke, the chief of staff, listening to reports that came in by wireless from carriers, submarines, and other warships in Admiral William F. Halsey's Third Fleet. Halsey's strategy was directed toward luring the Japanese home fleet out to do battle in defense of the Philippines and, in general, he succeeded. The flag plot on the *Lexington* showed that the Japanese were moving. Two enemy forces were approaching the Philippines from the west and another from the north. American carrier planes went out to strike at the ships in the north, while planes and submarines joined in the attack on the western fleets. For Jones it was something like watching a gigantic chess game on television as the operations were plotted, but in addition he was able to interview returning aviators who reported what appeared to be a powerful enemy battle fleet north of the islands. After being informed that our warships, submarines, and aerial bombs on October 24 had badly damaged and turned back the Japanese war fleets from the west, Halsey's task force set out at full speed in an effort to come to grips with the enemy force to the north. That was what the Japanese had hoped he would do in belief that it would leave the Leyte beachhead unprotected.

By noon on October 25, Halsey's airplanes had sunk four carriers, two cruisers, and a destroyer in the northern Japanese battle fleet. But then came disaster. Under cover of darkness, one western enemy force—badly battered by submarines and air attack and supposedly in retreat—had reversed its course and slipped through a series of narrow passages in the San Bernardino Strait to the east coast of the Philippines just north of Leyte. At dawn it fell upon the six American small carriers, three destroyers, and four small destroyer escorts supporting the Leyte beachhead. The little ships appeared helpless against the enemy's big guns. Halsey turned back from the north, but he was too far away. Admiral Kinkaid's ships just south of the Leyte beachhead had exhausted their armor-piercing ammunition.

The baby carriers launched their planes to attack the Japanese warships and maneuvered as best they could to escape the enemy rain of shells, but they were hard hit and the *Gambier Bay* was riddled by gunfire and explosions. In the end, only the daredevil tactics of the American destroyers and destroyer escorts, which laid down smoke screens to protect the carriers and then dashed into the muzzles of the Japanese heavy guns to fire their torpedoes, prevented total disaster. About 9 A.M. carrier planes from Kinkaid's fleet arrived to join in the battle, and half an hour later, when the Americans still felt that they might be wiped out at any moment, the Japanese commander unaccountably broke off the action and his ships retired through San Bernardino Strait. The Americans could hardly believe their eyes.

That night George Jones collected his notes on forty-eight hours of non-stop battle, discussed the entire action with Mitscher and Burke, and sat down at his typewriter:

BY GEORGE E. JONES
ABOARD ADMIRAL MITSCHER'S FLAGSHIP, October 25 (UP) *Today the Japanese fleet submitted itself to the destinies of war—and lost.*

Four enemy carriers have been sunk. Eight battleships have been damaged. . . .

Jones wrote for four hours, pulling together the threads of the greatest naval story of the war. The American aircraft carrier *Princeton* had gone down under a relentless attack by land-based Japanese planes, and at least six other ships were lost. The *Lexington* had weathered a heavy air attack, and Jones related how he had watched Mitscher maneuver the thirty vessels in his Task Force 38 through a rain of bombs. Reports from air-combat intelligence officers went into his story, as did the details of the Japanese attack off Leyte beachhead. The final returns, of course, were not in, nor would there be a full report on Japanese losses for months, but the United States was claiming to have knocked out twenty-five Japanese warships, including two battleships, six heavy cruisers, and three light cruisers.

Writing the story was only the beginning of Jones's job. He had to get it transmitted to New York, and he hoped to do it ahead of the only other correspondent—an Associated Press man—aboard the *Lexington*. No press copy could be sent by wireless from the *Lexington,* but arrangements had been made for carrying the correspondents' stories by courier plane to Guam, where they could be wirelessed to New York. Jones turned in one copy of his story to go in the courier plane, but he kept a couple of other copies in his pocket and on Friday, October 27, he got a break. Harold Stassen, who was Halsey's flag secretary, flew to the *Lexington* to talk to

Mitscher. Jones learned that Stassen was going on by air to Guam and asked him to deliver a copy of his story to the wireless office there. Stassen agreed and carried out his mission. The story began arriving in New York on Saturday in time for a headline splash in the afternoon newspapers. It was complete for Sunday morning newspapers. It was also exclusive.

It was early in February of 1945 before the Japanese were pushed back to the suburbs of Manila. At that point, there was grave concern for the Americans who had been interned by the Japanese in the capital for more than three years. Enemy troops were fighting fanatically and appeared ready to pull down all of Manila in ruins. There was obviously a great danger that the American prisoners would go down in the ruins too.

There were two ways that MacArthur's forces could approach the Santo Tomas prison camp, where some 3700 Allied internees were held in Manila. One was the direct assault from the north being conducted by the 37th Division. The second was by sending the 1st Cavalry Division on an "end run" around the Japanese flank in an effort to break into the city and reach Santo Tomas before the enemy was driven back through that section of the capital. MacArthur had ordered the 1st Cavalry to make the "end run."

Frank Hewlett had escaped from Manila just three years earlier and had been impatiently fighting his way back to his imprisoned wife ever since. When he learned of MacArthur's orders he sought out Bill Dickinson. "I'm going with the cavalry," he announced. Dickinson tried to dissuade him. "It's too big a chance to take," he argued, but he knew his words were hopeless. Dickinson yielded with misgivings and Hewlett joined the 1st Cavalry.

On the afternoon of Saturday, February 3, Unipresser H. D. (Doc) Quigg was trying to avoid a flurry of mortar fire behind the 37th Division front by lying in a roadside ditch with his face buried in the dirt. When he finally looked up he was staring at a four-star jeep that had halted on the road. MacArthur was sitting in the front seat, majestically ignoring the mortar fragments. Quigg got up and pulled out his notebook.

"When do you think we can get into Manila?" he asked the general.

MacArthur puffed on his corncob pipe. "We'll make it tomorrow," he finally said, thinking about his order to the 1st Cavalry.

Quigg scribbled a story and sent it back to headquarters, where Dickinson talked it through the censorship despite a ban on direct quotes from MacArthur. It hit the New York cable desk late Saturday morning and was a headline in afternoon and Sunday morning editions.

It was dark when the 1st Cavalry rescue column—sixteen tanks followed by jeeps and trucks—dashed into the "back door" of Manila, taking the enemy by surprise. They headed directly for Santo Tomas internment camp, a former university, and surrounded it. Japanese guards opened fire as a tank rumbled through the prison fence. Hewlett's jeep was immediately behind the tank and a soldier fired at him almost point-blank but missed. Sharp fighting was breaking out around the camp, and Japanese soldiers were shooting from one of the buildings as Hewlett and several others crept along a wall and dashed into the old auditorium.

Prisoners who had been huddled inside rushed to greet the Americans. "The cavalry is here!" somebody shouted. The first to arrive were lifted to the shoulders of the emaciated internees, who wept and cheered and hugged their liberators. Unipresser Robert Crabb and his wife and two small children—one born in Santo Tomas—were there. So was Mrs. Franz Weissblatt, wife of the United Press correspondent captured on Bataan. But Hewlett's wife was nowhere to be seen. When he could free himself from the crowd he asked a young girl he had previously known in Manila about her. She motioned him outside.

There was still sporadic firing on the grounds but they waited for a lull and then ducked across to the hospital building. Inside there was a dim light and Hewlett could see the top of the stairway. A thin, unfamiliar figure—a girl weighing no more than eighty pounds—was coming hesitantly down the stairs. Hewlett didn't recognize her at first. Then he looked again and was up the stairway in a few swift strides. His arms were around her and the long journey back was ended. The Hewletts were together again.

The next day the 37th Infantry Division drove into Manila from the north. The main Japanese forces had retired across the Pasig River to the southern section of the city, but strong rear-guard elements kept up a steady fire against the Americans while demolition squads wantonly wrecked and dynamited buildings in the business district. It was nightfall by the time Doc Quigg and a detachment of the 37th found themselves under the big stone walls of Bilibid Prison. The guards had fled but mortar fire was still heavy and the detachment took refuge in the prison archives building for the night. Quigg did a little exploring, feeling his way along a pitch-dark corridor. Somewhere ahead was the hum of voices and they sounded like American voices. In the blackness he slid along a wall toward a courtyard. He saw a shadowy form. He stopped and stuck out his hand.

Even as Stanley did in darkest Africa those many years ago [he wrote later], *I said:*
"I'm Quigg, United Press."
The Dr. Livingstone of Bilibid Prison grasped my hand fervently.
"I'm Weissblatt, United Press," replied the correspondent who had been wounded and captured by the Japanese on Bataan three years earlier.

With the battle for Manila still in progress, Dickinson appointed Bill Wilson manager of the Manila bureau and opened an office in a house across the street from Santo Tomas. The new office was frequently under severe enemy shell fire. There was no equipment for operation of a bureau, but

Wilson figured something would turn up. It did. Two men who had been radio operators for the United Press before the war wandered in with wireless sets that they had kept hidden since the fall of Manila. Rodolfo Nazareno, a former bureau employee, appeared and said he knew a couple of other capable newspapermen who wanted jobs. Wilson traded the staff's whisky supply for a gasoline generator and managed, by one means or another, to get gasoline from an army dump. Within a week the bureau was in action, picking up United Press newscasts from several different relay bureaus and translating them for Manila newspapers.

Two weeks later the United Press was serving eight local newspapers. Wilson, who insisted on cash payment in advance for the service, soon had a large box full of pesos under his bed. There weren't any banks operating, due to gunfire along the river, but the United Press was back in business in the Philippines.

3.

President Roosevelt died before victory was achieved in Europe, but everybody knew in April of 1945 that it could not be long delayed. The Russian armies were hammering at the gates of Berlin on April 22 and sweeping on westward toward the Elbe River. General Patton's armor rolled southward toward Regensburg and Salzburg. The Canadian First Army struck across the Meuse River. American Seventh Army troops crossed the Danube.

On April 25 Unipresser Ann Stringer climbed into a Piper Cub plane back of the American lines in Germany and, with two army officers, took off for the front. Miss Stringer was the first woman assigned to the front in Germany and had covered the American drive across and beyond the Rhine. Now the rumor had come that the Russians were at the Elbe and she intended to see for herself.

The little plane flew across the Elbe and landed in a clover field near the town of Torgau. The correspondent and the two officers climbed over two road blocks and started down the main street of Torgau. Toward them ran a strange figure in blue shorts and gray cap. As he came close they could see a red hammer and sickle on the cap. The rumor had been true; the Russians were at the Elbe!

"Bravo, Americanski!" the runner yelled. He pointed back to the river. It was practically full of Russians who had stripped down to their shorts and were ready to swim across to greet the American Army. Miss Stringer and her companions did their best to represent the American Army.

The Russian swimmers returned to the Torgau side of the river and, with a group of fully uniformed comrades, lined up in rigid military formation. One by one they stepped forward, saluted, shook hands, and stepped back into line. When this ceremony was completed they escorted Miss Stringer to their commander, a quiet, stocky man with jet-black hair. He said he had never before seen an American woman and invited the correspondent to the place of honor at luncheon. The toasts were frequent and drunk in everything from champagne to vodka.

Miss Stringer, however, was in a hurry to get back across the river and find some way to transmit her story to Paris, the little plane in which she had landed having gone back to its base. When she explained her problem to the Russians, they escorted her to the river, found a light German racing shell, lifted her in, and gave the boat a strong push toward the opposite bank. Unhappily, it was too strong a push. The shell overturned, pitching Miss Stringer into the river, ruining half of the ink-written notes she had taken and counteracting the warm sensation that had been created by champagne and vodka.

Wet and muddy, she crawled back in the shell and made it across on the second try. She also caught an airplane ride to Paris with the first story of the meeting of American and Russian troops in Germany.

The Italian city of Verona had always held a peculiar fascination for Unipresser James E. Roper because he thought of it as the storied home of Romeo and Juliet, the setting for Shakespeare's tale of eternal love. As he followed Allied forces through the Po Valley during the last brutal spasm of war in Italy in April of 1945, Roper decided it would be a good idea to write a feature story about Verona—something lyrical about the ravages of war and the love songs of poets. On the evening of April 26 he stumbled into Verona over the smoking bodies of German soldiers who had been killed in the destruction of a gasoline convoy—and found himself on the trail of quite a different kind of love story. Its principals were Benito Mussolini and Clara Petacci.

The whereabouts of Mussolini had been a mystery that every correspondent—and the Allied High Command—had been trying to solve for days. But when Roper separated from other correspondents and stopped in Verona he picked up a report that the Fascist leader had just fled from Milan. The next morning he set out by jeep for that city, joining forces en route with two newspaper correspondents following the same hunch. After a few miles they began passing German army stragglers, who dived into roadside ditches as the jeeps roared past. A few more miles and they passed a convoy of German army trucks carrying fully armed soldiers. They were too close to stop and turn around, so they put on speed and whirled past the trucks—seventy-one of them—without drawing anything more than surprised stares from the enemy. The war in Italy was over and the Germans knew it.

At Como they found Italian partisans in control and were told that a partisan leader, whose name was not given, knew Mussolini's whereabouts. They found the leader in a small office.

"Where is Mussolini?" they asked him.

"We have him," the leader replied. "We are moving him from place to ·

place. If you want to see him, go to Milan." To all other questions he only said grimly: "Go to Milan."

With a partisan guide the Americans drove on—far behind the German lines—to Milan. They saw many partisan armed bands, but no Germans. In Milan they were welcomed by joyous, friendly crowds of Italians and were given hotel rooms by the partisan "mayor." The next morning Roper was awakened by shouts of "Mussolini, Mussolini—in the square!" His boots still unlaced, he piled into his jeep and raced to Loreto Square. A howling crowd blocked the entrance until an Italian jumped up on the front fender and shouted: "American colonel! Official! Official!" Roper eased the jeep into the square and his escort leaped off, pointing toward the center of a milling crowd and exclaiming: "Mussolini!"

Roper couldn't see anything at first except angry, shouting men and women. For a moment he thought this might be a hoax; that it would be just his luck to be the only news-agency reporter within many miles when some impostor appeared and claimed to be Il Duce. He climbed slowly from his jeep, pushed through the crowd. Then he saw a bald head glistening in the early-morning sun. It was a broken head and it rested on the breast of a pretty girl stretched on her back on the ground, a girl whose hair was neatly curled in little ringlets but whose white blouse was dark with blood. A man stepped out of the crowd and aimed a vicious kick at the bald head.

BY JAMES E. ROPER

MILAN, April 29 (UP) *The people Benito Mussolini had ruled for two decades paid him their last tribute by hanging his remains head down from the rafters of a gasoline station in Milan's Loreto Square.*

There they spat upon their fallen leader, shot his body in the back and kicked his face into a toothless, pulpy mass. For hours after the body of the executed dictator was brought to Milan with that of his mistress and 16 other slain Fascist leaders, Mussolini lay in a pile of dirt in the center of the square. Then the mob tied wire about the ankles of Il Duce and Clara Petacci and suspended them upside down from the roof of the gasoline station.

On the day that Mussolini's body hung from a rafter in Milan, his Axis partner, Adolf Hitler, emerged briefly from his underground bomb shelter in the courtyard of the Reich Chancellery in Berlin. In the streets of Berlin, Russian guns were pounding closer and closer. The war was lost. But Hitler had decided to die in the ruins of his Chancellery.

Unipresser Jack Fleischer pieced the story together a little later when he succeeded in finding at Obersalzburg an official stenographer from Hitler's headquarters and, still later, when he located other members of the headquarters staff who had escaped at the last moment from Berlin. Fleischer's story was confirmed long afterward in almost every detail by official Russian and British reports.

Hitler informed his high command on April 22 that "I shall fall here in the Reich Chancellery." He ordered the others to try to escape to southern Germany and form a new government under leadership of Marshal Hermann Goering. He "seemed hazy" and would listen to no arguments. Later he married his mistress, Eva Braun, in the underground bunker. On May 1 they committed suicide in the bunker. Both bodies were carried to a shallow trench just outside the door of the bunker and burned with gasoline. No trace of their remains was found.

Ed Beattie was in prison camp Stalag III-A at Luckenwalde as the Hitler empire collapsed. He had been taken to Berlin soon after his capture and questioned for days. When officials were convinced that they would get nothing from Beattie, he was sent to the Luckenwalde camp. There his rotund figure slimmed down with amazing rapidity.

The last week in April, Russian troops overran Luckenwalde and moved on to the west, but instructed the Allied prisoners to remain in the camp for the time being. For the next few days they waited with undisguised impatience. It was May 3 before a Russian soldier told them that "we are about to meet the Americans thirty miles from here." Although there was strong evidence that prisoners who had tried to reach the American lines earlier had been killed or wounded, Beattie decided that afternoon to start for Wittenberg. He sat down for his final dinner in the camp but never finished it.

"There's some little guy in a jeep outside asking for you, Beattie," another prisoner informed him. "Name something like Bob Vermillion."

4.

Boyd Lewis, one of the United Press's most widely experienced correspondents, was in charge of the agency's European war staff as German resistance collapsed during the first week of May in 1945. On Sunday, May 6, Brigadier General Frank Allen, director of the SHAEF public relations division at Paris, summoned seventeen previously selected correspondents representing the world press to cover "an important out-of-town assignment." Lewis appeared for the United Press. The veteran Jim Kilgallen, once a Unipresser in Chicago, was the International News Service representative. Edward Kennedy, head of the Associated Press staff at SHAEF, was the third news-agency man. Once aboard a C-47 transport plane en route to Reims, General Allen told the correspondents that they were going to witness the signing of armistice terms.

"This group represents the press of the world," he reminded them. "The story is off the record until the heads of the governments have announced it. I therefore pledge each of you on your honor not to communicate the results of the conference or the fact of its existence until it is released on order of the Public Relations Division, SHAEF." No one objected.

Later, at Reims, Allen informed the correspondents there would be an embargo on the story until three o'clock Tuesday afternoon. This was on orders of President Truman and Prime Minister Churchill to General Eisenhower. Lewis protested the embargo. "Every bobtail radio from Ankara to Casablanca will have the story before Tuesday afternoon," he exclaimed heatedly. "We will be the most-scooped bunch of correspondents on the globe."

"That I cannot help, gentlemen," Allen replied. "The decision has been reached at a level very much higher than SHAEF. General Eisenhower's hands are tied."

Lewis realized that there was only one legitimate way to score a beat on the story and that was to file his dispatches first at the communications center on the mezzanine floor of the Scribe Hotel in Paris. The rule that had been established for the surrender story was that each agency would be permitted to file a twenty-five word flash. Then each agency could file 100 words additional and, finally, each could file 5000 words of detail. The flashes would be cleared in order of priority—that is, first come, first served —to New York with virtually no delay. But the agency that was first to file a 5000-word detailed story would be able to monopolize the transmission system long enough to knock its competitors out of the running in most newspapers.

The armistice was signed in a rambling, block-long school building at Reims at 2:41 A.M. on May 7. Lewis immediately began writing his story and had turned out several thousand words by the time the correspondents were summoned to start back to Paris. He had also figured out his strategy. He delayed leaving the big schoolhouse by writing additional material until everybody else had mounted the truck for transportation to the airfield. He was the last one in, sitting at the tailboard. At the airfield he was the first one out and easily the first on the plane, where he grabbed a seat next to the door. When the plane landed at Paris, Lewis was the first to reach his jeep, and raced into the city well ahead of other correspondents.

Running up the stairs to the Scribe communications room, he awakened the sergeant in charge. "Here you are, sarg," he said. "Your war is over. Start stamping these stories for first priority so they will be sent first when the embargo is lifted."

Lewis then turned in his flash, his 100-word add, and his long, detailed dispatches, each one marked to be sent on all five available wireless outlets to New York. This meant that the United Press would receive the same copy over five different routes and at five times normal cost, but it also meant that Lewis would, in effect, be blocking off the main dispatches of his competitors from the most satisfactory means of transmission for as long as it took to transmit his copy. Kilgallen puffed up the stairway a few minutes later and filed his story for second priority. Kennedy was third and thus became third in priority.

As a result, Kennedy was not in danger of being beaten on the surrender by more than a few minutes at most, but the fact that both Lewis and Kilgallen had filed their copy to move on all five outlets meant his detailed story would be behind the other two agencies. Kennedy went to Lieutenant Colonel Richard Merrick, the SHAEF censor, several times to complain about the embargo.

That Monday afternoon at 2 P.M. the Germans broadcast over the Flensburg radio instructions to their troops to cease fire, pointing out that they had been required by the terms of surrender to inform the troops by "every possible means" of the surrender. The broadcast was picked up in London and became available to the press, but it still was not confirmed by Allied officials.

When the British Broadcasting Company's account of the Flensburg announcement reached Paris, Boyd Lewis strongly protested to Merrick and General Allen in an effort to get the Reims stories released, but without success. Kennedy then told Merrick that he intended to send the story by whatever means he could because (1) the embargo was political censorship which the White House had disapproved, (2) the war was over and the end of censorship had been promised when the war ended, and (3) the Flensburg announcement obviously was authorized by SHAEF because Flensburg was under Allied occupation. "I give you warning now that I am going to send the story," Kennedy said, according to an article he wrote later.

Kennedy went to his room and instructed Morton Gudebrod, a member of his staff, to put in a telephone call for the Associated Press bureau in London. The call went through the Paris military switchboard—which the censorship was erroneously supposed to have under strict control—without difficulty and Kennedy dictated to his London office a brief version of the surrender. Then the phone went dead. It was midmorning in New York when Kennedy's story went out on the Associated Press wires, describing the surrender—oddly enough—as having taken place in a "little red schoolhouse" at Reims.

A short time later, correspondents at the Scribe, especially Lewis and Kilgallen, were all but buried under an avalanche of angry "call backs" or "rockets" from their home offices, most of them quoting "a little red schoolhouse." A quick check showed that Kennedy's story had not cleared through the communications room. He had obviously used some other communications route. But there were no words, no curses, no prayers that could persuade the censors to release the United Press or other stories. Lewis composed dozens of service messages to New York trying to say something informative but all were refused by the censorship. He couldn't even say that he had been at Reims.

Meantime, correspondents of agencies and of newspapers all over the world were angrily complaining to military officials, holding protest meetings at the Scribe, drawing up petitions to Eisenhower, and otherwise creating as great a rumpus as possible. General Allen suspended the operations of all Associated Press correspondents in the European theater for "a breach of confidence." This disciplinary action was lifted after six hours, but Kennedy and Gudebrod were permanently suspended. The next day an indignation meeting of fifty-three correspondents at the Scribe addressed a letter to Eisenhower protesting Kennedy's action and demanding that the blanket suspension of the Associated Press be reinstituted. Eisenhower declined their suggestion, but later he issued a statement saying that Kennedy "admits violation of his solemn commitment . . . I am informed the Associated Press appears to have taken the position of condoning and, in fact, praising this action of its representative when it actually was a self-admitted, deliberate breach of confidence. The Associated Press, therefore, takes the responsibility for clear violation of its word of honor to me as supreme commander of the Allied forces in Europe, and as a representative of the United States who had undertaken a firm commitment for his government in connection with its allies."

On May 10 the president of the Associated Press, Robert McLean, issued a statement that "the Associated Press profoundly regrets the distribution on Monday of the report of the total surrender in Europe which, investigation now clearly discloses, was distributed in advance of authorization by Supreme Allied Headquarters . . ." By that time, sentiment of many, but not all, newspapers was reflected in an editorial in the New York *Times* which said that the Associated Press membership

"must now make it clear, so that it is understood for all time, that they would prefer not to receive a story than have a 'news beat' even of such transcending importance obtained in such a manner . . . if it was a 'beat' it was one only because Mr. Kennedy's sixteen colleagues chose to stand by their commitments . . . We regret the incident as one which has done grave disservice to the newspaper profession."

Kennedy firmly insisted that his action was justified and in accordance with the policies, as he understood them, of the Associated Press. In July of 1946 the Army Chief of Public Information informed Kennedy that the revocation of his credentials would "no longer operate as a bar to your association with the War Department and the Army in your capacity as a professional writer."

5.

The war in Europe and Africa had been a costly one in many ways and United Press correspondents paid their share of the cost. Three Unipressers had died: Webb Miller in London, May 1940; Harry Leslie Percy, in Egypt, April 20, 1942; and Jack Frankish, killed by a German aerial bomb in Belgium, December 23, 1944. In addition the wounded correspondents included Leo S. Disher, in the Allied landings at Oran in 1942; Walter F. Logan, in a mine explosion near Medjez-el-Bab, Tunisia, in 1942; Richard D. McMillan, hit by a shell fragment near Cherbourg, June 25, 1944; Robert C. Miller, seriously wounded in the right arm by aerial-bomb fragments at Verdun in August 1944; Edward V. Roberts, struck in left shoulder and hip by shell fragments at Brest, September 1, 1944; James E. Roper, cut above the eyes in a dive-bombing raid near Rome, July 3, 1944, and Virgil Pinkley, struck in the neck by machine-gun bullets from a German plane in Libya, in December of 1941.

In the Pacific War, Brydon Taves was killed in the crash of a bombing plane in New Guinea on December 27, 1943, and John Julian Andrew was lost on a B-29 mission from India over the Bay of Bengal on November 5, 1944. Casualties included Franz Weissblatt, whose leg was fractured by Japanese mortar fire on January 7, 1942, just prior to his capture; Harold Guard, struck in the leg by bomb splinters in Malaya, January 30, 1942; Joe James Custer, who lost the sight of his left eye in the naval battle off Savo Island, August 8, 1942; Walter L. Briggs, struck in the hip by an explosive bullet during the Arakan campaign in Burma, February 2, 1943; and Evans O. Valens, who was struck in the face by flying coral when explosives blew up a Japanese cave on Okinawa.

6.

At dawn on July 15, 1945, there was an explosion on the New Mexican desert that changed everything, particularly the course of the war that was still in progress in the Pacific. Shortly after the explosion a public relations officer at the Pentagon in Washington telephoned the United Press bureau and talked to Milton Magruder. "Say, there's been an ammunition depot explosion out in New Mexico," he said. "There may be some reports of people hearing it out that way. Well, nobody was hurt but I thought I'd tell you about it. The Army public relations office in Denver is going to put out a statement about it."

Magruder said thanks and sent a message to the Denver bureau to check with army officials there—and that was about as close as anybody got to the story of the century until three weeks later when the first atomic bomb was dropped on Hiroshima, Japan. After that it was just a matter of days until the Japanese surrendered. The United Press radio listening post, operated by Reginald Tibbetts near San Francisco, had frequently given the agency the first break on big stories throughout the Pacific war. In 1942, for example, it had been twenty minutes ahead with a flash from Radio Tokyo that "Tokyo is being bombed . . . Tokyo is being bombed"—the first news of the famed Doolittle raid by carrier-based bombers. The station had also plucked

WA40

BULLETIN

WASHINGTON, AUG. 6.--(UP)--PRESIDENT TRUMAN TODAY ANNOUNCED THAT AN
"ATOMIC BOMB" HAS BEEN USED AGAINST JAPAN FOR THE FIRST TIME WITH
POWER EQUAL TO 20,000 TONS OF TNT.

MORECM1158A

WA41

ADD BOMB, WASHINGTON XXX TNT.

IN A STATEMENT ISSUED AT THE WHITE HOUSE MR. TRUMAN REVEALED THAT
16 HOURS AGO---SOMETIME SUNDAY---AN AMERICAN AIRPLANE DROPPED ONE OF
THE NEW BOMBS ON HIROSHIMA, AN IMPORTANT JAPANESE ARMY BASE.

"THAT BOMB HAD MORE POWER THAN 20,000 TONS OF TNT," THE PRESIDENT'S
STATEMENT SAID. "IT HAD MORE THAN 2,000 TIMES THE BLAST POWER OF THE
BRITISH 'GRAND SLAM' WHICH IS THE LARGEST BOMB EVER USED IN THE HISTORY
OF WARFARE."

THE PRESIDENT SAID THE NEW BOMB OPENED "A NEW AND REVOLUTIONARY
INCREASE IN DESTRUCTION" TO SUPPLEMENT THE GROWING POWER OF THE UNITED
STATES AGAINST JAPAN. THE NEW BOMB, HE ADDED, IS NOW IN PRODUCTION AND
"EVEN MORE POWERFUL FORMS" ARE UNDER DEVELOPMENT.

"IT IS AN ATOMIC BOMB," THE PRESIDENT SAID. "IT IS A HARNESSING OF
THE BASIC POWER OF THE UNIVERSE. THE FORCE FROM WHICH THE SUN DRAWS
ITS POWER HAS BEEN LOOSED AGAINST THOSE WHO BROUGHT WAR TO THE FAR
EAST."

MORECM1201P

*The two most significant dispatches carried on the wires of the United
Press in its first half century may have been those reproduced on these two
pages. Above is the story put on the wires by the Washington bureau a few
moments after official disclosure in 1945 that the Atomic Age had opened
with the harnessing of the basic power of the universe—the force from which
the sun draws its power.*

WA65B

BY JOSEPH L. MYLER

ABOARD U.S.S. MT. MCKINLEY OFF BIKINI, MAY 21.--(UP)--THE FIRST
GIANT UNITED STATES H-BOMB EVER DROPPED FROM A PLANE BURST OVER BIKINI
BEFORE DAWN TODAY WITH THE TERRIFYING BRILLIANCE OF A THOUSAND SUNS.

UNOFFICIAL ESTIMATES PLACED ITS POWER AT MORE THAN 10 MILLION
TONS OF TNT, ENOUGH CONCENTRATED VIOLENCE TO WIPE OUT THE HEART OF ANY
CITY.

HALF AN HOUR AFTER THE BURST A BEAUTIFUL PINK AND PEACH CLOUD HAD
SOARED TOWARD THE MAXIMUM HEIGHT OF 25 MILES. A VAST WEDGE OF
CAULIFLOWER TOP SPREAD RAPIDLY TOWARD A LATERAL MAXIMUM OF 100 MILES.
BUT IT WAS THAT FIRST FLASH OF LIGHT, ACCOMPANIED BY AN INSTANTANEOUS
WAVE OF HEAT, THAT SYMBOLIZED THE BOMB'S UNEARTHLY WEIRD POWER. THIS
WAS ELEMENTAL NUCLEAR FORCE THE SAME KIND OF FORCE THAT ENERGIZES THE
SUN AND STARS AND ALL THE GALAXIES.

IT SEEMED TO FILL THE UNIVERSE. AS SUDDENLY AS IT FLASHED, THIS
SUPERSOLAR LIGHT DISAPPEARED, FOLLOWED IN A TINY SPLIT SECOND BY THE
FIREBALL. SIMULTANEOUSLY WITH THE EXPANSION OF THE FIREBALL, IT BEGAN
RISING OFF THE HORIZON, WHILE SURGING UPWARD FROM BELOW APPEARED THE
GIANT STALK OF THE NOW FORMING BOMB CLOUD.

THE STALK WAS VISIBLE FIRST BELOW HEAVY CLOUD LAYERS. IT PIERCED
A FAT RAIN CLOUD LIKE A GIANT SPEAR. THE TIP OF THE SPEAR, GLOWING
LIKE A HEATED IRON, STABBED THROUGH THE TOP OF THE INTERVENING CLOUD
AND THEN WAS OBSCURED FOR A MOMENT. WHEN IT REAPPEARED IT HAD EXPANDED
INTO A NUCLEAR MUSHROOM TORN BY TITANIC TURBULENCE. SOME 30,000
FEET AND TWO MINUTES AFTER THE BURST THE CLOUD SHOULDERED INTO A CLEAR
SKY, FADING TO OLD ROSE, CERISE, AND A SORT OF ELECTRIC VIOLET.

CM1156A

*Eleven years later, in 1956, the above dispatch by one of the United
Press's top reporters disclosed the explosion of the first air-borne hydrogen
bomb. Even though the hydrogen bomb was far more powerful, it is interesting to note that the second dispatch makes similar references to the power
of the sun and the explosive force of TNT in describing its effect.*

out of the air news of the surrender of Hong Kong and Singapore, the first B-29 raids on Tokyo, and the first clash of Soviet troops with the Japanese in Manchuria.

Early on the morning of August 10, the station was receiving a news broadcast from Radio Tokyo and relaying it instantaneously on a wire to the San Francisco bureau, where Deskman Hennen Hackett was on duty. Hackett noticed a couple of routine news items in the broadcast. The third item started out routinely, too, but down in the middle of it was the big news—the Japanese government had advised the Swiss and Swedish governments that it was ready to accept terms of the Potsdam declaration in which the Allied powers had laid down the basis for ending the war. An instant later the flash was on the wires.

The Japanese capitulation came four days later. Sandor Klein was covering the White House when Charles Ross, the press secretary, called reporters into his office and told them a communication from the Japanese government, via Switzerland, was being translated. There was a wild dash of reporters for the door leading to their telephones. Klein was closest to the door but Douglas Cornell of the Associated Press grabbed him by the shoulder. Klein's elbow smacked him in the ribs and they tumbled out the door in a wild rush. Later, in another similar race from Ross's office with additional news, Robert Nixon of the International News Service was leading until he slipped rounding a corner. The pack simply ran over him, breaking his glasses and tearing off a large piece of the leg of his trousers.

It was not until almost seven o'clock that evening, however, that the reporters were ushered into the President's office, where Mr. Truman read a statement. When the double doors of the President's office were opened by secret-service men at the end of the conference there was a third and final heat in the telephone sweepstakes. The reporters fought for position running down the hallway to the big lobby of the White House executive offices. There a girl secretary was spreading out copies of the Truman statement on a big round table in the middle of the floor as the thundering herd rounded the corner. With a wild scream she leaped to the top of the table to escape being trampled underfoot. In the adjacent pressroom Charles Degges was opening a telephone line to the United Press news desk to dictate the Truman statement. Klein grabbed the phone:

"Flash!" he sputtered. "Japan surrenders."

CHAPTER THIRTY

The end of World War II opened the way for a tremendous job of rebuilding United Press services in Europe and the Far East, but that came second to the job of telling the story of postwar Japan. Frank Bartholomew arrived in Tokyo Bay with the first American forces on the cruiser *San Diego,* went ashore under the guns of the still-armed Japanese, and later headed the staff covering surrender ceremonies aboard the battleship *Missouri.* A few days later, on September 11, he went to the Tokyo suburb of Satagaya-ku and knocked on the door of Prime Minister General Hideki Tojo.

There was no answer, but a military guard patrolling the premises told Bartholomew and his companion, Toichiro Takamatsu of the newspaper *Mainichi,* that "the general is taking a walk." They went around to a garden on the south side of the house to wait. After a short time a window above them opened, sliding horizontally in the Japanese fashion, and the architect of Japan's war policy peered down at them through horn-rimmed spectacles.

"I am Tojo," he said slowly, nodding his bald brown head. Then he repeated: "Tojo."

Takamatsu was so emotionally upset that Bartholomew had difficulty in getting him to translate, but his request for an interview finally was made clear. Tojo did not reply but seated himself on the window bench and gazed thoughtfully at the two visitors. Just then several jeeps halted in front of the house and Major Paul Kraus of the United States Counter-Intelligence Corps walked to the garden. "Open the door," Kraus said to Tojo. "I am coming in to present my credentials."

Tojo waved his arms. "Unless this is an official order," he replied in Japanese, "I do not care to discuss it."

Kraus turned to his interpreter. "Tell him to open the door. Tell him to prepare for a trip to General MacArthur's headquarters in Yokohama."

Angrily Tojo slammed the window shut. Kraus, Bartholomew, and the rest of the party had just started for the front door when they heard a sharp, flat-sounding "whack!" from inside the house.

"What's that?" Kraus asked.

"Your pigeon just shot himself," Bartholomew replied. They raced to the front door, broke the lock, and went inside. The door of Tojo's study was also locked, and there was no answer to Kraus's demand that it be opened. He kicked it in.

Tojo sat in an easy chair, his legs crossed. He wore khaki whipcord military trousers and high boots and a white sports shirt that was stained with blood. An American air force pistol lay on the floor beside him.

Bartholomew pulled Takamatsu into the room and the Japanese newspaperman knelt beside the barely conscious war lord. Tojo's lips moved.

"I am happy to die," Takamatsu translated. "I wanted to die by the sword . . . but the pistol will do. . . . I assume responsibility for the war . . . banzai!"

But Tojo had blundered once more. He didn't die. Taken to a hospital, he was nursed back to health so that he could face a war-crimes trial—and the hangman's noose.

2.

Hugh Baillie arrived in Tokyo soon after the war ended and so did Miles W. Vaughn, who had returned to the Pacific area almost a year earlier as Far Eastern manager. Baillie talked General MacArthur into giving him an exclusive interview on his plans for the postwar occupation of Japan. Later he also interviewed Emperor Hirohito and China's Generalissimo Chiang Kai-shek. In the next few weeks Baillie extended his campaign for free exchange of news throughout the world by consultations with Japanese publishers as well as through talks with occupation officials, who were getting advice from American press association leaders on how to replace the wartime news monopoly of the Domei news agency. The Japanese newspapers had published many editions daily before the war. By the end of the conflict they were reduced to a single two-page edition each day, but they quickly began to revive in the postwar period. Almost immediately the United Press resumed special service to the *Mainichi* newspapers. Shortly afterward, it began world service to the Kyodo News Service, a newly organized co-operative that succeeded Domei. General and special service to nearly all the press and radio followed. Service was also re-established in Burma, Ceylon, Malaya, Thailand, Hong Kong, Indonesia, Indochina, Korea, and on the China coast.

The demand for service was so great in some areas of the Pacific that it was said Vaughn often opened a new United Press bureau by renting a grass hut, pulling a radio receiving set out of his suitcase, stringing an antenna between two palm trees, and announcing that he was ready to sign two-year contracts with all comers. While this version was somewhat exaggerated, it was true that various bureaus—Manila, for example—were opened with whatever meager equipment could be scrounged, borrowed, or bartered for and that service was resumed in many instances before the smoke of battle had quite faded away.

In Shanghai, Walter Rundle talked the Army out of one old radio receiver, bought a couple of battered typewriters and a secondhand mimeograph machine and opened a bureau in the only spot he could find—a three-room apartment on the fourth floor of a walk-up building. The important thing was that he could receive United Press newscasts from Manila and New York and that he had a staff of translators who could transfer the dispatches with a stylus to a mimeograph stencil for use by Chinese papers.

There were plenty of problems, of course. Rundle's contracts with Shanghai newspapers were for payment in United States dollars, but inflation of Chinese currency was in a runaway spiral and the contracts had to be renegotiated every few weeks. He also had to keep increasing the pay in Chinese currency of two dozen messengers who delivered the news service to the papers. The messengers eventually went on strike for still higher pay and plastered Shanghai with posters denouncing Rundle in particular and the United Press in general. Meanwhile the strikers lived on the roof of Rundle's office-apartment, sleeping under the sky and cooking their own meals. When Rundle began delivering his news reports in a jeep, the messengers compromised and returned to work, but they insisted that the hallway outside the office was haunted by the ghost of a Chinese girl who had been killed by a Japanese soldier.

"The only way to get rid of the ghost is with firecrackers," their spokesman said. When Rundle refused to buy firecrackers for them they threatened to strike again. In the end he had to buy the firecrackers. The messengers performed the ceremony of driving away the ghost and went back to work. Rundle sent in an expense account to New York:

FIRECRACKERS TO EXORCISE GHOST $20

3.

One of the remarkable chapters in United Press history was written in postwar Europe. As the cities of Europe were liberated the United Press went back into business as a news-distributing agency in lands that were eager for unbiased news of world affairs. European Manager Virgil Pinkley outlined the basic policy that, as rapidly as possible, a leased-wire system on the American pattern would be established to maintain constant communications among all European bureaus, both to collect and to distribute news.

The job of setting up the European news service while the war was still in progress started in Paris in September of 1944 after that city was liberated. At that time there was no way to receive news dispatches, but Joe Grigg and Jean DeGandt began signing up clients on the understanding that contracts would become effective whenever service could be started. The army newspaper, *Stars and Stripes,* helped solve their problem when it obtained permission to set up an elaborate radio monitoring station in the New York *Herald Tribune* plant in Paris, and began transcribing United Press newscasts that were beamed from New York to Africa and the Middle East. A copy of these dispatches was turned over to the Paris bureau. Later, Sam Hales, with the help of the *Stars and Stripes* editors, persuaded the Army to fly over from London two ancient Eddystone commercial short-wave receivers, 300 feet of coaxial cable, antenna wire, and other essentials—as well as two bicycles on which to deliver copy to newspapers.

Without asking for official permission, Hales, Haynes Thompson, and Robert Ahier slid around for several days in six inches of snow on the roof of the building at 2 Rue des Italiens, where the bureau was located, until they had an antenn. erected and a cable run down through a window of the office. They tuned in a receiver and found they could copy the United Press newscast from London to Buenos Aires. On January 1, 1945, the United Press was in business again in France, the first foreign agency in the field.

The Paris bureau was the first step in rebuilding the news gathering and distribution network under the direction of European News Manager William R. Higginbotham. Shortage of equipment made establishment of leased wires a technician's nightmare, and it was only the genius of a couple of experts—A. Hermet in Paris and Heinz Pfitzner in Germany—that made it possible to build the necessary switchboards. Everything from teleprinters to screws had to be bought on the black market, and, in many instances, American cigarettes may have been illegally used as currency in occupied areas, presumably without the company's knowledge or approval. On other occasions Art Watt turned up unexpectedly with equipment that he had found in unlikely places. One teleprinter was salvaged from a sunken barge in the Main River near Würzburg. Another had been discarded by the German Army and appeared beyond repair until Pfitzner got it reconditioned. A number were assembled from spare parts found in factories and supply shops at the end of the war, and two were machines that had been junked by the *Stars and Stripes*.

With ingenuity and a great deal of hard work, the service was established by a corps of Unipressers that included Sam Hales, Clinton B. Conger, Charles P. Arnot, Leo Disher, Frederick Laudon, Henry Tosti Russell, Tom Allen, and others. And gradually the leased wires were extended and the network sprouted legs reaching to Berlin, Brussels, Antwerp, Oslo, Vienna, Frankfurt, Hamburg, Copenhagen, Stockholm, Nuremberg, Munich, Prague, Zurich, Milan, and Rome. Sometimes in the early postwar days it seemed that the leased-wire system was held together by will power rather than sturdy equipment. Expert engineers swore it couldn't work. But it did, despite the fact that every imaginable kind of teleprinter collected at random in various countries and from the American Army was hooked into the same circuit—and occasionally Pat Conger even plugged in an electric coffee-making machine.

The effectiveness of the network was soon obvious. When the surviving leaders of the Nazi state were ordered to trial at Nuremberg, Conger arranged with the German postal authorities for a leased wire from Nuremberg to Paris. Then he looked around for another teleprinter. It happened there was an antiquated model that had been salvaged from the Berlin office by a prewar employee, Walter Wilke. This teleprinter had been used by Japanese correspondents who occupied the Berlin office of the United Press at one time during the war. It was equipped with the old time "Hier ist" and "Wer da?" buttons used on the prewar telex system. The buttons made it possible to determine quickly whether the post-office switchboard had connected you with the proper party. If you pressed the "Hier ist" ("This is . . .") button, it actuated an annunciator that automatically spelled out the name of the bureau that was making the call—in the case of Berlin like this:

UNIPRESS BLN

Without even removing the old printer from its wooden case, Conger loaded it in a jeep and drove to Nuremberg where, in the middle of the night, he set it up in the agency's allotted working space in the Palace of Justice pressrooms. It was several days before the trials started, however, and in that time a rival news agency spotted the teleprinter, complained to the authorities, and Conger was informed he would have to restrict the United Press file to army communications channels like everybody else. Regretfully he put a packing case over old UNIPRESS BLN and forgot about it until months later when Hugh Baillie arrived in Nuremberg just before the court announced the sentences of the convicted Nazis.

With Baillie's encouragement old UNIPRESS BLN was uncovered and hooked into a leased wire to Frankfurt, Paris, and London. The next morning it was ready to operate as a "secret weapon"—in fact, it enabled the agency to register a resounding beat on the verdicts and sentencing of the Nazi leaders—and Conger decided there should be a little ceremony in connection with opening the wire. When all was ready he invited Baillie to send the first message. The staff stood around respectfully waiting for the boss to think up something that would at least match Morse's famous telegraph message, "What hath God wrought!" But Baillie was intrigued by the "Hier ist" key.

"What's this thing?" he muttered, and his finger stabbed the button. Old UNIPRESS BLN shuddered to life with a gallant effort, but unhappily she had been brainwashed by the Japanese correspondents who occupied the office after Pearl Harbor. She hummed angrily, threw off a couple of tentative sparks and then spluttered her first words in four years:

S SS   SS SSSSSSSSMAINICHI SHIMBUN

Everybody stared. "My God," Baillie cried, "the thing is hissing at me in Japanese."

Baillie found plenty of action in connection with the Nuremberg trials. He was incensed when the Allied officials announced that no correspondents would be permitted to witness the executions of the Nazis sentenced to death, and he and Earl Johnson in New York immediately started a high-level campaign to get permission for news-agency reporters to be present. Johnson sent a telegram to Secretary of War Robert P. Patterson, urging that correspondents be permitte˜ to cover the executions as a matter of justice to the fighting men who gave or risked their lives to eliminate the criminals. Patterson referred the telegram to General Joseph T. McNarney, American member of the Allied Control Council in Berlin. Baillie then moved in on McNarney, urging him to use his office to have the ACC reconsider its decision. Shortly thereafter the decision was reversed and the ACC announced that one agency and one radio correspondent from each of the Big Four countries would be admitted. "The reversal . . . was a victory for the press of the United States," *Editor & Publisher* noted. "Credit is due the United Press which spearheaded the American protests."

Lots were drawn to select the American newspaper correspondent and J. Kingsbury Smith of International News Service won the draw. It was the only recorded occasion in history when Baillie did anything—even unintentionally—for the benefit of a competitor.

The postwar growth of the company was rapid. In 1947 the agency was serving 2689 newspapers and radio stations in seventy countries and territories. The news report was being translated into many different languages, and 144 bureaus were operating around the world. In the previous year the number of client newspapers in the United States had been increased by forty-six and in the rest of the world there had been a steady expansion into new territory as well as restoration of service in the war zones. In the Middle East, for example, the company had fifty-four subscribers as compared to one prior to the war. In Germany thirty-three newspapers were receiving the daily report, and a new relay bureau for Central European countries was established at Prague with an American staff directed by George Pipal.

By 1947 the volume of United Press newscasts to foreign countries also had been increased by about 30 per cent over prewar days. These newscasts originated at various key bureaus and could be picked up simultaneously by receiving stations in many cities. New York, for example, beamed multiple-destination newscasts to Europe, the Middle East, Africa, and Latin America. San Francisco beamed similar newscasts to the Far East. Still other newscasts originated in thirteen different foreign bureaus. As an indication of the tremendous growth of news distribution, the New York newscast carried approximately 5,500,000 words a year, while San Francisco fed

3,500,000 words a year to the Far Eastern bureaus and to newspapers from Korea to Java. In many instances this transmission had been so improved that mechanical relays operated teleprinters in the receiving stations. This meant that editors in distant cities—San Juan, Puerto Rico, for example—received news dispatches from New York instantly in the same complete typewritten form that copy was laid down on the desk of an editor in Pittsburgh or Kansas City.

The way was opened in 1946 for further spread of newscasting when the British Commonwealth agreed to license news agencies to have their own facilities for reception of multiple-destination newscasts. General Foreign Manager Joseph L. Jones and Communications Director Harry Flory had carried on a fight for such permission within the British Commonwealth since 1936. But it was only after their arguments had been strongly presented by Flory at the Anglo-American Communications Conference at Bermuda in 1945 that the London government permitted the United Press monitoring station at Barnet, for example, to be converted into a receiving station. This freed the agency of being forced to receive newscasts in England via government-monopoly facilities which were expensive and less efficient.

4.

In the first week of May 1946 about thirty prisoners at Alcatraz prison in San Francisco Bay rioted and killed two guards. Twenty guards were taken as hostages and Warden James A. Johnston finally called in Marines to help restore order. Fighting with guns, grenades, and even bazookas went on from May 2 until Saturday, May 4, by which time the rioters were subdued and a prison break avoided.

Ronald Wagoner, Dan Bowerman, and Roger Johnson of the San Francisco bureau had directed coverage of the story from outside the walls of Alcatraz. They had one reporter on a patrol boat that circled The Rock. Another with binoculars was stationed at the Coit Tower on top of Telegraph Hill overlooking the prison. Saturday afternoon Warden Johnston announced that he would admit one man from each press association and a few other local reporters for an interview.

Wagoner took the assignment and met with other reporters at the wharf to go aboard the prison launch. En route to The Rock he sat beside a man he didn't know, who turned out to be Al Ostrow, a new reporter on the Scripps-Howard San Francisco *News*. The *News* did not have a Sunday-morning edition, so Wagoner was able to enlist Ostrow's aid in covering the story for the United Press.

"There are two telephones in the warden's office," he told Ostrow, "but nobody will be permitted to use them. However, there must be other telephones around the place. Since nobody here knows you, the other reporters won't be watching you—they'll watch me to see I don't beat them to a phone. You sit close to the door. Then when the warden has talked enough to give us a good wire lead I will run my hand through my hair as a signal for you to leave quietly, try to find a telephone or get back to the mainland, and dictate your notes to the United Press bureau. Meantime I'll stay put as a kind of decoy."

The interview went off about as Wagoner had expected. After Johnston had given the highlights of the fighting, the number of dead, and other important information, Wagoner ran his hand through his hair. Ostrow calmly walked out the door. Nobody paid any attention, the other reporters thinking he was a member of the prison staff. He wandered around until he found a guard who told him there was a pay telephone in the locker room. Ostrow then discovered that he didn't have a dime with which to make a call. He borrowed one from another guard, called the bureau, and dictated the highlights of the warden's story. Then he returned to the press conference.

About fifteen minutes later Johnston was still talking when a guard broke in on the press conference.

"The Associated Press is on the phone," he said, "and insists on talking to their man."

"Okay," Johnston said, "but you take him to the phone and see that he does not say anything. All he can do is receive a message."

Shortly afterward the Associated Press reporter rushed back in and exclaimed, "Warden, the International News Service has broken this story already!" The INS reporter jumped to his feet and argued, correctly, that his service had done nothing of the sort. In fact, the Wagoner-Ostrow story was the only word that reached any newspaper until almost midnight, which was after eastern newspapers had gone to press and long after the United Press story had been delivered to western newspapers.

Even the San Francisco *Chronicle,* which had a reporter at the prison, headlined Wagoner's story under an editor's note which said:

Alcatraz broke its tradition of silence last night when Warden Johnston invited newspapermen and wire service reporters for a first-hand account of the uprising. Among the men given this unprecedented assignment was the Chronicle's *Stanton Delaplane. At a late hour last night, because of limited communications facilities, but one sparse report had been made from the island. It was the dispatch of Ronald W. Wagoner, printed below.*

Later, a number of reporters who had seen Wagoner sitting near the warden's desk throughout the interview asked him how he did it.

"Maybe," he replied to everybody, "we used carrier pigeons."

5.

One of the traditional skills of executives of the United Press was that of operating on an economical basis, of getting a high return for dollars expended. Economy had been unavoidable in the early years of the company. It continued to be a dominant factor in the successful operation of a profit-making corporation in later years because of the basic pattern of news-agency affairs. The service operated all over the world, and only close control of spending and of expenses could guard the exchequer against wide-open and unnecessary overspending when news broke at one or perhaps a dozen distant bureaus. The company also had to operate on a fixed income, whereas the important news of the world did not break on a fixed schedule that could be foreseen. As a result there were necessarily periods of heavy expenditure that had to be followed by periods of intense economy.

Some of the most cherished, if sometimes exaggerated, stories circulated among Unipressers, past and present, concerned the management's periodic economy waves, which were known as "downholds." When there was a downhold on, everybody was expected to slash controllable expenses to the bone. For years, when L. B. Mickel was superintendent of bureaus and director of downholds, a popular slogan in the lower echelons of the company was: "Save a Nickel for Mickel." Eventually former employees in Washington and Detroit—Steve Richards, W. H. Lawrence, Norman Nicholson, Anthony de Lorenzo, John Cutter and others—formed a social organization known as "The Downhold Club" of which Mickel became the executive secretary and often the guest of honor at annual dinners.

Meetings of The Downhold Club were occasions for recalling amusing—in retrospect, at least—incidents about expense accounts or about bureaus that had to operate shorthanded in an emergency. Most of the members had now risen into the relatively high-income brackets, and this enabled them to take a philosophic and sometimes appreciative view of their own early training in the merits of frugality. There was, for instance, the time Harold Jacobs sent in an expense account for "one mule shot out from under me" while covering a revolution in Mexico. There was Sports Writer Henry McLemore, who unfailingly started his weekly expense account with the same item—"Repair of typewriter, $5"—and managed to get away with it for years because his fast talk demoralized the accounting department. There was the time H. Allen Smith spent two hours composing a fake expense account in which he included every absurd and outrageous item he could think of. He presented it to Mickel for approval and then stood by to enjoy the explosion. It happened, however, that Mickel was very busy and, without more than a glance at the itemized expenses, he okayed it and handed it back. Smith was so depressed that he tore up the expense account and never did collect $1.35 for taxicab fare, which was the only legitimate item on the list.

One of the best-known stories of United Press operations in which one man was expected to do the work of several originated in the bureau at Raleigh, North Carolina. The bureau, headed by Warren Duffee, normally had four men but at one time was trying to survive temporarily with only two—Duffee and James Campbell. Campbell was known throughout the southern division as a newsman who went at full speed all the time. He also had a reputation as a fast teleprinter puncher, rivaled only by Chief Operator Paul Butler in Atlanta. There were two wire circuits out of the Raleigh bureau but one afternoon when a hot story broke there was nobody to punch the tape for the teleprinters except Campbell.

Undismayed, Campbell attempted to run both wires at once. He could do this by punching tape for the first teleprinter at a much greater speed than the tape could run through the machine. Then when a few feet of tape had accumulated, he would spin his chair around to the second teleprinter and punch out the story until he was a few paragraphs ahead of *that* machine. Then back to the first teleprinter, and so on. This kept both machines running but, in time, the 60-words-a-minute printer to Atlanta caught up with him and sputtered to a stop while he was punching on the other keyboard. In Atlanta, Butler realized what was happening but he thought he would have some fun with Campbell. He tapped out a message on the stalled wire:

WHATS MATTER? CANT YOU PUNCH?

There was a short pause on the wire, pregnant with frustration, and then came an answer from Campbell:

ONLY HAVE 2 HANDS

This was too good a chance for Butler to resist. He sent a message, not to Campbell but to Campbell's boss, Duffee:

SUGGEST YOU FIRE THE CRIPPLED BASTARD

CHAPTER THIRTY-ONE

Hugh Baillie was a kind of global reporter, but he managed to keep his eye on the news report, and he was never too far away to cable a few "red ants" messages to the top echelon editors in New York, London, or Tokyo. Baillie had a habit of discovering every so often, and frequently in the middle of the night, that the staff was in a slump everywhere, that the news report was falling apart, and that something had better be done about it in a hurry.

Once when he was burned up over a story that had gone wrong in Europe he returned to his office at nine o'clock that evening and telephoned European Manager Virgil Pinkley in London. Pinkley was awakened from a sound sleep and it took a minute or so before he understood what Baillie was talking about. By that time Baillie was still more impatient.

"What's the matter, Virgil?" he snapped. "Aren't you fellows on the ball? Don't you know what's happening with your crew?"

"But, Hugh," Pinkley protested, "it's almost three o'clock in the morning in London and . . ."

"Look, Virgil," Baillie interrupted, with high disdain for international time zones, "if the president of the United Press can be at work at this hour I don't see why his European manager can't be at work too."

On another occasion he arrived at work in New York with the firm conviction that during his absence abroad everybody in the organization had been resting on his oars. Baillie leaned back and dictated a memorandum, and, instead of addressing it to specific editors or bureau managers, he made sure that he was neglecting no one by his opening words:

TO ALL:

The United Press is the greatest news service in the history of journalism. It is our responsibility to keep it so.

But, what's going on here? I write this as we are in the midst of absorbing a licking on British planes shot down by the Israeli, which points up something I have been thinking over since I got back from South America.

The news report is in a down draft. A bad one.

I see no excuse for getting beaten on official announcements. I am sick of hearing that "the censor did it to us," or "the wire failed," etc., ad nauseam. When you are running a successful, surging news agency, the censor doesn't choose you out, your wire doesn't fail, etc.

Now, gentlemen, I also find that we don't hop to it on the rare and unusual. We turn up our noses too often. We don't lunge at opportunities for shooting legitimate entertainment into the service.

Sure, we have some world beats and we have some excellent worked-up wire features. Why not? Nothing new about that. It's par. . . .

I take it for granted we are planning in great detail to cover every big story we see coming and that we can extemporize superior coverage of any story that breaks unexpectedly anywhere in the world. Or am I wrong? Am I waxing nostalgic?

Let's have a big improvement effective today. If anybody can't be bothered to go along with this letter, let him quit. . . . Everybody get into the act.

Yes, you Unipressers, this is the alarm clock you hear ringing.

2.

Just how much effect Baillie's ultimata to the staff had on the news report over the years was difficult to judge, but it frequently seemed that things picked up noticeably following one of his broadside blasts. In any event there were occasions on which the staff displayed energy and initiative that might be ranked as above the call of duty. One such occasion was in Milan, Italy, in November of 1947.

At that time the government of Premier Alcide de Gasperi was in a bitter struggle with the Communist party for control of Italy, and Milan was a stronghold of the Communists. De Gasperi had "fired" the Milan prefect, A. Troilo, but Troilo refused to be dismissed. Communist party squads took over the prefecture palace, set up barbed-wire barricades at the entrances, put out guards, and announced that they would stay there in defense of Troilo. At the local police headquarters not far away all men were called to duty and armed with machine guns and antitank guns to guard against rioting.

There was almost nobody in the streets at midnight as Aldo Trippini left the United Press bureau in Milan and walked to the palace, where he was promptly surrounded by an outpost of workers armed with clubs, iron bars, and hand grenades. Trippini showed his press pass. He didn't expect it to do him much good, but in the dim light one of the guards misread it and mistakenly thought he was a reporter from the Italian Communist party newspaper *Unità*. He was immediately led into the building by a burly guard who informed him that a reporter from the "capitalist reactionary press" had been beaten up a few minutes earlier and taken to a hospital with serious injuries.

Inside the palace Trippini learned that Achille Marazza, the Italian Undersecretary of Interior, had arrived and insisted that Troilo must quit. The crowd threatened him and the workers appeared to be in the mood for a revolutionary outbreak. Trippini found a telephone in the switchboard room, but it was flanked by a dozen grim Communists. The reporter realized that he could not dictate his story without being overheard, and, once overheard, he felt reasonably certain that he would end up in a hospital if not in the morgue.

Nevertheless he couldn't stop at that point. In deadly silence he dialed the number of the United Press bureau. Deskman Enzo Peru answered and, upon hearing Trippini's voice, exclaimed: "At least, you are alive! We weren't sure." Trippini did not dare speak in English, which would arouse the suspicions of the guards. At the last moment he decided to take a chance on Peru's knowledge of the situation.

"The Milanese working people, rightly tired of Marazza's futile attempts to stem the Communist tide, are now protesting in the courtyard of the prefecture palace," Trippini dictated in Italian. "But Marazza, a henchman of reactionary forces . . ."

"What?" Peru yelled into the phone. "Has somebody got a gun at your back?"

"Well, more or less," Trippini replied, and continued his dictation. When he had told the story in terms that might have appeared in *Unità* he added: "Of course, if you see any paragraphs that are not correct, please correct them."

Peru then read back to him a straight factual account of what he had dictated, leaving out the pro-Communist flourishes and making clear that Marazza had refused to reinstate Troilo despite the threat of rioting by the Communists.

"Okay," Trippini said, and hung up. One of the guards walked over, slapped him on the shoulder and said: "You wrote a right story, comrade. We will smash in the teeth of all capitalist reporters."

Trippini wiped the sweat from his forehead and smiled.

Early the next day the Communists decided to call off their demonstrations and Troilo retired from office.

A political reporter can sometimes spend days and weeks working on a story and get nothing that can be printed. But at other times a story may fall in his lap by some freakish circumstance. In the case of Kirtland I. King the unusual circumstance was that he rather closely resembled James C. Hagerty, a member of the staff of Governor Thomas E. Dewey of New York.

At the Republican national convention at Philadelphia in 1948 Dewey's bid for the presidential nomination was being blocked at one point by a group of favorite-son candidates led by Senator Martin of Pennsylvania. King, manager of the United Press bureau at Albany, had spent all day trying to find out when and how the temporary road block would be removed and had learned nothing. Then, late in the day, he paused in a frustrated manner near the hotel suite in which Dewey had his headquarters. A member of Senator Martin's staff walked down the hall, addressed King by the name of Hagerty, and said:

"The senator is ready to release that announcement. When do you want me to give it to the reporters?"

"What announcement?" King asked.

"You know—announcement that the senator is withdrawing in favor of Governor Dewey."

"Oh, sure. Hold it up for thirty minutes. Then let it go."

King started down the hall to telephone the United Press news desk at the convention but was stopped by a leader of the Kansas delegation, who also mistook him for Dewey's aide.

"We're ready to swing twenty-three votes to Dewey," the Kansan said. "How do you want them—all on the first roll call or spread out?"

"According to plan," King replied, and continued his dash to the telephone with news that the blockade had been broken.

On the day before the presidential election of 1948 Henry Minott of the Boston bureau got some bad news. The Associated Press had worked up a good feature story for the next morning at the village of Hart's Location in New Hampshire. There were only eleven voters in Hart's Location and an Associated Press correspondent had arranged for all of them to be at the polls by 7:30 A.M. and thus to become the first community to report in the election. Minott was about to be taken for a ride on a feature story that would make every front page in the country the next day.

That afternoon Minott sent one of his staff members, Stanford Calderwood, and his wife speeding up to Hart's Location with instructions to take whatever action was necessary. They arrived about nine o'clock in the evening and found that the Associated Press reporter and photographer had gone to Conway for the night. Calderwood then called on all eleven of the town's voters and discovered how they would cast their ballots. He got a few quotes from each one and then visited the polling place, which was a house near the railroad tracks.

There was only one party-line telephone in Hart's Location, and Calderwood rented it for twenty-four hours for twenty-five dollars. He then telephoned a complete story to the Boston bureau at two o'clock in the morning, told the desk to hold it for later release, and went to bed. The next morning at seven o'clock two Associated Press reporters and a photographer arrived to collect their feature story. They were a bit grumpy when Calderwood got to the polling place because they had tried to use the telephone to call Boston and had been told it wasn't available. They had offered fifty dollars and, finally, one hundred dollars for use of the phone but had been refused. When the voting started, Mrs. Calderwood opened the telephone line to Boston and began describing the balloting. The eleven voters did exactly as they had said they would the night before. Once the Associated Press photographer asked a man who was marking his ballot to move from the sewing machine to a table for a better picture.

"Nope," the man replied. "I told Mr. Calderwood I would mark my ballot on the sewing machine and I aim to do it."

As Minott had foreseen, the story—by United Press—made the front pages everywhere.

There are times when luck plays a part in the success of a news-agency correspondent, but the reporter who stands around waiting for a lucky break very seldom gets one. Many hours and often weeks of advance planning and preparation are behind most beats. Take an example—and take it from Unipresser Norman J. Montellier.

Archbishop Alois Stepinac was put on trial in Yugoslavia in 1946 on charges of treason and collaboration with the Nazis. The Yugoslav government clamped down tight security around the gymnasium at Zagreb where the trial was held. There was a switchboard and a pressroom in the building, which appeared to give all reporters an even break, but Montellier was not satisfied with an even break. Before leaving Belgrade to cover the trial he spent a day at the Ministry of Communications, talking to the chief engineer. They went over every cable and telephone route on which the dispatches might be moved abroad. By the time the consultations were completed, Montellier knew that the fastest telephone communications were from point to point behind the Iron Curtain—to Prague, for example—and that the main telephone to Paris was routed via Zurich. This was important to him because the United Press bureau at Zurich was on the European leased-wire network and also because any calls to Zurich would block the main line to Paris. Some other facts he picked up were worrisome. There was a good separate line to Geneva, and the Associated Press had a bureau at Geneva. It was also possible to telephone Paris by way of Geneva or Prague.

At the end of the first day of the trial, Montellier put in a call to Zurich. Other American, French, and British correspondents simply booked their calls to Paris without designating the route, which meant that all of them were routed by way of Zurich. Montellier's call to Zurich, however, automatically blocked all the calls to Paris until he hung up the receiver. With considerable relief he observed that no other correspondent had investigated the routes and that they could not understand why their Paris calls were delayed.

After a few days Montellier's ability to get his story through long before anybody else prompted other reporters to take countermeasures. A group of French correspondents teamed up and booked so many calls to Paris in advance that Montellier could not get on the line to Zurich with his story.

But he simply switched his calls to Prague where George Pipal and Helen Fisher took his dictation and relayed the story to the European leased-wire circuit. The Prague calls were actually the quickest to go through, although they did not block the line to Paris, and Montellier continued to get his copy out ahead. The French correspondents then attempted to subvert the switchboard operator in the pressroom, wining and dining her lavishly and asking her for special consideration on the telephone. As it happened, she was a dedicated Communist, resented what she termed "capitalistic chicanery," and told Montellier that she would continue to play fair on his calls. In fact, on the day the archbishop was sentenced Montellier asked her to book a Zurich call for him the moment she saw him emerge from the courthouse. She did and the phone was open to Manager Ludwig Popper in Zurich by the time Montellier reached his desk. He dictated the final story from his notes directly to the European leased-wire network. Throughout the trial nobody in the press corps, except Montellier, ever discovered that calls could be made quickly to Paris via Geneva or, a bit more slowly, via Prague.

3.

In 1948 newspapermen and diplomats from fifty-three nations met in Geneva for an international Conference on Freedom of Information under auspices of the United Nations. Carlos P. Romulo, a veteran diplomat and newspaperman representing the Philippines, presided. Hugh Baillie, who had been carrying on the United Press campaign for free exchange of news in postwar Europe, was intensely interested in the conference and sent his executive assistant, Robert L. Frey, to Europe with the American delegation. Frey was invited to sit in on their discussions and was made an official consultant to advise the delegation on news-agency problems. Baillie also joined the delegation in Geneva as a consultant. He and Frey were the only American news-agency representatives participating in the conference.

The work of the conference represented a high-water mark in the long struggle to promote the free flow of news around the world, but at the same time it eventually led to a major disappointment for advocates of a free press in the councils of the United Nations. At Geneva the American delegation worked hard to draft "A Convention on the Gathering and International Transmission of News." Most of the nations were represented by newspapermen, and the language of the journalist rather than the language of the diplomat generally prevailed at the conference table, but there was a thread of contention throughout the meetings. The Western nations for the most part were seeking to formulate rules under which the press would have the least possible connection with government. The Communist countries took the position that a free press was one under government control.

Three draft treaties finally were adopted at Geneva—the American proposal and two parallel proposals by the British and French delegations. Baillie had labored with considerable success to have included in the American document the principle for which the United Press had fought for so many years: that news sources and transmission facilities should be competitively open and available to all with a minimum of official regulation of the free flow of news among all countries. At times, when there were proposals that threatened to cripple this principle, he had encouraged many editors and publishers in the United States to send cables to the American delegation urging them to stand firm. He also assigned Homer Jenks, one of the agency's European correspondents, to write daily dispatches from Geneva that kept American newspapermen fully informed of the trend of the discussions. In the end the documents drafted at Geneva represented perhaps the longest step forward ever taken by an international body toward establishing a method that would protect and encourage a freer flow of international news. There were amendments and reservations that the American delegation did not approve, but the net result was real progress toward elimination of the old official news-agency system.

Unfortunately the Geneva resolutions were merely the first step. They were then forwarded to the United Nations Economic and Social Council for examination and comment by its Committee on Human Rights. The committee's agenda was crowded, and it lacked the professional advice which had prevailed at the Geneva conference. The delegates took a restrictive tack and hastily modified the drafts before passing them on to the Committee on Social, Humanitarian and Cultural Matters of the General Assembly. When diplomats and government officials of the various nations saw what had come from Geneva, they made certain that the resolutions were further festooned with so many amendments of a restrictive nature that they became almost meaningless and were then left to wither away in pigeonholes.

"As far as concrete accomplishment goes," Frey summed up later, "the United Nations debates appear to have been a great boondoggle. But out of them have come at least two important contributions. One was the Geneva redefinition of freedom of the press and re-emphasis of its original meaning —freedom from government dictation. The other was the clear and unmistakable demonstration that in totalitarian countries the government and the press are one."

The long struggle between Generalissimo Chiang Kai-shek and the Chinese Communists for control of the mainland of China drew to a close in the first half of 1949. Peiping fell to the Communist armies in January and Mao Tze-tung, chairman of the Chinese Communist party, proclaimed the Chinese People's Republic in March. When Nanking fell on April 23 it was obvious that Shanghai, too, would soon be in the hands of the Red armies.

After the Nationalists had been driven from Nanking, Frank Bartholomew shuttled back and forth from Tokyo to Shanghai, trying to strengthen coverage around the borders of China and to keep the Shanghai bureau operating as long as possible. One of the problems Bartholomew faced at Shanghai was meeting the payroll in American money. Chinese employees of American and other foreign companies in Shanghai were demanding their pay in silver or gold and, in many instances, they seized the chief executives of American or British firms and held them as hostages until their demands were satisfied.

In this period Bart frequently collected a sackful of American silver coins in Tokyo and carried them to Shanghai to enable Bureau Manager Arthur Goul to pay his Chinese staff. He was ready to leave Tokyo in mid-May on such a trip when the Associated Press manager there asked him if he would also carry that agency's payroll to Shanghai. Bart agreed and departed with two bags of silver coins weighing about fifteen pounds each.

It was not a favorable time to return to Shanghai. The Communists were at the city outskirts and foreigners were unpopular. Obviously the time had come to close the bureau but the Chinese employees refused to permit Goul to leave unless claims were settled for an extra year's pay to each. This was more money than the bureau had, and all banks were closed. Goul decided to attempt to leave anyway, and the employees started a riot as he tried to get into an automobile to go to the airport. Sikh guards intervened, but the disorder ended only after Bartholomew agreed to return to the bureau with the Chinese employees. Goul left for Hong Kong and Bartholomew spent the rest of the day persuading the employees to settle for his available supply of "Big Heads"—Chinese silver dollars.

The employees then took over the United Press office, sleeping on the floor and cooking their meals there. Virtually all business was halted in Shanghai by May 20. Bart had a reservation on an American airline for that day, but when he arrived at Lunghwa airport, which was outside the wooden defensive line around the city, he discovered that the "last" plane from Shanghai was filled by Chinese refugees and airline personnel. He had no choice but to return to his hotel. The next day he walked the four miles to the airport and discovered that a number of Britons were still being evacuated by seaplane. When he inquired into the possibility of hitching a ride he was informed that there were already too many refugees and that there was no possibility of taking an American aboard.

The British planes had hardly taken off when Red Army advance forces captured the outer homing beacon of the airfield and reached a point near the end of the main runway. Bartholomew went back into the airport building. It was deserted, but a few minutes later an American—the local manager of Northwest Airlines—walked in. Then a priest and several nuns arrived and, after them, a photographer for International News Service. The gunfire around the airport was steadily increasing.

"There's a chance that one of our planes will come in," the Northwest Airlines manager said.

The day had been clear, but later heavy rain clouds formed and spread over more than half of the sky. Within another hour or so the airport would be closed in and a landing would be impossible because the ground-control approach equipment had been removed by the U. S. Navy. After a short wait they heard a plane overhead. When a battery of Communist antiaircraft guns fired on it, it continued across the airport and disappeared into the clouds. A moment later the airlines manager ran down from the tower.

"I talked to them," he shouted. "They're going to try to land. But it can be only for a minute. They won't even stop the outboard engines."

For ten tense minutes they waited. Then, flying low out of the dark clouds, the big DC-4 came straight for the main runway. It touched down abruptly and rolled to a halt where the little group of Americans waited. The door swung open. The men on the ground picked up the nuns and lifted them high. Hands reached out to drag them into the plane. The men were boosted and pulled through the door. The engines roared again. They were barely airborne when machine guns and antiaircraft batteries opened fire, but the foul weather quickly swallowed them up.

Bartholomew collapsed in a comfortable aisle seat, sweat pouring from his high forehead. His first thought was that they had made it. Then it occurred to him to wonder where they were going. He looked around for somebody to ask. A girl was walking down the aisle—a neat, smiling Filipino girl in the uniform of an airline stewardess. Bart motioned to her, the question already formed on his dry, stiff lips. He had to swallow hard before he could say a word and in that moment the stewardess leaned over with a question of her own:

"Sir," she said in a soft voice, "would you like a martini or a manhattan?"

Bart gulped. "I'll have a double martini," he managed. It was a couple of hours later before he found out that they were headed for Manila.

There are countless ways to hit the jackpot in covering a news story, and a correspondent must be able to discover the most suitable approach in each instance. One of the most widely read stories of 1950 was the romance of Actress Ingrid Bergman and Italian Director Roberto Rossellini, who were working on a motion picture on the volcanic island of Stromboli off the coast of Italy. Rumors of romance first appeared in gossip columns. Miss Bergman and Rossellini protested that the gossip misrepresented the facts, and, after a few weeks, both refused to talk to newspapermen. When Miss Bergman's husband rushed from California to Italy, the gossip seemed to be confirmed, and the actress and Rossellini were later besieged by reporters and photographers wherever they could be found. No reporter was getting any information, however, and after a short time Norman J. Montellier— then in charge of the Rome bureau—decided on an entirely different approach to the story.

Montellier assigned Aldo Forte, a veteran of the bureau and a long-time acquaintance of Rossellini, to visit Stromboli, but under instructions to write only about the motion picture being made there. Forte carried out this assignment without ever mentioning the romance in his stories. But he did have a couple of long talks with Rossellini in which he pointed out that, if the couple planned to marry, that fact could not be kept secret, and that it would be more pleasant for everybody if there were some way to check up on all the gossip and rumors. Rossellini agreed, and gave Forte several private telephone numbers where he could be reached at any time, on the understanding that the United Press would never quote him or Miss Bergman without their specific permission.

"Very well," Forte said. "We will trust you to tell us the truth and we will keep our word."

On September 1 the United Press broke the story that the couple would marry as soon as Miss Bergman was divorced, that she would "never" make another movie in Hollywood, and that she might quit the films entirely. The information, of course, came from Rossellini and Miss Bergman. But immediately thereafter there were rumors that Miss Bergman was pregnant, and the pressure from New York for confirmation mounted daily. Montellier and Forte had a meeting with Rossellini, who told them the entire story of the romance and said that the baby was expected late in January.

"You can write a sensational story now," he said. "But if you can keep faith and trust me, I will do everything I can to help you later."

Montellier agreed, withstood the heat from New York, and never carried the story of the expected child except as reported by "a friend"—actually Rossellini's sister. On February 2 Rossellini called the United Press bureau in Rome and put the staff in contact with a priest whom he had instructed to give Forte the details of the child's birth. The story was exclusive until the next day. For more than ten hours, the only other news of the event was a brief announcement carried by the Italian official agency forty-six minutes after the United Press story had cleared. A day later, Forte interviewed Rossellini and got his permission to quote him as saying: "I am the father."

4.

The Commercial Telegraphers Union (American Federation of Labor) and the United Press failed to reach an agreement in 1950 on terms of pay for teleprinter operators, and a serious strike threat developed in April. Hugh Baillie was in California at the time, but he returned to New York and, when it seemed unlikely that the deadlock could be broken, took charge of arrangements to keep service flowing to clients even if the operators struck.

This was possible because there were a number of chief operators who would stay on the job and there were many bureau managers and business representatives who could operate teleprinters in an emergency. Late in the month, Business Manager Jack Bisco advised Baillie that there was not much hope of avoiding a strike. Baillie then asked J. R. Mandelbaum, the federal mediation commissioner, to come to his office. He showed Mandelbaum a map on which he had plotted the consolidation of various news-wire circuits and the concentration of company executives at key points in such a manner that the news service would be delivered regardless of a strike by operators. He asked Mandelbaum to convey this information to the union leaders.

On May 1 the union called a strike of all United Press operators and they walked off the job. There was a brief interruption of service. Then the chief operators, business representatives, and bureau managers who had been moved to the main relay centers took over the teleprinters and resumed service on a slightly abbreviated scale to all newspapers. Union pickets began patrolling United Press offices.

At the end of the first week, the CTU announced that all United Press client newspapers would be picketed [Earl Johnson wrote later], *but Pittsburgh was the only city in which other unions observed the CTU picket line. The Pittsburgh* Press . . . *was prevented from publishing for two days. When the NLRB applied for an injunction to prohibit picketing as a secondary boycott, the Pittsburgh* Press *pickets were withdrawn.*

By this time, union handbills began calling the strike a "lockout." We sent a letter to strikers assuring them that the company had no desire to break the union, but on the contrary was still willing to consider a wage increase. The strike committee circularized all UP newspapers and radio stations urging them to quit the service. It warned that all would be picketed. . . . The Communist Daily Worker *in New York announced that it would use no UP copy during the strike.*

The San Francisco News *and the Pittsburgh* Press *asked us to move our bureaus out of their buildings to avoid picketing (this was done) but they continued to feature UP dispatches.*

After the first week we began hiring outsiders to man the keyboards and paid them the regular union scale. One classified ad in the New York papers brought 350 applicants in one day, more than enough to man our entire domestic wire system. CTU sympathizers in some bureaus frequently identified these temporary workers for the pickets and they were jeered in the street. . . . Some of their wives received threatening telephone calls. In the final week our teleprinter machines in several client offices in New Jersey and New York were sabotaged by men posing as repairmen for a rival service. The UP unit of the Washington Newspaper Guild announced that it was taking every legal step open to its members to help the striking punchers. . . . One member of the Washington unit refused to cross the CTU picket line.

On the night of May 25th, strikers in Chicago tried to delay our story of a streetcar fire in which more than 30 persons perished. They did this by putting calls through to all of the UP telephone numbers in Chicago and then "holding the line." Reporters at the fire had to dictate their stories directly by telephone to New York.

The strike ended the first week in June when the union accepted the offer the company had made just prior to the strike.

5.

One of the great battles for freedom of the press was waged in Argentina in the decade following World War II by the newspaper *La Prensa* of Buenos Aires. The relationship of *La Prensa* with the United Press had been a factor of the first magnitude in the development and improvement of foreign news service to the Americas since the end of World War I, due in great part to the vision of Don Ezequiel Paz and, later, his nephew, Dr. Alberto Gainza Paz.

The United Press had borne the main responsibility for providing a news service to *La Prensa* for almost a quarter of a century and, in turn, the newspaper had been a bulwark of the agency's strength in Latin America and, indirectly, in Europe. In 1943 Baillie sent Thomas R. Curran, an experienced business and news executive with the company, to Buenos Aires, where he later became vice-president in charge of South America. In 1944 Argentine army leaders, some of them under Nazi influence, staged a revolution and set up a military government. One of the members of the military junta was Colonel Juan Perón.

Perón had not yet established himself as dictator, but the military government quickly sought to exert influence over the newspapers, particularly *La Prensa*. This proved impossible, but in the struggle there were others who came into the line of fire. The United Press operated a subsidiary company in Argentina, Prensa Unida. This company was attacked by government officials as a "subterfuge" and as a device for circumventing the tax laws.

At about the same time in 1944 the United Press carried a report that the Argentine Navy was preparing to act against the military government leaders. This led to the closure of the agency in all of Argentina for eighteen days, and a threat that it would never be permitted to reopen. Curran and his staff arranged for the news report to be cabled to Montevideo during this period and it was delivered, in one way or another, to *La Prensa* every day.

The closure order in Argentina, however, was a stunning blow. The agency then had about 190 client newspapers in Latin America, but Argentina was its biggest single source of revenue and Buenos Aires its South American headquarters. The United States Government at that time had not extended recognition to the Argentine military regime, which was eager to establish diplomatic ties with Washington. At one point a high government official suggested to Curran that he "get the United States to intervene in your behalf and then we will start you up again." Curran declined on the ground that he did not intend to try to use the United Press to get Washington to recognize the Buenos Aires government.

A couple of weeks later the Buenos Aires junta dictated for United Press signature a statement that started with a correction of the naval-intervention story and extended to a plenary confession of whatever other imaginary sins the junta could attribute to the agency. Upon signature of the statement, the agency was reopened. United Press officials immediately acted to prevent any repetition of such a situation. The entire communications system was changed, and Buenos Aires operations were streamlined and decentralized. The next closure of the United Press by an Argentine dictator, in 1953, lasted longer, but did not affect service in any other country.

The ascension to power of Dictator Juan Perón in 1946 left no doubt that the government was afraid of a free press. Perón soon realized that he could not subvert *La Prensa*. But he knew that it was a powerful threat to his kind of rule and he set out to destroy its owners. Perón tried to sway working newspapermen to his aid by requiring employers to raise their pay by 20 per cent. Then he took possession of all newsprint, including that imported by *La Prensa,* and apportioned it on almost a day-to-day basis. In 1948 all newspapers were limited to sixteen pages—a heavy blow to *La Prensa* but a big help to some weaker newspapers that supported Perón. Later the number of pages was reduced to eight by government order.

Perón frequently urged the people not to advertise in or buy *La Prensa*— circulation went up to a record 575,000 in this period—and sent organized gangs of hoodlums to attack the offices. Once Curran was in the office of Alberto Gainza Paz when gangs gathered outside, shouting "traitor." A piece of iron had been thrown through the window into the director's office. Gainza Paz picked it up and used it on his desk as a paperweight.

"Perón," he said, "may close us but he is not going to change us."

Finally, in 1951, the Perón-dominated newspaper-vendors' union issued an ultimatum to Gainza Paz demanding monopoly of distribution of *La Prensa,* elimination of all direct subscriptions, and 20 per cent of the revenue from classified advertising. The ultimatum was presented to the director shortly before the forty-eight-hour time limit set by the union expired. This was Perón's intended death blow, and it was an effective one. The union refused to negotiate, called a strike, and closed the newspaper on January 26. Employees who attempted to go to work were beaten up or shot at, and one was killed.

At about this time, Joseph L. Jones had gone to Buenos Aires and arranged a "suspension of service" agreement with Gainza Paz. The agreement was not made public, but it specified that United Press service to *La Prensa* would be suspended, effective upon Gainza Paz's loss of control of the newspaper. It also agreed that service would be resumed when and if he regained control. This, of course, was designed to relieve the agency of any legal obligation to continue service if Perón succeeded in ousting Gainza Paz and tried to use the newspaper's great influence for his own purposes.

One day in March of 1951 Gainza Paz summoned Curran and gave him a message advising Hugh Baillie that the end was in sight and asking him to make the facts clear to the world—that *La Prensa* had been struck for political purposes and not because of labor trouble. On March 20 a committee of the Congress took possession of the newspaper, barred all employees, and refused to permit Gainza Paz to enter the building. Gainza Paz escaped to Uruguay, having been convinced that he could do more good at liberty abroad than in jail at home.

The closing of *La Prensa* deprived the United Press of revenues of around half a million dollars a year. The Peronistas published their own version of *La Prensa* and made overtures to the agency to resume service, which had been halted as soon as Gainza Paz lost control. Service was not resumed. Curran and South American News Director William H. McCall launched an intensified sales campaign in other Latin American countries that partly made up for the loss of revenue from Buenos Aires. By that time the company also was expanding rapidly in other foreign areas that had been opened up after the war, but its foreign revenues were greatly reduced over the next five years.

The harassment of the United Press and its personnel continued throughout most of the Perón dictatorship, although Perón himself on several occasions had sent for Curran and talked to him in comparatively pleasant fashion. In 1953 two Argentine secret-police officers attempted to take Curran off a boat leaving for Rio de Janeiro. He telephoned the United States Ambassador, and the foreign office persuaded the police to withdraw. Two months later the police ordered an airplane on which Curran was flying to Montevideo to turn back to Buenos Aires. The radio message arrived after the plane had landed in Uruguay, however, and failed of its intention.

Only the fall of the Perón dictatorship, five years after *La Prensa* was closed, enabled Gainza Paz to return from exile and resume publication on February 3, 1956, of the newspaper that his grandfather had founded in 1869. United Press service also was resumed. In the pressroom of the newspaper stood Gainza Paz, pale with emotion, and Frank Bartholomew of the United Press. The publisher pressed a button on the first unit of the big presses. They moved slowly—then faster and faster. *La Prensa* lived again. At midnight, on July 8, 1956, thousands of persons stood in the street in front of *La Prensa* and sang the national anthem as the Lamp of Liberty on the Freedom statue atop the building was lighted again for the first time since a dictator's hand extinguished it in 1951.

CHAPTER THIRTY-TWO

A couple of years after World War II, Earl Johnson made a tour of inspection through the Far East. He conferred with many United Press correspondents, listened to the ideas of political and military experts—including General MacArthur and Generalissimo Chiang Kai-shek—and wrote a story predicting that there would be trouble along the line that divided American troops from Russian troops in Korea.

On January 3, 1950, Earnest Hoberecht, manager of the Tokyo bureau, turned up an unusual story about United States policy in the Far East. It said that the State Department had "notified its attachés that the loss of Formosa to the Chinese Communists was to be anticipated."

Hoberecht's story blew the lid off in Washington. Senator Knowland of California, a strong friend of the Chinese Nationalists, demanded that the State Department make public the document from which Hoberecht had quoted. At the next White House press conference Mr. Truman acknowledged the accuracy of the policy indicated in the story. The whole trend of the administration's policy toward China came up for debate that grew increasingly bitter. But Formosa was only one facet of the whole; decisions were impending in the Far East that would entail far greater consequences.

2.

Sunday was a dull day for correspondents in Korea, and Sunday, June 25, 1950, started out about as usual. Jack James, in charge of the Seoul bureau, had planned to break the monotony of the weekend by going on a picnic, but when he woke up it was raining. Furthermore, he had set his alarm clock for 7 A.M. because he intended to finish writing a mail story that morning before setting out on the picnic. Once awake, he got dressed and looked around for his raincoat. It was missing. He decided that he had left it at the United States Embassy and he stopped there en route to the office. Jumping out of his jeep, he ran to the door where he met an army intelligence officer. The officer showed no surprise at seeing James so early on Sunday morning. Instead, he asked, "What have you heard from the border?"

James stopped and thought hard for a moment. The officer obviously had heard something from the border. Just as obviously, he mistakenly believed that James had come running in not because of the rain but because he, too, had heard something.

"Not much," the correspondent finally replied. "What have you heard?"

"Hell, I've heard nothing since the report that the North Koreans had crossed the 38th Parallel everywhere except in the area of the 8th Division. It's pretty vague as to details."

"That's more than I had heard," James replied, and ran on to the communications room. There he discovered that a number of reports had come in from South Korean police to the effect that Communist troops from the north had launched an attack into South Korea. For months there had been rumors that such an invasion was imminent and all of them had proved false. James had no intention of going off half cocked on the basis of messages from jittery frontier police officers. He began calling various American and Korean officials who might have more definite information. None of them did, but he urged them to check and to call him back. By 9:30 A.M., additional information had been received and there was no longer any doubt that some kind of offensive had been launched from the north.

Although James had waited an hour and a half for more substantial reports before filing his story, it was the only dispatch that reached the United States in time for Sunday morning newspapers. By 11 A.M. his story had gone around the world and was rebroadcast from Manila to South Korean newspapers, which used it in extra editions announcing the invasion. By that time James had sent one of his Korean staff members, George Suh, to the front area and was receiving an eyewitness report of the invasion. By that time, too, Washington was on the telephone to the Seoul embassy asking whether the United Press report of an invasion was correct.

The Tokyo bureau of the United Press was no more prepared for covering a war than the South Koreans were for fighting one, but it lost no time in getting started. Manager Hoberecht immediately arranged for virtually solid around-the-clock radio-teletype transmission to the United States over facilities of the Japanese Ministry of Communications. By being the first applicant, he was able to tie up the best available frequencies on what quickly became an overcrowded communications route. Rutherford Poats and Peter Kalischer, of the Tokyo bureau, were started for Korea so quickly that Poats caught an airplane to Itazuke still wearing the white sports shirt in which he had answered the telephone at home. A hurry call was sent to New York for reinforcements.

Kalischer accompanied raw troops to the Korean front—or what was supposed to be the front—on July 5, the first day American infantrymen went into action. He picked a ringside seat on a hill overlooking the main road near Osan, dug himself a foxhole, and waited for the big show to start. Unhappily it was started first by a column of twenty Russian-made tanks that crunched down the road as the spearhead of the North Korean advance. Crouching in his hole, Kalischer watched the tanks open fire on American positions. They were answered with ineffective artillery fire and then by everything that the American battalion had—mortars, recoil-less 75-millimeter rifles, machine guns, and bazookas. These missiles seemed to bounce off the tanks like ping-pong balls. Bazooka teams later crept close to the road and damaged three tanks, but by that time North Korean artillery was firing into the American lines and several thousand enemy troops could be seen leaping from trucks and starting an advance against the strategic hill on which Kalischer crouched.

Kalischer crawled out of his foxhole and saw enemy soldiers in green and brown uniforms about a hundred yards away. He ran down a slope overlooking a rice paddy. American soldiers fell back, stumbling and sobbing, across the crest of the slope. Kalischer joined a file moving southward through heavy rain. The front line had vanished and they had been bypassed by the North Korean troops when they holed up in a farmhouse for the night.

The next day radio monitors in Tokyo heard an enemy broadcast listing Kalischer as a prisoner, but, in fact, he was slogging through gumbo-thick rice paddies and over hills toward the village of Itchang. His shoes had become a pulp and he hadn't eaten for two days when he and his companions staggered into a kind of no man's land not far from Chonan on the morning of the third day. They made contact with an American artillery observer and, that afternoon, Kalischer arrived, bearded and filthy, at the pressroom in Taejon with the story of how North Koreans had clobbered the first American battalion to go into action.

The news from Korea was terrible as the Communist armies advanced past Seoul and the communications lines were an indescribable jumble. Within a week after American infantry went into action, there were seventy correspondents at the 24th Division command post at Taejon. They had the use of one military telephone to Japan when and if the Army didn't need it. Headquarters was a dingy, rat-infested provincial government building and the reporters had a single big room for sleeping, writing, waiting, and fighting. They stood in line a dozen at a time to get a chance to use the telephone. Everybody heard exactly what everybody else was dictating. There were no secrets and no exclusives over that communications route, and there were times when a correspondent went through a special kind of torture—hearing a competitor dictate a hot bulletin to Tokyo with a dozen long-winded reporters still in line in front of him.

Some reporters occasionally licked the communications jam. Bob Bennyhoff turned out to be skillful at getting his stories back from the front line, due in large measure to his ability to make friends with the Signal Corps. Once a Signal Corps man fixed up a line for Bennyhoff on a hill overlooking the scene of a stiff battle, handed him the telephone, and told him he was connected with his Tokyo office direct. Lying on the hill above the Naktong River, Bennyhoff turned in what probably was the quickest play-by-play report ever made from a remote battle front.

Later, when MacArthur started his counteroffensive, Bennyhoff carefully studied the forces in action and decided that the Republic of Korea Capital Division moving up the east coast of the peninsula might well be the first to reach the 38th Parallel. He decided to join the ROK division on the theory they would be a front-page story when they forced the North Koreans back into their own territory. There was an American officers' mission from the Korean Military Advisory Group with the ROKs and they were so pleased to have somebody covering their almost forgotten action that they gave Bennyhoff any kind of communications facilities available. These included a mobile radio-teletype in a van, and Bennyhoff, who had learned to punch a teletype in Reno, was given carte blanche to use it at any time. Since he proved to be more skillful at the job than the regular army operator, they also gave him military messages, including top-secret material, to transmit to headquarters.

Much to the surprise of all correspondents, except Bennyhoff, the ROK Capital Division became the first to drive into North Korean territory. This made it big news and brought several other correspondents dashing to the scene. Bennyhoff was tipped off by Rutherford Poats that competition was coming and made a few special preparations. With the co-operation of the KMAG officers, he concealed the radio-teletype van in a heavily wooded area. The newly arrived reporters were unaware of its existence and, for several days, sent their dispatches back to headquarters by air or any other way they could. And for several days they were bombarded by their Tokyo offices because they were running hours behind the United Press stories.

One evening, after covering the front, Bennyhoff nonchalantly sauntered away from the other reporters and circled around to his hidden van, where he began transmitting his copy. This time, however, he had failed to shake off the opposition. One of the correspondents had shadowed him and had seen him slip into the van. Bennyhoff was hunched over the keyboard and hard at work when he heard the door open. He knew he had been discovered.

"Okay," he growled without even looking up. "So you found it. Come on in and shut the goddamn door."

Hugh Baillie went to Korea when the United Nations forces were penned up in the Pusan area and General MacArthur, in Tokyo, told him he had better carry a pistol. Later, when the offensive northward was in progress, Baillie flew with MacArthur to recaptured Seoul and wrote a story about how the general delivered a speech of thanksgiving in the remnants of what had been the capitol building of the Republic of Korea.

The war air was tainted with smoke and death. The route of the "triumphal procession" had been past smashed and burning buildings, through dense clouds of the infamous Korean dust, past columns of refugees now heading for home . . . In the seated crowd before MacArthur, squeezed into benches where the legislators used to sit, were many wearing camouflaged helmets or caps, and most were keeping them on their heads because shards of glass tinkled down from the wrecked dome of the hall at intervals.

Then MacArthur said: "In humble and devout manifestation of gratitude, I ask that all present rise and join me in reciting the Lord's Prayer."

There was the rumbling shuffle of many feet. Off came the camouflaged helmets, the canvas caps, the snappy blue Air Force hat, the Navy caps. Every head was bowed and, as from the rear I looked over the assembly, many carbines were sticking up. The man directly in front of me wore two pistols and had a knife dangling at his back . . . MacArthur's voice uttered the words which have come down the ages, slowly and with great feeling.

Baillie's dispatch caught a lot of attention in the United States the next morning, and Earl Johnson sent him a message of congratulations on a unique achievement:

THIS IS FIRST TIME ANY CORRESPONDENT EVER SCORED FRONT PAGE PLAY WITH LORDS PRAYER

Bob Vermillion jumped once too often with the paratroopers. Somewhere over North Korea, Vermillion bailed out behind the enemy lines and was doing fine until another jumper floated against his parachute and caused him to drop like a rock for the last few yards. He hit the ground hard enough to break his ankle, but fortunately there were few North Korean soldiers in the area, and, with other casualties, he was moved back to a first-aid station, where he was safe but in great pain.

At this point Ralph Teatsorth was frantically telephoning all advanced bases in an effort to locate his missing correspondent. He finally found him at the end of a shaky field-telephone line to the first-aid station and persuaded a Signal Corps man to put Vermillion on the phone. The correspondent gave him the highlights of what had happened, but Teatsorth wanted a more comprehensive story and, because the connection was bad, finally said: "Bob, if you can talk, I guess you can write, so why don't you get off a long story and send it to me."

Although neither Vermillion nor Teatsorth regarded this suggestion as out of order, it quickly became the favorite legend of the press camp (in a version that was later picked up by Novelist James Michener) and elaborated as follows:

TEATSORTH (on the telephone): *Bob, you bastard, stay alive until you give me this story or I'll see that you never get another job as a reporter.*

VERMILLION: *I'll try. . . .*

DOCTOR (interrupting): *This man is in critical condition and we are preparing to operate.*

TEATSORTH: *Don't you dare give my man morphine, you dumb horse doctor, until I get that story out of him. If you don't get off that line I'll sue you, and the whole U. S. Army. Get him up there so he can talk.*

It made a good story.

3.

Throughout the Korean conflict there was concern in United Nations capitals that the Chinese or Russian Communist armies would intervene directly in the war and thus touch off another world conflagration. MacArthur's natural desire to strike at the enemy air bases in Manchuria was a point of sharp debate in Washington, and especially in London, where the general sometimes seemed to be suspected of attempting to evade his directive to wage a limited war confined to Korea. In October President Truman decided to fly to Wake Island for a personal meeting with his Far Eastern commander.

Merriman Smith, the United Press White House correspondent, was one of three news-agency reporters who accompanied Mr. Truman to the secret conference on October 15. Smith had a decade of White House experience behind him, but he discovered that it was still possible to get into the biggest jam of his career without even trying. The Truman-MacArthur conference, which turned out to be reasonably harmonious, was at so remote a spot that communications immediately became the major problem for correspondents. There was only a single navy wireless channel for use by news-agency reporters. The three news-agency men agreed that their only course was to "pool" their story on the official communiqué to be issued at the end of the conference. They delegated Robert Nixon of the International News Service to write this story and Smith to see that it moved as rapidly as possible over the single circuit to Honolulu. There the story would be delivered directly to commercial communications companies, which would relay it simultaneously to the offices of the three agencies.

When the communiqué was released, Smith took it by jeep to the navy wireless shack and told the operator to send it as a single story, but addressed to the three agencies. The operator was inexperienced and the Honolulu station signaled that something was wrong with the transmission. Finally Smith took over the teletype machine himself and sent the last half of the copy addressed to all three agencies. He figured he had probably violated all the rules in the book but he was pleased that he had bulled the copy through without much delay.

Meantime the United Press manager in Honolulu, Dave Belnap, had been doing a little planning on his own. He knew the communications setup from Wake was shaky and at the approximate hour the communiqué was due he appeared at the Honolulu receiving station which was relaying the press copy to commercial channels. The story was just coming in from Wake, but it was in terrible shape. The third take was ahead of the first take and the copy was jumbled throughout. Belnap watched until he had enough copy to give him the highlights of the communiqué. Then he put in a telephone call to San Francisco and began dictating the story.

The next day the reporters from Wake arrived in Honolulu and discovered that the United Press had been forty minutes ahead of everybody else on the results of the President's conference with MacArthur. Smith was promptly accused of a double cross in handling the copy from Wake and nothing that he could say convinced his competitors that he had not done them dirt. They abused him and ostracized him all the way back to Washington and never accepted the fact that they had been outsmarted not by deception at Wake Island but by a simple display of initiative and advance planning at Honolulu.

4.

Not long after President Truman returned to the White House and a short time before Phil Newsom took over as war desk editor in Korea, there were ominous developments on the Korean front. On October 24 Marine fliers reported they had been fired on by Chinese antiaircraft batteries near the Yalu River boundary of Manchuria. The next afternoon near Sinanju, an intelligence officer whispered to Glenn Stackhouse that "we've got a Chinese prisoner." Stackhouse rode with him to a makeshift stockade and listened to the questioning of a Chinese soldier in cotton-quilted coat, baggy pants, and tennis shoes. Early in November, Joe Quinn was covering the American 1st Cavalry Division and the South Korean 1st Division when Chinese Communist and North Korean troops on horse and on foot slipped through the advance lines and made an Indian-style massacre attack on two American combat regiments at Usan. Quinn woke up with the wild notes of an enemy bugle call in his ears and discovered that the Americans were fighting against overwhelming odds. Both regiments were badly cut up—"they murdered us," he quoted a soldier as saying—and hundreds of civilians were killed before Quinn and other survivors swam the icy Kuryong River and escaped. For the next few days the front-line area was "fluid" and there was severe fighting before the Eighth Army could re-form on the south bank of the Chongchon River.

It was not until the second week in November that the Eighth Army renewed a limited offensive. Meanwhile, the 7th Division of the 10th Corps pushed all the way to the Yalu River. Unipresser Charles R. Moore was with them and became the only American correspondent "to spit in the Yalu"—a distinction that almost led to his capture. On November 27 a Chinese army of some 250,000 men hiding in the hills north of Chongchon launched a powerful offensive against the United Nations forces. They broke through the center of the Eighth Army line and soon had cut off all but three escape routes to the south. The great retreat began.

For correspondents the next ten days were a nightmare of confusion, of bitter cold, of impossible communications and, always, of great danger. The retreat of the 24th Division down the Sukchon road, which Stackhouse accompanied, was a tortuous crawl through clouds of choking dust, with vehicles moving bumper to bumper. Moore was on the Northeast Front at Hyesanjin when the 7th Division troops fell back from the Yalu, trying to escape Chinese traps on a long narrow road winding through icy mountains in the Chosin reservoir area. The enemy soon cut the road and isolated the 1st Marine Division headquarters at Hagaru. There was a 2900-foot airstrip at Hagaru, bulldozed out of the side of a hill, and Moore flew in on a C-47 carrying Marine replacement troops.

When he reached General Oliver P. Smith's command post it was riddled by enemy machine-gun bullets, but the commander was imperturbably drinking a cup of coffee and had time to give Moore a couple of stories, one of them about the rescue under fire of an ambushed army battalion on the ice of Chosin. Moore flew back southward that evening—on a plane carrying the frozen bodies of men killed in action at Chosin—with a pocketful of stories about the most desperate action of the Korean War, including one that was destined for front-page attention everywhere. It didn't come from the general but from a Marine, who quoted Smith as saying:

"Retreating? Hell, we're not retreating. We're just attacking in another direction."

By December 23 Seoul was being abandoned for the second time, and there was talk of total evacuation from Korea. On that day Peter Webb was riding with David Walker of the London *Daily Mirror* near the South Korean capital when their jeep skidded around a sharp bend in the road and almost ran into the wreckage of another vehicle. A wrecked jeep was a common sight along that frozen road, but this one was different. It had the four stars of a general painted on its front. And in a pool of congealing blood on the road lay a pair of dark sunglasses—the trademark of General Walton H. Walker, commander of the United Nations Eighth Army.

Webb and David Walker hurried to a field hospital where General Walker had been taken and found it surrounded by military police who were keeping everyone out. Webb, however, was wearing a British uniform and had on a jacket that covered his war correspondents' insignia. He also wore a peaked cap with a gold letter "C" on it, resembling a British regimental badge. Taking a deep breath, he jumped out of the jeep and walked to the main gate, with the air of an officer on a grave mission. After a momentary hesitation the American guard at the gate flashed his hand up in a snappy salute. Webb returned an even snappier salute and walked briskly inside past the police cordon. Just as he reached a group of staff officers standing outside a large hospital tent, a surgeon emerged, stripped off his rubber gloves, and said: "I'm sorry, gentlemen. We did everything we could, but he's dead."

Webb was stunned. The United Nations commander dead at the very moment when the enemy was about to renew his offensive? Wars had often been lost for lesser reasons. But he had to make sure. He stepped forward to the surgeon.

"Do you mean General Walker?" he asked.

"Yes. Who else did you think?" the doctor replied, looking at him curiously. Webb retired as gracefully as possible and hurried back to Seoul, trying to plan some way to get the story out without tipping off other correspondents and without avoiding censorship. His only hope, he decided, was to telephone Tokyo and have them submit the story to MacArthur's headquarters for clearance. But he also knew that the only telephone he could use was in the Seoul pressroom, where a dozen other correspondents would overhear him.

"David," he said as he and Walker reached the pressroom, "Can you sing?"

"I guess so, why?"

"I've got to use that telephone and not be overheard. When I get Tokyo on the line you start singing, and loud."

Walker took up a strategic position in the pressroom and in an off-key but wonderfully loud voice rendered "The Road to the Isles" with such enthusiasm that everybody in the room complained bitterly—except Webb. He was in the flimsy phone booth, talking to Bob Vermillion in Tokyo. An hour later Vermillion had the story cleared and on the wireless. When the news got back to Seoul, Webb was promptly arrested and held for eighteen hours until it was proved that he had not violated censorship.

If Frank Bartholomew had not happened to be in Korea in 1951 newspapers outside of the Iron Curtain might have had their news of the Korean armistice negotiations only by courtesy of the Communist press. Negotiations leading to an armistice began at Kaesong in North Korea in 1951 and Bart went there prior to the opening of actual truce talks. A number of documents had been drawn up by United Nations and North Korean representatives and, in reading through them, he observed that the correspondents and photographers of United Nations countries were to be barred from covering the meetings. Bartholomew immediately sent a written protest to the United Nations commander, General Matthew Ridgeway, and as a result

Ridgeway insisted that the bar be lifted at Kaesong and, later, at Panmunjom.

The armistice negotiations dragged on and the war was not officially ended until July 27, 1953. On that date General William K. Harrison, representing the United Nations, and General Nam Il of North Korea met in the so-called "peace pagoda" at Panmunjom to sign an official armistice. Only one American reporter was present—LeRoy Hansen of the United Press, who dictated over a field telephone a running story of the ceremonies for the information of all other correspondents.

As the first copy of the truce document was signed by the two generals, Hansen looked at his watch and called out that the war ended at one minute after ten o'clock in the morning. That time was made official in the United Nations Command documents. When the ceremonies were completed, Hansen checked his watch and discovered that it was one minute slow, but he never told anybody.

CHAPTER THIRTY-THREE

By 1955 Hugh Baillie had been president of the United Press for an unprecedented twenty years—a momentous, history-making period in world affairs and in news-agency affairs. He had taken over when the company had 1360 newspaper clients and at a time when the way had been opened for the sale of news to radio stations. He had developed a new advertising slogan—"The World's Best Coverage of the World's Biggest News"—and he had scoured the byways as well as the highways of the globe in a campaign to live up to that goal. The United Press service had been extended to most of the nation's biggest newspapers and now included the Philadelphia *Bulletin,* the St. Louis *Post-Dispatch,* the San Francisco *Chronicle,* the Los Angeles *Times,* and the Gannett newspapers in the East.

During his administration the agency pioneered in development of a special style of writing news and features for radio—writing for the ear instead of the eye—and established leased-wire radio-television circuits that covered the country. By 1955 the United Press was serving 4515 newspaper and radio clients. After World War II, the company in collaboration with Twentieth Century-Fox Movietone set up United Press Movietone to record news events on motion-picture film for use by television stations. In 1952 Acme News Pictures was purchased and the name changed to United Press News Pictures, which pioneered the distribution of photographs to newspapers and television stations by facsimile process. The simplicity of the process enabled many small newspapers to receive telephoto pictures. In the same period the agency led the way in developing the use of the teletypesetter, by means of which news stories sent on the wire could be automatically transmitted to linotypes in newspaper offices and set into type without being handled by editors or linotype operators.

Baillie had never ceased to be a reporter. He made headlines many times over these years by interviewing world leaders in Europe and the Far East, and he was so often on the spot when big crises were developing that one London newspaper announced his arrival just before the war with a headline saying: "Look Out! Baillie's In Town." As the chief executive of a world press association, Baillie was unique in that he spent about as much time at the war front and other hot spots as he did at his desk in New York.

By 1954 Baillie had pretty well covered the field as a newspaperman and had even found time to persuade Bandmaster Paul Lavalle to write "The United Press March" which was distributed to radio clients for use as the "signature" on broadcasts of United Press news. But his long, strenuous career had exacted a price. In the early 1950s he was hospitalized several times by a stomach ailment. He was still the kind of fighter who came out swinging when the bell rang, but, early in 1955, he stepped aside. Frank H. Bartholomew, first vice-president of the company, had been covering still another war front in French Indochina, but he was summoned to New York. On April 6, 1955, he succeeded Baillie as president of the company.

Two years after Bartholomew took over the United Press, with Mims Thomason as business manager and LeRoy Keller as sales manager, the company was spending about $28,800,000 a year on the collection and distribution of news to approximately 4800 clients. These clients were about equally divided between newspapers and radio-television stations. There were 117 bureaus in the United States and 96 in other countries.

Bartholomew, a tall, soft-spoken, fast-moving man with a balding dome and a quick smile, gave an impression of ease and informality in almost any job, but he approached management problems with the direct skill of an engineering expert plus the inquiring mind of a reporter. Like earlier presidents of the company, he was a newsman at heart as well as a skillful writer and editor. Unlike other presidents, he had never worked in the New York office, and that fact was of importance in his climb to the top management job. The Pacific Coast Division, which he had directed for thirty years, was large, varied, and, in practice, more independent of New York headquarters than any other United Press division.

The mere fact that he was comparatively remote and less directly under the domination of whatever strong personality was in the home office gave Bartholomew greater personal identity and more room for executive growth. Under these circumstances he developed his own administrative practices and ran his own show. He quickly gained a reputation for energetic operation on an economical basis.

Under Bartholomew's guidance in western states the United Press served every daily newspaper (with one exception) in the state of Nevada, for example; and served twice as many clients in California as all other agencies combined. Furthermore, Bart had spread his wings beyond the Pacific Coast Division and by 1930 was in charge of the Pacific area including Australia, Alaska, Mexico, Central America, and Honolulu. In supervising news-service operations in this spacious area, Bartholomew demonstrated an ability to delegate authority and to develop executive staff talent. He planned carefully for the future and, more than any other regional executive of the company, kept his area of operation abreast of modern concepts of corporate management. His initiative and his inclination to make the most of modern technological and administrative methods particularly fitted Bartholomew to take command as the United Press approached its fiftieth anniversary.

The company had been founded at a time when strongly individualistic leadership was a necessity. It could then compete with the established Associated Press only by introducing many new ideas and a high degree of boldness—sometimes it may have been closer to cockiness—into the news-agency business.

It attracted attention and increased its business by doing something different; by introducing by-lines of its reporters, by a lively, colorful style of writing, by developing human-interest stories, by pioneering many ingenious methods (the use of wireless, for instance) of collecting the news economically and efficiently, by using American methods and American reporters to cover foreign news. These and other innovations were developed of necessity in the heat of competition, but they were to leave their mark on the journalistic world as they caught on and became standard practice.

Now, as the agency grew and the pattern of leadership began to change, one man could no longer keep his finger on everything in the routine of daily operation. Individualism gave way to executive teamwork in a company that operated a multitude of services all over the world. A greater and greater dispersion of authority became essential as the organization expanded beyond the scope of any single personality.

Bartholomew fully understood this expanding pattern and was well equipped to direct it. He could and sometimes did handle any job in the service, but he had, too, a skill for co-ordinating the work of his subordinates, an ability to put the right executive in the right spot with full command of operations, a keen sense of client relations, and a knack for keeping an eye on many boiling pots. He emphasized that the first responsibility of management was to accent quality in the news report. He also launched a program designed to release the full potential of his executive staff.

The United Press had been fortunate for fifty years in having leadership that was peculiarly fitted to the time and circumstances. The second half of the twentieth century called for change, for new ideas and new methods. By training, experience, and temperament, Bartholomew was uniquely prepared to provide such leadership.

2.

Fortunately, one thing that did not change over fifty years was the rivalry between the United Press and the Associated Press, which had been so essential to growth of a free and robust press in the United States. Nor had the basic requirements of press-association reporting changed. The agency reporter of 1957 had many advantages over the correspondent of 1907, but both were judged by the same standards—accuracy and factuality, integrity, skill in presenting the news, and the ability to present it first. These were hard, demanding standards requiring a specialized ability even among newspapermen, yet they were met day after day by news-agency reporters all over the world. The successful press-association correspondent would always need a kind of dedication to the task of telling—honestly and swiftly—the manner in which history was made this day.

Gene Symonds, the United Press manager for Southeast Asia, was in Singapore in May of 1955 when a bus strike led to violent Communist demonstrations, particularly by Chinese students. A number of persons had been injured and the city was almost paralyzed on the evening of May 11 when Symonds stopped at a restaurant for dinner. Later he telephoned the Singapore bureau and was informed that the rioting was intensified, that automobiles had been burned in the street, and that several persons, including two detectives, had been killed.

The desk man at the bureau added that there was a cable message asking for motion pictures for use on television, but nobody had been able to get through police lines to get pictures.

"I'll get them," Symonds said. Other newspapermen at the restaurant tried to persuade him to keep away from the rioting and one asked: "Why risk your life with that mob?"

"That's where the story is," Symonds answered. He got his 16-millimeter movie camera and found a friendly taxi driver, Abdul bin Ali, who took him to Alexandra Road. There Symonds was told that a policeman, trying to save himself and three constables from being trampled underfoot, had fired a shot that killed a young student. The mob grew still more angry. Police refused to let Symonds past a road block leading to the center of rioting but he circled to another street and approached a corner of Alexandra Road. The taxi driver stopped when he heard shouts and a number of shots. Around the corner came 600 rioters, carrying the body of the student who had been killed. They were chanting, wailing, screaming.

Symonds got out of the taxi and walked toward the mob, which stopped in sudden silence. He raised his camera—and the mob went wild. A moment later he had been battered to the pavement, struck with bicycle chains, sticks, bamboo rods, and rocks. It was an hour before rescuers got him to the hospital, where nurses wept when they saw his broken body. He died early the next morning.

There are certain kinds of stories that might be described as classical in the history of journalism, stories that are certain to attract and hold the interest of readers everywhere. Of these perhaps the most perfect illustration is the disaster at sea. A sinking ship—the *Titanic* scraping an iceberg, the *Morro Castle* aflame—represented from the time of the first reporter all of the elements of a dramatic story. Tragedy, heroism, cowardice, suspense were almost always present and theatrically outlined on a small stage in the wake of distress signals from a ship at sea. This was true in the era of sailing ships. It was no less true in the modern day of wireless telephones and radar and aerial rescues.

On the night of July 25, 1956, the new Italian transatlantic liner *Andrea Doria,* sliding through fog patches south of Nantucket Island, collided with the Swedish American Line's *Stockholm.* At 11:25 P.M., a distress call was sent out from the Italian ship and rescue operations were launched from New York and Boston. The first United Press bulletin on the collision contained only meager information received by the Coast Guard in New York. But James Hudson, on the late night desk, immediately started his assistant, James W. Carroll, checking the offices of the two steamship lines and sent a message to the Boston bureau to move in on the story.

Carroll could provide only brief bulletin service for newspapers on the night wire, but by the time Overnight Editor William Laffler reached the office around one o'clock in the morning, it was evident that a major story was breaking. Laffler began calling in reinforcements and recruiting help among reporters and wire filers who worked late on the night service or in the sports department. Wireless telephone calls were booked to both the *Andrea Doria* and the *Stockholm.*

Sam Donnelon, overnight editor of the local desk, telephoned Ed McCarthy at his home and instructed him to dash to Coast Guard Search and Rescue headquarters and, if possible, get aboard a rescue cutter. Jack Woliston, day manager of the New York bureau, was summoned to the office, where he began assigning additional reporters to key spots. Jerry Brazda welded together the early day story gathered from a dozen different sources. By the time Frederick M. Winship took over from Brazda shortly after dawn, the *Andrea Doria* was about to be abandoned, but most of her 1134 passengers had been taken aboard rescue boats in calm seas.

Now the basic facts of the disaster had been gathered, but the real work of digging out the dramatic details and reporting the death of a great ship had just begun under direction of Day News Manager Gene Gillette in New York and Bureau Manager Stanton Berens in Boston. Berens assigned Joseph Phelan and Miss China Altman to Coast Guard headquarters in Boston and sent James Geggis in a chartered airplane over the scene of the collision. Meantime McCarthy had talked a New York Coast Guard public-relations officer into arranging a flight over the scene. However there were so many reporters on hand by the time the plane was ready that the Coast Guard officers decided to send only one reporter and to require him to return to base and share his information with all other reporters before writing his story. McCarthy won the draw and climbed aboard an amphibian plane with television and newsreel photographers.

But it was Geggis who became the first newsman to fly over the scene of the collision. His pilot then landed on Nantucket Island and Geggis relayed to Boston the first exclusive description of the *Andrea Doria,* the *Stockholm,* and the ships that had sped to the rescue.

Shortly afterward McCarthy, too, looked down at the sinking Italian ship as water poured into her tilting funnels about ten o'clock. At the same time, still another Unipresser—Bureau Manager James Whelan of Providence—arrived over the *Andrea Doria* in a navy plane from Rhode Island. He then landed on Nantucket and turned in the first eyewitness story of the sinking— "I saw a great ship die today"—while McCarthy was flying back to his New York base with a "pool" descriptive story. Shortly afterward Berens got through a wireless telephone call to the *Ile de France,* one of the rescue ships, and produced the first interview with a survivor. Then Fred Winship in New York reached the *Stockholm* by telephone for additional details of the collision. By that time a list of passengers on the *Andrea Doria* had been compiled and correspondents in Rome, Stockholm, and a score of cities in the United States were contributing additional information to the story.

Many thousands of words about the disaster had now gone on the wires, but there was much, much more to come. The survivors were being brought ashore. Hundreds of families were clamoring for information about relatives. The injured were scattered in a dozen different places. More and more United Press reporters scattered to docks and hospitals and steamship-line offices to gather the details. When the *Ile de France* approached New York, Tom Zumbo was on a Coast Guard cutter that pulled alongside her. With other reporters he went aboard and began interviewing men, women, children. One man had on nothing but a topcoat. Actress Ruth Roman was wearing a borrowed T shirt and oversize khaki pants, having torn her clothes to shreds escaping from the sinking ship. After the ship docked, Zumbo was on the telephone for a solid ninety minutes dictating his stories.

The work went on throughout Thursday night and Friday and Friday night. The details were pieced together, the death list of almost fifty was compiled, the heroism and the tragedy were reported. The confused scenes of action were described to the Boston and New York offices in a torrent of facts and figures that were sifted and funneled into a single channel. The product of scores of men and women was processed swiftly into an orderly procession of facts and the story of disaster at sea rolled out to United Press clients around the world.

In October of 1956 there was trouble behind the Iron Curtain that Soviet Russia had drawn to separate its European satellite nations from the West. A bloodless uprising in Poland against Russian domination was followed on October 23 by a kind of spontaneous revolution against the Communist dictators of Hungary. For three days, while civilians fought with mounting intensity against Russian tanks, communications were disrupted and almost the only word reaching the outside world was picked up from fragmentary broadcasts over Radio Budapest.

During most of those three days Unipresser Anthony Cavendish was trying to get from Warsaw to Budapest, and Unipresser Russell Jones was trying to reach the same destination from Vienna. Cavendish finally bluffed his way aboard an airplane leaving Warsaw airport with a cargo of blood plasma. He flew to a small military airfield near Budapest and walked into the revolution-torn capital, just as long lines of Russian tanks were withdrawing in momentary defeat. By the time he had trudged to the center of the city, the reporter had the first installment of the story the world was anxiously awaiting, but he had no way to send it. There were no telephones, no telegraphic or wireless communications in operation; nobody was quite sure whether there was any government either, so great was the confusion.

Cavendish began a search of government offices and, at the Ministry of Foreign Affairs, he struck pay dirt. There was a telex wire still in operation and it could be hooked up to London. It was, to be sure, a telex for transmission of diplomatic messages only, but this was an emergency. Cavendish talked rapidly and eloquently. In the end the call was put through to London and the first eyewitness story from the battered city in three days was transmitted to the outside world on October 29. On the same day Jones arrived from Vienna by automobile.

For the next few days, as telephone communications were restored, the two reporters covered a story of confusion and violence and high hopes among the "freedom fighters" of Hungary. But on November 4, reorganized and reinforced Russian military forces smashed their way back into the city, reinstated a Communist government and again stopped all communications with the outside world. American and British correspondents in Budapest tried to get permission from the Russians to return to Vienna, but the Russians held them up several days. On November 8 Cavendish and Jones decided to divide their strength. Cavendish climbed into a battered old German automobile and headed for the Czechoslovak frontier. He was fired on as he raced out of the suburbs of Budapest and at Gyoer he was arrested by Russian soldiers who held him two days before permitting him to continue to Vienna. By that time the Russians also had given the correspondents remaining in Budapest permission to return to Vienna and all American reporters departed—except Jones.

At first it appeared Jones would have no way to get his stories to the outside world. But with a generous outlay of money, a communications official was persuaded to set up a temporary teleprinter connection with Vienna, over which some news was moved on the day Cavendish and other reporters arrived in the Austrian capital. Two days later telephone service was restored, but each call was limited to six minutes. Jones got around this by booking calls to Vienna, Frankfurt, Belgrade, and Stockholm. He dictated for six minutes on the first call that came through. When the next call was ready he picked up his story where he had left off and dictated another six minutes. And so on. As a result his story was scattered in three or four different cities, each of which relayed its section to Vienna to be assembled into a complete dispatch. On some occasions, he also dictated dispatches directly to the Press Wireless office in Prague. The Prague operator sent the story to New York, which relayed it back to London from where it went on the European leased wires and was eventually received in Vienna, only 200 miles from Budapest.

Jones and Cavendish repeatedly had been under fire during the early Budapest fighting, but they were among friendly freedom fighters and willingly took their chances. Once the Russians had returned, the shooting was gradually reduced, but the danger often seemed still greater. Soviet troops protected the new Communist regime of Janos Kadar and Russian patrols on the street had nervous fingers on their guns. On December 4, Jones watched more than thirty thousand women of Budapest gather at Heroes Square to lay wreathes and flags at the tomb of the unknown soldier. Many of them carried children in their arms. Then, at the height of the demonstration, Soviet soldiers stationed around the square in armored cars leaped from their vehicles with submachine guns, their officers drew pistols, and the whole mass of troops charged into the crowd.

For one desperate minute Jones was convinced that everybody in the square, including himself, was marked for slaughter. But the women held their ground and even threw flowers at the soldiers. The command to fire was never given.

Jones got the story to Vienna by telephone. But the next day he was expelled from Hungary after three weeks in which he had been the only American reporter covering the first dramatic and tragic postwar revolt against Communist dictatorship. For his work in Budapest, Jones won journalism's triple crown—the George Polk Memorial Award from the Overseas Press Club, the Sigma Delta Chi Award for international reporting, and the Pulitzer Prize for "excellent and sustained coverage . . . at great personal risk" of an international story.

CHAPTER THIRTY-FOUR

Fifty years is a long span for reporters who have a deadline every minute. In the half century after the United Press Associations was founded in 1907, history moved at a headlong pace. Empires crumbled and new empires sprang up, collapsed, and gave way to still newer concentrations of power. Nations were created and destroyed and created again in unfamiliar patterns. Everywhere there was ferment and change. But perhaps nothing changed more rapidly or radically than the business of collecting and distributing news around the face of the globe.

The first news dispatches bearing the credit line "By United Press" went out over a one-wire Morse telegraph system or by regular mail to 369 newspapers. The leased telegraph lines were tenuous ties linking a few big cities of the East and Middle West, a few cities on the Pacific Coast. News limped, often painfully, along these wires, through relays, and across gaps that had to be spanned by ordinary telegrams or telephone.

But by the time the 1950s rolled around, the miracle of transmission of news and photographs by radio to multiple destinations had made it possible to bring the whole world into almost instantaneous contact. In 1949, for the first time in history, a dispatch was transmitted directly from the United Press bureau in London to clients on three continents. A few years later, an operator seated at a radio teleprinter keyboard in New York could send a dispatch to newspapers anywhere by means of radio signals that traveled around the world in approximately one seventh of a second.

This technological progress enabled the company simply to "blanket" the world with a constant flow of news dispatches transmitted at the rate of sixty words a minute and immediately plucked out of the air by bureau and client automatic receiving equipment in any country—or at the South Pole, for that matter. In practice, of course, the daily foreign news report of some 60,000 words had to be "tailored" differently for different areas, and, by 1957, United Press dispatches were being broadcast by radio from fifteen key cities around the world. Over all, a total of 260 radio transmitter hours a day were required to serve clients in foreign countries and to transmit foreign dispatches to the United States.

The vast change in communications since the time when Ed L. Keen covered Great Britain on a cable budget of one hundred words a day was demonstrated during the 1956 Olympic games at Melbourne, Australia. Sports Editor Leo H. Petersen took a staff of twenty-seven reporters—drawn from eleven different countries—to Melbourne and set up special radio tele-printer circuits to San Francisco, Manila, Tokyo, and London for the dura-tion. As a result, the outcome of sports contests held on the other side of the world reached newspapers in Chicago, for example, just about as quickly as if the games had been staged in Detroit or Milwaukee. Flashes filed by Petersen in the press box at the Olympic stadium in Melbourne could be laid down in newspaper offices all over America in approximately ninety seconds.

Faster communications at lower cost per word opened the way for a great increase in the volume and variety of the news agency's product. By 1957 the United Press complex of 375,000 miles of leased channels across the United States carried a daily news report of about 260,000 words on the main trunk lines, including a regular budget of feature and interpretative articles, science and women's stories, sports and market news. The company also operated a special service bureau directed by C. Edmonds Allen and a daily news report for ships at sea, compiled under supervision of William Manley.

These and other expanding services gradually boosted United Press per-sonnel to around 6000. The Washington bureau, as an example, had grown from five men in a one-room office over a haberdashery in 1907 to a staff of 115 under direction of Vice-President Lyle C. Wilson and News Editor Julius Frandsen. That bureau's foreign department, headed by Carroll Ken-worthy, employed a dozen reporters, and John M. Vogt headed a staff of four others operating the affiliated Washington Capital News Service. The single Morse wire of earlier days had grown into a battery of twenty-six teleprinters under supervision of Chief Operator Robert K. MacCormac.

2.

The men who founded the United Press Associations in 1907 dreamed big. They wanted to build a world service that would be free to gather news anywhere at any time and to sell it anywhere they could find a buyer. It was a commercial idea, but it was a great deal more than just a means to make a profit. It was an idea or a dream, if you please, shared with many others—a belief that if the truth could be told to all, without bias or preju-dice, peoples everywhere would understand each other better and would move closer to realization of man's aspirations.

The existence of the United Press, or something like it, was essential and inevitable in the evolution of a strong and independent press in America and, eventually, in the struggle for a free press in many other lands. The agency provided strong leadership and was a significant factor in progress toward that goal; in fact, because of the peculiarities of its position, progress had to be made if the company was to expand and flourish in a highly competitive field. Even after fifty years nobody would contend that the goal had been reached or the dream realized. But it had not been forgotten either. The struggle for unrestricted exchange of information went on. It would go on as long as free journalists survived.

All around the world today, now, at this moment men and women of the United Press Associations are tracking down, collecting, writing, and processing the news that you will read in your newspaper this afternoon or tomorrow morning, or that you will hear on your radio or television in a few minutes or a few hours. They are looking for the small nugget of news that will be printed only in your home town, as well as for the headline that will blacken the front page of every newspaper in the country. By the very nature of their business they are always consciously or subconsciously looking for news, always aware that the next moment could bring them the breathless adventure of today's biggest news story. For such men and women there's a deadline every minute.

J.A.M.
Guilford, Conn.
April 15, 1957

INDEX